Carl Schmitt and *The Buribunks*

In 1918 a young Carl Schmitt published a short satirical fiction entitled *The Buribunks*. He imagined a future society of beings who consistently wrote and disseminated their personal diaries. Schmitt would go on to become the infamous philosopher of the exception and for a while the 'Crown Jurist of the Third Reich'. *The Buribunks* – ironically for beings that lived only for self-memorialisation – has been mostly lost to history. However, the digital realm, with its emphasis on the informatic traces generated by human doing, and the continual interest in Schmitt's work to explain and criticise contemporary constellations of power, suggests that *The Buribunks* is a text whose epoch has come.

This volume includes the first full translation into English of *The Buribunks* and a selection of critical essays on the text, its meanings in the digital present, its playing with and criticism of the literary form, and its place within Schmitt's life and work. *The Buribunks* and the essays provide a complex, critical and provocative invitation to reimagine the relations between the human and their imprint and legacy within archives and repositories. There is a fundamental exploration of what it means to be a being intensely aware of 'writing itself'.

This is not just a volume for critical lawyers, literary scholars and the Schmitt literati. It is a volume that challenges a broad range of disciplines, from philosophy to critical data studies, to reflect on the digital present and its assembled and curated beings. It is a volume that provides a set of fantastically located concepts, images and histories that traverse ideas and practices, play and politics, power and possibility.

Kieran Tranter is chair of law, technology and future in the School of Law, Queensland University of Technology. Kieran researches the legalities of technology and the technologies of legality. His current projects concern the motor vehicle in the governance of the Australian settler state, mobile connectivity and everyday life in the Global South.

Edwin Bikundo is a senior lecturer in the Law Futures Centre, Griffith Law School, Griffith University. Edwin's research addresses international and comparative law, legal theory, and law and the humanities. He is currently finalising a book about Giorgio Agamben, international law and Johan Wolfgang von Goethe's *Faust.*

TechNomos

Part of the
TechNomos: Law, Technology and Culture
series

series editors

Kieran Tranter, *School of Law, University of Queensland, Australia*
Edwin Bikundo, *Griffith University, Australia*

for information about the series and details of previous and forthcoming titles, see weblink to be inserted

A GlassHouse book

Carl Schmitt and *The Buribunks*

Technology, Law, Literature

Edited by
Kieran Tranter and Edwin Bikundo

Routledge
Taylor & Francis Group
a GlassHouse book

First published 2022
by Routledge
2 Park Square, Milton Park, Abingdon, Oxon OX14 4RN

and by Routledge
605 Third Avenue, New York, NY 10158

a GlassHouse book

Routledge is an imprint of the Taylor & Francis Group, an informa business

British Library Cataloguing-in-Publication Data
A catalogue record for this book is available from the British Library

Library of Congress Cataloging-in-Publication Data
A catalog record has been requested for this book

ISBN: 978-0-367-54887-2 (hbk)
ISBN: 978-0-367-54891-9 (pbk)
ISBN: 978-1-003-09106-6 (ebk)

DOI: 10.4324/9781003091066

Typeset in Bembo
by Taylor & Francis Books

Contents

Illustrations

Figures

Tables

Contributors

Nour Benghellab is a lecturer and LLD candidate in the Département des sciences juridiques, Université du Québec à Montréal. Nour researches legal modernism as a literary and legal movement, and more generally the history of twentieth-century European legal thought. She is presently completing an LLD dissertation on Carl Schmitt as a modernist author.

Carla Biondi is a postgraduate student in the Professional Translation for European Languages Master's degree in the School of Modern Languages, Newcastle University, United Kingdom. Carla is currently specialising in literary and technical translation from English to Italian and vice versa.

Fabrizio Grasso is a PhD candidate in political sciences in the Department of Political and Social Sciences, University of Catania. Fabrizio researches political theology. He is currently focusing his studies on the principle of immanence and the problem of atheism.

Attila Gyulai is a research fellow, Centre for Social Sciences – Institute for Political Science (Budapest); associate professor, Corvinus University of Budapest. His research focuses on realist political theory, democratic theory, and the Hungarian political system.

Charles Lawson is a professor in the Law Futures Centre and Environmental Futures Research Institute, Griffith Law School, Griffith University. Charles researches intellectual property and public administration law with a current focus on synthetic biology. His current projects are considering 'facts' in science and law discourse, a bibliometric analysis of access and benefit sharing genetic resources law and a quantified account of plant breeders' rights in Australia.

Vittorio Lubrano is a PhD candidate, member of the Thinking Documentary Film Research Group and collaborator of the Art of Living Research Group, Political Philosophy, NOVA University of Lisbon. Vittorio researches the political implications of posthuman studies. His current projects concern continental political philosophy, animality and non-human perspectives in documentary films and post-Deleuzean forms of subjectivity.

Desmond Manderson is a professor who is jointly appointed to the ANU Colleges of Law and of Arts & Social Sciences at the Australian National University. He directs the Centre for Law, Arts and the Humanities.

Michael P.A. Murphy is SSHRC doctoral fellow in international relations and political theory, University of Ottawa. Michael's research focuses on the philosophical foundations of international relations theory. He is the author of two dozen peer-reviewed articles and the book *Quantum Social Theory for Critical International Relations Theorists: Quantizing Critique* (Palgrave Macmillan, 2021).

Matteo Negro is professor of philosophy in the Department of Political and Social Sciences, University of Catania. He has studied and researched in Cologne, Freiburg, Paris and Geneva. Matteo researches political theology, metaphysics and practical philosophy.

Joseph Owen is a doctoral researcher in the Faculty of Arts and Humanities, School of English, University of Southampton. Joseph researches the intersections of early twentieth-century political philosophy and artistic modernism. He is currently completing his thesis on images of sovereignty in Carl Schmitt's writing, buttressed by textual analyses of works by Virginia Woolf, William Faulkner and Samuel Beckett.

Timothy D. Peters is a senior lecturer in law in the School of Law and Society, University of the Sunshine Coast and president of the Law, Literature and the Humanities Association of Australasia. Tim researches the intersections of legal theory, theology and popular culture, as well as critical examinations of the corporation and the corporate form. He is the recipient of an Australian Research Council Australian Discovery Early Career Award (project number DE200100881) funded by the Australian Government, examining 'New Approaches to Corporate Legality: Beyond Neoliberal Governance'.

Laura Petersen is a PhD candidate in the Institute for International Law and the Humanities at the University of Melbourne. Her research is cross-disciplinary, combining approaches to jurisprudence with German studies, literature and art.

Karen Petroski is a professor of law, Saint Louis University School of Law. Karen's scholarship broadly addresses law and language; her publications have considered, among other matters, doctrines of legal interpretation and the roles played by discursive activity in legal professionalisation. Her recent work has focused on fictionality, both in and beyond legal settings, and includes *Fiction and the Languages of Law: Understanding Contemporary Legal Discourse* (Routledge, 2018) and *Fictionality* (New Critical Idiom series, Routledge, 2021).

Catherine Pickering is a professor in the Environmental Futures Research Institute, Griffith University. Catherine researches alpine ecology, climate change, recreation ecology, protected area management, human–nature interactions, biodiversity conservation and innovative literature review methodology. Her current projects include using social media in natural and protected area management.

Richard Polt is professor of philosophy at Xavier University, Cincinnati, Ohio. His research focuses on Heidegger, with interests including technology and memory. Recent books include *The Task of Philosophy in the Anthropocene* (edited with Jon Wittrock, Rowman & Littlefield, 2018), *The Typewriter Revolution: A Typist's Companion for the 21st Century* (W.W. Norton, 2015) and *Time and Trauma: Thinking Through Heidegger in the Thirties* (Rowman & Littlefield, 2019).

Gert Reifarth is a teacher of German at Scotch College Melbourne. Born in the former East Germany, Gert has also worked in academia and theatre.

Lachlan Robb is a PhD candidate in the School of Law, Queensland University of Technology. Lachlan's research involves exploring technology through a legal anthropological lens. His PhD focuses on an ethnographic study of blockchain as an emerging technology.

Francine Rochford is an associate professor in the School of Law, La Trobe University. Francine researches the legal and governance aspects of universities, along with the law of torts and environmental law. Her current projects include the relationship between soft regulation, risk and tort law, and the relationship between markets and law.

Carl Schmitt (1888–1986) was a conservative, controversial German legal jurist, constitutional, scholar and political theorist. He is noted for his polemical work and acerbic critique of liberalism. His legacy will forever be tainted by his association with National Socialism, despite being expelled from the party after only three years of membership.

Karen Schultz is a lecturer in the Griffith Law School, Griffith University. Karen researches in legal theory, constitutional law and legal history. Her current projects concern intergenerational justice and Sir Samuel Griffith's utopian and Dantista dimensions.

Ernesto C. Sferrazza Papa is a postdoctoral fellow in the Instituto de Filosofía, Pontificia Universidad Católica de Chile. Ernesto's research deals with the relationship between space and power and with Carl Schmitt's philosophy and its contemporary legacy. His latest monograph has been consecrated to a philosophical critique of walls. His current project concerns the notion of 'element' in contemporary philosophy.

Preface

This preface is non-Buribunkian. The Buribunks are all 'I': ego-selves stamping their life into the pages of world history. They are self-curators and memorialisers *par excellence*. Their life, their thoughts, their hopes and fears are dutifully diarised, published and archived. A life lived as recording. Buribunkdom is not a society but rather a machine of atomistic content producers, a nation of noise-making, text-producing individuals.

There is no 'we' for the Buribunks.

This preface is about all the others who have engaged and been involved in the process of discovery and engagement with Carl Schmitt's enigmatic and alarmingly prescient text that led to this collection. Buribunks might be islands, but we decidedly are not.

Griffith Law School in the 2010s was a location for creativity and critique broadly within the discipline now known as cultural legal studies. Through the deanship of William P. MacNeil, text, context and a particular form of playful praxis with popular cultural legalities were fostered and encouraged. It was into this community that Schmitt's 1918 tale of *Die Buribunken*, forgotten in English, was remembered.

The first substantive step was achieving a full translation of Schmitt's *Die Buribunken* from the original German. In 2016, together with Timothy D. Peters and Edward Mussawir, we were surprisingly successful in convincing the Dean (Research) Gerry Docherty to provide funds for a translation and a small workshop. Through Shaun McVeigh, the president of the Law, Literature and Humanities Association of Australasia, we were put into contact with Gert Reifarth and Laura Petersen, who completed the initial (and now subsequent) translations of the text. The workshop was held on 24 November 2017. First reflections and draft papers were presented by Timothy D. Peters, Karen Schultz, Lachlan Robb, Catherine Pickering, Charles Lawson, Daniel McLoughlin, Roshan da Silva, Chris Butler and us. The opening keynote was by Wouter G. Werner and special thanks were also due to Mark Antaki, who was a fantastic discussant.

But like the Buribunks, who must publish to live, we who live to publish had to publish from the workshop or perish. The translation and the first round of manuscript was reviewed and collated and published in the *Griffith Law Review* 27(2) (2019). This included fuller versions of some of papers presented at the workshop and work by Michael P.A. Murphy, Vittorio Lubrano, Attila Gyulai, Francine Rochford and Desmond Manderson. Particular thanks are owed to Edward Mussawir as managing editor and Kate Edmonds as production editor of the *Griffith Law Review*, who had the patience and forbearance to work with us and the contributors on the volume.

Which comes to this volume. This book owes its existence to the interest that has come from the translation of *The Buribunks* and the workshop. There has emerged a community of scholars who find the text hard to put down and harder to stop thinking about. Ironically, it is a text that inspires writing.

We wish to specifically thank the executor of the Carl Schmitt estate, Professor Dr Jürgen Becker, for granting permission to publish this translation.

Further, we wish to thank the following who have been readers and commentators on various manuscripts in this project: Afshin Akhtar-Khavari, Nour Benghellab, David Caudill, Maria DiBattista, Thomas Giddens, Daniel McLoughlin Francine Rochford, Lachlan Robb, Joseph Owens, Mark Thomas, Vittorio Lubrano, Matthew Specter, Pedro Tereso de Magalhães, Attila Gyulai, Karen Petroski, Steven S. Kapica, Richard Joyce and Morshed Mannan.

We would also like to thank Collin Perrin at Taylor & Francis for his support and belief in the project (and for finally getting us to commit to a subtitle), and Susan Jarvis, Kristina Chelberg and Hamish Ironside for their editorial work.

Edwin Bikundo and Kieran Tranter
Gold Coast, Queensland, Australia
30 May 2021

Part I

Introducing *The Buribunks*

Chapter 1

The Buribunks as law, technology and literature

Kieran Tranter and Edwin Bikundo

> Let us, true to our method, start with what is, with the facts. Both are facts: the Buribunks keep a diary and also have an enlarged mouth.[1]
>
> Carl Schmitt, *The Buribunks* [1918]

Diary entry 21δ1010W: Carl Schmitt and diary people

Carl Schmitt seemingly looms over contemporary legal and political theorising.[2] Marginalised after the war through his refusal to participate in de-Nazification coupled with his pre-war engagement with the Nazi regime, Schmitt was seen as a dangerous thinker.[3] His Weimar works presented to post-war legal and political culture a dangerous critique of cosmopolitan liberalism through recognition of the irredeemable violence inherent in Western politics. The twenty-first century, with its politics of terror, nationalism and naked institutional violence, has resulted in a growing appreciation of Schmitt's intellectual output accompanied by appropriate caution. While this has not been a blind reassessment of the man, let alone a re-evaluation of his political choices in Germany in the 1930s, theorists – particularly Giorgio Agamben, Judith Butler, Chantal Mouffe and Jacques Derrida – have led to a reconsideration of how Schmitt and his core contributions can help make sense of the contemporary world, law, politics and being.

One of Schmitt's first publications was *The Buribunks* ('*Die Buribunken*'), published in the journal *Summa* in 1918.[4] Readers otherwise familiar with Schmitt's later writings would nonetheless be surprised by its tone and content. *The Buribunks* is a piece of speculative fiction. In it, a 30-year-old Schmitt discusses the future emergence of a specific type of posthuman – 'the Buribunks' – humans who have become integrated into a global system of information production through continuous diary writing and dissemination. The text, written in the voice of a celebratory pamphlet for the Buribunks' global ascendency, describes

1 Chapter 2 of this volume, p 14.
2 Meierhenrich and Simons (2017).
3 Müller (2003).
4 Schmitt (1918).

DOI: 10.4324/9781003091066-2

the cultural origins of the Buribunks, the organisational features of 'buribunkdom' and the central tenets of the Buribunks' manifesto. It is a tightly packed text. A (dys)utopian world of *logos* fixated elites. A parody of intellectuals. A critique of modernity through the forms of modernism. A triumphant promethean ontology that, in its extremity, seems ludicrous. An insight into the developing thoughts of the man and his complicities.

Until now, *The Buribunks* has only been a footnote in the work of Schmitt scholars. Mentioned in passing, it is generally regarded as an early work peripheral to Schmitt's later opus. Friedrich Kittler included a substantial extract from it in *Gramophone, Film, Typewriter.*[5] Kittler's use of *The Buribunks* is insightful. For Kittler, it provocatively identified the transformation from analogue existence to the informational age of the digital.[6] Contemporary readers of *The Buribunks* are particularly struck by its imagining of an information culture of the real-time self-dissemination of personal details as highly suggestive of living in, and with, the digital. Given the general lack of scholarly attention, little is known about Schmitt's motivations for the text. Schmitt's biographer suggests that the 'realm of buribunkerism' is an institution inspired by Schmitt's wartime bureaucratic experience in the Army General Command in Munich.[7] As a parody of an output- and publicity-obsessed academia, it could also suggest Schmitt's struggle for a position within the German academy at the time.

One possible reason for the passing over of *The Buribunks* is that, until now, there has not been a full English translation. A partial translation did appear in *Gramophone, Film, Typewriter*, but the full text has not been available to English-speaking scholars. In recognition of the centenary of publication, Griffith University commissioned a full English translation of *The Buribunks*. This translation has been approved by the Schmitt estate for publication. The latest version of this translation is reproduced in Chapter 2 of this volume.

Diary entry 21δ1010X: buribunkian activity about Buribunks

> Copies of all diary entries are submitted daily and collated by local councils. Their simultaneous inspection results in indexation according to subject matter as well as authorship … Due to an ingenious scheme, later inspection through a card catalogue makes it possible straight away to determine every circumstance of interest pertaining to each person … The diaries thus arranged and inspected are submitted in regular monthly reports to the head of a Buribunk department who … is thus able to record buribunkologically all of buribunkdom. Depictions of one another in photographs and films, constant traffic of diary exchanges, readings from diaries, visits to art studios, conferences, establishment of journals,

5 Kittler (1999)
6 Kittler (1999), p 231.
7 Mehring (2014), p 82.

> theatre festivals with homages to the personality of the artist staged before and after the show – in short, many adequate precautions ensure that the interest of the Buribunk in himself and everything buribunkian does not dry up.[8]
>
> Carl Schmitt, *The Buribunks* [1918]

This volume is the final outcome of a series of activities relating to the full English translation of *The Buribunks*. Like good Buribunks, we undertook presentations and conferences and symposia. There was reporting of progress to funding bodies. There was publishing of the interest in the project and exchanges of texts and commentaries. The central penultimate activity was the publishing in the *Griffith Law Review* of the translation and early versions of several of the chapters that are in this volume. The Buribunks write, type and record in the present to acknowledge their doing in the past, so that it is available, searchable and transparent to the future. In the fullness of this spirit, it is important that we acknowledge the chapters that have had an earlier iteration in the *Griffith Law Review*.

Earlier versions of the translation and the translators' notes were published as:

- Carl Schmitt (2019), '*The Buribunks*. An Essay on the Philosophy of History' 28 *Griffith Law Review* 99.
- Laura Petersen and Gert Reifarth (2019), '*The Buribunks:* A Translators' Note' 28 *Griffith Law Review* 113.

Iterations of Chapters 4, 7, 9, 10, 14, 15 and 16 were published as:

- Kieran Tranter (2019), '*Die Buribunken* as Science Fiction: The Self and Informational Existence' 28 *Griffith Law Review* 118.
- Michael P.A. Murphy (2019), 'What Does It Mean to be Anti-Social? Potentiality and Political Ontology in *The Buribunks*' 28 *Griffith Law Review* 154.
- Francine Rochford (2019), 'Negative Space: The Paradox at the Heart of Buribunkology' 28 *Griffith Law Review* 247.
- Vittorio Lubrano (2019), 'On the Normality of Writing: Inscription/Description of Everyday Life' 28 *Griffith Law Review* 173.
- Karen Schultz (2019), 'Schmitt's Satire in *The Buribunks*: Intertextual Links in Diary-Writing's Dystopia' 28 *Griffith Law Review* 206.
- Desmond Manderson and Edwin Bikundo (2019), 'Forms of Irony in Carl Schmitt's Political Romanticism, *The Buribunks* and Ex Captivitate Salus' 28 *Griffith Law Review* 189.
- Attila Gyulai (2019), 'It's a Fact: The Buribunks are the Enemies of the Political' 28 *Griffith Law Review* 231.

8 Chapter 2 of this volume, p 24.

Diary entry 21δ1010Y: The chapters

> In each second of world history, under the rushing fingers of the World-I, the letters rush from the keyboard of the typewriter onto the white paper and continue the historical narrative.[9]
>
> Carl Schmitt, *The Buribunks* [1918]

The chapters that follow are divided into four parts. Along with this introductory chapter, Part I comprises the translation of *The Buribunks* by Gert Reifarth and Laura Petersen, along with an extended note by the translators. In the note, Petersen and Reifarth discuss the challenges and choices they made in bringing *The Buribunks* to an English readership. They particularly map and note the intertextualities used by Schmitt and introduce Schmitt's own focus on diarising.

The chapters in Part II all consider and explore *The Buribunks* as typeset. Typesets are models, masters and measures, something hard that leaves a mark and allows for copies. Typesets represent an ideal against which the fidelity of copies can be determined. In this part, the Buribunks as Schmitt's fictional creations with their informatic and archive management priorities are embossed. Each of the chapters considers the Buribunks and the social, institutional and ontological worlds that Schmitt creates around them as typesets for contemporary concerns. The Buribunks as invocative creations are the focus.

This is seen directly in Chapter 4 by Kieran Tranter, which essentially takes the Buribunks as the imagery of informatic existence seriously. He argues that, notwithstanding the textual apparatus of buribunkdom, they provide a measure for contemporary anxieties and transformations from the digital. He suggests that the Buribunks' sole focus is on mastering their imprint in the collective archive; this highlights both the transition zones between the actual and the digital and the institutional pressure for the formation and maintenance of perfect digital twins emanating in both the Global West and East.

Where Tranter takes an approach of the Buribunk as a measure – indeed, a cypher for the digital – Chapter 5 by Timothy D. Peters builds beyond this relationship. Peters sees in *The Buribunks* a science fictional examination of the theological commitments of bureaucracy and its practices of archiving. Connecting with Schmitt's responses to Max Weber in *Political Theology*,[10] Peters draws parallels between *The Buribunks* and the science fiction of Philip K. Dick, arguing that both point beyond the economic theology of omnipresence to a need to celebrate the unseen and the unrecordable.

In Chapter 6, Richard Polt draws a parallel suggestion from *The Buribunks.* However, rather than reading it through the political/economic theology lens like Peters, he regards the Buribunks as shallow, jumpy creatures that manifest Kierkegaard's and Heidegger's criticisms of modern life as unauthentic. Like

9 Chapter 2 of this volume, p 26.
10 Schmitt (1985).

Tranter, he sees the Buribunks as exemplars of the hyper-connected, hyper-stimulated, hyper-surveilled data-self of the digital. Like Peters, Polt embraces the speculative invitation presented by *The Buribunks*, imagining a resistive and grounded practice of 'privacing' as a possible escape from the 'hyper-buribunkist age'.

In Chapter 7, Michael P.A. Murphy also sees in *The Buribunks* a speculative imagining of a dystopian society of total surveillance and total control; a backwards facing society of actuality rather than potentiality. Murphy identifies in Schmitt's buribunkdom a parallel with Aristotle's account of the Megarians. The Buribunks over-emphasise the actual, the archive of doing, rather than the possibility of doing. He shows how this establishes a totalised and absolute sovereignty. But, like Peters and Polt, he also identifies that *The Buribunks* contains strands that could be woven into resistance. Murphy concludes by exploring how anti-social Buribunks – those that refuse to participate in the collective enterprise of diarising – represent an emancipatory challenge to the Megarian metaphysics of buribunkdom.

Karen Petroski identifies in *The Buribunks* an anti-intellectual parody in Chapter 8. With their obsessive focus not just on text production but on being cited and referenced in texts, the Buribunks do seem to capture the shallow narcissism of institutional academia. However, Petroski goes further, viewing *The Buribunks* as belonging to the tradition of Menippean satire where learned discourse and attitudes are parodied through linguistic complexity, rational irrationality and hyperbole. Identifying that *The Buribunks* is also generative of the academic hoax tradition, famously represented by Alan Sokal's *Social Text* incursion,[11] Petroski suggests that these forms of anti-intellectualism reveal a conservative agenda.

Like Tranter, in Chapter 9 Francine Rochford sees in the hyperconnectivity and data-sharing of the digital a coming to pass of buribunkdom. She observes a set of profound disjunctions. First, the continual depositing of facts reveals a crisis of facticity. Second, this diarising of self is audience-less. There are no readers, just producers. She then identifies how these Buribunk realities have infused the modern university – not so much in the older publish-or-perish survivalism, but in the dance of performance management, of accounting for hours as moments of discrete value creation. The diary becomes an auditing weapon and iron frame, where commitments in the present about the future become fact through the creation of data that solidify the promised future as a past. In common with Murphy, Rochford concludes with the hope that purposeful absence can be a form of resistance and escape.

Part III involves chapters that consider *The Buribunks* as writing and particularly as revelatory of modernist literature. The themes of 'truth', power and technology identified in the earlier chapters are present; however, the emphasis shifts to the complex paradox of parody and performance in *The Buribunks*. It is writing about the awareness of writing.

11 Sokal (2010).

Vittorio Lubrano sees this clearly. In Chapter 10, he identifies *The Buribunks* as a reaction to modernist projects in philosophy and writing, in particular the mechanisation and commodification of writing, as attempts to capture and know life. He identifies that to write is to control in a context of fundamental uncertainty about the efficacy of control. The Buribunks want to control their lives, but in doing so do not live at all. They create dead texts from zombie people. Lubrano transitions the level of engagement with *The Buribunks* in the chapters of this book. Where the earlier chapters regarded the text as suggestive of the digital contemporary, its anxieties and politics, the subsequent chapters peer more deeply into the text as a text.

This theme, particularly *The Buribunks* as celebrating a particular mode of writing, is emphasised by Joseph Owen. In Chapter 11, Owen focuses on Schmitt's relationship with the diary as a particular modernist form. He tracks how Schmitt's lifelong preoccupation with diarising was forged during his war years. He notes how modernist impulse infused Schmitt's relationship with the diary. Rather than realism and surface, Owen identifies how the influence of avant-garde cinema from that time manifested within Schmitt's practice of dairying, but also his excessive, distorted account of the diarising as totality in *The Buribunks*.

In Chapter 12, Nour Benghellab makes the distinction between the critique and criticism of parody and the empty formalism of pastiche. For her, *The Buribunks* is less parody and more pastiche. But she distinguishes pastiche from more contemporary entanglements of postmodern literary theory as empty, ahistorical appropriation. In examining *The Buribunks* as a retelling of Hegel and Kierkegaard, Benghellab both presents a revitalised account of pastiche as a literary technique and identifies the traces of Schmitt's future theorising of the progression of history towards mechanisation and automation. For her, *The Buribunks* is not only a manifestation of pastiche deployed as critique but anticipatory of Schmitt's later work.

Whereas Benghellab identifies the techniques of pastiche in *The Buribunks* as a form of writing, Ernesto C. Sferrazza Papa, following Reinhart Koselleck,[12] is prepared to distinctly call the text satire in Chapter 13. For him, the text is ultimately a satire of modern thought that involves talk and counter-talk, ending with the quantification and mechanisation of the world and life. Like Petroski, Sferrazza Papa identifies an anti-intellectual target of *The Buribunks*: a satire on the forms and cultures of a removed and *logos*-centric community.

Karen Schultz undertakes a similar argument in Chapter 14. In a substantial and detailed contribution, Schultz takes Schmitt's known classical influences and identifies the deep and immediate manifestations in *The Buribunks*. Specifically, she focuses on how the classic satires of Tacitus and Juvenal, both referenced by Schmitt in *Dictatorship*, [13] directly influence *The Buribunks*. From Tacitus, Schultz

12 Koselleck (2002), p 84.
13 Schmitt (2014).

forensically identifies the criticism of historians as pandering to ego and power, and from Juvenal, she takes the diminishing vitality of intellectual life through repetitive and marginal writing.

As can be seen in Chapters 12 and 14 by Sferrazza Papa and Schultz, the satirical registry of *The Buribunks* seems well acknowledged and through Benghellab, Schmitt's use of pastiche as a literary technique in support of this satirical agenda was identified. In Chapter 15, Desmond Manderson and Edwin Bikundo examine Schmitt's use of irony. Their chapter marks the beginning of Part IV of this volume, which reads and considers *The Buribunks* from within Schmitt's wider oeuvre. Manderson and Bikundo identify in *The Buribunks* an ironic Schmitt, whose broader writings tend to be read as direct and brutal. The friend/enemy distinction, his decisionism, the anti-romanticism and anti-liberalism are denoted in the concrete. Manderson and Bikundo show that the irony of *The Buribunks* is not an exception, but rather a feature of Schmitt's broader work. Following on from Petersen and Reifarth's identification of Schmitt's borrowing from Faust in *The Buribunks* (Chapter 3), they suggest a Faustian persona to Schmitt in the way irony is deployed as a sword in *Political Romanticism*[14] and a shield in *Ex Captivitate Salus*.[15] As with *The Buribunks*, both reveal a complex, cynical distancing between self and responsibility.

In Chapter 16, Attila Gyulai also considers *The Buribunks* in proximity to *Political Romanticism*. He argues that *The Buribunks* tells of the impossibility of positivism, of self-enclosed and self-referential systems, remaining pure. For him, *The Buribunks* prefigures Schmitt's concept of the political. As a text, it tells a fable of an apolitical society, yet there are two cracks that rupture this smooth world of facts. The first is the tension in the text regarding the accredited author, 'C.S.', who writes of the Buribunks for an imagined audience of non-Buribunks – an imagined other as addressee in the midst of the triumphant, large-mouthed diarists. The second is the named intra-textual other, the failed Buribunks who refuse to contribute to the archives of buribunkdom.[16]

In their provocative compound Chapter 17, Fabrizio Grasso and Matteo Negro use *The Buribunks* to interrogate Schmitt's ontological engagements with history. In the first part of the chapter, Grasso establishes that *The Buribunks* presents an embolden factuality of history – history as concrete and simultaneously boundless. He then sets up through identifying Schmitt's indebtedness to Aquinas the way Christian hope and mystery complement, indeed give meaning to, a universe of facts. This leads to the second part of the chapter, in which Negro suggests *The Buribunks* invokes a Promethean world-view, a politics of fact and will imposed on the world. Like Peters, Negro sees an awareness and emphasis on the theological within Schmitt. Negro then traces through Schmitt's major works how this brutal ontology is counterpoised by

14 Schmitt (1986).
15 Schmitt (2017).
16 On this point see also McLoughlin (2019).

the figure of the Christian Epimetheus (a persona Schmitt explicitly adopts in *Ex Captivitate Salus*). Where the Buribunks as Promethean moderns think they can make the world through writing, fixing the future with a plan, the Christian Epimetheus does not disengage from world-making and politics, but only knows the meaning and effect of that engagement at the end. Unlike the meek Christian passively awaiting the end, or the *Katechon* who delays the end, the Christian Epimetheus functions in the absence of certainty of outcome.

In summary, *The Buribunks* provides a rich text. The beings and their civilisation animated by Schmitt suggest a template and a structure to make sense of the digital. It is a satire and critique of a modern orientation to both thought and writing. Further, it helps appreciation of Schmitt's broader oeuvre. Ending with the pitiful, problematic imago of the Christian Epimetheus as the Schmittian counterpose to the Buribunks seems like a fitting conclusion. Except. As Tranter and Rochford suggested in their chapters, the buribunkian ethos of worth and meaning only in quantity of citation is an even more intense paradigm in the contemporary academy than it was for the scholars of his own age that Schmitt seemed to be lampooning. The cold calculous of worth through metrics dominates.[17] Which opens to the postscript by Lachlan Robb, Charles Lawson, Catherine Pickering and Edwin Bikundo. In Chapter 18, they present an analysis of Schmitt's influence on the academy since 2001. Directly asking the question of how a Buribunk would consider Schmitt, they present a 'mixed methods' analysis of citations to Schmitt since the commencement of the 'War on Terror'. They find that Schmitt is 'no Ferker dominating the archive, rather his impact is fragmented, spread across disciplines and presented in heterogeneous company'. The Schmitt considered as a Buribunk is revealed more as Christian Epimetheus than Prometheus. His influence and remembering seem to be incidental and accidental, surfing the currents of history rather than making waves. A Buribunk in decline, slowly leaching out of the archive, or a cynical anti-Buribunk who sowed enough ambiguous seeds that they seem to keep sprouting in the gardens of subsequent generations. Furthermore, the rigorous data-gathering, counting and digital-aided analysis of this chapter should also give pause. Like the authorial 'C.S.' in *The Buribunks*, how much of the enthusiastic and earnest tabulating and analysis should be taken as such – or is there an ironic parody at play?

As less than successful Buribunks, we leave it to others, in future 'rat' seconds,[18] to make the next entry.

References

Zeena Feldman and Marisol Sandoval (2018) 'Metric Power and the Academic Self: Neoliberalism, Knowledge and Resistance in the British University' 16 *tripleC: Communication, Capitalism & Critique* 214.

17 Feldman and Sandoval (2018).
18 Chapter 2 of this volume, p 26.

Attila Gyulai (2019) 'It's a Fact: The Buribunks are the Enemies of the Political' 28 *Griffith Law Review* 231.

Friedrich A. Kittler (1999) *Gramophone, Film, Typewriter*, Stanford University Press.

Reinhart Koselleck (2002) *The Practice of Conceptual History: Timing History, Spacing Concepts*, Stanford University Press.

Vittorio Lubrano (2019) 'On the Normality of Writing: Inscription/Description of Everyday Life' 28 *Griffith Law Review* 173.

Desmond Manderson and Edwin Bikundo (2019) 'Forms of Irony in Carl Schmitt's Political Romanticism, "The Buribunks" and Ex Captivitate Salus' 28 *Griffith Law Review* 189.

Daniel McLoughlin (2019) 'The Biopolitics of "The Buribunks": The Digital Archive and the End of History' 28 *Griffith Law Review* 137.

Reinhard Mehring (2014) *Carl Schmitt: A Biography*, Polity Press.

Jens Meierhenrich and Oliver Simons (eds) (2017) *The Oxford Handbook of Carl Schmitt*, Oxford University Press.

Jan-Werner Müller (2003) *A Dangerous Mind: Carl Schmitt in Post-War European Thought*, Yale University Press.

Michael P.A. Murphy (2019) 'What Does it Mean to be Anti-Social? Potentiality and Political Ontology in "The Buribunks"' 28 *Griffith Law Review* 154.

Laura Petersen and Gert Reifarth (2019) '"The Buribunks": A Translators' Note' 28 *Griffith Law Review* 113.

Francine Rochford (2019) 'Negative Space–The Paradox at the Heart of Buribunkology' 28 *Griffith Law Review* 247.

Carl Schmitt (1918) 'Die Buribunken' 1 *Summa: Eine Vierteljahresschrift Viertes Viertel* 89.

Carl Schmitt (1985) *Political Theology: Four Chapters on the Concept of Sovereignty*, MIT Press.

Carl Schmitt (1986) *Political Romanticism*, MIT Press.

Carl Schmitt (2014) *Dictatorship: From the Origins of the Modern Concept of Sovereignty to Proletarian Class Struggle*, Polity Press.

Carl Schmitt (2017) *Ex Captivitate Salus: Experiences, 1945–47*, Polity Press.

Carl Schmitt (2019) 'The Buribunks: An Essay on the Philosophy of History' (trans Gert Reifarth and Laura Petersen) 28 *Griffith Law Review* 99.

Karen Schultz (2019) 'Schmitt's Satire in "The Buribunks": Intertextual Links in Diary-Writing's Dystopia' 28 *Griffith Law Review* 206.

Alan Sokal (2010) *Beyond the Hoax: Science, Philosophy and Culture*, Oxford University Press.

Kieran Tranter (2019) 'Die Buribunken as Science Fiction: The Self and Informational Existence' 28 *Griffith Law Review* 118.

Chapter 2

The Buribunks

An essay on the philosophy of history

Carl Schmitt

Translated by Gert Reifarth and Laura Petersen

Buribunkology as a science

Before anything else, it should be the ambition of every science to justify its existence through actual achievements and to ensure that an imposing body of work stands in the way of any subversive doubt regarding its potential as a science. If the value of any methodological discussion about the scientific nature of human intellectual activity lies only in reflecting upon the intellectual methods and aims of the work, then this presupposes a body of work in the first place – in the same way, it is self-evident that there would be no study of America if America had not been discovered, and no buribunkology if there were no buribunkologists.[1] Such historicity planted with both feet on solid ground is, at first glance, certainly convincing and does not have to fear any objections. However, we do not intend for the apparent evidence to deter us from discovering the hidden difficulties of the situation, so that our careful scepticism will be rewarded with an insight into the finest nuances. For it is the essence of true buribunkology not only to understand the actual facts in the fullness of their interpretations but also to capture itself with luminous clarity as the object of buribunkology – in this way, it advances to the highest heights of human intellectuality, thus joining the course of history in full awareness of its own embeddedness in the historical. Every buribunkological publication is in turn part of buribunkology and thus constitutes a reality in the buribunkological sense.

Out of these observations an argument needs to be developed, whose rigour would only be denied by ultramontane ignorance or old-fashioned Lutheran stubbornness. If it is true that there is a point where – to express it in Hegel's brilliant phrase – quantity turns into quality, then the discussion of the question of buribunkology as a science has to revolve around the cardinal point of

1 In this way, the existence of the Buribunks themselves, which is occasionally denied by hypercritical doctrinists in a manner that can hardly be taken seriously, is *a priori* put beyond doubt. As the existence of America follows from the fact that American Studies exists, the existence of the Buribunks follows from the fact that buribunkology exists.

DOI: 10.4324/9781003091066-3

whether the factual quantity of buribunkological actualities has reached such an extent that it is only sensible to address it as a quality (which here means as a science). In response, we would therefore have to supply a bibliography of buribunkological research. However, we restrict ourselves to mentioning that already more than 400,000 buribunkological dissertations (20 divisions!) have been published and for years the weekly competitions of the International Buribunkological Institute for Ferker and Related Research (IBIFERR) have always culminated in numerous prizes and laudatory recognition. Apart from this, the buribunkological publishing house represents one of the most flourishing branches of our highly developed publishing industry and – last but not least – the Buribunk and Ferker Research Panel Commission (BAFREPAC) has a standard yearly budget of several billions. Especially this powerful fact provides impressive evidence. According to the well-known, wise remarks by Simmel, the great philosopher of money, it is money, in a supreme sense, to which the transition of quantity into quality is most applicable. Therefore we may use this considerable sum as the cornerstone of our argument; it puts it beyond any scientific doubt that if quantity can turn into quality at all, then this point has already been reached for buribunkology.

Of course, we shall not deviate from the position of cautious historicism in our own science, and shall not cease to keep before our eyes the relative correctness and relative incorrectness of all human insight in the never-ending developmental process of the World Spirit. This enables us to eliminate an obvious objection, which we do not want to fail to mention. The dead, life-opposing, formulaic mud of scholasticism also reached a considerable quantitative volume, and doubtlessly was a real historical force for centuries. But scholasticism belongs to a stage of development whose position has long been negated by the unstoppably forward-moving World Spirit as it lies not only 10 or 20 years behind us, but – here too the quantity of the number transitions into the quality of the value – several hundreds of years. Therefore it cannot be difficult for us to recognise the difference between today's buribunkology and obsolete scholasticism – it lies exactly in the essence, the spirit: buribunkology is alive, scholasticism is dead, the Buribunks live and the scholastics are long buried.

Scientific buribunkology is in an especially advantageous position towards its subject, Buribunkdom, as a similar spirit breathes life into both and unites them in a harmonious marriage. What would all research be without the secret weaving of the spirit which fuses lifeless details into a living organism and aids empathic understanding by transforming every act of perception into a genuine internalisation of memory. There is a good deal of true Buribunkdom in every single one of the 400,000 dissertations and we do not deem it irrelevant that the reward for the lowly intellectual drills is no different from that which history pays the ingenious organiser for the high flights of his mind – the reward rests in the certainty of entering oneself into history and to be still quoted in aeons. So here the most immediate spirit lives everywhere and grants us an understanding of the true meaning of life, namely life itself, life as it is historically present or was historically present, in its concrete factual actuality and positivity. Hence our subject matter is an overwhelming reality, nothing from the realm into which dreamers gaze but fact and fact again. After the sad experiences of the scholastic centuries we can no longer doubt it: a big effort was wasted foolishly, a nearly immoral waste of strength lured humankind from the green fields of secularity into the grey theories of speculation. Naturally this was also a necessary stage of development and not without relative value and appeal. We will also not lose the superiority of our objectivity here and protest in an emotional fashion or become enraged.[2] Therefore metaphysics no longer poses a danger for us. But nevertheless we are aware of our duty to buribunkology, and every attempt to bring back the sad speculations of those bygone days will face the united front of buribunkologists, who come together under the victorious battle cry: buribunkology is more than theology, jurisprudence or philosophy, it is indeed more than a science, it is a fact.

The Buribunks

Let's go *in medias res*, let's tackle the problem at its central, most interesting point: what is the criterion, the *differentia specifica*, the big distinctive feature? Is it intellectual or physical? Is it, in other words, the fact that every Buribunk keeps a diary or the fact that he has an enlarged mouth?

Let us, true to our method, start with what is, with the facts. Both are facts: the Buribunks keep a diary and also have an enlarged mouth. But which is the more meaningful fact? At first glance, it could appear as if the keeping of diaries were displaying such an enormous intellect that we have to locate the more meaningful buribunkological value in this, rather than in the enlarged mouth, which appears to be merely a physiological fact. If, however, we consider that lesser peoples, Polynesians, Tierra del Fuegians, Baronga Negroes and other tribes incapable of an education, have a relatively small mouth, even though they are cannibals, the close connection between the enlarged mouth and a higher intellect becomes a probability. This probability reaches its ethical certainty through the further assertion that if a small mouth is already sufficient to elevate those primitive races above the level of apes and birds, a bigger mouth (again according to the theory of quantity becoming quality) has to lead to a decisive divide between two different sorts of humans, so that the sort on this side (on the side of the big-mouthed Buribunks) relates to the unkempt kind on the other side no differently than that kind does to apes and birds. It would

2 Schmitt allows himself the outright unbelievable statement that every remaining respect for the spiritual on earth was the inheritance of the Christendom of the Middle Ages from which we kept living for a few short centuries *in dulci jubilo* (similar to apprentices who have stolen the petty cash) – only to then realise what a de-Christianised world really thinks about art and science. In the name of the whole of buribunkology, I reject this brazen statement in the strongest terms.

therefore be careless, to say the least, to simply deem the diary to be the decisive fact in an intellectual sense rather than the enlarged mouth – it would indeed betray ignorance of most valuable ethical insights if one were to deny that (even if intellect is needed to keep a diary) the enlarged mouth leads to the assumption of a particularly productive intellect, as it is the intellect that designs the body. If we now, fully conscious of the intellectual importance of the enlarged mouth, nevertheless lean towards preferring the diary, we are guided in this by a decidedly historical appreciation of progress whose stages can indeed be proven historically by the spreading of the idea of keeping a diary – whereas the gradual enlargement of the mouth would require a physiological-anatomical, in short a more medical, consideration.

Today, as we are able to enjoy the radiant high noon of the idea of keeping a diary in its full delightfulness, we gladly overlook the achievement of the person, who (perhaps an unknowing instrument of the World Spirit) planted in an unassuming primordial fashion the seed that now shades the earth as a powerful tree. A certain, I may say, moral feeling of responsibility forces upon us the question of which historical person we have to acknowledge as the predecessor of this glorious epoch – the dove which the World Spirit sent prior to its last and most advanced period. We will have to address this central question through a general investigation.

For buribunkology, it would be a proud triumph to be able to call a hero like Don Juan their ancestor and thus (in opposition to the accusation of scholarly unworldliness) to achieve the paradox of hailing from this life-mocking and truly unscholarly gentleman. Indeed a record is kept of Don Juan's conquests, but the *punctum saliens* is to whom the intellectual ownership of this idea is to be attributed. Don Juan himself sings in his Champagne Aria:

> Ah, la mia lista doman mattina
> d'una decina devi aumentar –

a sentiment that frequently courses through the true buribunkologist when he considers the ever-increasing extent or number of his publications. Therefore, he will be tempted to compare such a victorious feeling with the brash self-confidence of the frivolous conqueror of women. In spite of this, we must not be deterred from our incorruptible seriousness by a seductive similarity and must also never forget to keep a distance to our possible ancestor which is proscribed by calm objectivity and unemotional scientific endeavour. Did Don Juan really have this specifically buribunkian attitude which led him to keep a diary – not for superficial, boastful fun but rather out of, dare I say, a sense of damned duty and obligation towards history? We are unable to believe it. Don Juan had no interest whatsoever in the past, indeed just as little as in the future, which for him barely extended beyond his next rendezvous; he lived in the immediate present and his interest in the singular erotic experience did not contain anything in which we could glimpse the beginning of self-historicisation. We do not notice anything of that attitude which distinguishes the Buribunk and which springs from the urge to preserve every single second of one's own being for history: the creating and viewing of oneself as a monument. The diary-keeping Buribunk pounces on every second, as does Don Juan – their psychological impulse is certainly similar. But instead of consecrating his prey on the altar in the light-filled temple of history, he drags it into the murky depths of brutal hedonism, devouring it like an animal satisfying its base instincts.[3] At no point does he have the, as I call it, buribunkian cinematic attitude – he never understands himself as history's subject-object, in which the World Soul has become action through writing itself. He only acknowledges in passing the record that Leporello keeps for him as an amusing spice to his base pleasures. We may rightfully doubt whether, for example, among the 1003 representatives of Spain as few as three owe their inclusion to the existence of the record; in other words, whether Don Juan was moved to act in as few as three cases through the inner longing to generate or continue the record – in the same way as numerous grand deeds of art, science and daily life owe their existence to the thought of the diary or the newspaper (the diary of the general public). The record was never *causa finalis*; for the relevant acts of innervation in question – within the parallelogram of psychological forces – it played at most the supporting, marginal role of an accompanying incentive. Thus we are finished with Don Juan.

Leporello's behaviour is all the more interesting. He takes the sensual pleasures which are leftovers from the table of his master, a few girls, a few tasty bites – other than that he merely serves his master. A Buribunk does not do this as the Buribunk is unconditionally and absolutely his own master, he is himself. However the desire awakens by and by in Leporello to participate in the experience of his master through his writing down of it, taking note of it – this is the moment when the dawn of Buribunkdom begins. Through an admirable ruse, he rises above his master and even if he does not become Don Juan himself, he becomes more than that – he advances from being his wretched servant to his biographer. He becomes a historian, he drags him before the bench of world history, that is, the world court, to appear there as defender or prosecutor depending on the result of his observations and interpretations.

Is Leporello really aware of the fact that with his catalogue he made the first step towards an enormous development? Surely not. We do not want to belittle the powerful attempt that is the little list of the poor buffo, but we cannot under any circumstances address him as a conscious Buribunk – how indeed should he come to it, he the poor son of that beautiful but culturally so

3 In this way, one could say Don Juan did not chew over his experiences, if indeed one were to accuse the buribunkian diary-keeping of being a sort of intellectual rumination. However the falseness of such an accusation is easily proven as the diary-keeping Buribunk does not actually experience anything beforehand, but it is the entry into the diary and its publication that constitutes the experience. To speak of chewing over is thus outright nonsensical because there has been no chewing in the first place.

backward country, in which the terror of papal inquisition trampled down and destroyed the last remainders of intelligence. Thus he was not able to bring to fruition his intellectual achievement (even though it was still important); he has in his hand the chest full of treasures but is lacking the key. He missed the essential point and did not utter the magic words that open up the way to Aladdin's treasures. He lacks awareness of the writer's higher consciousness, the awareness of being the author of a piece of world history and therefore having become an associate judge of the world court – and even having influence over the judgment of this world court as through his written documents he submitted evidence which cannot be refuted by a hundred oral witness statements. Had Leporello possessed the strong will to this power, if he had dared to attempt this fabulous leap to be an independent writing personality, he would have first of all written his autobiography, he would have made a hero out of himself, and instead of the easy-going cavalier who fascinates superficial minds, we may well have the impressive image of a superior manager who pulls the colourful marionette Don Juan on the strings of his superior business skills and intelligence. But instead of taking the quill into his fist, the poor devil clenches his fist in his pocket.

On closer inspection, the utter inadequacy of Leporello's cataloguing becomes obvious to us in the form of countless errors. He places one photograph after the other, but nowhere is there an attempt to form a homogeneous continuum out of the heterogeneous discontinuum of successive conquests – there are no linking thoughts or accounts of development. We notice no evidence of causal connections, or of the psychological, climatic, economic and sociological conditions of the singular incidents, or of an aesthetic account of the rising and falling curve of the development of Don Juan's taste. Neither do we notice any specific historical interest in the singularity of every procedure. His lack of interest is completely incomprehensible; he does not even express any consternation when he sees every day how the phenomenal sexuality of his master vanishes in an aimless rush instead of being channelled into the rational direction of a purposeful policy of population growth. There is even less of an urge to gather reliable research into details – nowhere does he trace the deeper connections of the specific conquest, nowhere does he collect sociologically useful data about social status, origin, age and so on of Don Juan's victims or about their previous lives – at the most he remarks that they were 'of every social status, every shape and every age', which appears to be far too general for scientific research. We also don't hear anything about the fact that these victims may later have united in large collective mass action and provided mutual economic support, which in view of the large number would doubtlessly have been the only appropriate thing to do. Also missing, of course, is any statistical breakdown within the individual numbers, which would have been so obvious when considering a figure as high as 1003; even more obviously absent is a reference to how social welfare, which had become necessary in so many cases, took care of the abandoned girls. Naturally there is also no trace of the thought that the introduction of women's suffrage would be a basic demand of justice in view of this brutal exploitation of the social superiority of man towards the defenceless women. We look in vain for the fundamental laws concerning development of the collective mental state of society, the subjectivism of the time and the degree of its sensitivities. In a word, imperfection here becomes reality. Leporello is deaf to the sheer mass of the most urgent scientific questions – to his own detriment, as he has to pay dearly for his deafness in front of history. Because he disregards these questioning voices, he did not even conduct a single investigation (the opportunity which today even the most immature student of humanities would not have missed), and therefore he has not become aware of the importance of his own personality. The dead matter has not been conquered by the intellectual activity of its editor, and the theatre posters on the advertising pillar still read: *Don Juan, The Libertine Punished,* and not *Leporello's Tales.*

Let us, then, leave the good buffo behind and turn to the representatives of Buribunkdom, whose development has advanced and evolved in a logical way. It is self-evident that at all times there were people who kept diaries and had a feeling of responsibility towards history. Marcus Aurelius's writings have been mentioned in this respect,[4] and someone even went back to the Confessions of Saint Augustine[5] without sensing that in such catholicising trivialities we merely encounter the phosphorescence of African–European race mixing which, sinking into decadence, finds a last biological lifeline through a morbid clinging to God and unmanly self-deprivation. It makes more sense to mention

4 Ulrich Finnig, *The Origins of Buribunkdom*, Halle an der Salle 1912, p 208 ('a fledgling seed of true buribunkian spirit already graces the pages of this noble philosopher in an emperor's coat'). As a result of the authors' fondness for their hero (which has been noticed so often of late), F. too cannot bring himself to conclude that Marcus Aurelius's writings suffer greatly from moralising auto-pedagogical constructions which render the reading of it all into a serious test of patience for the buribunkologist.

5 P. Expeditus Schultze, *Was Saint Augustine a Modern Author?* Cologne 1911, p 385. In my opinion, Sch. is far too lenient towards Augustine. Obviously no researcher in their right mind will expect from an author from the fourth century the height of the intellectual level of our time, but this excuse should never lead us to give up on all essential expectations. Otherwise we declare all people of whom we have fixed written statements to be Buribunks, even Pythagoras with his duty of confidentiality, which is so anti-buribunkian. Also obsolete to the point of anachronism is the remark of H. Reuter, *Augustinian Studies*, Gotha 1887, p 4: 'That Augustine should have made the days of conversion the subject of reflection immediately after they occurred is improbable for psychological reasons alone. Processes of this kind may indeed have repercussions which permeate the future inner life, but towards a critical analysis of their own self-consciousness … towards a written account that would correspond to that interest, the people in question do not usually feel well-disposed. We know of no such analysis from Paul, Luther or Calvin.' Faced with this naïve psychology of R., we cannot help but smile; the novel *Ascension to Heaven* by H. Bahr and also the extensive written account of Bahr's recent conversion renders it simply *ad absurdum.*

here Pliny the Elder,[6] a number of details from whose life appear indeed to be eminently buribunkian (he read when he wasn't writing, and wrote when he wasn't reading). We also observe a rather positive sign of the new spirit in Richard Wagner's autobiography, in which the master recounts the fact that he had not been able to bear his loneliness without lively correspondence and had waited from one postal delivery to the next. The real development, however, only begins, and immediately on the largest of scales, with the great Ferker.

Only Ferker developed the diary into an ethical-historical possibility; he holds the rights of the first-born in the realm of Buribunkdom. Be history yourself! Live so that every single one of your seconds can be recorded in your diary and fall into the hands of your biographer! Coming from a mouth like Ferker's, those were big and strong words which humankind had never heard before. A world confederacy for the distribution of his ideas, which was organised with great skill and which had at its disposal an intelligent press, paved the way for this thought to reach the last corners of the most remote villages. No hamlet is so small for no smith to be there at all, to quote an old folk tune; today we may say with pride that no hamlet is so small for a puff of buribunkian spirit not to blow there. The extraordinary man[7] who towered over thousands of aides like a field marshal and guided enormous activity with a steady hand, at one instance deploying platoons of researchers to a threatened spot, at the next supervising (with unheard-of strategic ability) pioneering dissertations as a means of digging trenches into difficult problems – this incredible personality had gone through truly sensational life events. Born as the son of poor people and educated in the Latin-less school of his small hometown, he in turn became a dentist, a book maker, a newspaper editor, a heavy construction contractor in Tiflis, a secretary in the central office of International Organisations for the Increase of Tourism to the Adriatic Sea, a cinema owner in Berlin, an advertising manager in San Francisco, and finally a lecturer for Advertising and Arrivistics at the Business School in Alexandria. It was there that his cremation took place, as well as the utilisation of his ashes for the production of printing ink (which was organised in grand style and had been strictly regulated by himself in his will), from which a small part was sent to all printing presses on earth. Then the whole of civilised humankind was educated about this

6 Kuno Lifschitz, *On the Methodology of Buribunkology*, Berlin 1909, p 32.

7 There is rare agreement about this in all relevant documents. Maximillian Sperling, in his diary (*Sperling's Diaries*, edited by Alexander Bumkotzki, Vol. XII, Breslau 1909, p. 816) calls him 'a smart fellow'. Theo Timm in his letter of 21 August to Kurt Stange (*Timm's Letters*, edited by Erich Veit, Vol. XXI, Leipzig 1919, p 498) calls him 'a fabulous bloke'. 'I find him marvellous,' writes Mariechen Schmirrwitz in her diary (edited by Wolfgang Huebner, Vol. IV, Weimar 1920, p 455). 'He is enormous, every way you look at it,' cries Oskar Limburger, enraptured after their first meeting (*Recollections From My Life*, edited by Katharina Siebenhaar, Stuttgart 1905, p 87). A 'demonic type', writes Prosper Loeb, Königsberg 1899, p 108. A 'tremendous guy' writes Knut vom Heu in his letters to his bride (edited by her son Filip), Frankfurt am Main, 1918, p 71, etc.

event through leaflets and illuminated advertising and warned with unsurpassable poignancy to always remember that in every single one of the billions of letters, which the eye encounters over the years, there is an atom of the ashes of the immortal man. Thus the trace of his earthly days cannot disappear in aeons; through a grand, shall we say, anti-metaphysical-positive gesture, he secured for himself (even in death a genius of actuality) his continued existence in the memory of humankind, which is even more solidly secured by the library of diaries, part of which he already published in his lifetime and part of which he had edited after his death. For in every moment of his eventful life, he knows himself to be eye-to-eye with the writing of history or the press; in the midst of nerve-wracking events, he cranks changing film images into his diary with cool calmness in order to incorporate them into history. Thanks to this foresight, but also thanks to the selfless research that followed, we are informed about nearly every second of the life of the hero.

We will not address its details here,[8] as we are interested only in the specifically buribunkian state of the soul in its historical crescendo which gradually develops in its intensity over time. We see a wildly agitated life, filled with nerve-wracking experiences without Don Juan's mindless addiction to pleasure, in full awareness of its own wild agitation, I would even say of its own modernity and suitability for the theatre; this self-awareness begins with abstaining from all ideology and still marvelling at the fact that life is (to speak in the crude tone of this time) a grand old thing. This knowledge of oneself as a subject of interest (artistic, scientific and historical interest), this heightened self-awareness, connected inextricably with completely dissolving into the community – those are the characteristic contours of a great life. In the sharpest rejection of every thought of a diary, Ferker had devoted himself in the beginning to reckless work and thoughtless self-enjoyment after he had been filled with a deep loathing for every ideology even as a seven-year-old pupil at his Latin-less school. Although this loathing was justified, it initially led to an unacceptable disregard of the factual meaning of the spiritual/intellectual. Until

8 See mainly the still authoritative Ferker biography by Pielenpiep in 200 volumes, a work of the noblest buribunkological observance. Also John Puffke, *Ferker's Mouth*, Göttingen 1898 p 33ff (proficient work!); Emil Sterker, *Our Ferker*, No. 78029 in the collection 'Intellectual Heroes', Leipzig 1900; Gustav Maria Adolf Mayer, *Ferker's Work as a Maker of Books*, Hamburg 1892; Max Hirschberg, *Ferker's Bowel Movement*, Wiesbaden 1913; Aenne Schwitz, *Ferker and Us Women*, Marburg an der Lahn 1910 (with interesting psychological empathy!); Eduard Fuchs, *Ferker in the Cartoons*, Munich 1914; Florence Marson Cassel, *Is There a Real Ferker Problem?*, New York 1913; Gaston Maquaque, *Ferker et le Ferkerianisme*, Lyon 1912; Heinrich Ritter von Kistemaker, *Ferker as a Dentist* (with important compilations of his client lists) in BAFREPAC's 253rd session report from 15 November 1911. More populist and pedagogical: Herbert Eulenberg's silhouette 'Ferker' in his fine collection of silhouettes, Berlin 1912; Maria Züttkemaier, *What Do I Tell My Little Ones About Ferker?*, Paderborn, 1910; Richard Knorp, *Ferker in Primary School*, Jena 1907.

the logic of the facts turned this Saul, too, into a Paul and nudged him with the soft force of historical experience towards the insight that makes the egg of Columbus stand: all the big hustle, the tireless drive to utilise everything and the expansive drive to produce can be transferred without the slightest loss of power and intensity to the spiritual/intellectual, the ethical. In this way, not only was the human being Ferker ethically elevated, but also the most incredible scientific progress accomplished and a splendid example provided of the truth that the progress of humankind can only be expected when everyone only thinks of themselves and lets everything else run its own course. Only now we are able to define historically the crucial achievement of the ingenious man: not only has he utilised the world-changing idea of the modern corporation for human intellectual activity without leaving moral ideals behind; not only has he – demonstrating through his life that one can follow a purposeful career and still be an ethically complete person – connected mind and matter through the abolition of a dualism hostile to life and removed (through a victorious new idealism) the constructions of theologising metaphysics which were unsuited for the intellectual climate of the twentieth century; he found (and that is the most essential aspect) a form of contemporary religiosity while strictly retaining an exclusive positivism and an unflinching belief in nothing but the facts. And the spiritual region where the synthesis of these numerous contradictory elements, of this tangle of negated negatives, takes place – the inexplicable, the absolute, the essence of every religiosity – is none other than the buribunkian.

No buribunkologist, who is a true Buribunk at the same time, will utter the name of such a man without the deepest reverence. Before we continue, we have to strongly emphasise this. Because if in the following we contradict the opinions of commendable Ferker researchers with regard to the critical classification of the hero, we do not want to do so without emphatic protest against the misunderstanding that we would misconceive the formidable impulses which came from Ferker, as if we had not yet grasped his full greatness. Nobody can be more permeated by and filled with it than us. Even so, he is not the hero of Buribunkdom, he is only the Moses who was allowed to see the Promised Land but not to enter it. There are still starkly alien elements circulating as foreign bodies in Ferker's otherwise pure blood; atavistic reminders still cast their shadows onto large periods of his life and cloud the pure image of autarkic noble Buribunkdom. Otherwise it would not be plausible that the great man, despairing over his most inner self, lowered himself shortly before his death not only to enter a bourgeois Christian marriage but even to marry his own housekeeper, a woman who we know to have been an utterly uneducated, even illiterate person who, in the end, in sanctimonious bigotry, tried to prevent the cremation in the same way that she generally hindered the free development of his personality. It need not be repeated that our buribunkological discipline must not let us down when faced with this fact. As nothing human is alien to us, we are able to understand even such perversions of the human heart and accordingly enter them *sine ira et studio* into the book of history. It must, however, be stressed that this point, which the Ferkerologists treat with understandable silence as a *pudendum* – as if there were *pudenda* in buribunkology! – is not discussed even superficially in Ferker's diaries. We know from an impeccable source[9] that he was afraid of death; neither about this nor about the motives behind his marriage did he leave a diary entry. We are faced with a conundrum.

The only possible solution to the question contains, in turn, the seed of new questions. Whether Ferker married the housekeeper out of a depression which can be traced back to his neuro-psycho-pathological disposition or whether the neuro-psycho-pathological illness is a result of his marriage – we are restricted to mere speculation about this question because of the lamentable lack of any diary entries. There is something to be said for the first assumption, because if the neuro-psycho-pathological disposition had not existed, at least a hint about the approaching decision to marry should be found in the diaries.[10] The fact that the assessment of his character, otherwise so straightforward, is severely disturbed in this instance, suggests the conclusion that the psychological abnormality manifests itself in locking up the torments of his soul – instead of writing them down and externalising them in a publication – and allowing them to create poisonous dreams of an atavistic fear of death and of a moral sense of responsibility. Ferker had not yet recognised with the urgently required rigour what today is common practice for every one of us: turning the intellectual-spiritual struggles and cramps that hinder free creativity into an object of creativity. This was the reason why he stumbled and, acting with unbearable caprice, once again allowed the old times to raise their head. To have overcome such caprice and to have moulded Buribunkdom in its purest form into a historical reality is the achievement of Schnekke.

As a fully ripened fruit of the noblest Buribunkdom, this genius fell from the tree of his own personality. With Schnekke we no longer find the hint of a stumble, no deviation, however small, from the noble lineage of the proto-buribunkian. He is nothing but a diary-keeper, he lives for the diary, he lives in and through the diary – even though in the end he keeps a diary about the fact that he has run out of ideas about what he could write in the diary. On a level where the I – projecting itself onto a tangible You-World – streams back into the World-I with powerful rhythm, the highest harmony is reached through the absolute devotion of all powers to the inner self and its identity. As ideal

9 From the memoirs of Ferker's doctor, Dr Friedlieb (edited by his daughter Erika, Cairo 1899, Vol. VII, p 95).

10 F. Rappaport, *Ferker as a Psychopath*, Geneva 1908 (highly interesting study, but probably not really up to its subject matter), also F. Scheiner, *Ferker and Marriage*, Leipzig 1900. Sch.'s assumption that the housekeeper suppressed all diary entries relating to Ferker's marriage I consider unproven, as the housekeeper could neither read nor write (which becomes obvious from her school reports edited by Boldt (Munich 1911)).

and reality have melted into one in unheard-of perfection, any peculiarities – which made Ferker's life so sensational, but in a considered view should attract doubt rather than praise – are missing. Schnekke is a personality in an even higher sense than Ferker, and exactly for that reason he vanished fully into the most unobtrusive sociability; his distinct originality, his I, which resonates in extreme autonomy, rests in an indistinctive generality, in a uniform lack of colour which is the result of the will to power at its most sacrificial. Here the last and absolute height is reached, and we do no longer have to fear a regression as in Ferker's case.[11] The realm of Buribunkdom has been established. For Schnekke, with his strong feeling of commonality and his universal instinct, found opportunity in the midst of his perpetual diary-keeping to sever the diary from its restrictive tie to the single person and elevate it to a collective organism. The organisation of the obligatory collective diary on a large scale is his achievement. Through this, he set and secured the external conditions for buribunkian interiority, and elevated the resounding chaos of unconnected individual Buribunkdom to the harmonious perfection of a buribunkian cosmos. Let us trace the outlines of this sociological architecture.

Every male and female Buribunk is obliged to keep a diary for every second of their existence. Copies of all diary entries are submitted daily and collated by local councils. Their simultaneous inspection results in indexation according to subject matter as well as authorship. Not only are the entries of an erotic, demonic, satirical, political and so on nature grouped together (under the strictest observation of the copyright law pertaining to each entry), but the authors are also catalogued according to their place of residence. Due to an ingenious scheme, later inspection through a card catalogue makes it possible straight away to determine every circumstance of interest pertaining to each person. If, for example, a psycho-pathologist was interested in the dreams of a certain class of Buribunks during their puberty, the relevant materials could be compiled in no time at all with the help of the card catalogues. The work of the psycho-pathologist would, however, itself be subject to registration so that, say, a historian of psycho-pathology could reliably determine in a matter of hours which kind of psycho-pathological studies have so far been conducted

11 What a difference between Ferker's and Schnekke's behaviour towards women! With Schnekke, there is never a thought of Christian marriage, he recognises it with instinctive certainty as a ball and chain on the leg of his genius and knows how to avoid it with unfailing certainty, despite his numerous erotic relationships which have taken on a definite shape in his inner life. He always remains aware of his debt to the free development of his uniqueness, and rightfully calls on Ekkehard, when he writes in his diary that marriage would restrict his essential I-ness. However we must also not overlook the enormous progress on the part of the women from Ferker to Schnekke. In Schnekke's life, there is no woman who is illiterate, none that would dare in a laughably petit bourgeois way to obstruct the genius's desire for being unrestrained, none who would not have been proud to have served a man like Schnekke as a muse for his artistry and enjoyed in this the noblest reward for her femininity.

and at the same time – this is the biggest advantage of double registration – which psycho-pathological motives led to these psycho-pathological studies. The diaries thus arranged and inspected are submitted in regular monthly reports to the head of a Buribunk department who, in this way, has constant control over the course of psychological development in his province, and he himself reports to a central agency which creates master catalogues published simultaneously in Esperanto, and is thus able to record buribunkologically all of Buribunkdom. Depictions of one another in photographs and films, constant traffic of diary exchanges, readings from diaries, visits to art studios, conferences, establishment of journals, theatre festivals with homages to the personality of the artist staged before and after the show – in short, many adequate precautions ensure that the interest of the Buribunk in himself and everything buribunkian does not dry up; they also prevent a detrimental anti-social digression of this interest, and thus it does not have to be feared that the sublime rotation of this buribunkian world will ever come to an end.

A rebellious spirit, however, also expresses itself here, albeit rarely. But it needs to be taken into account that in the realm of the Buribunks there rules a limitless, all-understanding, uncomplaining tolerance and the highest respect for personal freedom. No Buribunk is prevented in any way from freely creating his diary entries; not only may he state that he lacks the intellectual strength for entries and that only the sadness about this lack of strength gives him the necessary strength – this is even a very popular type of entry that is especially recognised and highly regarded. He can also note, without having to fear even the slightest pressure, that he regards the diary as a pointless and burdensome institution, as a silly harassment, as a laughable custom; in short, he is not barred from using the strongest expressions. For the Buribunks know very well that they would damage the nerve centre of their existence if they were to restrict the unconstrained freedom of expression. There even exists a well-regarded organisation that sets itself the task to buribunkially record anti-Buribunkdom. In the same vein, a separate enterprise has been established in order to accommodate (in impressive diary entries) the disgust and revulsion towards the whole enterprise and the protest against the duty of diary-keeping. And whenever the diary entries threaten to suffer from a certain uniformity, the leaders of the Buribunks stage an initiative at periodic intervals, which usually re-establishes the individual-personal character with great success.[12] The apex, however, of these liberties lies in the fact that no Buribunk is prevented from writing in his diary that he refuses to keep a diary.

Needless to say, this freedom must not become unrestrained anarchy. Every entry of the refusal to keep a diary needs to be justified and described in detail.

12 In connection with this, the brave neo-buribunkian attempts deserve special attention: they have led to the periodically repeated competition on the question 'What real progress has Buribunkdom achieved since Ferker?' and to decisive action designed to aid this progress.

Whoever, instead of writing that he refuses, really stops writing, makes inappropriate use of the general freedom of mind and will be eliminated due to his anti-social disposition. The wheel of progress passes silently over the silent one; he will no longer be mentioned, he can therefore no longer make himself heard until he finally, sinking step by step, is forced into the lowest class, to help create the external conditions for the possibility of noble Buribunkdom, for example making by hand the paper on which the most valuable diaries are printed … This is a strict but entirely natural selection of those who are better, as he who doesn't succeed in the intellectual struggle of the diaries will fall behind progress and be absorbed by the masses who create those external conditions; as a result of these physical labours, menial services and so on, he is also no longer able to use every second of his life buribunkologically and thus his fate plays out with merciless inevitability. As he no longer writes, he can no longer defend himself against possible slurs regarding his person, he is no longer up to date, and eventually he vanishes from the screen of the monthly reports and ceases to exist. As if the earth has swallowed him, nobody knows him anymore, nobody mentions him in their diary, no eye sees him, no ear hears him; and may his lament be ever so harrowing and drive him into madness, the iron law does not know mercy against the unworthy one who has excluded himself, in the same way as the fundamental laws of natural selection know no exception.

Thus the Buribunks hope through tireless and eager work to reach such perfection of their organisation that an unheard-of refinement is ensured, even if perhaps only in hundreds of generations. Bold calculations – may progress grant that they do not turn out to be utopian! – see the culture already at such a height that, as a result of the unlimited progress, the ability to keep a diary gradually appears with the Buribunk-foetus. The foetuses could then inform each other about their unique perceptions through means of communication yet to be created – and could thus supply the necessary factual base for a refined ethics of sexuality, unveiling the last secrets of sexual research. All this lies of course still in the far distance, however it is a historical fact that today there already exists a powerful Buribunkdom that is highly organised and thus contributes to the most intense enjoyment of one's innermost personality – a Buribunkdom that is talking, writing and enterprising, triumphantly entering the dawn of its own historicity.

Outline of a philosophy of the Buribunks

I think, therefore I am; I speak, therefore I am; I write, therefore I am; I publish, therefore I am. This does not contain a contradiction, but is merely the ascending order of identities, which develop beyond themselves according to the laws of logic. For the Buribunk, thinking is nothing other than soundless speech; speaking nothing but scriptless writing; writing nothing but anticipated publishing and therefore publishing is identical with writing, with such minor differences that they may safely be disregarded.

I write, therefore I am; I am, therefore I write. What do I write? I write myself. Who writes me? I myself write myself. What is the content of my writing? I write that I write myself. What is the big engine lifting me above this self-sufficient circle of I-ness? History!

I am therefore a letter on the typewriter of history. I am a letter writing itself. But strictly speaking I do not write that I write myself but only the letter that I am. But, writing, the World Spirit captures itself in me – so that I, capturing myself, at the same time capture the World Spirit. In fact I do not capture myself and it through thinking, but writing – for in the beginning there is the deed and not the thought. That means: I am not only the reader of world history but also its writer.

In each second of world history, under the rushing fingers of the World-I, the letters rush from the keyboard of the typewriter onto the white paper and continue the historical narrative. Only in the second in which the single letter leaves the senseless and meaningless indifference of the keyboard, and hits the lively connections on the white page, a historical reality is created; only this second is the birth hour of life. That is to say, of the past, as the present is only the midwife who delivers the lively historical past from the dark body of the future. Until it has been reached, the future lies there as dull and indifferent as the keyboard of a typewriter, like a dark rat hole from which one second after another (like one rat after another) steps into the light of the past.

What does, ethically speaking, the Buribunk do who keeps a diary every second of his life? He wrests every second from the future in order to incorporate it into history. Let us remind ourselves of the full magnificence of this procedure: from second to second, the blinking young rat of the present second creeps out of the dark rat hole of the future, out of the nothing of what has not yet been, in order to enter with sparkling eyes in the next second the reality of the historical. In contrast to the mindless human being, for whom millions and billions of rats stream into the immensity of the past without plan or aim and become lost there, the diary-keeping Buribunk is able to capture them one by one and have their well-organised legion perform the big parade of world history. Thus he secures for himself and humankind the biggest possible quantum of historical factuality and awareness. Thus the fearful anticipation of the future loses its horror, for whatever may be, one thing is certain, namely that no second emerging from the future is lost, no letter of the typewriter will miss the page.

The death of the individual is also merely such a rat-second; it does not carry within itself its content – happy or sad – but only receives it through the writing of history. In the rat-second of my death, however, quill and diary fall from my hand and I seem to be no longer actively involved in this writing of history; the essence of diary-keeping, the will to power over history fades and makes room for a foreign will. If we disregard here the pedagogical side of the matter, that means the urge not to lose a second in order to impose our will to power onto the future writing of history, we need to admit that the termination of our will to history arrives very much against our will, as the will to power always only signifies the will to one's own power, not to the power of some historian in the coming centuries. Such doubts will however cause heavy confusion and we have already seen how even in the case of the great Ferker the fear of death had a catastrophic influence on his historical fame; today the true Buribunk is hardly in any danger of confusion thanks to the growing awareness whose sunlight exterminates the germs of the fear of death.

We see through the illusion of singularity. We are the letters that have rushed from the hand of the writing World Spirit and we consciously surrender ourselves to this writing power. In this we see true freedom. But in this we also find the means to put ourselves into the place of the writing World Spirit. The single letters and words are but the tools of world history's cunning. Many a defiant 'Not' which is thrown into the text of history feels proud in its opposition and considers itself a revolutionary, when perhaps it merely negates the revolution. But by consciously becoming one with world history which writes, we grasp its spirit, we become its equal and – without stopping to be written – nevertheless at the same time position ourselves as writers. In this way we outwit the cunning of world history – writing it while it writes us.

In the realisation that there is true reality only in history, we seek real immortality in history. Not in some after-world. Christianity had 'shifted' the heads of people in a literal sense (in full acknowledgement of the relative value of its sublime teachings this needs to be stressed) as it had turned the gaze from the factuality of the past to an after-worldly future, where there is, as we saw, only the dark rat hole of that which not yet exists, but no reality. Therefore we restore the correct direction for the heads towards the real by seeking immortality where it really is: behind us not before us.

The thought of posterity begat many heroic deeds. But who was posterity up until now? An imaginary person, a scheme, a fiction? The heroes who lived before Homer, as is well known, may also have hoped for posterity, for immortal fame. They have been cheated out of it. Who until now had a guarantee of fame in posterity? Most names have been preserved through curious accidents. *Festum breve gloria mundi.* And in spite of this, the instinct was right and only needed a more solid factual foundation. For a life without fame is a dance without music, a carousel without a street organ. However we are able, thanks to the buribunkian institutions, to transform fame,[13] which until now really was only a fleeting shadow, into a solid state and stabilise it in the form of a compact mass of diaries and printed material, instead of empty talk. A

13 Schmitt allows himself the unbelievable assertion that in view of eternity all earthly fame was merely a worthless illusion, but no replacement for immortality – if, indeed, in fortunate cases fame were to still grow for centuries after death, this would be the same as the hair and nails of a corpse continuing to grow. We refuse to tolerate such disgusting comparisons (which we liken to those of the church fathers) and reject them in the strongest terms in the name of buribunkology.

noble motive of human greatness is in this way relocated from the uncertain sphere of metaphysical illusion and returned to solid ground.

This is the true ethics, true because it is anchored deeply in the facts. The Buribunk does not need Christianity or any other ideology. He is smilingly above that, without emotion, without complaint. He is among many other things also a Christian, but he knows more about Christianity than a thousand theologians. For he is not only a Christian; he is a Christian as well as a Buddhist, a Muslim, an Agnostic, he is everything as he recognises all things in their reality, which means in the relativity of their historical conditions. Thus he is more than all these things, and more than all human beings who do not rise above them – and through writing he gains the viewpoint of the absolute, understanding everything and also himself in his relativity. He is the World Spirit writing itself, perpetuating itself, outwitting itself in its immediate irrefutable factuality.

C.S.

Acknowledgements

Originally published as 'Die Buribunken' in (1918) 1(4) *Summa* 89. An earlier version of this translation was published in (2019) 28(2) *Griffith Law Review* 99. Thank you to the executor of the Carl Schmitt estate, Professor Dr Jürgen Becker, for granting permission to publish this translation.

Chapter 3

Behind the words of *Die Buribunken*

Translators' comments

Laura Petersen and Gert Reifarth

Contemporary readers would have found Schmitt's essay in the fourth and last issue of the journal *Summa* (1917/18), which was a collection of 'essays, marginalia and reprints of famous texts from philosophy, theology and political science'.[1] *Die Buribunken* was published in the section entitled 'Marginalien' (marginalia).[2] Both the English and German words have the same connotations and are derived from the Latin *margo* (on the side). However, marginalia in *Summa* were not annotations but substantial texts. They belong to a genre of German writing called the gloss, which has long been used for religious, legal and literary commentary.

Our aim was to recreate the experience of a present-day German reader picking up the text and to replicate Schmitt's pervasive nominal style. Where possible, we consciously attempted to retain Schmitt's distinctive phrasing and other formal and stylistic elements that characterise the original. In order to enhance readability, we occasionally introduced en dashes and parentheses to help structure the long, convoluted sentences, but attempted to keep the same length and flow. Regarding the style of the text, we draw your attention to two examples. First, the text contains a number of military phrases.[3] This

1 Schmitt (2005b), p 430. (This translation and all others in this piece are our own.) Hüsmert and Giesler also note that *Summa* had stylish typography and high-quality binding: Schmitt (2005b), p 430. Alongside the editor Franz Blei and Schmitt, other authors published in *Summa* included Ernst Bloch, Robert Musil, Konrad Weiss and Hermann Broch.

2 The text is signed with the initials C.S. Using initials rather than full names was not unusual for texts published in this section of *Summa*. About half the authors included their full names and the other half are only identifiable by their initials. Schmitt had three pieces published in *Summa*: 'Recht und Macht' (issue 1); 'Die Sichtbarkeit der Kirche. Eine scholastische Erwägung' (issue 2); 'Die Buribunken' (issue 4). Schmitt and Blei were collaborators, with some of Schmitt's work also published (under the pseudonym Dr Negelinus) in Blei's literary satire *Das große Bestiarium der Literatur* (1920): see Schmitt (2005b), p 12.

3 'divisions [of dissertations]' (*Divisionen*); 'lowly intellectual drills' (*Gamaschendienst*); 'united front' (*die geschlossene Phalanx*); 'under the victorious battle cry' (*unter dem sieghaften Schlachtruf*); 'who towered over thousands of aides like a field marshal' (*der*

DOI: 10.4324/9781003091066-4

perhaps reflects the military tone of an era of war and may also have their origin in Schmitt's own experience of World War I.[4] Second, it is noticeable that when Schmitt shifts his discussion regarding writing to include a specific technology – the typewriter – the sentences become much shorter.[5] We retained this stylistic effect: the words become a staccato imitation of mechanical keys hitting paper.

Close reading of selected words and phrases

There are well-known German terms in Schmitt's text that present one with numerous different possible translations. *Wissenschaft* is one such word, which can be understood as an 'academic discipline', but can also mean 'study' as well as a more general reference to intellectual endeavour, translated as 'science', applying to both the natural sciences and the humanities disciplines. *Das Geistige* can be read as 'the spiritual', 'that which concerns the intellect' or 'that which concerns the mind'. Our translations of these terms attempt to capture the meanings we feel are most fitting in each instance.

In the section titled 'The Buribunks', we translated the Buribunks' physical feature that is *ein erweitertes Maul* with the phrase 'an enlarged mouth'.[6] Different to *Mund*, the standard German term for a human mouth, *Maul* is a term used for animal mouths and for name-calling – for example, *Halt's Maul* is an insulting command similar to the English 'shut your trap' and *Großmaul* is used for a boastful person. Later in the text, Schmitt includes the similar term *großmäulig* (big-mouthed).[7]

In the passage about *Don Giovanni*, when Leporello's strategy of list-making is scrutinised, Schmitt mentions the *Individualität des einzelnen Vorgangs*, which means 'the individuality of each procedure'. The word choice *Vorgang* seems oddly technical here; we decided to use 'conquest' with its overtones of sexual endeavour.[8]

When Schmitt attempts to convey the imperfections of Ferker, he disparages his education at a *lateinlose Realschule*, a 'Latin-less school'.[9] While today in

wie ein Generalstabschef über den Tausenden von Hilfskräften thronte); 'deploying platoons of researchers to a threatened spot' (*bald die Kolonnen der Forscher an eine bedrohte Stelle warf*); 'digging trenches into difficult problems' (*die Eingrabung in schwierige Probleme*). Chapter 2 of this volume, p 19.

4 Schmitt was in the army from February 1915. He was put in charge of a division of the Bavarian Army Corps responsible for censoring printed materials and monitoring the peace movement: Schmitt (2005b), pp 6–7; Mehring (2014), pp 61–71. Official army documents written by Schmitt are reprinted in Schmitt (2005b), pp 181–399, as well as diary entries from the Army Barracks, pp 19–60.

5 Chapter 2 of this volume, pp 25–6.

6 Chapter 2 of this volume, p 14.

7 Chapter 2 of this volume, p 14.

8 Chapter 2 of this volume, pp 15, 17.

9 Chapter 2 of this volume, pp 19, 20.

Germany a *Realschule* is a non-academic type of secondary school that finishes after Year 10, in former times it was school that focused on a 'real' – that is, 'factual' – approach to education. In Reformation times, the opposite was a *Lateinschule*, Latin school, which focused on religious education conducted in Latin and was seen as preparation for university.[10] By virtue of his Latin-less education, Ferker becomes an unscholarly figure.[11] In addition, Ferker's imperfection is likened to an impurity of blood. We learn that there are starkly alien elements that circulate as *Fremdkörper* (foreign bodies) *in Ferkers doch wirklich rassigem Blut*. The adjective *rassig* may mean 'hot-blooded', 'sleek', 'fiery', yet any of these translations would not establish a logical sequence with the preceding sentences. Our translation is, 'There are still starkly alien elements circulating as foreign bodies in Ferker's otherwise pure blood.'[12] A term like *rassiges Blut* for the modern-day German reader is impossible to separate from the later use of the terms *rassig, rassisch* and *reinrassig* (racially pure, of pure breed) in the National Socialist ideology and its devastating consequences.[13]

Ferker's successor, and indeed buribunkology's saviour, Schnekke, is said to have managed his private life *trotz seiner zahlreichen zu innerer Definivität gediehenen erotischen Beziehungen*. We retain the rather convoluted style here, a little unsure of the passage's exact meaning, and introduce the word 'life' so the sentence reads 'despite his numerous erotic relationships which have take on a definite shape in his inner life'.[14] It may well be that Schmitt simply means 'despite his many actual erotic relationships'. Likewise, towards the end of the text, we introduce another word, 'relocated', to assist with the meaning of the passage: 'A noble motive of human greatness is in this way *relocated* from the uncertain sphere of metaphysical illusion and returned to solid ground.'[15]

When Schmitt writes that some Buribunks may deem diaries *einen lächerlichen Zopf*, the literal translation of the phrase would be 'a laughable pigtail/plait/braid'. It refers to a hairstyle that was common, for example, in the Prussian army in the eighteenth century and also known in England as a 'queue', when soldiers braided their long hair.[16] The expression later became a metaphor for something that is obsolete and unnecessary and hence has to be abolished; one must *alte Zöpfe abschneiden* (cut off old braids). In light of this background, we translated the expression as 'a laughable custom'.[17]

10 See Hammerstein (1996), pp 376–8, 408–10.
11 We may also find a hint here to the first half of the seventeenth century as the time of his fictional life, as it was then that the opposition of the two school types was at its most pronounced.
12 Chapter 2 of this volume, p 21.
13 It is striking, given Schmitt's later association with National Socialism, to read descriptions regarding race and 'pure blood'.
14 Chapter 2 of this volume, p 23, n 11.
15 Chapter 2 of this volume, p 28.
16 See Stocqueler (1871), p 103.
17 Chapter 2 of this volume, p 24.

Further, in the process of becoming one with the spirit of world history, the text asserts that we (as Buribunks) *setzen uns dennoch gleichzeitig als Schreibende* (nevertheless at the same time position ourselves as writers).[18] Note the connotations in German regarding the meaning of *setzen*, which is 'to type-set', and a typesetter used to be known as a *Setzer*.

The names of the two fictional heroes of buribunkology in the text prove to be one of the various displays of Schmitt's sense of humour. 'Ferker' brings to mind the German word *Ferkel* (meaning piglet but can also be used to call a human a 'swine'), while 'Schnekke' is close to *Schnecke* (meaning snail and also referring to a person who is slow to act).[19] Schmitt also cites an extensive archive of pretend research – for example, his footnotes are peppered with amusing inventions such as the book title *Ferker's Bowel Movements* or a researcher named Knut vom Heu (Knut of the Hay). This parody of the conventions of academia adds a key element to the playfulness of *The Buribunks*.

We made two small adjustments to the text.[20] First, in the passage that states *kein Dörflein so klein ist, daß nicht ein Hauch buribunkischen Geistes darin webe*, we took *webe* (to weave) to be a typographical error for *wehe* (to blow) and translated thus: 'no hamlet is so small for a puff of buribunkian spirit not to blow there'.[21] This takes into account the German noun *Windhauch* (puff of wind) as well as the expression *Hier weht ein Hauch von …* (Here blows a puff of …).[22] We also corrected one instance where the terms 'Buribunk' and 'buribunkologist' appeared to be mixed up.[23]

18 Chapter 2 of this volume, p 27.

19 There is also a personal intertextual connection with this character. Schmitt seems to have invented a figure called Schnekke, sometimes spelled Schnecke, years earlier. The editors of Schmitt's diaries refer to a similarly named theatre character that Schmitt used in plays written with his friends in early 1910, and in late 1911 he was a character in a novel Schmitt wrote and circulated among his friends: Schmitt (2005b), p 11. Note those friends (Fritz Eisler, Eduard Rosenbaum, Franz Kluxen) are also called 'the real Buribunks' by the editors of the volume (p 11).

20 Other typographical errors in the original text, which we implicitly corrected, are: *Bühengerechtigkeit* should be *Bühnengerechtigkeit*, a comma is missing between *Zeitschriftengründungen* and *Festspielaufführungen*, and *mit groBem Erfolg* should be *mit großem Erfolg*.

21 Chapter 2 of this volume, p 19.

22 We thank the anonymous reviewer of the 2019 version of the translation published in the *Griffith Law Review* for their suggestion that perhaps 'webe' is correct. If the translation was to read 'no hamlet is so small for a puff of buribunkian spirit not to weave through' then, as they suggest, this would fit the references in the text to the 'weaving' of material together into a totality through an organiser. However, we find that it is more likely to be a printing mistake.

23 Chapter 2 of this volume, p 14. Schmitt mentions *großmäulige Buribunkologen* (big-mouthed buribunkologists) when he clearly refers to the object of the study of buribunkologists, namely Buribunks.

Intertextuality and form

Schmitt employs three different types of exponents of Buribunkdom: historical figures, existing fictional characters and Schmitt's own inventions. He refers to some historical figures as early – and imperfect – Buribunks, namely Marcus Aurelius, Saint Augustine, Pliny the Elder and Richard Wagner. To steer closer to an ideal Buribunkdom, he then invents two weighty figures (Ferker and Schnekke) and fabricates sources in order to provide them with an extensive biographical as well as academic background. Furthermore, Schmitt anchors his text firmly in the tradition of European art and philosophy by referring to and quoting from key (and actually existing) works in both fields. References include Simmel's philosophy of money, key ideas by Hegel and the phrase 'will to power', which points to Nietzsche.

There are also two more extensive examples of intertextuality on which we want to comment. First, Schmitt offers a buribunkological reading of Mozart's darkest opera, *Il dissoluto punito, ossia il Don Giovanni* (1787), two characters from which he exploits for his own purposes.[24] After Don Giovanni himself is hailed as an ancestor of the Buribunks but then discarded, Leporello, man-servant of Don Giovanni, provides the initial example that enables Schmitt to introduce the idea of how diary keeping should be practised. By rejecting the servant's unscientific approach to the recording of events, Leporello provides a negative template: a proper Buribunk should do whatever Leporello fails to do.[25] This includes going beyond the mere disinterested recording of events; it

24 The opera is commonly known just as *Don Giovanni*. The full title, referred to by Schmitt at the end of the section on Leporello, translates as *The Rake Punished, or Don Giovanni*. The biographical assertions that Schmitt himself may be viewed as a Don Juan adds an unexpected resonance to this section of the text. According to his latest biographer, Reinhard Mehring, Schmitt was a womaniser who 'developed more and more into a questionable Don Juan, rushing from conquest to conquest' (Mehring 2014, p 210). In a further twist, Schmitt's friend Alice Berend included in her 1918 novel *Der Glückspilz* ('The Lucky One') well-disguised intimate details from Schmitt's first marriage (see Schmitt 2005a, p 13 n 36 and an excerpt in Schmitt 2005b, pp 521–3). Schmitt in his own diaries lists his sexual encounters with his first wife and even his ejaculations rather bluntly (see Schmitt 2005a, pp 96, 98, 100, 102, 105, 153; Schmitt 2005b, pp 113, 174). His diaries also feature much private pettiness and an outburst against women voicing political opinions (by which they 'shed their femininity') and female artists who put art in danger: Schmitt (2005a), p 190.

25 In fact, Leporello appears to be much more of a Buribunk than Schmitt gives him credit for. In the *Catalogue Aria*, he sings, 'There are farm girls, chambermaids, women from the city, countesses, baronesses, marchionesses, princesses … He likes plump girls in winter and slim ones in summer … The older ones he conquers just to add them to the list, but his first passion are the young and inexperienced ones. He doesn't care if they are rich, ugly, beautiful – as long as they wear a skirt.' Leporello's account thus includes size, social status, age and other personal characteristics of Don Giovanni's conquests.

involves making broader connections, detailed analysis and even the drawing of practical conclusions.

Second, Schmitt frequently borrows expressions (without reference) from a drama that is arguably the German language's most famous, namely Goethe's *Faust* (1808/1832).[26] The play's devil figure, Mephistopheles, enjoys Schmitt's particular interest. For instance, his enraged outcry after Faust's soul is 'stolen' from his devilish grip, 'a big effort was wasted foolishly',[27] is directed by Schmitt towards the uselessness of scholasticism, which Schmitt accuses of having produced only 'grey theories of speculation'. This refers to a scene in which the devil messes with the mind of a young scholar-to-be, who he confuses with these words: 'All theory, dear friend, is grey, / And green life's golden tree.'[28] To bemoan the inferiority of Leporello's buribunkian efforts, Schmitt adapts the devil's comment on unsatisfactory philosophical efforts: 'Alas, the linking thoughts are missing.'[29]

In addition to these intertextual references and borrowings, Schmitt's footnotes are a key formal element of the text. From the 13 footnotes, most are a straightforward spoof with (fictional) references or comments on the proposition in the text. There are also two footnotes that are self-reflexive.[30] Taken at face value, these footnotes add a layer of commentary from the perspective of a buribunkological colleague who is reviewing the text, who refers directly to 'Schmitt'. Tommissen contends that these two footnotes contain the personal position of Schmitt himself.[31] We suggest, however, that these two footnotes are meant to be read as if they were fictional editorial interjections. In any case, their presence extends the narrated time of the text and its process of creation: it gives the appearance of having been reviewed. Therefore, despite the narrator's professed fidelity to the discipline of buribunkology, the text is not written in the professed buribunkian style where words hit the page in a rush of letters. Instead it takes the form of an academic style of argument with a polyphony of other textual and fictional influences.

26 Schmitt was also enthusiastic about a drama that brings Don Juan, Faust and the devil together – Christian Dietrich Grabbe's *Don Juan und Faust* (1828). See his diary entry from 19 December 1915: Schmitt (2005b), p 170, and also p 6.

27 Chapter 2 of this volume, p 14. 'Ein großer Aufwand, schmählich! ist vertan' (*Faust* line 11837).

28 Chapter 2 of this volume, p 14. 'Grau, teurer Freund, ist alle Theorie, / Und grün des Lebens goldner Baum' (*Faust* lines 2038–39).

29 Chapter 2 of this volume, p 17. See *Faust* line 1939. Beyond quoting the devil, Schmitt also takes two lines from the play's closing *Chorus Mysticus* – 'Imperfection / Here becomes reality' (Chapter 2 of this volume, p 18; see *Faust* lines 12106–7) – and quotes the dying Faust to refer to Ferker's attempt to secure posthumous fame: 'The trace of my earthly days / Cannot disappear in aeons' (see *Faust* lines 11583–4). Schmitt uses Goethe's rather than the Gospel of John's wording when examining the Buribunks' capturing of the World Spirit: 'In the beginning there is the deed' (Chapter 2 of this volume, p 26, see *Faust* line 1237).

30 Footnotes 2 and 13.

31 Tommissen (1993), p 354.

For us, Schmitt's *The Buribunks* reads as a satirical form of commentary, a gloss. Our suggestion for a legal audience is to read it as a marginalium that broadly continues this genre of the gloss, of commentary, and comments on it as a form. Rather than glossing a particular proposition of law, however, we propose that his description of the character of the Buribunks could make a statement regarding commentary as a specific mode of writing. For instance, we invite you to read the writing practice of Schmitt's Buribunks in parallel with the practice of legal commentary, characterised by Vismann and Krajewski thus:

> Commentaries, which provided the material for codifications, consist in a self-observing, self-constituting, and yet at the same time self-deconstructing and permanently self-optimizing practice.[32]

Conclusion: Schmitt's own writing practice

Even in his later years, Schmitt remained unapologetic about his attitude towards (and conduct during) the National Socialist era.[33] The more we engaged with Schmitt's personal life, reading his diaries and some of his other papers, the more we fought to retain a veneer of academic disinterest and separation between our academic personas, our personal histories, and our opinions of him as a jurist, a philosopher and a husband. Engaging with *The Buribunks*, we also struggled with the problematic discussion of race and gender. We have constrained our comments here to discussions of content and form. However, we acknowledge and applaud the decision by Daniel Steuer, the English translator of Mehring's biography of Schmitt, to dedicate his translation to the victims of 'delusional fanaticism, exaggerated self-importance and senseless and meaningless crimes'.[34]

In conclusion, we wish to briefly allude to Schmitt's own writing practices in light of the themes of *The Buribunks*. He himself was an avid diary keeper, with the earliest entries dating from 1912.[35] According to the German editors of his early diaries, Schmitt 'made his decision to no longer keep a diary the topic of his satire "The Buribunks"'[36] in 1917 and stuck with this decision until 1921 before writing again intermittently over various intervals.[37] The diaries were

32 Vismann and Krajewski (2008), p 107.
33 See especially Schmitt (1991); Schmitt (2000); Mehring (2014). For details on Schmitt's life, see the biographies by Noack (1996) and especially Mehring (2014).
34 Mehring (2014), p xiii.
35 Five volumes have been published in Germany. See Schmitt (1991, 2005a, 2005b, 2010, 2018).
36 Schmitt (2005b), pp vii–viii.
37 Schmitt's diaries were written using an obsolete and extremely difficult-to-read form of stenography. Mehring's biography on Carl Schmitt is dedicated to Hans Gebhardt (1925–2013): 'the only reader of Schmitt's shorthand': Mehring (2014). See also Schmitt (1991), p v.

not his only method of recording his life and thoughts. For example, there is a compilation of writings that (in contrast to the private nature of the diaries) appears to have been intended for some form of posthumous publication, namely *Glossarium*.[38] Schmitt wrote in 1948:

> My aversion to diaries and diary-keeping is too great. Most diary writers seem to me like children who suck their fingers … mere babies, even when they are real self-torturers and not, like Samuel Pepys, narcissists.[39]

In his reflections on the Schmitt archive, Petar Bojanić contends that Schmitt was 'perhaps the last great *documentalist* of the 20th Century'[40] and describes how 'Schmitt counts and writes down everything. He counts and notes his ejaculations, his expenses and debts, quotes, meetings, drunkennesses, restaurants, travels, hatreds, fears … everything.'[41]

Even though Schmitt was often secretive about his notes and diaries, Bojanić asserts that Schmitt in his later years attempted 'to preserve, put together and connect his writings' as a way to consciously curate his future archives: his was a 'complex and complicated life, a life at once revealed and concealed by writing'.[42]

This piece of writing is another work in the genre of 'marginalia', a layering on top of the English translation and Schmitt's original text: an aside, a comment. We invite your own commentary to continue the cycle.

References

Petar Bojanić (2011) 'Scribomania: On the Wife, on the Archive. Carl Schmitt and the Secrets of his Handwriting', https://ifdt.bg.ac.rs/wp-content/uploads/2015/05/Bojanic_CSchmitt_archives.pdf (English translation, uploaded in 2015 on the website of Belgrade University, Institute for Philosophy and Social Theory also published in Serbian and Russian).

Notker Hammerstein (ed) (1996) *Handbuch der deutschen Bildungsgeschichte*, vol I, C.H. Beck.

Reinhard Mehring (2014) *Carl Schmitt: A Biography*, trans Daniel Steuer, Polity Press.

Paul Noack (1996) *Carl Schmitt: eine Biographie*, Ullstein.

Carl Schmitt (1991) *Glossarium. Aufzeichnungen der Jahre 1947–1951*, ed Eberhard Freiherr von Medem, Duncker & Humblot.

Carl Schmitt (2000) *Antworten in Nürnberg*, ed Helmut Quaritsch, Duncker & Humblot.

38 See Schmitt (1991), p VI. The same publisher released in 2015 a second edition of *Glossarium*, which was expanded, amended and annotated, covering the years 1947–58 (see Schmitt 2015).

39 Schmitt (1991), p 96.

40 Bojanić (2011), p 1 (italics in original).

41 Bojanić (2011), pp 2–3.

42 Bojanić (2011), p 5.

Carl Schmitt (2005a) *Tagebücher Oktober 1912 bis Februar 1915* (2nd ed), ed Ernst Hüsmert, Akademie Verlag.

Carl Schmitt (2005b) *Die Militärzeit 1915 bis 1919.* Tagebuch Februar bis Dezember 1915. Aufsätze und Materialien, eds Ernst Hüsmert and Gerd Giesler, Akademie Verlag.

Carl Schmitt (2010) *Tagebücher 1930 bis 1934*, ed Wolfgang Schuller, Akademie Verlag.

Carl Schmitt (2015) *Glossarium. Aufzeichnungen aus den Jahren 1947 bis 1958*, eds Gerd Giesler and Martin Tielke, Dunker & Humblot.

Carl Schmitt (2018) *Tagebücher 1925 bis 1929*, eds Martin Tielke and Gerd Giesler, Duncker & Humblot.

Joachim Hayward Stocqueler (1871) *A Familiar History of the British Army*, Stanford University Press.

Piet Tommissen (1993) 'Über die satirischen Texte Carl Schmitts', in Volker Beismann and Markus Joseph Klein (eds), *Politische Lageanalyse, Festschrift für Hans-Joachim Arndt zum 70. Geburtstag*, San Casciano, 339–380.

Cornelia Vismann and Markus Krajewski (2008) 'Computer Juridisms' 29 *Grey Room* 90.

Part II

The Buribunks as typeset

Chapter 4

The Buribunks, post-truth and a tentative cartography of informational existence

Kieran Tranter

Introduction

The digitalisation of human existence – through surveillance capitalism or state surveillance – has triggered an increased awareness of how human doing knowingly and unknowingly generates data, and how data become used for corporate and political purposes.[1] Earlier forms of digital engagement were discrete and innocent. The digital was a virtual 'play space' where users could create and experiment without much consequence in the real.[2] A series of developments, in both the West and the East, the Cambridge Analytica controversy and the emergence of the social credit system[3] have made it obvious that distinctions between the virtual and the real are misleading because of the datafication of life.[4]

This chapter begins the task of providing a tentative cartography of informational existence. 'Information existence' refers to the relation, connection and possibly truth of the lived human and their record in the archive. An understanding of informational existence refers to the being of beings thrown into a datafied world. This chapter does not yet claim a complete account; rather, it is a step along the way towards understanding how to be as datafied beings having an informational existence. The guide for this sojourn is unexpected: Carl Schmitt's *The Buribunks* is presented as a cypher for conceiving informational existence.

The first part of this chapter will briefly introduce Carl Schmitt's *The Buribunks* as a celebration of informational existence as the memorialisation of the self in time. The second part, drawing upon Schmitt's account of the Buribunks, maps the ways whereby the self is recorded in the digital. However, the present is not buribunkian: the self and its data-doubles are fragmented and conflicted, generated by surveillance, the data serfdom of worker-nodes, curatorial social media practices and 'dark' activities that try to hide personal responsibility. Nevertheless, the

1 See, for example, Pasquale (2015); Zuboff (2019).
2 Castronova (2004, 2007).
3 Wong and Dobson (2019).
4 Sadowski (2019); Southerton et al. (2019).

DOI: 10.4324/9781003091066-6

Buribunks' drive to master the archive encapsulates a tendency in the digital towards correspondence and unity within data repositories of the self.

Carl Schmitt's *The Buribunks*

The Buribunks is a brief text. Written as a celebratory pamphlet for the Buribunks' global ascendency, it describes the cultural origins of the Buribunks, the organisational features of 'Buribunkdom' and the central tenants of the Buribunks' manifesto. In terms of genre, it is in the form of science fiction's 'future history' genre,[5] telling the future history of humanity through a parody of academic conventions including the citing of fictional references. Through this, the Buribunks emerge as beings infused with a specific technicity: they are beings (possibly merged with typewriters)[6] that practise 'buribunkology' – the compulsive keeping of a diary of one's life that is immediately public.[7] Further, the Buribunks form the Buribunkdom – a total structured repository to which the daily diary is submitted, coded to make it searchable and archived[8] for 'History!'[9]

In this future, the Buribunkdom dominates the world as the techno-managerial elite. There are seemingly two classes: the Buribunks, who write history and do the important jobs of archiving, ordering the archive and studying the archive; and those of inferior intellect, who do menial physical activities.[10] The world described reminds us of Herman Hesse's *Glass Bead Game* – a society run by the philosopher kings of the global intellectual-bureaucratic class.[11] It is also tempting to see in *The Buribunks* some of E.M. Forster's celebrated short story 'The Machine Stops', published in 1909.[12] Forster conjures a vision of a locked-down, networked society with a physical and communication infrastructure that is degrading.[13] It is a tale of the possible endurance of the individual human outside of the global informatics machine.[14] There is no such sentimentality or redemption for the liberal human in a text typed by Schmitt.

The informatics machinery of Buribunkdom is described as total:

> Every male and female Buribunk is obliged to keep a diary for every second of their existence. Copies of all diary entries are submitted daily

5 Canary (1974).
6 Kennedy (2004), p 44.
7 Chapter 2 of this volume, pp 12–4.
8 Chapter 2 of this volume, p 23.
9 Chapter 2 of this volume, p 26.
10 Chapter 2 of this volume, p 25.
11 Hesse (2000); Roberts (2007).
12 Forster (1909).
13 Forster's 'The Machine Stops', with its cocooned networked humanity, has become a go-to text for reflections of 2020 COVID-19 public health isolation and lockdowns. See Batty (2020); Canavan et al. (2020); Merrin (2020).
14 Caporaletti (1997); Seabury (1997).

> and collated by local councils. Their simultaneous inspection results in indexation according to subject matter as well as authorship. Not only are the entries of an erotic, demonic, satirical, political and so on nature grouped together (under the strictest observation of the copyright law pertaining to each entry), but the authors are also catalogued according to their place of residence. Due to an ingenious scheme, later inspection through a card catalogue makes it possible straight away to determine every circumstance of interest pertaining to each person.[15]

After this description of an archive amenable to Boolean searches, Schmitt's author turns to what it should mean to be a being within this network. The self only comes to the present in the act of publishing:

> I think, therefore I am; I speak, therefore I am; I write, therefore I am; I publish, therefore I am … I write, therefore I am; I am, therefore I write. What do I write? I write myself. Who writes me? I myself write myself. What is the content of my writing? I write that I write myself.[16]

The essential concern of the publishing and archiving Buribunks is time, precisely the fixing of the historical record for future historians. Buribunkdom is dedicated to the managing of the material record of a Buribunk's life with the desire to stamp that narrative into the future: 'I am therefore a letter on the typewriter of history.'[17] The enemies of the Buribunks are biographers and revisionist historians – beings from the future who misrepresent, slander or otherwise do not present the 'truth' of a person and their life in their writings. The Buribunks seem to inhabit a 'post-post-truth' world, where the possibility for misinterpretation and misrepresentation of the traces of the self that have accumulated in the archive is countered through total control by a Buribunk of their material record.

To communicate this buribunkian essence, the narrator – known only by the initials 'C.S.'[18] – uses exhortations and slogans. It is not just the material fact of keeping and disseminating a diary that goes to the buribunkian essence; rather, it is a temporal orientation, a sense of history and historiography, a desire to 'seek real immortality in history'.[19] In celebration, the narrator invokes a hybrid horror composed of time, typewriters and rats. The rat imagery scurries in two directions. The first is an allusion to the cascading of temporal quanta from the future into the past:

> the present is only the midwife who delivers the lively historical past from the dark body of the future. Until it has been reached, the future lies there

15 Chapter 2 of this volume, p 23.
16 Chapter 2 of this volume, p 25.
17 Chapter 2 of this volume, p 26.
18 Chapter 2 of this volume, p 28.
19 Chapter 2 of this volume, p 27.

> as dull and indifferent as the keyboard of a typewriter, like a dark rat hole from which one second after another (like one rat after another) steps into the light of the past.[20]

The contrast with the Buribunks' human ancestors cannot be clearer:

> Whereas with the mindless human being ... millions and billions of rats stream into the immensity of the past without plan or aim and become lost there ... the diary-keeping Buribunk is able to capture them one by one and let their clearly well-arranged army present the big parade of world history.[21]

The second direction relates to the lives of individual Buribunks. The life and death of an individual Buribunk is merely a 'rat-second',[22] mostly inconsequential to world history. However, concern for self in the real is not a true Buribunken orientation; instead, the individual has been subsumed into the flow of the historical record: 'We are the letters that have rushed from the hand of the writing World Spirit and we consciously surrender ourselves to this writing power. In this we see true freedom.'[23]

This celebratory conclusion – the last lines are '[A Buribunk] is the World Spirit writing itself, perpetuating itself, outwitting itself in its immediate irrefutable factuality'[24] – is distinctly illiberal. The trappings of the liberal subject, grounded on the fear of death, have been extinguished by the 'sunlight'[25] of the Buribunks. The writing/disseminating units for Buribunkdom are less individuals than their mere human ancestors, but in their active, 'heroic'[26] writing, they are much more. The contrast with the liberal human is in the relationship with time. A liberal is 'prudent':[27] he uses freedom, rights and property in the present to plan, contract and acquire for the future.[28] The liberal is future focused: the mind and activity of the present are driven by the vision of the future-self enjoying the benefits of present work.[29] The Buribunks have a more complicated relationship with time: they labour in the present to order the material record to dictate to the future. Whereas the liberal looks towards the future, a Buribunk has their typewriter facing the past.

20 Chapter 2 of this volume, p 26.
21 Chapter 2 of this volume, p 26.
22 Chapter 2 of this volume, p 26.
23 Chapter 2 of this volume, p 27.
24 Chapter 2 of this volume, p 28.
25 Chapter 2 of this volume, p 27.
26 Chapter 2 of this volume, p 27.
27 Hobbes (2008), p 44.
28 Tranter (2018), pp 71–2. The gendered pronoun is deliberate. The liberal is, as generations of feminist scholars have established, is distinctly masculine in its doing in the world. See West (1988).
29 Shum and Tranter (2017), p 485.

Although *The Buribunks* was typed a century ago, and predates the digital computer by 30 years, in its illiberal celebration, in its temporal awareness, in its comprehension of a total, searchable archive of 'world-history', in its funny, irascible exploration of the features of the beings networked into such an actuality, *The Buribunks* presents as an iteration of informational existence. This is what Friedrich Kittler glimpsed in 1991 when he inserted a substantial extract from *The Buribunks* into his seminal *Gramophone, Film, Typewriter* [30] to connect the material on the typewriter to Alan Turing and the digital.[31] As a description of what it means to be informational beings, there are some parallels with Donna Haraway's 'Manifesto for Cyborgs'.[32] Both are ironic:[33] there is a playing with the expectations of academic conventions and a meditation on how technology radically changes the subject, subjectivity and the social. Both are also illiberal.[34] This is not to suggest any greater parallels between Haraway and Schmitt, except for these aesthetic similarities and a perceived common enemy in the liberal. Whereas Haraway sees the complexities and complicities, along with the possibilities and promises, of cyborgs born from the war-machines of the twentieth century,[35] Schmitt's Buribunks are much less transitional.[36] There is a confident writing onto world history with the Buribunks that is absent from the cyborg. To paraphrase Schmitt's narrator, there is a 'factuality',[37] a concreteness to the form of informational existence denoted by the Buribunks. Whereas the cyborg is an unstable and shifting form, the Buribunk is about unitary identity and the entrenching of that unitary self within the data-stream. The cyborg rejects any absolutes from which a correspondence theory of truth could be grounded, while the Buribunk labours towards absolutes and correspondence.

It is this deep desire for correspondence, manifest in care of the self's informational record, that defines the Buribunks as a form of informational existence. Having come to this appreciation of the Buribunks, their relation to the archive will be used in the next part as a cypher for living a datafied life in the early twentieth-first century.

The Buribunks as a cypher of informational existence

Human life becomes translated into the digital at four identifiable transition zones. The first is the digital's system of everyday surveillance that hoovers data

30 Kittler (1999).
31 Kittler (1999), pp 198–260.
32 Haraway (1985).
33 On *The Buribunks* as irony, see Schultz (2019); Manderson and Bikundo (2019).
34 Schneider (2005). On the opposition and possible reinscription of the liberal man within Haraway's cyborg, see Hayles (2006).
35 Haraway (1985).
36 Braidotti (2006), p. 78.
37 Chapter 2 of this volume, pp 26, 27, 28.

from human activity. The second is the institutional expectations of audit culture, where work-nodes frantically contribute to the data-stream. The third occurs through social media, where prosumers actively manage and curate representations of the self. The fourth is the generating of anonymous data for malevolent 'dark' purposes. There are possibly further zones and other ways of grouping life to data transition points; nevertheless, these four – everyday surveillance, data-generation of work, the curation of self at (and as) play and digital malevolence – capture the broad swathe of how human life and doing generate a record in the digital archive. *The Buribunks* presents as a tentative cartography for ordering and making sense of these digital entanglements.

The first transition zone is the unknowing, uncaring or compulsory leaving of data through triggering a surveillance point of the digital.[38] The site of doing by the human is irrelevant. This generating of data can occur by walking down a CTV-enhanced path, scanning a ticket at a public transport booth, engaging with an Internet of Things (IoT), GPS or cellular-enabled device, or actively interacting with the infosphere by googling.[39] In a 'sensor society',[40] questions of will and wilfulness are irrelevant. Often, depositing data is the cost of participation. This can be as simple as the price of walking or driving in public,[41] knowing that images of self and vehicles will be recorded. It can be as subtle as the unobtrusive recording of search histories by search engines or as obvious as the brutal requirement that valid data are entered in all fields before a transaction can be progressed.

There is a bizarre ghost of liberalism in this unwilling contribution to the digital. There is often an allusion to 'choice'. The choice to be physically present in public spaces, to choose to search the internet, to choose to engage with online portals to access public and private services rests with the self. This is the charade of the digital's click to accept end user licence agreement.[42] Such myth-making is mischievous: there is a compulsion to engagement. Even assuming an individual managed the troglodyte dream of unplugging from the digital, their movements in the real would still be caught by surveillance networks. Further, physical disguises such as Guy Fawkes masks or false number plate on vehicles are likely to trigger active investigations. As Kevin Haggerty and Richard Ericson remarked 20 years ago, the then emerging system of rhizomic surveillance sees the 'disappearance of disappearance'.[43] To live life in the present involves the leaving of a data trail that cannot be avoided. The digital has imposed an information tax.

38 The relationship between the Buribunks and contemporary emergent regimes of digital surveillance has also been made by McLoughlin (2019), pp 145–9.
39 Kitchin and Dodge (2011); Lyons (2010).
40 Andrejevic and Burdon (2015)
41 Guzik (2013).
42 King (2016); Phillips (2020), pp 216–18.
43 Haggerty and Ericson (2000), p. 619.

This form of unwitting informational existence is not that of the Buribunks. Yet it is the fact that humans leave material and informatics traces that Schmitt identified as the seed of the Buribunks. The Roman who lost a coin, the Victorian drunk discarding a spirit bottle, the letter back home from a sailor serving during the Pacific war, these haphazard material moments of life can become preserved through time to become the primary sources for history. The digital has merely intensified and magnified this process. Every day, the digital's information tax gathers 2.5 quintillion bytes of data.[44] These data are both more permanent and more vulnerable than the coins, bottles and paper left in time stream by earlier humans. They are more permanent because they can be effortlessly copied, backed up and archived on storage devices. They are more vulnerable because the programs that code and decode them are updated, replaced and then unsupported, rendering past stored data gibberish.[45] Storage space also costs, so data are often archived for a period, then overwritten with newer data. Further, material physicality does affect digital data as it does the passage of coins, bottles and paper within the time stream.[46] Servers do crash, data become corrupted, systems are hacked and backups fail. What was once stored can become lost to history, notwithstanding firewalls and backups. It is possible that the digital could experience an informational catastrophe of the magnitude of the fire at Alexandria.[47]

As Schmitt makes plain in *The Buribunks*, this shedding of data to history is incidental to humanity. What makes humans lesser to Buribunks is the thoughtlessness and carelessness through which they allowed these 'rat-second' moments to scurry out of the time hole. Schmitt captures a point that is often overlooked in anxious analyses by liberals of the surveillance apparatus of the digital. In these analyses, the digital demarks something radically new – a potential mega-machine of total surveillance – that must be constrained by technologies that traditionally have safeguarded liberal freedom – rights, property, permission and contract. There is a slip between the fact of the existence of big data archives and the ends that those with computation power and access to the archives can achieve. In *The Buribunks,* it was the individual becoming self-aware of how their inevitable contribution to the archive could be used by later analysts that awoke the Buribunks' spirit. The liberal anxieties with privacy and the uses of data carelessly disclosed to the digital that crystallised in the Cambridge Analytica controversy of 2018 could be a similar awakening.[48]

The second transition zone resolves around certain digital manifestations of audit culture. 'Audit culture' is a contested term. It has been deployed in the

44 Bulao (2020).

45 The unreadability of data stored on legacy media and systems from the 1970s and 1980s has been noted as a problem for biographers. See, for example, Menéndez (2016).

46 Iraci (2017).

47 Casey (2014), p 62.

48 Berghel (2018); Ward (2018).

context of the neoliberal university and indeed in the Buribunks' concern with metrics of academic impact and performance.[49] In this deployment, audit culture refers to analysis of the archive to determine the value or worth of an academic publication, and by implication of the author. However, this specific site for the application of metric-based management does not exhaust the scope of audit culture. As Marilyn Strathern identifies, 'audit culture' emerged as a framing concept within the ethnographic study of institutions, capturing how financial and data-driven management structures, expectations and protocols were particularly changing the responsibility and ethical decision making of professionals.[50] The emphasis on rankings, h-indexes and impact factors that are problematised in the literature exploring audit culture within the academy is a manifestation of a deeper trajectory within institutional governance. Techno-managerial modes of organising and wielding power have always been tied closely to practices of the archive: with files, filing and file-notes implementing the practice of leaving records of actions and decision.[51] Indeed, Reinhard Mehring suggests that Schmitt's inspiration for *The Buribunks* was his wartime experience in the bureaucracy of the Army General Command in Munich.[52] What should be recorded, and how those recordings become computed to determine efficiency and productivity, have been a consistent feature of the institutionalisation of techno-managerial work.[53] The aggressive accounting for billable hours in the twentieth-century law firm is a pre-audit culture manifestation of this tendency.[54]

However, what was identified in the studies of audit culture from the 1990s and early 2000s was an intensification of this process and an explicit use of data and statistics in the governing ideal.[55] These studies anticipated the rollout and remaking of institutional practices due to the introduction of enterprise management software,[56] which presents the promise of a single institutional-wide interface and a single data repository, as well as the automation of auditing activities[57] – the coded embodiment of audit culture.[58] In practice, enterprise software tends towards hierarchy in decision making and information management. It works by creating vertical chains of information flow, where different users have differential access to the data-stream. The introduction of enterprise software has therefore seen the hardening of hierarchy within institutional work

49 Shore and Wright (1999); Wright and Shore (2003). On how the Buribunks prefigure contemporary academic concerns with metrics, see Rochford (2019), p 254. Also see Chapter 18 in this volume.
50 Strathern (2003), pp 2–3.
51 Vismann (2008). pp 88–101.
52 Mehring (2014), p 82.
53 Shore and Wright (2015a), pp 423–6.
54 Fortney (2000).
55 Shore and Wright (2015b).
56 Wagner et al. (2006), pp. 286–8.
57 Saxena and McDonagh (2017).
58 Petelin (2008).

environments, and with that a predilection to selective disclosure, passing of responsibility and the establishment of offline, analogue 'shadow systems'.[59]

Enterprise software is an obvious transition zone in the digital. The worker-nodes of an enterprise-software-driven organisation operate in a constant presence of workflows, notifications, web-forms and data entry. The form of informational existence being wrought out in bits and bytes by the worker-nodes is different from the data trail shed by humans in the digital in the sense of self that goes with the depositing. The worker-node knows the data they upload will be linked to their corporate identity as a worker-node. Others up the data stream will know a specific worker-node (employee ID number xxx) made a particular contribution. Contributions are made with an awareness that auditing algorithms are already processing the data for employee evaluation and productivity analysis. This awareness of contributing to the archive seems more Buribunks. Indeed, the mass intensification of the digitalisation of work in response to public health lockdowns has made this more obvious. There has been a need to demonstrate productivity to nervous line managers, who have been robbed of their familiar industrial-era surveillance of seeing busy worker-nodes in cubicles, through intensive and intensified Zoom meetings, shared calendars, email chains, contributions to Google Docs and so on. This has made obvious a Buribunks spirit to be seen *and recorded* in the work archive.[60]

However, this form of informational existence lacks specific Buribunks features. First, unlike the Buribunks, it cannot be said that the worker-nodes are their own masters, for their data generation and depository are for others. The information serfdom of a worker-node hardwired into an enterprise software system and work from home platform is much more the dystopian existence in Forster's 'The Machine Stops' than the master of the self that is celebrated by the narrator in *The Buribunks*.[61] Second, the worker-node enters data not to celebrate their self and life, but rather to comply with the extraneous demands of the system. This is not the writing of reflective life narratives, or marshalling the rat-seconds of a life into an unassailable memorial for history. Ashley Pearson and Kieran Tranter have used the platform video game genre, epitomised by Nintendo's Super Mario Bros franchise, to describe the worker-node in the digital.[62] There is a consistent flow of instant tasks to be navigated. If the task is not completed, it restarts. A timer counts down how long is being spent on a task and the rigidity of code means that there can only be set number of structured resolutions to that task.[63] Within this transition zone, the human occupying the site of a worker-node is aware of their contribution to the archive but is mostly lost in a frenzy of responding to digital stimulation.

59 Skoumpopoulou and Waring (2017), pp 821–5.
60 Hodder (2020); Maalsen and Dowling (2020); Waizenegger et al. (2020).
61 Chapter 2 of this volume, p 13.
62 Pearson and Tranter (2015).
63 Pearson and Tranter (2015), pp 831–3.

Rather than being Buribunks ordering the rat-seconds, they are the rats being organised by the master code.

Which comes to the third transition zone of the digital, the beings manifested through social media. The informational existence disclosed through social media seems to have distinctly buribunkian features. Participation in social media involves the conscience addition to the archive, unlike the human enmeshed in the rhizomic surveillance of a sensorial ecosystem. Further, it involves the voluntary disclosure of details of the self to the archive,[64] not the compulsory workflow production of a worker-node. Research on social media has tended to fall into two categories. The first concerns social media as *media*. In this research, social media is identified as a specific form of mass or public communication. There tends to be a binary assessment of social media within this literature. The other relates to its possibility to enhance public life, through better communication in disaster management[65] or for greater forms of participatory democracy,[66] or as a forum for progressive social and political movements such as the '#MeToo movement'[67] or the Arab spring of the early 2010s.[68] Balanced against this enhancing of the public potential and actuality of social media is research that identifies its corrosive effects on public institutions, particularly how social media echo chambers have contributed to a fake news-fuelled divisive and aggressive political culture[69] or how they undermine the jury system.[70] Liberalism and its political apparatuses tend to be the focus of this literature, exploring as had happened with older media forms, how technologies of mass communication enhance or undermine individual freedom of choice and action.[71]

The second focus is more on the informational existence brought into being by social media, specifically the *social* in social media. This literature shares a symmetry with the other focus in that there are contrasting assessments of the social of social media. The first is that, by providing an informational avatar, social media enriches the self through providing meaningful and beneficial social interactions.[72] There have been claims that social media interactions can enhance public diversity and personal empowerment[73] and contribute to positive mental health outcomes.[74] However, these are contested claims,[75] with

64 Van Dijck (2013), pp 29–44.
65 Houston et al. (2015); Yates and Paquette (2011).
66 Linders (2012); Oliveira and Welch (2013).
67 Tippett (2018); Lăzăroiu et al. (2018).
68 Howard et al. (2011).
69 Allcott and Gentzkow (2017); Quandt (2018); Sunstein (2018). Such phenomena are not restricted to Western nations: see Lim (2017).
70 Braun (2017).
71 Siapera (2017), pp 39–59.
72 Chambers (2013); Cornejo et al. (2013); Hooghe and Oser (2015).
73 Morrison (2011); Poletti (2011).
74 Ellison et al. (2007).
75 Sidani et al. (2016); Woods and Scott (2016).

recent studies suggesting that social media engagement has negative mental health effects.[76]

The identified reason for this relates to the curatorial nature of social media content.[77] Prosumers of social media do not treat it as a confessional space that records the rawness of their life in its factuality.[78] Rather, there is increased awareness that social media users construct a specific image of the self in the text, images and likes within an account.[79] This drive to present details of the self within an overarching narrative is distinctly Buribunks. It is not the base recording of a chronology of events that distinguishes the Buribunks, but an awareness of how events are interpreted by others further down the time-stream and a desire to dictate meaning to that. Mikaela Pitcan, Alice E. Marwick and danah boyd report how young New Yorkers from non-white backgrounds carefully manage their online presence according to mainstream notions of respectability.[80] The participants showed a buribunkian awareness to 'self-censor … in a manner they described as presenting a "neutral" or "vanilla" face, catering to the respectability norms of the most powerful potential viewers – often potential employers or high-status community members – rather than peers'.[81] The participants show that the Buribunks-like activity of constructing digital representations of the self tends to be focused around socially conservative narratives of mainstream respectability, material success, and personal health and happiness.[82] This is not correspondence truth but a post-truth project of self-positioning according to underlying narratives and framing. Social media content generally shows happy and healthy successfulness.[83] This triggers the negative mental health effects of social media consumption. There is an over-representation of 'perfect' people with 'perfect' bodies living 'perfect' lives. This curating results in the informational existence disclosed on a social media platform often having a highly selective and tenuous relationship with the complex, contested, messy everydayness of a human life.[84]

The post-truth, curating social media prosumer is not entirely buribunkian. The Buribunks compulsorily record the minutia of daily existence. Selective withholding in the name of curating seems prohibited.[85] Rather than doctoring and selective disclosure, the Buribunks are encouraged to write about why and how they desire to doctor and selectively disclose. This is embodied in the principle

76 Andreassen et al. (2017); Hawi and Samaha (2017).
77 Hogan (2010).
78 Tifentale and Manovich (2015).
79 Fox and Rooney (2015); Kang (2000); Page (2011).
80 Pitcan et al. (2018).
81 Pitcan et al. (2018), p 170; see also Duffy and Chan (2019).
82 Dobson (2016).
83 Lambert (2016); Trottier (2012); Bararova and Choi (2014); Duguay (2016).
84 A problem when decision makers treat social media representations as a true history of the person. See Sleep and Tranter (2018).
85 Chapter 2 of this volume, p 24.

of keeping a diary about not wanting to keep a diary.[86] The Buribunks manifest strict correspondence between lived reality and the material record that is not evident in the practices of social media prosumers – it is a fidelity to correspondence truth between life and record. Nevertheless, the buribunkian features of the social media prosumer are telling. There is a distinct illiberalness to the nature of their disclosing. There is an implosion of the division of public and private that liberalism policed by rights, property and contract. There is a confident writing oneself, or at least posting a curated avatar of the self, into the digital.

A tempting sense of informational sovereignty is disclosed by the buribunkian activity of the social media prosumer. The concept of informational sovereignty comes from international law as the need for nation-states to have sovereignty over their data.[87] It is suggestive to interrogate the curatorial activities of a social media prosumer in sovereign terms familiar from Schmitt's later work. The diligent social media prosumer polices the informatics of the cultivated digital self. There is an everyday managing – the posting of content and the network labouring of liking – and more extreme 'exceptional'[88] actions around the suspending and deleting of accounts. Further, deeply embedded in the network-generative logic of social media is another familiar concept: the friend/enemy distinction.[89] There is a brutality of sovereign-like violence embedded in the decision to link with 'friends' or not-link with 'not-friends'. In positioning the prosumer as the loci for everyday data management and more extreme exceptional activities, and couching the networking switch according to 'friends' and 'not-friends', there are allusions to Schmitt's sovereign.

However, in this the limits of *The Buribunks* as a cypher for informational existence are revealed. The human unwittingly and carelessly shedding data to the digital, the worker-node responding to the digital stimuli of the master-code and the social media prosumer can all be the same self – indeed, could be the same self at almost the same time. It is a fundamental percept for Schmitt that the sovereign is a unity. Sovereignty is not capable of division, and signs of splintering and contestation are terminal symptoms.[90] This unity is also evidenced in the Buribunks' confident management of the rat-seconds of the present for the memorialisation of the self. Schmitt's characters impose a singular imprint onto the world. Yet this is not the reality for the data-doubles spawned by the same human when encountering transitional points in the digital: there are shifting and conflicting accounts of the self. The imprint of the

86 Chapter 2 of this volume, pp 24–5. On the political significance of this, see Murphy (2019).
87 Polčák and Svantesson (2017). On how *The Buribunks* might inform international law scholarship, see Werner (2019).
88 Schmitt (1985), p 5.
89 Schmitt (1996a), p 26.
90 Schmitt (1996b), p 74.

self through digital surveillance might only have a loose relationship with the data-flows emanating from the same self as a work-node or the avatar of the self that is strutting about social media. There is a nomadic form[91] to the transient, changing and conflicting traces of the self in the digital.

This is before a fourth transitional point to the digital is introduced, that of false accounts and trolling. Through the diary, the Buribunks 'transformed [fame] into a solid state'.[92] The users of false accounts and trolls seek personal pleasure through causing anonymous harm.[93] While the social media prosumer presents an avatar of the self to the digital, the users of false accounts and trolls have a distinctly un-buribunkian desire to hide from history, to radically disconnect and quarantine their lived self from the record of their toxic digital activities. With these contributors to the digital, the narcissism manifest in the Buribunks is replaced by darker motivations.[94] Any relation to a Buribunk is in the negative. There is no archiving of the self to history; rather, as seen directly in the trolling of Facebook memorial sites,[95] there is antagonism towards other disclosures of self in the digital. Trolls are not liberals prudently striving in the present for a better future, nor are they Buribunks compulsively diarising in the present so the future archive records their past. Rather, the troll is present, indulging in gratification of the self, indifferent to the record being left behind.

The existence of false accounts, trolls and even the 'dark web' of hidden identities[96] highlights that some data in the digital is, by design, disconnected from a human life in the real. This reinforces the disunity of representations of the self in the digital; that coherence and correspondence is not currently possible. For all the spin around 'big data', the reality is that big data is yet to be that big – yet to be a merged totality.

However, the final significance of *The Buribunks* rests in its suggestive teleology. Buribunkdom came to be through an impulse to care for the record of a self in the archive. The text highlights the incongruence between a unitary sense of self in the real and the disunity of the self's digital representations, which generates a desire for digital unification. This desire is manifest in the liberal reforms around regulating digital surveillance through permissions and implementing rights to forget. It can also be seen in the name-and-shame actions of troll hunters in connecting anonymous offensive and damaging digital activity to real persons.[97] For the tradition that takes Haraway's cyborg as its progenitor, such drifting back to unity is possibly regressive. In the splintering of representations of the self in the digital, a transitional – and possibly a more ethically responsive – being was capable of growing, away from the old

91 Braidotti (2006), p 78.
92 Chapter 2 of this volume, p 27.
93 Buckels et al. (2014); Dynel (2016).
94 Humphrey (2017).
95 Phillips (2011).
96 Gehl (2016), pp 1225–6.
97 Humphrey (2017).

totalities of self, body, gender, sex, race, class or biota.[98] There is a terrifying sameness to the Buribunks. It is a world composed of narcissists banging out self-aggregating platitudes on the typewriter of history that could be coming to pass with the interchangeability of cat memes, GIFs, selfies and ritualised emoji posts on social media. The Buribunks laboured for unity and mastery of self through correspondence between the real and a total, authoritative archive.

This seems to capture the motives and drives behind attempts to achieve greater digital correspondence to the real and unification of representations of the self in the digital. At one level, this is the emerging reality of the digital East, where previous surveillance society desires of aptly named totalitarians are supposedly building a total sensorial net that truthfully records the doings of humans in the digital.[99] It is also the motivating desire of Western forms of the digital. Surveillance capitalism thrives when the data and real coincide, so the algorithmic nudges deliver consumers and profits, and benefit various forms of state apparatus keen to track, trace, know and manage individuals in the real world. The danger of these desires for 'truth' in the digital is the energy for progressive transformations of the self. In particular, its relations with others that come from playing, experimenting and fragmenting expected unitary identities could be lost.[100] A future of bland, ever-archiving persons in the real, reflected in bland, safe and curated representations in the digital, is not something to be celebrated.

References

Hunt Allcott and Matthew Gentzkow (2017) 'Social Media and Fake News in the 2016 Election' 31 *Journal of Economic Perspectives* 211.

Cecilie Schou Andreassen, Stale Pallesen and Mark D. Griffifths (2017) 'The Relationship Between Addictive Use of Social Media, Narcissism, and Self-Esteem: Findings from a Large National Survey' 64 *Addictive Behaviors* 287.

Mark Andrejevic and Mark Burdon (2015) 'Defining the Sensor Society' 16 *Television, New Media and Society* 19.

Natalyn N. Bararova and Yoon Hyung Choi (2014) 'Self-Disclosure in Social Media: Extending the Functional Approach to Disclosure Motivations and Characteristics on Social Network Sites' 64 *Journal of Communication* 569.

Michael Batty (2020) 'The Coronavirus Crisis: What Will the Post-Pandemic City Look Like?' *Environment and Planning B: Urban Analytics and City Science*https://doi.org/10.1177/2399808320926912.

Hal Berghel (2018) 'Malice Domestic: The Cambridge Analytica Dystopia' 51 *Computer* 84.

Rosi Braidotti (2006) *Transpositions: On Nomadic Ethics*, Polity Press.

Kerstin Braun (2017) 'Yesterday is History, Tomorrow is a Mystery: The Fate of the Australian Jury System in the Age of Social Media Dependency' 40 *University of New South Wales Law Journal* 1634.

98 Braidotti (2006), pp 77–9.
99 Qiang (2019); Xu (2020); Yu (2020).
100 Lyons (2018), p 835.

Erin E. Buckels, Paul D. Trapnell and Delroy L. Paulhus (2014) 'Trolls Just want to Have Fun' 67 *Personality and Individual Differences* 97.

Jacquelyn Bulao (2020) 'How Much Data is Created Every Day in 2020?' *Tech Jury*, https://techjury.net/blog/how-much-data-is-created-every-day/#gref.

Robert H. Canary (1974) 'Science Fiction as Fictive History' 16 *Extrapolation* 81.

Gerry Canavan, Jennifer Cooke, Caroline Edwards and Paul March-Russell (2020) 'Apocalypse Now: COVID-19 and the SF Imaginary' 136 *Foundation* 84.

Silvana Caporaletti (1997) 'Science as Nightmare: "The Machine Stops" by E.M. Forster' 8 *Utopian Studies* 32.

Eric Casey (2014) 'Collecting the Cosmos: The Apocalypse of the Ancient Library' in Cathy Gutierrez and Hillel Schwartz (eds), *The End That Does: Art, Science and Millennial Accomplishment*, Routledge, 41.

Edward Castronova (2004) 'The Right to Play' 49 *New York Law School Law Review* 185.

Edward Castronova (2007) *Exodus to the Virtual World: How Online Fun is Changing Reality*, Palgrave Macmillan.

Deborah Chambers (2013) *Social Media and Personal Relationships: Online Intimacies and Networked Friendship*, Palgrave Macmillan.

Raymundo Cornejo, Mónica Tentori and Jesús Favela (2013) 'Enriching In-person Encounters Through Social Media: A Study on Family Connectedness for the Elderly' 71(9) *International Journal of Human–Computer Studies* 889.

Amy Shields Dobson (2016) *Postfeminist Digital Cultures: Femininity, Social Media, and Self-Representation*, Palgrave Macmillan.

Brooke Erin Duffy and Ngai Keung Chan (2019) '"You Never Really Know Who's Looking": Imagined Surveillance across Social Media Platforms' 21 *New Media & Society* 119.

Stefanie Duguay (2016) '"He Has a Way Gayer Facebook Than I Do": Investigating Sexual Identity Disclosure and Context Collapse on a Social Networking Site' 18 *New Media & Society* 891.

Marta Dynel (2016) '"Trolling is Not Stupid": Internet Trolling as the Art of Deception Serving Entertainment' 13 *Intercultural Pragmatics* 353.

Nicole B. Ellison, Charles Steinfield and Cliff Lampe (2007) 'The Benefits of Facebook "Friends": Social Capital and College Students' Use of Online Social Network Sites' 12 *Journal of Computer-Mediated Communication* 1143.

E.M. Forster (1909) 'The Machine Stops', in Rod Mengham (ed), *The Machine Stops and Other Stories*, Andre Deutsch, 87.

Susan Saab Fortney (2000) 'Soul for Sale: An Empirical Study of Associate Aatisfaction, Law Firm Culture, and the Effects of Billable Hour Requirements' 69 *UMKC Law Review* 239.

Jess Fox and Margaret C. Rooney (2015) 'The Dark Triad and Trait Self-Objectification as Predictors of Men's Use and Self-Presentation Behaviors on Social Networking Sites' 76 *Personality and Individual Differences* 161.

Robert W. Gehl (2016) 'Power/Freedom on the Dark Web: A Digital Ethnography of the Dark Web Social Network' 18 *New Media & Society* 1219.

Keith Guzik (2013) 'Taking Hold of the Wheel: Automobility, Social Order, and the Law in Mexico's Public Registry of Vehicles (REPUVE)' 47 *Law and Society Review* 523.

Kevin Haggerty and Richard V. Ericson (2000) 'The Surveillant Assemblage' 51 *British Journal of Sociology* 605.

Donna Haraway (1985) 'A Manifesto for Cyborgs: Science, Technology and Socialist Feminism in the 1980s' 80 *Socialist Review* 65.

Nazir S. Hawi and Maya Samaha (2017) 'The Relations Among Social Media Addiction, Self-Esteem, and Life Satisfaction in University Students' 35 *Social Science Computer Review* 576.

N. Katherine Hayles (2006) 'Unfinished Work: From Cyborg to Cognisphere' 23 *Theory, Culture, Society* 159.

Hermann Hesse (2000) *The Glass Bead Game*, Vintage.

Thomas Hobbes (2008) *Leviathan*, Pearson Longman.

Andy Hodder (2020) 'New Technology, Work and Employment in the Era of COVID-19: Reflecting on Legacies of Research' *New Technology, Work and Employment*https://doi.org/10.1111/ntwe.12173.

Bernie Hogan (2010) 'The Presentation of Self in the Age of Social Media: Distinguishing Performances and Exhibitions Online' 30 *Bulletin of Science, Technology and Society* 377.

Marc Hooghe and Jennifer Oser (2015) 'Internet, Television and Social Capital: The Effect of "Screen Time" on Social Capital' 18 *Information, Communication and Society* 1175.

J. Brian Houston*et al.* (2015) 'Social Media and Disasters: A Functional Framework for Social Media Use in Disaster Planning, Response, and Research' 39 *Disasters* 1.

Philip N. Howard, Aiden Duffy, Deen Freelon, M.M. Hussain, Will Mari and Marwa Maziad (2011) *Opening Closed Regimes: What Was the Role of Social Media During the Arab Spring*, working paper, Project on Information Technology and Political Islam, University of Washington.

Michael Lee Humphrey (2017) '"I Am in No Way This": Troll Hunters and Pragmatic Digital Self-Reference' 3 *Persona Studies* 21.

Joe Iraci (2017) 'The Soaking Resistance of Electronic Storage Media' 38 *Restaurator. International Journal for the Preservation of Library Archival Material* 33.

Jerry Kang (2000) 'Cyber-Race' 113 *Harvard Law Review* 1130.

Ellen Kennedy (2004) *Constitutional Failure: Carl Schmitt in Weimer*, Duke University Press.

Chelsea King (2016) 'Forcing Players to Walk the Plank: Why End User Licences Agreements Improperly Control Players' Rights Regarding Microtransactions in Video Games' 58 *William and Mary Law Review* 1365.

Rob Kitchin and Martin Dodge (2011) *Code/Space: Software and Everyday life*, MIT Press.

Friedrich A. Kittler (1999) *Gramophone, Film, Typewriter*, Stanford University Press.

Alex Lambert (2016) 'Intimacy and Social Capital on Facebook: Beyond the Psychological Perspective' 18 *New Media & Society* 2559.

George Lăzăroiu, Zuzana Rowland and Viera Bartosova (2018) 'Gendered Power Disparities, Misogynist Violence, and Women's Oppression: The #Metoo Movement Against Workplace Sexual Harassment' 10 *Contemporary Readings in Law Social Justice* 57.

Merlyna Lim (2017) 'Freedom to Hate: Social Media, Algorithmic Enclaves, and the Rise of Tribal Nationalism in Indonesia' 49 *Critical Asian Studies* 411.

Dennis Linders (2012) 'From e-Government to We-Government: Defining a Typology for Citizen Coproduction in the Age of Social Media' 29 *Government Information Quarterly* 446.

David Lyons (2010) 'Surveillance, Power and Everyday Life: Properties of Technology', in Phillip Kalantzis-Cope and Karim Gherab-Martín (eds), *Emerging Digital Spaces in Contemporary Society*, Palgrave Macmillan, 107.

David Lyons (2018) 'Engagement, Exposure, and Ethics in Digital Modernity' 11 *International Journal of Communication* 821.

Sophia Maalsen and Robyn Dowling (2020) 'COVID-19 and the Accelerating Smart Home' 7 *Big Data and Society*, https://doi.org/10.1177/2053951720938073.

Desmond Manderson and Edwin Bikundo (2019) 'Forms of Irony in Carl Schmitt's Political Romanticism, The Buribunks and Ex Captivitate Salus' 28 *Griffith Law Review* 189.

Daniel McLoughlin (2019) 'The Biopolitics of The Buribunks: The Digital Archive and the End of History' 28 *Griffith Law Review* 137.

Reinhard Mehring (2014) *Carl Schmitt: A Biography*, Polity Press.

José Menéndez (2016) 'Loose Fingers Sink Ships: 15 Years of E-mails from Manuel Cardona', in Klaus Ensslin and Luis Viña (eds), *Manuel Cardona*, Springer, 87.

William Merrin (2020) 'Anthropocenic War: Coronavirus and Total Demobilization' *Digital War*, https://doi.org/10.1057/s42984-020-00016-9.

Aimée Morrison (2011) '"Suffused by Feeling and Affect": The Intimate Public of Personal Mommy Blogging' 34 *Biography* 37.

Michael P.A. Murphy (2019) 'What Does it Mean to Be Anti-Social? Potentiality and Political Ontology in The Buribunks' 28 *Griffith Law Review* 154.

Gustavo Henrique Maultasch Oliveira and Eric W. Welch (2013) 'Social Media Use in Local Government: Linkage of Technology, Task, and Organizational Context' 30 *Government Information Quarterly* 397.

Ruth Page (2011) *Stories and Social Media: Identities and Interaction*, Routledge.

Frank Pasquale (2015) *The Black Box Society: The Secret Algorithms that Control Money and Information*, Harvard University Press.

Ashely Pearson and Kieran Tranter (2015) 'Code, Nintendo's Super Mario and Digital Legality' 28 *International Journal for the Semiotics of Law* 825.

George Petelin (2008) 'Can We Trust Our Ground Control?' 11 *Junctures: The Journal for Thematic Dialogue*, www.junctures.org/index.php/junctures/article/view/32/368.

Andelka M. Phillips (2020) *Buying Your Self on the Internet: Wrap Contracts and Personal Genomics*, Edinburgh University Press.

Whitney Phillips (2011) 'LOLing at Tragedy: Facebook Trolls, Memorial Pages and Resistance to Grief Online', *First Monday*, https://firstmonday.org/article/view/3168/3115.

Mikaela Pitcan, Alice E. Marwick and dahah boyd (2018) 'Performing a Vanilla Self: Respectability Politics, Social Class, and the Digital World' 23 *Journal of Computer-Mediated Communication* 163.

Radim Polčák and Dan Jerker B. Svantesson (2017) *Information Sovereignty: Data Privacy, Sovereign Powers and the Rule of Law*, Edward Elgar.

Anna Poletti (2011) 'Coaxing an Intimate Public: Life Narrative in Digital Storytelling' 25 *Continuum* 73.

Xiao Qiang (2019) 'The Road to Digital Unfreedom: President Xi's Surveillance State' 30 *Journal of Democracy* 53.

Thorsten Quandt (2018) 'Dark Participation' 6 *Media Communication* 36.

Peter Roberts (2007) 'Conscientisation in Castalia: A Freirean Reading of Hermann Hesse's The Glass Bead Game' 26 *Studies in Philosophy and Education* 509.

Francine Rochford (2019) 'Negative Space: The Paradox at the Heart of Buribunkology' 28 *Griffith Law Review* 247.
Jathan Sadowski (2019) 'When Data is Capital: Datafication, Accumulation, and Extraction' 6 *Big Data Society*, https://journals.sagepub.com/doi/full/10.1177/2053951718820549#.
Deepak Saxena and Joe McDonagh (2017) 'A Systematic Literature Review of the Enterprise Systems Research in Leading IS Journals (2000–2015)', *Proceedings of the Twelfth Midwest Association for Information Systems Conference 2017*, http://aisel.aisnet.org/mwais2017.
Carl Schmitt (1985) *Political Theology: Four Chapters on the Concept of Sovereignty*, MIT Press.
Carl Schmitt (1996a) *The Concept of the Political*, University of Chicago Press.
Carl Schmitt (1996b) *The Leviathan in State Theory of Thomas Hobbes: Meaning and Failure of a Political Symbol*, Greenwood Press.
Joseph Schneider (2005) *Donna Haraway: Live Theory*, Continuum.
Karen Schultz (2019) 'Schmitt's Satire in The Buribunks: Intertextual Links in Diary-Writing's Dystopia' 28 *Griffith Law Review* 206.
Marcia Bundy Seabury (1997) 'Images of a Networked Society: E.M. Forster's "The Machine Stops"' 34 *Studies in Short Fiction* 61.
Cris Shore and Susan Wright (1999) 5 'Audit Culture and Anthropology: Neo-Liberalism in British Higher Education' 5(4) *Journal of the Royal Anthropological Institute* 557.
Cris Shore and Susan Wright (2015a) 'Audit Culture Revisited: Rankings, Ratings, and the Reassembling of Society' 56(3) *Current Anthropology* 421.
Cris Shore and Susan Wright (2015b) 'Governing by Numbers: Audit Culture, Rankings and the New World Order' 23 *Social Anthropology* 22.
Annie Shum and Kieran Tranter (2017) 'Seeing, Moving, Catching, Accumulating: Pokémon GO, and the Legal Subject' 30 *International Journal for the Semiotics of Law* 477.
Eugenia Siapera (2017) *Understanding New Media*, 2nd edn, Sage.
Jaime E. Sidani*et al.* (2016) 'Association Between Social Media Use and Depression Among US Young Adults' 33 *Depression and Anxiety* 323.
Dimitra Skoumpopoulou and Teresa Waring (2017) 'Cultural Change Through the Implementation of an Enterprise System: A UK University Case Study' 30 *Journal of Enterprise Information Management* 809.
Lyndal Sleep and Kieran Tranter (2018) 'Social Media in Social Security Decision Making in Australia: An Archive of Truth?' 22 *Media Arts and Law Review* 442.
Clare Southerton, Maja Sonne Damkjaer and Anders Albrechtslund (2019) '*Living Big Data: Datafication in Everyday Practices of Participatory Surveillance*', paper presented at Big Data and the Power of Narrative, Copenhagen.
Marilyn Strathern (2003) 'Introduction: New Accountablities', in Marilyn Strathern (ed), *Audit Cultures: Anthropological Studies in Accountability, Ethics, and the Academy*, Routledge, 1.
Cass R. Sunstein (2018) *#Republic: Divided Democracy in the Age of Social Media*, Princeton University Press.
Alise Tifentale and Lev Manovich (2015) 'Selfiecity: Exploring Photography and Self-Fashioning in Social Media', in David M. Berry and Michael Dieter (eds), *Postdigital Aesthetics: Art, Computation and Design*, Palgrave Macmillan, 109.
Elizabeth Chika Tippett (2018) 'The Legal Implications of the MeToo Movement' 103 *Minnesota Law Review* 229.

Kieran Tranter (2018) *Living in Technical Legality: Science Fiction and Law as Technology*, University of Edinburgh Press.
Daniel Trottier (2012) *Social Media as Surveillance: Rethinking Visibility in a Converging World*, Ashgate.
José Van Dijck (2013) *The Culture of Connectivity: A Critical History of Social Media*, Oxford University Press.
Cornelia Vismann (2008) *Files: Law and Media Technology*, Stanford University Press.
Erica L. Wagner, Susan V. Scott and Robert D. Galliers (2006) 'The Creation of "Best Practice" Software: Myth, Reality and Ethics' 16 *Information and Organization* 251.
Lena Waizenegger, Brad McKenna, Swenjie Cai and Taino Bendz (2020) 'An Affordance Perspective of Team Collaboration and Enforced Working from Home During COVID-19' 29 *European Journal of Information Systems* 429.
Ken Ward (2018) 'Social Networks, the 2016 US Presidential Election, and Kantian Ethics: Applying the Categorical Imperative to Cambridge Analytica's Behavioral Microtargeting' 33 *Journal of Media Ethics* 133.
Wouter G. Werner (2019) 'Buribunks and Foundational Paradoxes of International Law' 28 *Griffith Law Review* 259.
Robin West (1988) 'Jurisprudence and Gender' 55 *University of Chicago Law Review* 1.
Karen Li Xan Wong and Amy Shields Dobson (2019) 'We're Just Data: Exploring China's Social Credit System in Relation to Digital Platform Ratings Cultures in Westernised Democracies' 4 *Global Media and China* 220.
Heather Cleland Woods and Holly Scott (2016) '#Sleepyteens: Social Media Use in Adolescence is Associated with Poor Sleep Quality, Anxiety, Depression and Low Self-Esteem' 51 *Journal of Adolescence* 41.
Susan Wright and Cris Shore (2003) 'Coercive Accountability: The Rise of Audit Culture in Higher Education', in Marilyn Strathern (ed), *Audit Cultures: Anthropological Studies in Accountability, Ethics, and the Academy*, Routledge, 69.
Xu Xu (2020) 'To Repress or to Co-opt? Authoritarian Control in the Age of Digital Surveillance' *American Journal of Political Science*, https://doi.org/10.1111/ajps.12514.
Dave Yates and Scott Paquette (2011) 'Emergency Knowledge Management and Social Media Technologies: A Case Study of the 2010 Haitian Earthquake' 31 *International Journal of Information Management* 6.
Ai Yu (2020) 'Digital Surveillance in Post-Coronavirus China: A Feminist View on the Price We Pay' *Gender, Work and Organization*, https://doi.org/10.1111/gwao.12471.
Shoshana Zuboff (2019) *The Age of Surveillance Capitalism: The Fight for the Future at the New Frontier of Power*, Profile Books.

Chapter 5

The theological-bureaucratic science fiction of Philip K. Dick and Carl Schmitt

An economic theology of omniscience in *The Buribunks*

Timothy D. Peters

Introduction

In this chapter, I take-up the consideration of Carl Schmitt's satirical essay, *The Buribunks*, as a form of science fiction.[1] My reference points in doing this are twofold. The first relates to Schmitt's famous work on the nature of political theology and its companion work, *Roman Catholicism and Political Form*, [2] understood specifically as a response and riposte to the work of Max Weber and his theses on the bureaucratisation and disenchantment of modernity.[3] The second is in relation to the very structure of the speculative fiction in which Schmitt engages in his satirical essay, linking this to the speculative fiction of American author Philip K. Dick. I therefore seek to examine both the nature of political theology as a response to secularisation and the work of Dick's critical satire of capitalist bureaucracy. The significance of doing so unpacks how each engages in a form of what Giorgio Agamben refers to as economic theology, which is prescient of our digital modernity.

The theological presuppositions of buribunkology's secularisation

The Buribunks is a satirical essay written by the young Carl Schmitt and published in 1918.[4] Schmitt's work of this period, which culminated a few years later in his much-quoted *Political Theology*, as well as the companion piece *Roman Catholicism and Political Form*, is, among other things, a critical response to the work of Max Weber and to the sociology of the period (his 1914 dissertation took aim at the sociological arguments regarding truth and the

1 Chapter 2 of this volume; Tranter (2019).
2 Schmitt (1996b, 2005).
3 See Weber (1946b, 1958, 1978).
4 Chapter 2 of this volume.

DOI: 10.4324/9781003091066-7

relation of the individual to the state).[5] In November 1917, the year before The *Buribunks* was published, Schmitt attended Max Weber's lecture on 'Science as Vocation', which sets forth his concept of modernity's disenchantment of the world – the 'fact' that everything has become knowable and the continuous and (in principle) never-ending progress of science and scientific knowledge.[6] Weber's lecture, as well as his broader work, including *The Protestant Work Ethic and the Spirit of Capitalism*, sought to analyse the processes of secularisation and bureaucratisation that accompanied the emergence of capitalism and the modern state.[7] He famously identified that formative aspects of the 'ethic' of capitalism could be found in the Protestant Reformation, in particular the notions of predestination, asceticism and rejection of the world that was part of Calvinism. These provided the 'preconditions and consequences of a specific type of rationalism that became a dominant force when inner-worldly asceticism fused with the capitalist economic system'.[8] This was not to suggest, for Weber, that such a theological undergirding continued. Rather, modernity's disenchantment of the world and the processes of secularisation have meant that belief and theological presuppositions are no longer required, replaced by the knowability of science and the scientific method.

While Weber emphasises secularisation, in his outlining of political theology, Schmitt – the famed and notorious jurist – did not so much dispute the influence of Protestantism on the emergence of both capitalism and liberalism as provide supplementary counter-narratives. In his work on *Roman Catholicism*, his focus was on the political forms of representation that the 'publicness' of Catholicism provided, as opposed to the 'privateness' of Protestantism's economic forms.[9] In *Political Theology*, however, Schmitt presented a counter-position to Weber's secularisation. This can be seen in terms of his famous claim that:

> All significant concepts of the modern theory of the state are secularised theological concepts not only because of their historical development – in which they were transferred from theology to the theory of the state, whereby, for example, the omnipotent God becomes the omnipotent lawgiver – but also because of their systematic structure, the recognition of which is necessary for a sociological consideration of these concepts.[10]

5 See Schmitt (1914). See the discussion of this work in Ulmen (1996), pp xii–xiii; Ulmen (1985), pp 11–13.
6 Weber (1946b). Schmitt also attended Weber's later lecture on 'Politics as Vocation' in 1919, to which Schmitt's famous *The Concept of the Political* is, in part, a response: Weber (1946a); Schmitt (2007). For a summary biography of Schmitt, including noting his attendance at both the Science as Vocation and Politics as Vocation lectures, see Meierhenrich and Simons (2017).
7 Weber (2005).
8 Ulmen (1996), p xxiii, n 14; Weber (2005).
9 Schmitt (1996b).
10 Schmitt (2005), p 36.

The methodological focus on systematic structure is important here, and goes not only to Schmitt's point about the disciplinary and structural parallels between theology and law, but also to the nature of the analogies that he draws.[11] However, the trajectory of his argument is one that challenges what secularisation means. As Giorgio Agamben points out:

> While, for Weber, secularisation was an aspect of the growing process of disenchantment and detheologization of the modern world, for Schmitt it shows on the contrary that, in modernity, theology continues to be present and active in an eminent way.[12]

For Agamben, this is not to 'necessarily imply an identity of substance between theology and modernity, or a perfect identity of meaning between theological and political concepts; rather, it concerns a particular strategic relation that marks political concepts and refers them back to their theological origin'.[13]

Agamben argues, however, that Schmitt's thesis about political theology needs to be supplemented in 'a way that would extend its validity well beyond the boundaries of public law, extending up to the fundamental concepts of the economy and the very idea of the reproductive life of human societies'.[14] Agamben seeks to examine not just *political* theology, which founds the transcendence of sovereign power on the single God, but *economic* theology, which replaces this transcendence with the idea of an *oikonomia*, conceived as an immanent ordering of both divine and human life. Despite Agamben critiquing Weber's notion of disenchantment, this would seem to emphasise the theological understanding of the economic as opposed to the political – and Agamben aligns in part with Erik Peterson's critique of Schmitt when he notes that 'the living being who was created in the image of God in the end reveals himself to be capable only of economy, not politics ... that history is ultimately not a political but an "administrative" and "governmental" problem'.[15]

Yet Schmitt's *Political Theology* is *already* a critical response to the economic theology that he identified with Weber. Such is a point that G.L. Ulmen made in working through aspects of the fraught relationship between the two.[16] He highlighted how Schmitt was engaged in a critique not simply of liberalism, but of the rationalisation and neutralisation of economic thinking that it promoted. Schmitt attacked Weber's 'prognosis' in which 'the future belongs to the

11 For a consideration of the parallels between theology and jurisprudence, see Schmitt (2008).
12 Agamben (2011), pp 3–4.
13 Agamben (2011), p 4.
14 Agamben (2011), p 3.
15 Agamben (2011), p 3.
16 Ulmen (1985), p 44. He notes that whereas, 'Weber was fundamentally concerned with what might be called economic theology; Schmitt concerned himself with "political theology."'

intelligent, professionally-educated bureaucracy because it is the essential bearer of the thoroughly-technicalized "state" with its rational consistency based on the legal norms of a going concern. Legality is the positivistic functional *modus* of bureaucracy.'[17] Schmitt argues that such a neutralisation overlooks the political. He explains that no bureaucracy simply 'works in an empty space and in pure ether; it exists under foreign and domestic political conditions and in a concrete situation'.[18] The vision of a thoroughly secularised, rationalised and neutralised economy is to forget both the political foundations of such an economy *and* its theological origins.

It is in understanding Schmitt's critical engagement with Weber that I come to his satirical essay. As Karen Schultz has highlighted, *The Buribunks* has as an object of its satire, three targets: the 'romantic occasionalist diary-writing'; a 'progressivist philosophy of history'; and 'positivist social science'.[19] The first two, which Schultz deftly situates in their intertextuality with Schmitt's work of the time, emphasise the *content* of the essay: the analysis of buribunkology as an obsessive keeping of diaries *and* its articulation in relation to a particular philosophy of history. My focus here, however, is on the way in which the formal and structural presentation of *The Buribunks* provides a critique of the modes of scholarship and ways of knowing produced by modern sociology in its positivised form. In his 1914 work, Schmitt describes sociology as 'the new science of factual correlations, without which the individual cannot be conceived and in which he completely disappears'.[20] It is this methodology of drawing 'factual correlations' that the first part of Schmitt's essay satirises. The narrator of the essay, after establishing the 'scientific' legitimacy of 'buribunkology' (determined primarily by the quantity of dissertations, publications and research funding that the field garners),[21] turns to a

17 Ulmen (1985), pp 42–3. Ulmen is quoting from Schmitt (1996a). The later English translation by George Schwab and Erna Hilfstein differs slightly as follows: 'the future belongs to the intelligent, professionally trained bureaucracy because it is the actual carrier of the thoroughly technologized plant called "state" that operates according to an inner rational logic in compliance with legal norms. Legality is the positivistic mode of operation of the bureaucracy'. Schmitt (1996a), p 66. I have retained Ulmen's translation because of its emphasis on the state's taking up of the 'rational consistency' and 'legal norms of a going concern', which better captures the underlying economic dynamics to which Schmitt is speaking, rather than simply the physicality evoked in the reference to a 'technologized plant'.

18 Schmitt, quoted by Ulmen (1985), p 43.

19 Schultz highlights the way Schmitt destabilises each of these three concepts, and provides a detailed and insightful analysis of the first two. She notes that 'he abrades diary-writing for its embrace of romantic occasionalist subjectivism, endless conversation, and vanity; he challenges history's progressivist philosophy for its repetition and utopian thinking; and he deprecates positivist social science for its socio-technical rationales and empty form'. Schultz (2019), p 207.

20 Schmitt (1914), p 6. Quoted in Ulmen (1996), p xxx, n 17. Schmitt also aligned this concept of sociology with contemporary epistemology, which sought 'the epistemological subject that can only be found in a supra-individual consciousness'.

21 Chapter 2 of this volume, p 13.

systematic consideration of the subject of the field: the 'Buribunks'. The narrator begins by asking what is significant about a 'Buribunk', a seemingly appropriate question that proposes a distinction between intellectual and physical differences. However, the potential answers then provided – 'is it ... the fact that every Buribunk keeps a diary or the fact that he has an enlarged mouth?' – while presented in the objective language of the sociologist or anthropologist, calls into question the nature of those disciplines and their concrete factual actuality and positivity.[22] The narrator goes on to work through the causal possibilities of these 'facts', pointing in a critical fashion to the way in which it is possible that the 'intellect ... designs the body' and thus, while one would think that the keeping of diaries would be the key focus, the physiological changes are still of potential significance.[23] This satirises the sociological science of 'factual correlations'.

It is with such a satirical approach in mind that one must read the rest of the essay, which conducts first a historiographical tracing of the origin of what could be termed the 'ethic of the Buribunk' (whether it is found in Don Juan, his servant Leporello or the later 'heroes of Buribunkdom', the fictional Ferker and then Schnekke), and then the elaboration of the 'sociological architecture' of the Buribunk in terms of the process of keeping and collating of diaries. The latter presents a form of bureaucratised record-keeping of everything that the Buribunks do for every second of every day of their lives. While satirising sociology in general, the methodological structure presented in the essay parallels Weber's own format in *The Protestant Ethic*, which sought to find the origins of the particular 'ethic' that undergirded capitalism, before going on to determine when it had become 'fully developed' and then secularised.[24]

Such parallels are further highlighted by the way the narrator methodically applies Weber's description in 'Science as Vocation' of the primary task of a 'useful teacher', which is 'to teach his students to recognize "inconvenient" facts' – facts that are inconvenient for a particular viewpoint (including one's own).[25] The narrator notes such a fact in relation to Ferker, the figure often held up as the hero and originator of Buribunkdom. While an avid diary-keeper, Ferker apparently *did not* record everything. There are gaps in his diaries that do not explain, for example, the reasons for his marriage.[26] Although certain inferences can be made, it is the presence of such gaps that leads the narrator to position Ferker as only a *forerunner* of Buribunkdom, not the presentation of it as fully developed. The supreme example of the Buribunk (which he reserves for the later figure of Schnekke) is one who captures *all* components of life within their diary. This leads to a historiography of the fictional study of buribunkology, which is the obsessive and exhaustive keeping

22 Chapter 2 of this volume, p 14.
23 Chapter 2 of this volume, pp 14–5.
24 Weber (2005).
25 Weber (1946b), p 147.
26 Chapter 2 of this volume, p 21.

of diaries so that every second of one's life may be kept and recorded. Schnekke is the 'hero' of Buribunkdom because he

> is nothing but a diary-keeper, he lives for the diary, he lives in and through the diary – even though in the end he keeps a diary about the fact that he has run out of ideas about what he could write in the diary.[27]

This incessant diary-keeping is then accompanied by bureaucratic processes of categorisation that go with it. Diary entries must be submitted daily and collated by local councils, which will immediately index them, then collate monthly reports for the head of each Buribunk department, who then reports to a central agency that creates master catalogues.[28]

In this formal and structural sense, the essay satirises the sociological emphasis on the trajectory of rationalisation, where the 'ethic' of Buribunkdom is traced from its emergent states to a 'fully developed' hierarchy of society. More specifically, Schmitt is satirising Weber's analysis of the modes of secularisation and rationalisation that aligns with his articulation of modernity and its 'disenchantment of the world'. That this fits within the particular paradigm of scientific knowledge upon which Weber draws is clear from the way Schmitt's narrator declares that buribunkology is 'more than theology, jurisprudence or philosophy, it is indeed more than a science, it is a fact'.[29] Buribunkology's displacement of Schmitt's own disciplinary reference points (theology, jurisprudence and philosophy), as well as 'science', is therefore presented as a form of secularisation. Yet how are we to understand this secularisation? Is it in the form of Weber's disenchantment of the world, or is it in terms of Schmitt's political theology, via which theology – although secularised – is active in an eminent way?

The essay itself makes little reference to either jurisprudence or theology until the end, when the narrator notes a 'shifting of the head' away from that which Christianity has posited, to that of buribunkology and its relation to immortality:

> In the realisation that there is true reality only in history, we seek real immortality in history. Not in some after-world. Christianity had 'shifted' the heads of people in a literal sense (in full acknowledgement of the relative value of its sublime teachings this needs to be stressed) as it had turned the gaze from the factuality of the past to an after-worldly future, where there is, as we saw, only the dark rat hole of that which not yet

27 Chapter 2 of this volume, p 22. What's more, Schnekke (apparently) severed 'the diary from its restrictive tie to the single person and elevate[d] it to a collective organism' of which Schmitt's narrator then traces the sociological architecture. Chapter 2 of this volume, p 23.
28 Chapter 2 of this volume, pp 23–4.
29 Chapter 2 of this volume, p 14.

> exists, but no reality. Therefore we restore the correct direction for the heads towards the real by seeking immortality where it really is: behind us not before us.[30]

This encompasses an immanent secularisation, which occurs not by dismissing the theological but by articulating it on a different level. That is, the narrator does not dismiss the seeking of immortality or eternal life, but rather argues for a turning of the gaze from some after-world deemed unreal in the same way that any point of the future is unreal, to the only reality and factuality being in the past. The reader is thus invited to seek 'immortality where it really is: behind us not before us'.[31] This process of secularisation sheds light on the essay itself.

If we are to take Schmitt's later critique of secularisation seriously, then it is not so much the secular that is significant, but the theological or metaphysical world-view that undergirds its concepts. In the context of buribunkology, what undergirds it is a particular economic theology. For what matches the vision of a complete record-keeping, in which the entire history and interiority of the subject is captured and objectified within the diary, is an underlying presupposition about the readability or knowability of such content. A particular theological or divine view aligns with the sense or desire for a completeness of the record-keeping. At the level of the secular, this completeness of record-keeping is a reflection of bureaucratised disenchantment in which everything about the Buribunk becomes *knowable*. As Weber points out in 'Science as Vocation', the scientific paradigm of knowledge is *not* that each individual has greater knowledge of the way in which things work – most individuals who get on a street trolley, or today who get in a car, know little about the actual workings of these modes of transportation.[32] Rather, it is that the world is disenchanted because it is *knowable* – mystery has been removed from the world. However, the completeness of the record-keeping – that it is a keeping not of particular notable points of information, but of *everything* no matter how trivial – invokes a theological presupposition. The records themselves constitute a complete knowledge, which *someone* may know, and which the divine knows in its completeness.

As such, the vision of buribunkology, while encompassing a critique of the philosophy of history and a secularised claim to immortality, presupposes a sense of divine omniscience. If Schmitt's later example of 'political theology' is the shift from the omnipotent God to the omnipotent lawgiver, we find here a parallel shift from the omniscient God to an omniscient archive. The theological trajectory that tracks the implications of such omniscience is linked, according to Agamben, to the genealogy of the theological-economic-

30 Chapter 2 of this volume, p 27.
31 Chapter 2 of this volume, p 27.
32 Weber (1946b), p 139.

providential paradigm that can be contrasted with the theological-political paradigm in which Schmitt engages in his *Political Theology*.[33] Such distinctions are *not* between two completely opposed paradigms, but rather between 'two poles' of the 'bipolar machine', which correlates a transcendent principle with an immanent order (the two poles of 'Kingdom' and 'Government' in Agamben's work).[34] Liberalism's emphasis on the immanence of economic order, and then the secularisation of this paradigm by modernity, does *not*, according to Agamben, result in emancipation from the providential paradigm – because it is still caught in the intertwining of sovereignty and economy.[35]

Schmitt's satirical essay can therefore be understood as engaging and critiquing liberalism's attempt to eliminate the theological-political paradigm of sovereignty in terms of an economic theology of omniscience and the archive. Such a vision of a divine archive, and a complete capturing of all that occurs in history, itself has certain precursors. In addition to various religious visions of the all-encompassing knowledge of God, one could point, as John Durham Peters does, to Charles Babbage's nineteenth-century vision of the air capturing and recording all of history.[36] In the mid-twentieth century, such visions were then reproduced by the Argentine writer Jorge Luis Borges's story *The Library of Babel*, encompassing a universal library that contains all possible combinations of 410-page texts.[37] For Peters, the contemporary relevance of such visions of complete archives or databases is in terms of understanding today's modes of digital record-keeping and data-mining. In this context, he highlights Sergey Brin's suggestion that 'the perfect search engine would be the mind of God'[38] and places Google's organising of the world's data within a 'distinguished family of religious media'.[39] That is, 'Google's project is to build a temple to meet the sky, anchor remembrance, and serve as a canon of all knowledge.'[40] For Peters, 'Google revives the ancient dream and nightmare of a "book of life" in which every human deed is recorded for the Day of Judgment and thus stands in a long line of sacral and bureaucratic bookkeeping.'[41] Schmitt's 'buribunkology' not only fits within this tradition, but in satirising it provides a critique of it.

The prescience of Schmitt's essay and the parallels between buribunkology and today's 'informational existence', the biopolitics of the digital archive and the (self-)surveillance of the post-millennial have been taken up and

33 Agamben (2011), p 277.
34 Agamben (2011), p 284.
35 Agamben (2011), p 284.
36 Peters (2015), pp 347–8.
37 Peters (2015), pp 352–4.
38 Peters (2015), p 339.
39 Peters (2015), p 339.
40 Peters (2015), p 339.
41 Peters (2015), p 346. He also notes that, 'God and Google are both passive miners of data; not a sparrow falls nor a click occurs without their notice' (p 341).

highlighted by Kieran Tranter, Daniel McLoughlin and Francine Rochford.[42] In various ways, each of these authors point to the limitations of today's buribunkology – the contrast between a particular vision of the completely written and captured subject and the fragmentary and multiple natures of such digital existence. Yet the underlying vision – the economic theology of omniscience – persists. In the next section, I will take-up these arguments in general, and, in particular, Tranter's analysis of Schmitt's essay as a form of science fiction – a thinking about the impact of certain forms of technology and technological thinking – by making some comparisons between Schmitt's essay and the work of the twentieth-century American speculative fiction writer Philip K. Dick (1928–82).

The Buribunks as science fiction: Schmitt the Phildickian

Eulogised by Frederick Jameson in the 1980s as the 'Shakespeare of Science Fiction',[43] Dick has provided much material for the makers of Hollywood blockbuster films since Ridley Scott's acclaimed release of *Blade Runner* in 1982 (based on Dick's *Do Androids Dream of Electric Sheep?*).[44] However, as Ethan Mills argues, the films based on Dick's work tend to present a Hollywoodified form of individualism where 'good defeats evil, free will secures the triumph of the human spirit and our heroes discover knowledge of reality and virtue (all before the credits roll)'.[45] This contrasts with what Mills describes as the 'Dickian worldview', which encompasses a 'universe of paranoia, ignorance and a lack of true freedom.[46] Dick's 'heroes' only 'occasionally discover the truth', 'wonder if they make any genuine free decisions' and generally accept that they do not.[47] Jason Vest, who has studied both Dick's work and the films based upon it, argues that it is these latter themes that have associated Dick with postmodernism.[48] He situates Dick's work in relation to twentieth-century literary writers such as Franz Kafka, Jorge Luis Borges (referred to above) and Italo Calvino, noting that there is a cross-over in themes associated with all four of them: 'ontological doubt, epistemological uncertainty, the necessity of creative art, the dehumanizing aspects of technological proliferation, the ambiguity of human identity, and the inability to distinguish reality from fiction'.[49] While associated with postmodernism, Dick retains a certain humanism in his work – not necessarily in terms of Hollywood's triumph of the individual, or 'a naïve faith in the individual's ability to create his or her future no matter what

42 McLoughlin (2019); Rochford (2019); Tranter (2019).
43 Jameson (1982, 2005).
44 Dick (1968); Scott (1982) *Blade Runner.*
45 Mills (2011).
46 Mills (2011).
47 Mills (2011).
48 Vest (2007, 2009).
49 Vest (2009), p xvi.

obstacles may arise, but rather a profound compassion for the individual's difficult struggle to overcome these obstacles'.[50] Such (postmodern) humanism arises, according to Christopher Palmer, 'out of a critique of the society, politics and psychology of modernity'.[51]

At a broad level, it is this emphasis on a critique of modernity that draws a connection between Schmitt and Dick, although such a direct connection has yet to be taken up or substantially explored. Francesco Ragazzi has analysed the notion of pre-emption in the post-9/11 US National Security Strategy in light of Dick's short story 'Minority Report' (upon which the 2002 film starring Tom Cruise was based) and, in particular, its displacement of the traditional criminal justice system by the new concept of 'pre-crime'.[52] Ragazzi compares the attempts to rewrite international law principles around a notion of pre-emptive war in terms of an internationalisation of Schmitt's emphasis on sovereignty and the exception.[53] My interest in Dick's connection to Schmitt, however, lies in the way both encompass an intertwining of politics with theology. As Palmer notes, Dick's writing

> situates itself on territory contested between politics and religion: politics, wherein a certain cultural practice or way of explaining the world can be seen as ideological, that is, an invention or production helpful to those in power; and religion, wherein the same thing can be seen as illusory, that is, the sign that secular, experienced reality is not really real. Behind a social ideology there may be nothing more than another fabrication, but behind a secular illusion there is, perhaps, a spiritual reality.[54]

This question of the connection between the 'fragile and deceptive' nature of experience and the possibility of a 'true reality' that may lie behind it is one that reappears throughout Dick's work. As is frequently noted, Dick's later work, and specifically his final novels (*VALIS, The Divine Invasion* and *The Transmigration of Timothy Archer*), are overtly theological in nature, engaging in a form of Gnosticism that seeks a true reality behind the illusion of our experience.[55] However, an engagement with the questions of theology and reality appear throughout Dick's work. This takes up a classic trope of science fiction

50 Vest (2009), p xi.
51 Palmer (2003), p 9.
52 See Ragazzi (2004). Spielberg (2002) *Minority Report*. For an alternative analysis of the (il)legality of 'pre-crime' in terms of the film based on Dick's short story, see MacNeil (2007).
53 Ragazzi (2004).
54 Palmer (2003), p 6. He continues: 'If so, politics and religion crucially diverge, but for the moment we note that in both realms ordinary experience is taken to be fragile and deceptive, and the social, the basis and conditioner of ordinary experience, is seen as a fabrication or a fake. In addition religion is often itself a fabrication in Dick's novels, yet not necessarily less consolatory for being a fabrication.'
55 Dick (1981a, 1981b, 1982). See, for example, Durham (1988); Vest (2009).

as engaged in a process of secularisation: providing technological or social explanations for that which, in the past, may have been attributed to the divine. It can be seen at its most explicit in the science fiction trope of a technologically enabled 'eternal life'.[56] In a number of places, Dick presented a more sophisticated version of this by, for example, describing both drug-induced and technological modes of different people coming together and inhabiting a single body as a realisation of the theology of the Eucharist.[57]

At one level, Dick's work reflects Weber's notion of disenchantment, rationalisation and secularisation, with the development of science and technology moving to explain and even achieve what theology in the past has only alluded to as mystery. At the same time, Dick's engagement with theology and theological themes also encompasses the *reverse* of Weber's disenchantment. This takes the form not so much of a revealing of the 'knowability' of the world as explained by science, but rather the bureaucratisation of our vision of the divine. Dick's work thus engages in modes of political and economic theology – looking both to the ways in which theological notions inform secular concepts and *also* the way in which *modern* conceptions come to inform *modern* theological notions. Dick's theological speculation, therefore, is not an escape from the challenge of contemporary times and late capitalism but, as Scott Durham notes, a critical engagement with and understanding of them.[58] If Schmitt's *Political Theology* is about recognising the continuity of theology in the context of 'secular' modernity's law and politics, Dick is engaged in a critique of economic theology through his bureaucratic articulations of the divine. In this way, the themes of Dick's science fiction and Schmitt's *The Buribunks* overlap. I will focus here on three examples from Dick's short stories that provide explanations of divine mystery in the context of the bureaucratic experience of mundane modernity.

In 'The Adjustment Team', the short story upon which George Nolfi based his 2011 *The Adjustment Bureau*, Dick takes aim at the notion of divine providence and foresight.[59] Ed Fletcher, an employee of a small real estate firm, is the 'victim of a clerical error' in that a divine 'summoner' (his pet dog) fails to make a call (bark) at the correct time. The result is that Ed is late to work on a day on which an 'adjustment' is being made to 'Sector T137'.[60] Ed therefore discovers that his office building and all those in it appear to be made of ash and are disintegrating. Fleeing the scene (and chased by strange men in suits), Ed believes he has suffered a psychotic episode or nervous breakdown – a point

56 This is nicely captured by an advertisement from Palmer Eldrich in *The Three Stigmata of Palmer Eldrich*: 'God only promises eternal life; we can deliver it.' Dick (1966/1983), p 127.
57 See, in particular, Dick (1966/1983).
58 Durham (1988).
59 Dick (1954a); Nolfi (2011) *The Adjustment Bureau*. For a critical reading of Nolfi's film, see Peters (2022), Ch 6.
60 Dick (1954a), p 82.

further supported by the fact that when he later returns to the office, everything appears normal. However, on closer inspection Ed discovers that things are not quite as they were. There are a range of slight alterations to individuals, their clothing and appearances, the layout of offices and furniture. Startled by these changes, Ed flees once again; however, when he tries to call the police from a nearby phone box, he is instead taken up to 'the heavens'. There he meets with the 'old man', who presents their operations as a mass bureaucratic divine plan, which necessitates the making of a number of 'adjustments' to reality – adjustments that they are 'full licenced' to make.[61] Ed was supposed to have been adjusted with the rest of his office. Having now seen 'behind' the curtain of reality and given privy to these grand plans, Ed is warned not to tell anyone on pain of being adjusted himself – an order to which he willingly agrees.

This story presents a version of the divine plan not so much as an all-powerful God who, through the ministry of the angels, is carrying out his infallible will, but rather as a divine bureaucracy that succumbs to all the potential fallibilities of bureaucracy itself. The story thus transforms the traditional theological position, which is a perfect, infallible, omnipotent and omniscience divinity, with angels proclaiming and reflecting God's glory into a well-meaning and well-intentioned, but only semi-powerful and partially knowing, bureaucratic operation carried out by fallible clerks. If we read Dick's narrative as a parable of secularisation, then one of the dynamics of the shift from the theological to the secular can be identified: that which is presented as infallible, all-powerful and all-knowing becomes subject to error, failures and gaps. In one sense, this is the problem of the secularisation paradigm – in attempting to secularise certain theological, political and economic concepts, it transfers from a perfect divinity to an imperfect humanity without recognising the effects of such shifts (a point emphasised by Agamben in relation to the secularisation of the theological-providential paradigm in the economy and its government).[62]

It is the trajectory of this shift that is satirised by Schmitt's The *Buribunks*. The supposed infinite and onward march of the progress of science and the becoming knowable of all misrecognises what is a divine trait that has been secularised and forgets the very dynamic of the problem: both in terms of the very impossibility for the complete recording of the self, but also the impossibility for there to be a human knowledge of all. If we return to the example of Google, as Peters notes, aspects of this problem *are* recognised. For the way Google's indexing and archiving function is *not* to ensure a complete knowledge of everything on the internet, but rather to focus on the *links* and *connections between* content.[63] This reflects, at one level, Dick's vision of a bureaucratised divine omniscience. If Google is a god, then it is a particular

61 Dick (1954a), p 97.
62 Agamben (2011).
63 Peters (2015), p 334.

secular and modern one bound by the limitations of its existence, including the limitations of knowledge. Such limitations can be seen in the way the subject brought *within* the archive of buribunkology, the archive of 'big data' or Google's indexing, is *not* capturing the internality of the subject, but rather their projected and observed avatar or data double.[64] As Eric Trozzo points out, what Google's algorithms and the data mining of 'big data' presuppose is the conflation between the recorded data and the experience of the subject that it represents. Its goal is to 'reduce us to our data double'.[65]

This point is demonstrated by Dick's short story, 'We Can Remember It For You Wholesale', upon which both the 1990 and 2012 *Total Recall* movies are loosely based.[66] There, Douglas Quail longs for adventure – to take a trip to Mars and to be an inter-planetary spy. However, as his wife continually emphasises, given his miserable role as a clerk he has no means of affording or accomplishing such a dream. A solution presents itself in terms of 'Rekall, Incorporated', a company that specialises in inserting memories of certain events into one's brain. While Quail has doubts about how effective such a process will be, the manager of Rekall emphasises that Quail has 'no chance, no possibility in the slightest, of ever actually getting to Mars'.[67] Rekall is the only way of achieving his 'life long dream'. More importantly, the memories to be inserted are 'more than the real thing' because 'real' memories are forgotten. What Rekall provides is not a second-best option: 'The actual memory, with all its vagueness, omissions and ellipses, not to say distortions – that's second-best.'[68] However, when Quail is sedated to have these memories inserted, it is discovered that he *already* has such memories – but they had been overridden in an attempt to wipe out his recollection of such activities. That is, Quail *had* been an inter-planetary spy and gone to Mars, but his memories were wiped out by the spy agency after he completed an interplanetary assassination. The recovery of these memories results in the spy agency trying to catch up with him, tracking him via an implant that had been placed in his brain, which enables all his thoughts to be 'read' by someone else.

Dick's story, in its meditation on the nature or 'reality' of memory, provides certain parallels to buribunkology and the way it connects memory to the experience of the subject. The lure of Rekall is that it gives a mundane and ordinary individual who does not and will not achieve anything of note the ability to *remember* experiencing a life of adventure and significance – that is, the ability to enter into the 'buribunkian cinematic attitude', the experiencing of oneself 'as history's subject-object', the star of one's own film.[69] The contrast between Quail's apparent existence as a mundane clerk and his desire for the

64 Trozzo (2019), pp 131–3.
65 Trozzo (2019), p 132.
66 Dick (1987); Verhoeven (1990) *Total Recall*; Wiseman (2012) *Total Recall*.
67 Dick (1987), p 361.
68 Dick (1987), p 361.
69 Chapter 2 of this volume, p 16.

adventure parallels Ferker and Schnekke: the first, who engaged in a 'wildly agitated life, filled with nerve-wracking experiences', but who still had not achieved the ideality of Buribunkdom by externalising all experience and internalities into his diary;[70] the second, who seemed to have achieved nothing except the complete diarisation of his non-achieving of anything, his 'indistinctive generality'.[71] In Dick's story, the mundane character of Quail appears initially to desire a Ferker-style life, escaping a Schnekke-style mundanity, only to discover that he has *already* engaged in such a life of adventure but can no longer remember it. The historiographic trajectory from 'exciting Ferker' to 'mundane Schnekke' that Schmitt's narrator outlines is thus paralleled – but instead of this being accompanied by an evolution in the recording of *memories*, what is emphasised is the *loss* of memory: not so much the 'right to be forgotten', but the 'right to forget' is central to the story. When it is discovered that any replacing of such exciting memories with a mundane existence will likely *not* displace the desires that drove Quail to Rekall in the first place, it is suggested that they be replaced with alternative memories, with one suggestion being that he could be given memories of having been an inter-planetary Don Juan with a girl in every city on Earth, Lunar and Mars, who had given up the lifestyle due to exhaustion.

What is key to the story is the connection between one's memory and thoughts, and one's experience as a subject. Both the implant that enables the spy agency to 'read' Quail's thoughts and the technology of inserting memories by Rekall encompass a particular vision of memory and reality – one that aligns with buribunkology. Particularly significant is the emphasis on the way both the recorded memory of the Buribunk and the 'artificial' memory implanted by Rekall become more real than ordinary memories. The 'reality' of a memory for buribunkology is in its recording, its rendering for posterity in a fashion that will not be diminished or forgotten. Rekall provides a further extension of this by enabling such secure memories to be reinserted into the individual in a way that exceeds ordinary memories, which *do* fade. The ability to read or adjust the internality of one's own thoughts is an extension of the very paradigm of knowledge captured by the diary itself. For the diary is an externalised internality, a rendering visible of one's thoughts for *others* to read and a capturing of them in a way that sustains their existence beyond the fallibilities of one's own memory.[72] The result is that the 'diary', the 'memory insert', has – as Trozzo notes about Google and 'big data' – a 'better memory … than we do ourselves'.[73] This process of externalising memory not as an aspect of recording but as a complete rendering visible of the subject has two results. First, it means that the ability to 'read' the thoughts or manifest memories of a subject takes the

70 Chapter 2 of this volume, p 20.
71 Chapter 2 of this volume, p 23.
72 Rochford (2019).
73 Trozzo (2019), p 110.

place of the subject, but in a way that limits or eliminates the process of evolving change and self-construction of the subject, flattening out *all* records and *all* data. Second, it calls into the question the *authenticity* of both one's own memories *and* the recording of such memories in diarised form. The first challenges our understanding of the subject, the second the way in which we presume the 'authorship' of that subject's actions and record-keeping.

This question of authorship is key to my third example, Dick's story 'Prominent Author'.[74] In this story, an employee of the company 'Terran Developments' is given a prototype 'Jiffi-scuttler' to test prior to its release to market. The Jiffi-scuttler is a new form of transportation device that, once set up, enables one to move hundreds of miles in a matter of seconds by walking through its 'wavery gray tunnel'.[75] The device 'bridge[s] distances non-spatially, through another dimension', although exactly *how* had not been explained clearly to Henry Ellis, the main character of the story.[76] In fact, when Henry questions one of the engineers about how it works, he gets frustrated that all he is presented with is an analogy, not 'a factual answer' to his question of *where* his Jiffi-scuttler goes.[77] Henry's *lack* of knowledge of how the device that he now uses every day to travel 160 miles to work in a matter of seconds is reflective of the scientific paradigm of knowledge that Weber associates with disenchantment.[78] While he knows little about this mode of transportation, other than it works in the fourth dimension, he presumes that such information is *knowable* – although he is told, as a consumer, not to worry about it.

The 'prominence' of the 'Prominent Author' is the way it engages with a sense of mystery in the context of a disenchanted world. When using the Jiffi-scuttler, Henry discovers groups of tiny people that can partially see him through the walls of the tunnel. They provide him, on a *very* small wisp of parchment, a number of questions in another language. He takes these to his company's linguistics department and asks to use their translating machine (with the story that he is trading letters with a friend on Centaurus VI). He then calls the 'Federal Library of Information' to get answers to the questions, re-translates them and returns them to the group that he found through the wall of the Jiffi-scuttler. Except that each time he goes through the device, the people have changed, as if numerous years have gone by. After doing this a number of times, it appears that the 'little people' have developed a cult around him and start presenting burnt offerings. Henry's actions are eventually discovered and he is fired by his boss. He was supposed to disclose any 'malfunctions' with the Jiffi-scuttler, which clearly he had not. What is noted is that the language was not some alien dialogue, as Henry suspected and had translated by the

74 Dick (1954b).
75 Dick (1954b), p 30.
76 Dick (1954b), p 30.
77 Dick (1954b), p 31.
78 Weber (1946b), p 139.

company's machines, but rather ancient Hebrew. Henry had, by answering these questions in written form, been writing Holy Scripture – a point emphasised in the final scene when one of his wife's friends asks what he has been working on and he presents a copy of the *Holy Bible*.

This final example provides a contrasting account of writing and authorship to The *Buribunks*. One of Schmitt's narrator's criticisms of the forerunners of the Buribunks is their *lack* of awareness of the writer's higher consciousness. He refers to Leporello, the servant of Don Juan, who goes in part towards a buribunkology by writing down the 'conquests' of his master, but does not have that sense of the writer's higher consciousness, of being 'author of a piece of world history and therefore having become an associate judge of the world court'.[79] At one level, Dick's tale provides an example of how those who are engaged in the writing of world history themselves are not necessarily aware of it – the simple translating and responding to questions is actually the writing of what becomes scripture. At the same time, this highlights the nature of scripture and authorship. As Tracy Strong points out in his analysis of Schmitt and Thomas Hobbes, the significance of scripture – at least from a Protestant perspective – is that its authority is *not* dependent on any (human) author: 'for a Protestant the truth of Scripture does not depend on knowing what its author meant (for God cannot be known). Scripture is authoritative in and of itself, not because we know the intentions of the author.'[80] He argues that Hobbes, with his *Leviathan*, attempted to produce a secular form of scripture that, like the Bible, could be read '*and to which the intentions of the author can be of no concern*'.[81] Significant in this context was also the Protestant rejection of a metaphorical understanding of scripture, privileging instead a literal understanding, for 'metaphor cannot be at the basis of a correct understanding'.[82]

Such a turn to a literal understanding prefigures the later mode of 'knowability' of the scientific paradigm. We can see this in terms of Henry's desire to know the 'true facts' about the nature of the Jiffi-scuttler, rather than merely an analogy, as well as a representation of the way in which he went about 'writing' what became scripture: the providing of 'his answers, the precise, correct responses he obtained from the Federal Library of Information and had the Linguistics Machine translate into their language'.[83] The 'Prominent Author' would thus seem to be a parable of secularisation: the writing of Scripture, and even the descriptions of the appearances of 'God' that it describes, are explained by a defective futuristic technological apparatus that allows for communication to go back in time. Instead of being the 'word of God', the Bible is actually precise responses from a futuristic librarian to a series of questions from the past.

79 Chapter 2 of this volume, p 17.
80 Strong (2010), p 260.
81 Strong (1993), p 149, emphasis in original.
82 Strong (1993), p 149. As Strong notes, 'The claims made for a literal understanding of the Bible have to do with the nature of a text, not the nature of God.'
83 Dick (1954b), p 37.

The story thus presents, in a similar fashion to buribunkology, a secular account of omniscient knowledge. It is important to note that Henry's 'authorship' is called into question – he *did not* write the responses to the questions. Rather, he relied on both an apparently unlimited and infallible Linguistics Machine to translate the text and the ability for complete and correct responses from the 'Federal Library of Information'. That is, he was able to engage analogue versions of Google's search and translate functions, presumed to be able to capture and provide all answers completely. Dick's tale presents a vision of Google writing scripture. This reflects not simply the archive of buribunkology, presumed to be a complete capturing of all the information about the Buribunks, appropriately categorised and sorted to make for easy searching, but Schmitt's satirical critique of the 'objective' methods of social science, which is the structural framework of *The Buribunks*.

At the same time, there is an aspect of Dick's tale that structurally undermines its form of secularisation. If the Bible was written in the form of precise anthropological responses to specific questions, why does it retain as much theological and literary symbolism as it does? The premise of Dick's story would only seem to function as a mode of secularisation if we are to believe that the Bible contains simply 'precise' answers that could be provided from future librarians and *not* metaphor. If, however, we take scripture seriously as *both* literal and metaphoric, historic and symbolic, then Dick's tale ceases to present a scientific and disenchanted narrative, but is rather one of mystery. Such secularisation would point back to divinity – a divinity working through both human and technological agents.

Conclusion

Schmitt's satirical account of buribunkology, Dick's science fiction and what could be referred to as the theology of the digital archive all point to a particular presupposition: that of the possibility of the universe as completely knowable and captured in an archive that is all-encompassing. However, the problem with this secularisation of the theological concept of omniscience is that it encompasses blind spots. The 2020 Netflix documentary *The Social Dilemma* features a range of past and present members of the tech industry who seek to 'out' the issues of social media, search engines and the psychology of software design.[84] But, even in their *critique* of social media companies and their technological paradigms, they remain caught within the paradigm of buribunkology: that *everyone* is included, connected and captured by the archive. As such, their critique is of algorithms that can determine how frequently or infrequently someone has engaged with a particular app or platform and target them to get them to re-engage. What such a critique *forgets* is the subject that

84 Orlowski (2020) *The Social Dilemma*.

exceeds the presupposed data double – those that are *not* connected, or that are connected only in part.

Where Schmitt's satire becomes *most* prescient is in the way it articulates the vision of the excluded. His narrator notes that the one who stops writing 'is no longer up to date, and eventually he vanishes from the screen of the monthly reports and ceases to exist'.[85] Existence here is in being included in the archive, writing and engaging with it. For those who cease to do so, those who, because they do not or cannot continue to write, are rendered to subordinate tasks such as making the paper for the diaries, the result is:

> As if the earth has swallowed him, nobody knows him anymore, nobody mentions him in their diary, no eye sees him, no ear hears him; and may his lament be ever so harrowing and drive him into madness, the iron law does not know mercy against the unworthy one who has excluded himself, in the same way as the fundamental laws of natural selection know no exception.[86]

We find here an articulation of a law without exception, which Schmitt famously goes on to critique in his *Political Theology*. At the same time, as Agamben's work has made clear, the figure who is excluded is not, as a result, completely detached from the law. Instead, they are caught in the relation of the 'ban'. Those who are abandoned are not set before a specific law, but rather brought before a sovereign power. Abandonment 'is a compulsion to appear absolutely under the law, under the law as such and in its totality'.[87] Those who are excluded – or, rather, who have excluded themselves – from such a vision remain caught within the paradoxes of the sovereign ban, included via their exclusion.[88]

At the same time, the words of Schmitt's narrator that describe the excluded as those who are 'as if the earth has swallowed' them allude instead to *another* vision of those who are not captured. For that which 'no eye sees' and 'no ear hears' is also that which is 'seen' and 'heard' by the divine. As St Paul, quoting the book of Isaiah, in 1 Corinthians 2:9, notes, 'What no eye has seen, nor ear heard, nor the human heart conceived, what God has prepared for those who love him.'[89] That which is not seen or heard, that which exceeds what is

85 Chapter 2 of this volume, p 25.
86 Chapter 2 of this volume, p 25.
87 Nancy (1998). Quoted by Agamben (1998), p 58.
88 Agamben (1998), p 59. Agamben argues that, 'Only if it is possible to think the Being of abandonment beyond every idea of law (even that of the empty form of law's being in force without significance) will we have moved out of the paradox of sovereignty towards a politics freed from every ban.'
89 1 Cor 2:9 NRSV; cf Isaiah 64:4 'From ages past no one has heard, no ear has perceived, no eye has seen any God besides you, who works for those who wait for him.'

captured by the archive, written by the Buribunk, or tweeted, posted or searched by the user of the digital, is that of the divine itself. In this light, we potentially find the need to return to a theological understanding as a mode of challenging the secularised economic theology of omniscience. Such is not to turn to a paradigm of sovereignty, surveillance or a stark and uncaring archival omniscience, but rather, as Trozzo notes, to highlight the 'glory of God' not as 'a dismissal of what is not seen, but a celebration of it'.[90]

Acknowledgements

My utmost thanks and gratitude go to Kieran Tranter and Edwin Bikundo for the invitation to be part of this project, their editorial prowess and their endless patience. For their supportive and useful comments, I acknowledge and thank Chantelle Peters, the anonymous reviewer and each of the participants in the 2017 Symposium 'The Buribunks Project – a Translation of Carl Schmitt's *Die Buribunken*', hosted by the Law Futures Centre, Griffith University. Thanks also to Michaella Duggan and Eloise Turnbull for research assistance in completing the chapter. This research was partially supported by the Australian Government through the Australian Research Council's Discovery Early Career Researcher Award funding scheme (project DE200100881).

References

Giorgio Agamben (1998) *Homo Sacer: Sovereign Power and Bare Life*, Stanford University Press.

Giorgio Agamben (2011) *The Kingdom and the Glory: For a Theological Genealogy of Economy and Government*, Stanford University Press.

Philip K. Dick (1954a) 'Adjustment Team' *Orbit*, September–October, 81.

Philip K. Dick (1954b) 'Prominent Author' *IF: Worlds of Science Fiction*, May, 27–41.

Philip K. Dick (1966/1983) *The Three Stigmata of Palmer Eldritch*, DAW.

Philip K. Dick (1968) *Do Androids Dream of Electric Sheep?*Doubleday.

Philip K. Dick (1981a) *The Divine Invasion*, Timescape Books/Simon & Schuster.

Philip K. Dick (1981b) *VALIS*, Bantam.

Philip K. Dick (1982) *The Transmigration of Timothy Archer*, Timescape Books/Simon & Schuster.

Philip K. Dick (1987) 'We Can Remember It for You Wholesale', in Philip K. Dick (ed), *The Philip K. Dick Reader*, Citadel Press, 358.

Scott Durham (1988) 'P.K. Dick: From the Death of the Subject to a Theology of Late Capitalism' 15 *Science Fiction Studies* 173.

Frederic Jameson (1982) 'Futuristic Visions That Tell Us About Right Now' *In These Times*, 5 May, 17.

Frederic Jameson (2005) 'Philip K. Dick, in Memoriam', in Frederic Jameson (ed), *Archaeologies of the Future: The Desire Called Utopia and Other Science Fictions*, Verso, 345.

90 Trozzo (2019), p 143.

William P. MacNeil (2007) 'Precrime Never Pays! Law and Economics in *Minority Report*', in William P. MacNeil (ed), *Lex Populi: The Jurisprudence of Popular Culture*, Stanford University Press, 80.

Daniel McLoughlin (2019) 'The Biopolitics of the Buribunks: The Digital Archive and the End of History' 28 *Griffith Law Review* 137.

Jens Meierhenrich and Oliver Simons (2017) 'Carl Schmitt's Life: A Chronology', in Jens Meierhenrich and Oliver Simons (eds), *The Oxford Handbook of Carl Schmitt*, Oxford University Press, xix.

Ethan Mills (2011) 'Hollywood Doesn't Know Dick', in D.E. Wittkower (ed), *Philip K. Dick and Philosophy: Do Androids Have Kindred Spirits?*, Open Court, 3.

Jean-Luc Nancy (1998) 'Abandoned Being', in Victor E. Taylor and Charles E. Winquist (eds), *Postmodernism: Disciplinary Texts: Humanities and Social Sciences*, Taylor & Francis, 337.

George Nolfi (dir) (2011) *The Adjustment Bureau*, Universal Pictures.

Jeff Orlowski (dir) (2020) *The Social Dilemma*, Netflix.

Christopher Palmer (ed) (2003) *Philip K Dick: Exhilaration and Terror of the Postmodern*, Liverpool University Press.

John Durham Peters (2015) *The Marvelous Clouds: Toward a Philosophy of Elemental Media*, University of Chicago Press.

Timothy D. Peters (2022) *A Theological Jurisprudence of Specualtive Film: Superheroes, Science Fictions and Fantasies of Modern Law*, Edinburgh University Press.

Francesco Ragazzi (2004) '"The National Security Strategy of the USA" or the Improbable Meeting of Grotius, Carl Schmitt and Philip K. Dick' 56 *Cultures & Conflicts* 141.

Francine Rochford (2019) 'Negative Space: The Paradox at the Heart of Buribunkology' 28 *Griffith Law Review* 247.

Carl Schmitt (1914) *Der Wert des Staates und die Bedeutung des Einzelnen*, JCB Mohr.

Carl Schmitt (1996a) *The Leviathan in the State Theory of Thomas Hobbes: Meaning and Failure of a Political Symbol*, Greenwood Press.

Carl Schmitt (1996b) *Roman Catholicism and Political Form*, Greenwood Press.

Carl Schmitt (2005) *Political Theology: Four Chapters on the Concept of Sovereignty*, University of Chicago Press.

Carl Schmitt (2007) *The Concept of the Political*, University of Chicago Press.

Carl Schmitt (2008) *Political Theology II: The Myth of the Closure of any Political Theology*, Polity Press.

Karen Schultz (2019) 'Schmitt's Satire in The Buribunks: Intertextual Links in Diary-writing's Dystopia' 28 *Griffith Law Review* 206.

Ridley Scott (dir) (1982) *Blade Runner*, Warner Bros.

Steven Spielberg (dir) (2002) *Minority Report*, Twentieth Century Fox.

Tracy B. Strong (1993) 'How to Write Scripture: Words, Authority, and Politics in Thomas Hobbes' 20 *Critical Inquiry* 128.

Tracy B. Strong (2010) 'The Sacred Quality of the Political: Reflections on Hobbes, Schmitt and Saint Paul' *Politisches Denken*, Jahrbuch 1, https://elibrary.duncker-humblot.com/publication/b/id/34431.

Kieran Tranter (2019) 'Die Buribunken as Science Fiction: The Self and Informational Existence' 28 *Griffith Law Review* 118.

Eric Trozzo (2019) *The Cyberdimension: A Political Theology of Cyberspace and Cybersecurity*, Wipf and Stock.

G.L. Ulmen (1985) 'The Sociology of the State: Carl Schmitt and Max Weber' 1 *State, Culture, and Society* 3.

G.L. Ulmen (1996) 'Introduction', in Carl Schmitt (ed), *Roman Catholicism and Political Form*, Greenwood Press, vii.

Paul Verhoeven (dir) (1990) *Total Recall*, Caroclo Pictures.

Jason P. Vest (2007) *Future Imperfect: Philip K. Dick at the Movies*, Praeger.

Jason P. Vest (2009) *The Postmodern Humanism of Philip K Dick*, Scarecrow Press.

Max Weber (1946a) 'Politics as Vocation', in H. Gerth and C. Wright Mills (eds), *From Max Weber: Essays in Sociology*, Oxford University Press, 77.

Max Weber (1946b) 'Science as Vocation', in H. Gerth and C. Wright Mills (eds), *From Max Weber: Essays in Sociology*, Oxford University Press, 129.

Max Weber (1958) *The Protestant Work Ethic and the Spirit of Capitalism*, Charles Scribner's Sons.

Max Weber (1978) *Economy and Society: An Outline of Interpretive Sociology*, University of California Press.

Max Weber (2005) *The Protestant Ethic and the Spirit of Capitalism*, Routledge.

Len Wiseman (dir) (2012) *Total Recall*, Columbia Pictures.

Chapter 6

Inauthentic temporality and the age of hyperburibunkism

Richard Polt

Introduction

The Buribunks is an experiment in speculative fiction – an extrapolation from a 'what if?'. What if publishing became a society-wide obsession and expectation? What if the private, undocumented experiences of every individual were recorded and made available to the public? In Schmitt's satirical vision, the effect would be a catastrophically inauthentic existence – to the point where we can even ask whether the Buribunks are still human.

Schmitt's vision can be clarified and enriched through some kindred analyses of inauthenticity: Kierkegaard's verdict on the public; Nietzsche's critique of antiquarianism; and Heidegger's phenomenology of inauthentic temporality and the chatter of the 'they'. But in turn, *The Buribunks* enriches these points of view by focusing on the practice of constant, universal publishing. It is not writing *per se* that is inauthentic (all four thinkers were prolific writers, even graphomaniacs), or all forms of publishing, but a kind of representation that is addressed immediately to others, and that aims to turn all subjective experience into objective, public data that can be correlated, analysed and exploited.

In 1918, buribunkism was a bold projection from print culture, film technology, and the nascent science of data analysis. A century later, nearly everyone in the industrialised world has the capacity to make any information accessible to anyone, at virtually no cost and with no delay. Anyone who has used the internet is familiar with what we might call *hyperburibunkism*.

We have not yet experienced, much less thought through, all the implications of the hyperburibunkist revolution, which certainly exceeds the limits of Schmitt's speculation. However, he offers a prescient vision, including a striking account of buribunkist temporality. The Buribunks' obsession with documenting their existence reduces time to a series of 'rat-seconds' – fleeting conditions to be trapped and recorded. The past becomes analysable information, rather than a living heritage. The present becomes a data point, rather than an opportunity for action or insight. Perhaps most disturbingly, the future becomes merely a trove of as-yet-unknown information, rather than meaningful possibilities to be pursued with a clear understanding of one's own

DOI: 10.4324/9781003091066-8

finitude. The Buribunks are even robbed of the significance of their own death, which is converted into just another upcoming event awaiting dissemination and analysis. Our own hyperburibunkist age offers striking examples of each of these points.

In addition to its effects on individual existence, inauthentic buribunkist temporality has political implications – as does any attempt to resist it. None of the thinkers I discuss advocated liberal or leftist points of view, and Heidegger and Schmitt embraced Nazism as a movement that would supposedly restore authenticity to Germany, cutting through chatter to put the people's 'being' at stake. In our own times, inauthentic temporality serves to exacerbate divisions, spread conspiracies, consolidate blind loyalties and establish near-total surveillance. The question that faces us is how to foster liberty, truth, community and authenticity in the information age.

I argue that one contributor to a more authentic temporality, and indirectly to a more genuine public sphere, must be a counter-practice to hyperburibunkism that I call privacing: the cultivation of experiences that resist publication.

Inauthenticity in Kierkegaard, Nietzsche and Heidegger

Schmitt was neither the first nor the last to perceive the trend in modernity that is often called 'inauthenticity'. A look at three philosophical explorations of inauthenticity can provide context and depth for his vision in *The Buribunks.* I make no claims here about influence; I am simply exploring some related views.[1]

The Present Age (1846) is Kierkegaard's fiercest denunciation of 'the public' and its effects. For Kierkegaard, the public is a collective consciousness that allows us to slip away from individual responsibility. It dissolves commitment and personal experience into empty chatter, spreading ready-made interpretations of everything – interpretations that invite ever more talk, and distract the individual from making a genuine choice of how to live.

Trapped in public opinion, the individual 'finds himself in the vast prison formed by the reflection of those around him'.[2] This prison, the public, is 'a phantom … a monstrous abstraction, an all-embracing something which is nothing, a mirage'.[3] It consists of 'unreal individuals who never are and never can be united in an actual situation or organization – and yet are held together as a whole'.[4] 'Made up of such individuals, of individuals at the moments when

1 The pompous authorial voice of *The Buribunks* employs a philosophical jargon that incoherently blends Hegel, Comte, Nietzsche and others – including several references to the will to power, but with no overt allusions to Nietzsche's essay on history.
2 Kierkegaard (1962), p 48.
3 Kierkegaard (1962), p 59.
4 Kierkegaard (1962), p 60.

they are nothing, a public is a kind of gigantic something, an abstract and deserted void which is everything and nothing'.[5]

From Kierkegaard's point of view, the primary function of public discourse, as embodied in newspapers and journals, is not to keep the masses informed or to foster reasonable debate, but to dictate what the predominant opinions and concepts should be, and to postpone decisions indefinitely by way of inexhaustible blather. There is endless observation and reflection, but never the genuine silence required by 'the inner life', and nothing real is at stake. 'When nothing important ever happens to gather the threads of life together with the finality of a catastrophe: that is the time for talkativeness.'[6]

Every impulse to take an individual stand or make an unconditional leap is absorbed and neutralised by the public. Thus, '*everything continues to exist factually whilst [the age] supplies a secret interpretation – that it does not exist*'.[7] Real existence, for Kierkegaard, would require seizing one's own individuality with passion and commitment. It is existence in the first person, so to speak – whereas, in the public, everyone becomes 'a third party (an onlooker)'.[8]

Nietzsche offers a kindred critique of the present age: it is surfeited with historical consciousness. He makes his case in one of his *Untimely Meditations* (1874): *On the Advantage and Disadvantage of History for Life* (often known as *The Use and Abuse of History*).[9] For Nietzsche, we know too much about our past, and we know it in the wrong way – we suffer from the sickness of ironic historicism, and our overabundance of knowledge saps our strength.

Nietzsche distinguishes three types of historical research: monumental history seeks inspiration and role models for action; critical history exposes and denounces the roots of the oppressive present order; and antiquarian history preserves and admires what we have inherited.[10] Each of these practices can be useful or harmful to the vital needs of a community, depending on how they are deployed, and under what circumstances. For example, critical history may liberate those who are oppressed by the establishment, but it may also leave people in a state of uprooted cynicism and despair.[11] Monumental history can excite action, but it also involves unjust, unrealistic distortions that can lead to practical pitfalls.[12]

The mode of history that is most relevant to *The Buribunks* is antiquarianism. Healthy antiquarianism can helpfully preserve local traditions, encouraging us to cherish our home.[13] But antiquarianism can also become an unhealthy

5 Kierkegaard (1962), p 63.
6 Kierkegaard (1962), p 69.
7 Kierkegaard (1962), pp 42–3.
8 Kierkegaard (1962), p 64.
9 Nietzsche (1980).
10 Nietzsche (1980), p 14.
11 Nietzsche (1980).
12 Nietzsche (1980), p 16.
13 Nietzsche (1980), pp 19–20.

obsession with accumulating and analysing every last detail of the past, applying no criterion for what is *worth* preserving but instead taking 'everything to be equally important'.[14] This inauthentic antiquarianism stifles growth, letting the past overwhelm the present and future. The artefacts and records of the past – which are largely the effects of human action and creativity – ironically end up discouraging us from acting and creating in the present, because we are so weighed down by the bric-a-brac of bygone efforts. 'Antiquarian history ... degenerates the moment that the fresh life of the present no longer animates and inspires it ... Then you may well witness the repugnant spectacle of a blind lust for collecting, of a restless raking together of all that once has been.'[15]

For both Kierkegaard and Nietzsche, authentic existence requires action. Kierkegaard mainly argues that the public dissolves the commitment required by action; for Nietzsche, inauthentic antiquarianism kills action's creativity.

In *Being and Time* (1927), Heidegger incorporates Kierkegaard's and Nietzsche's analyses of inauthenticity in his account of the human way of being in general. For Heidegger, we tend to fall into inauthentic existence; this tendency is ineradicable, but its 'domination' waxes and wanes from one historical period to another.[16] Heidegger's technological examples – public transportation, newspapers, the radio[17] – show that he is particularly concerned with his own day.

For Heidegger, human existence is a way of being in which one's own being is an issue. That is, each of us is constantly faced with the questions: Who am I? How am I to live? But we can disregard these questions, as we do when we exist inauthentically; we can let them fade into the background while we go about our daily tasks in an environment whose meaning seems to be settled. Heidegger claims that no negative value judgements are implied in his analysis of inauthenticity, which is simply a description of everyday reality.[18] In fact, we could hardly function at all if we were in a constant state of anxiety, consumed by the awareness of our guilt and mortality, as we are in the rare moments when we are impelled to exist authentically. Furthermore, Heidegger insists that authentic existence is a modification of ordinary, inauthentic life rather than its abolition.[19] Nevertheless, it is fair to characterise inauthenticity as a superficial condition in which we are oblivious to the deeper dimensions of existence and avoid acting in a decisive, 'resolute' way that clarifies the practical situation.

Heidegger's analyses of the 'idle talk' of the 'they' are particularly vivid descriptions of inauthentic experience that parallel Kierkegaard's account of the

14 Nietzsche (1980), p 20.
15 Nietzsche (1980), p 21.
16 Heidegger (1953), p 129. The German pagination is also found in all available English translations.
17 Heidegger (1953), pp 105, 126.
18 Heidegger (1953), pp 175, 222.
19 Heidegger (1953), p 130.

public. The 'they' (*das Man*) is the default identity on which we fall back in everydayness: we do as 'they' do, or as 'one' (German *man*) does, rather than taking responsibility for who we are. We also speak as 'one' speaks, and write as 'one' writes: we repeat truisms without seriously inquiring into their truth, and participate in a shared interpretation of the world without ever having to commit ourselves, on a deep and fundamental level, to that interpretation. We are curious about what will come next, but too impatient to dwell on things and discover them more deeply.

For Heidegger, human existence is fundamentally temporal. This does not just mean that we are born, live for a while and die, but that we are continually 'thrown' into some situation in which we 'project' possibilities. We thus extend 'ecstatically' into the future (we are always appropriating possible ways to exist), into the past (we have always already been thrown into a context) and into the present (we are always operating in our current world).[20] Above all, we make sense of our lives in terms of guiding possibilities, and we are necessarily exposed to death, the possibility of having no more possibilities at all.[21] Only you can face up to your own mortality. 'Authentic' temporality, then, is ecstatic, primarily futural and finite (mortal).

This understanding of time is a far cry from the typical picture of time as a timeline or a fourth dimension. In this 'inauthentic' interpretation, time consists of a continuum of 'nows', point-like instants of presence.[22] We can observe and analyse what is present at various moments, order these observations chronologically, graph the results and so on. Time becomes merely a measurement of change, or difference 'over time'; factors such as death, guilt, thrownness and projection do not appear in this picture, or we take them as merely 'subjective' considerations that are irrelevant to the 'objective' course of events.

What is the origin of the inauthentic interpretation of time? How does it derive from authentic temporality? Heidegger argues that in everyday, inauthentic living, we become absorbed in our current practical concerns and forget about the bigger existential questions. If theoretical questions arise – questions that require us to ascertain objective facts – we are no less absorbed in the present, and no closer to existential insight. We then focus not on ourselves as temporal beings, but on 'present-at-hand' (*vorhanden*) objects, whose behaviour and transformations we can document and describe. Time is merely something that we count as we order those transformations into sequences of earlier and later 'nows'.[23] But none of this would be possible if we were not constantly engaged in thrown projection. Ecstatic, authentic temporality is thus

20 Heidegger (1953), p 329.
21 Heidegger (1953), p 262.
22 Heidegger (1953), pp 420–4.
23 Cf. Aristotle, *Physics* IV.10–14.

presupposed by linear, inauthentic temporality, and can never be explained in terms of it.[24]

One more line of thought in *Being and Time* is particularly relevant to *The Buribunks* as 'an essay on the philosophy of history'. For Heidegger, ecstatic temporality applies to the social life of human beings, where it takes the form of a contest over the meaning of a collective 'destiny' in light of a shared 'heritage'.[25] This movement of history (*Geschichte*) takes place whether or not we engage in 'historiography' (*Historie*) – the explicit study of the past.[26] Such research is made possible by the deeper happening of history, and the development of a highly refined scholarly discipline pursued by historians in no way guarantees that a community is wrestling authentically with its destiny and heritage. In turn, a community might be authentically historical (*geschichtlich*) without having a particularly historiographical (*historisch*) consciousness. Antiquarianism, in Nietzsche's sense, is certainly not equivalent to authentic collective historicity.

Inauthentic temporality in *The Buribunks*

Let us turn to Schmitt's satirical extrapolations. From the start, *The Buribunks* imagines a world where the analysis of data about the past (*Historie*, in Heidegger's terminology), of a basically 'antiquarian' kind (in Nietzsche's terms), has come to dominate and overwhelm genuinely historical existence (*Geschichte*) and present experience – to the point where *Historie* and *Geschichte* become 'indiscernible'.[27]

For the Buribunks, perception becomes remembrance or 'internalisation' (*Er-innerung*).[28] There is no longer any experience independent of historiographical representation: 'it is the entry into the diary and its publication that constitutes the experience'.[29] The element of publication is crucial here: buribunkist historiography constantly feeds and reinforces what Kierkegaard terms 'the public'. Nothing is considered a real experience until it is recorded and shared.

We can go further: existence itself consists only in public representation. 'The existence of the Buribunks follows from the fact that buribunkology exists' and not the other way around.[30] The Buribunks *are* only because they are the subjects and objects of historical research. The very meaning of being shifts from living presence into re-presentation, and 'the true meaning of life' is to be found only in 'life as it is historically present [*da ist*] or was historically

24 Heidegger (1953), pp 424–5.
25 Heidegger (1953), pp 383–4.
26 Heidegger (1953), p 392.
27 Lubrano (2019), p 177.
28 Chapter 2 of this volume, p 13.
29 Chapter 2 of this volume, p 16 n 3.
30 Chapter 2 of this volume, p 12 n 1.

present [*da war*]'.[31] Since historical presence is essentially available to the public, privacy becomes obsolete: 'confidentiality' is 'anti-buribunkian';[32] there are no '*pudenda* in buribunkology!'.[33] This implies 'an increasingly perfected surveillance'.[34]

Thinking is writing is publishing, so only the publication of my diaries assures me of my own consciousness and being.[35] I am free to publish my opposition to publishing – but a real refusal to play the game brings dire consequences. The non-writer 'vanishes from the screen of the monthly reports and ceases to exist [*ist nicht mehr vorhanden*]'.[36] 'Screen' here translates *Bildfläche*, literally 'image surface'. The word refers to a domain within which items may make a noticeable difference. For instance, when a company introduces a new product to the market, it appears on the economic *Bildfläche*. To 'vanish from the *Bildfläche*' is to become irrelevant and effectively non-existent, as when an industry becomes non-viable. The word is perfectly suited to buribunkism, with its insistence on public visibility as a mark of existence. The claim that non-writers are no longer 'present-at-hand' (*vorhanden*) does not seem to mean they are physically eliminated; rather, they are reduced to menial jobs such as paper-making, and in the absence of records about them, they effectively become unpersons. These are the 'Bartleby Buribunks' who prefer not to participate – or, in Agamben's terms, the 'abjected' *homo sacer* of the Buribunk system.[37]

The ambition of buribunkism is truly boundless. The phrase 'every second' recurs as a refrain in the text, as Schmitt emphasises that not a single moment of the Buribunks' existence may be allowed to escape the regime of historiographical representation. The supply of information and the ways to analyse and use it are virtually infinite, guaranteeing that 'interest … does not dry up'.[38] Research and entertainment can always be carried farther, generating more data as they go – so 'it does not have to be feared that the sublime rotation of this buribunkian world will ever come to an end'.[39] The proliferation of recorded information guarantees that, in Heidegger's terms, there can always be more idle talk. Buribunkism is, as it were, immortal.

Yet, despite the illusion that 'the Buribunk is unconditionally and absolutely his own master, he is himself',[40] buribunkian existence is empty and inauthentic. The so-called 'genius' Schnekke,[41] the true founder of buribunkism, is

31 Chapter 2 of this volume, p 14.
32 Chapter 2 of this volume, p 18 n 5.
33 Chapter 2 of this volume, p 22.
34 Koselleck (2002), p 96.
35 Chapter 2 of this volume, p 25.
36 Chapter 2 of this volume, p 25.
37 Murphy (2019), pp 164, 169.
38 Chapter 2 of this volume, p 24.
39 Chapter 2 of this volume, p 24.
40 Chapter 2 of this volume, p 16.
41 Chapter 2 of this volume, p 22.

in a fact a nobody whose purported 'extreme autonomy' and 'will to power' take the form of 'a uniform lack of colour'.[42] The Buribunks' supposed 'internalisation' is in fact an externalisation, an objectification and a loss of self. Like Nietzsche's lifeless antiquarians, the Buribunks have lost the ability to make value judgements and to engage in fresh, creative activity – which requires a certain dose of forgetting. Although their goal is purportedly 'the creating and viewing of oneself as a monument',[43] the idea of documenting every second makes the goal unattainable: antiquarian history, which wants to preserve what has happened simply because it has happened, is antithetical to monumental history, which selects a few moments and actions as paradigms worthy of imitation. A record of every second is a record that cannot possibly be surveyed, interpreted and curated by a human mind.[44] It overwhelms human judgement and choice.

Genuine action is thus paralysed by buribunkism, as life is hollowed out and sacrificed to the obsession with documentation. Every Buribunk subscribes to the notion that his or her own experiences are unique, precious and worth publishing; ironically, though, the universal dominance of this notion flattens everyone out and robs them of truly personal and significant experiences. The cult of superficial uniqueness is just a higher-order conformism, and the semblance of individualism masks a de-individualisation. Thus Schnekke, the 'fully ripened fruit of the noblest Buribunkdom', ends up keeping 'a diary about the fact that he has run out of ideas about what he could write in the diary'.[45] (One imagines a bleak, absurd anticipation of Samuel Beckett.) As Kierkegaard puts it, 'Nothing ever happens but there is immediate publicity everywhere.'[46]

For the buribunkian mentality, the institution of marriage and the mythology of an afterlife are absurd, unrealistic throwbacks. But recording erotic experiences and amassing representations of oneself are no substitute for committed love and personal survival after death. Love and death are the great facts of life that resist incorporation into buribunkist history. Thus Ferker's marriage, for unknown motives, to 'an utterly uneducated, even illiterate person' and his fear of death are the saving graces that keep him from complete descent into Buribunkdom.[47]

Buribunkism flattens not only individual existence, but also collective life. The Buribunks are indeed 'the enemies of the political'.[48] They have all retreated obediently from political action into the documentation of their personal experiences; they conform to a superficial individualism. In Heidegger's

42 Chapter 2 of this volume, p 23.
43 Chapter 2 of this volume, p 16.
44 McLoughlin (2019), p 151.
45 Chapter 2 of this volume, p 22.
46 Kierkegaard (1962), p 35.
47 Chapter 2 of this volume, p 21.
48 Gyulai (2019).

words, 'We draw back from "the great mass" as "one" draws back.'[49] Meanwhile, the community is regulated by a bureaucratised, technocratic state that leaves no room for genuine contests over the collective future.

Perhaps the most striking aspect of this inauthentic, objectified existence is the way it reduces time to a stream of fleeting conditions to be trapped and recorded – or, in Schmitt's unforgettable term, 'rat-seconds':

> only this second [of historical recording] is the birth hour of life. That is to say, of the past, as the present is only the midwife who delivers the lively historical past from the dark body of the future. Until it has been reached, the future lies there as dull and indifferent as the keyboard of a typewriter, like a dark rat hole from which one second after another (like one rat after another) emerges into the light of the past ... the blinking young rat of the present second creeps out of the dark rat hole of the future, out of the nothing of what has not yet been, in order to enter with sparkling eyes in the next second the reality of the historical ... Thus the fearful anticipation of the future loses its horror, for whatever may be, one thing is certain, namely that no second emerging from the future is lost, no letter of the typewriter will miss the page.
>
> The death of the individual is also merely such a rat-second ... today the true Buribunk is hardly in any danger of confusion thanks to the growing awareness whose sunlight exterminates the germs of the fear of death.[50]

Writing amid global war and pandemic, Schmitt understands how people try to evade the horror of death – which always comes for *you*, as an irreplaceable individual – by seeking the prolonged publicness of fame, which seemingly blends the individual into the deathless *we*.[51] With modern technology, fame – of a diluted and quite unheroic sort – is available to everyone. One tries to transcend death by multiplying representations of oneself.

But this banal, routinised posterity has the effect of draining significance from the individual's death – and thus from life. The meaning of one's own, singular existence is reduced to a dull, prolix stream of data that can be accessed by anyone. Life and death no longer have absolute significance.

Instead, 'history' reigns supreme. Thus, among the Buribunks, the future and present are monstrously subordinated to the past – of a certain kind. This is the past reduced to re-presentation, turned into a form of presence-at-hand, in Heidegger's terms. Bygone facts are captured and kept constantly available for use and analysis, as if they were present objects. Buribunkism, then, is not the elimination of presence, but the triumph of a certain sort of inauthentic present.

49 Heidegger (1953), p 127.
50 Chapter 2 of this volume, pp 26–7.
51 Chapter 2 of this volume, pp 26–7.

To employ more of Heidegger's terminology: the authentic future is a realm of possibility that allows one to decide who one is while facing one's own mortality, while the buribunkian future is 'only the dark rat hole of that which not yet exists'.[52] The authentic present is a meaningful context, a world or 'there' in which we may act insightfully and resolutely; the buribunkian present is a mere delivery slot for historiographical representations. The authentic past is a legacy from which we can draw inspiration for the future; the buribunkian past is only an endless collection of preserved traces of events. The past the Buribunks have documented appears to them to be full of life, while in fact it is a vast graveyard, a desert of dead data, or at best a rat haven. Of course, its records can be exploited to generate new experiences, but these in turn find their *raison d'être* in the accumulation of more historical information. In the end one must ask: what for?

The temporality of hyperburibunkism

In some respects, Schmitt accurately extrapolates from his day to our own. The buribunkian diaries are multimedia creations incorporating 'photographs and films';[53] the scope of big data is vast ('more than 400,000 buribunkological dissertations');[54] advanced 'card catalogue' technology enables sophisticated search and analysis.[55] (We may think here of the punched-card information-processing systems pioneered by Herman Hollerith for the 1890 US census; Hollerith's enterprise was eventually incorporated into IBM.) With the refinement of such recording and computing technologies, we are now equipped to make a boundless 'antiquarianism' accessible to a pervasive 'they'.

Once the internet reached large numbers of users in the 1990s, personal webcams and blogs began broadcasting buribunkian diaries to the world. By now, the average twenty-first century human is all too familiar with what we can call hyperburibunkism. As the slogan has it in Dave Eggers's *The Circle*, a dystopian depiction of the death of privacy, 'All that happens must be known' – where knowledge means digital storage, publishing and analysis.[56] This ideal is celebrated with a naive enthusiasm worthy of BAFREPAC in popular manifestos such as *Total Recall: How the e-Memory Revolution will Change Everything*, whose authors celebrate the idea of digitally documenting every moment and fact in one's life.[57] Despite the warnings of authors such as Eggers and Viktor Mayer-Schönberger,[58] recording technology marches on, and we generally acquiesce or embrace it. Smart speakers (which would more

52 Chapter 2 of this volume, p 27.
53 Chapter 2 of this volume, p 24.
54 Chapter 2 of this volume, p 13.
55 Chapter 2 of this volume, p 23.
56 Eggers (2014), p 68.
57 Bell and Gemmell (2009).
58 Mayer-Schönberger (2009).

accurately be called smart microphones) gather the utterances in our households and put them to unknown uses. Our smartphones track our location and behaviour. We voluntarily publish images of our experiences, our bodies and our trail of metadata as we hope to become 'influencers' skilled in self-promotion – or, in Schmitt's term, 'arrivistics'.[59] We enter a Kierkegaardian prison of reflections – of others and ourselves. The self risks becoming a series of selfies – and, like true Buribunks, we fantasise about a pseudo-immortality through the digital preservation of our data.

Like the Buribunk who 'cranks changing film images into his diary',[60] we document and publicise our lives through our digital devices. In turn, we scroll through the assorted rat-seconds of those we follow on social media. 'Keeping up' with the events of the day really means surveying the recent past, the collection of daily occurrences that have been absorbed into the global digital history. That record persists – although not as reliably as we may imagine – and remains available for analysis, remixing and reappropriation.

In hyperburibunkist culture, we are all journalists documenting ourselves and each other. The present appears to have no meaning until it is published. Events are non-events until images, measurements and accounts of them go online. Experience has no reality until it is publicly documented – thus armies of smartphones come out at concerts or other events, intervening between their owners and what they are recording. Meals aren't worth savouring unless an image of them is posted to social media. Showing that one was 'there' becomes more important than actually, fully being there.[61] Thus we fulfil the buribunkian imperative: 'Be history [for] yourself! [*Sei dir selbst Geschichte!*] Live so that every single one of your seconds can be recorded in your diary and fall into the hands of your biographer!'[62]

The future starts to seem like nothing but a typewriter waiting to type – or, rather, the screen (*Bildfläche*) of a smartphone just before the next post or message appears. We wait for a 'notification' that something has happened, that some digital rat has left its dark hole. This constant expectation and reaction create a jumpy, inattentive mentality.

In this environment, it becomes ever more difficult to undertake resolute, authentic action. Any choice, statement or gesture can be absorbed efficiently into public 'ambiguity',[63] where it is impossible to tell what is genuine and what is mere reproduction. Decisiveness becomes ever more elusive in the digital atmosphere, where it seems that everything can be replayed, undone, duplicated and modified. It appears that no act is subject to the pressure of the

59 Chapter 2 of this volume, p 19.
60 Chapter 2 of this volume, p 20.
61 For an effective dramatisation of this alienated culture, see Crawford (2013).
62 Chapter 2 of this volume, p 19.
63 Heidegger (1953), pp 173–5.

'finality of a catastrophe'.[64] We float in an endless, tepid sea of ironic ambivalence.

It is not just individual minds that are affected by hyperburibunkian temporality; it also has significant political implications. As Schmitt foresaw, the proliferation of information tends to consolidate the power of those who can aggregate and analyse it. In our own day, massive data flows reinforce corporate and governmental structures.

In much of the world, the information age takes the form of what Shoshana Zuboff calls 'surveillance capitalism', which treats us as consumers whose behaviour is minutely scrutinised:[65] 'Nothing is too trivial or ephemeral for this [data] harvesting.' As in Buribunk society, there is freedom – within limits: for instance, 'Google is "formally indifferent" to what its users say or do, as long as they say it and do it in ways that Google can capture and convert into data.' As our small choices and preferences are recorded, quantified and monetised, 'Subjectivities are converted into objects that repurpose the subjective for commodification.'[66]

Surveillance capitalism is a vast and supremely efficient way of establishing the mild, modern despotism predicted by Tocqueville, which 'would degrade men without tormenting them':[67]

> I see an innumerable crowd of like and equal men who revolve on themselves without repose, procuring the small and vulgar pleasures with which they fill their souls … Above these an immense tutelary power is elevated, which alone takes charge of assuring their enjoyments and watching over their fate. It is absolute, detailed, regular, far-seeing, and mild … It willingly works for their happiness; but it wants to be the unique agent and sole arbiter of that … can it not take away from them entirely the trouble of thinking and the pain of living? So it is that every day it renders the employment of free will less useful and more rare; it confines the action of the will in a smaller space and little by little steals the very use of free will from each citizen.[68]

For Tocqueville, mature freedom involves 'pain and trouble'; the constant provision of pleasure and entertainment thus reduces freedom and hampers authentic individuality. Of course, this does not rule out a *superficial* individuality that is, in fact, necessary for surveillance capitalism to function. By making tiny choices in our hyperburibunkist environment, we make it increasingly easy for algorithms to feed us a steady stream of agreeable products

64 Kierkegaard (1962), p 69.
65 Zuboff (2020).
66 Zuboff (2015), p 79.
67 Tocqueville (2000), p 662.
68 Tocqueville (2000), p 663.

and opinions. Our 'diaries' generate a trickle of contentment, with just enough novelty to keep us amused. This form of domination, with its manifold pleasures and the constant exercise of consumer preferences, is far more effective than a traditional tyranny based on fear and force. It goes against the grain to rebel against a system that mirrors your own habits.

Then there is surveillance socialism, the more heavy-handed yet highly sophisticated form of control that is now being perfected in China. Here, every citizen is constantly monitored by pervasive identification technology, especially in regions that are considered politically problematic. Hundreds of millions of cameras deploy facial recognition systems and can be linked to a genetic database. A 'social credit system' assesses the reliability of every citizen.[69] Like surveillance capitalism, surveillance socialism leaves some room for individual choice and expression, and it is often a soft and silent dictatorship – but there is always a threat of violence.

Of course, contrary to the buribunkian vision, an informational asymmetry is built into these systems of surveillance. The relevant information is not accessible to all; once-private data are not made public to everyone, but only to those in control of vast data-collection systems.[70] What, then, are the political effects of *public* data sharing in our hyperburibunkist age?

First, as we have all become amateur journalists, professional journalism has suffered. Well-researched news is drowned in chatter, including misinformation and disinformation ('fake news'). The constant stream of data from countless sources creates pressure to 'keep up' rather than 'missing out', so it becomes burdensome to pause, reflect and analyse. With no generally accepted epistemic authority, we tend to choose to listen to those with whom we already agree.

Accordingly, all behaviour and expression tend to become raw matter for propaganda and ideology. Anything can be taken out of context, warped and weaponised. Processes of selection and distortion create polarised political camps. In its early days, the information age seemed to promise a more enlightened citizenry, but we have found that it facilitates the formation of rival cliques that share no standards of trust or legitimacy. Conspiracy theories and incommensurable world-views fight to dominate our splintered 'they'.[71]

In this environment, is it possible to take action – to begin creative initiatives and undertake commitments that will inspire others? To take a stand on the meaning of a 'destiny' and 'heritage', in Heidegger's terms? Yes, certainly, and such action can spread 'virally' thanks to hyperburibunkist technology: consider the Arab Spring or the Black Lives Matter movement.

69 A growing list of over 100 sources on the topic can be found in the Wikipedia article 'Mass surveillance in China', https://en.wikipedia.org/wiki/Mass_surveillance_in_China.

70 McLoughlin (2019), pp 144–9.

71 For jaded views of the online public sphere, see for example Morozov (2013); Taylor (2015).

However, there are also obstacles to such initiatives. Speaking out and taking action can be more difficult when your every act becomes public information. First, your trail of recorded utterances and choices creates an image, a persona, that may be hard to escape. It can be easier to conform to the persona than to do something new. If you do try to take action, it is very difficult to be heard and have an effect amidst the hyperburibunkist cacophony. If you start to have an influence, the more embarrassing data about you will be marshalled by your opponents and put to use within hostile spheres of information, not to mention by the governmental or corporate interests that you may be threatening. The more impact your new action has, the more it will be taken out of context, parodied, pilloried or turned into a trivial meme. Given these obstacles, the path of least resistance is to stay within the boundaries that have been so well defined by the trail of your own past behaviour, and to hope to avoid the curse of drawing excessive attention.

One could also argue that the hyperburibunkist system itself has become so strong that it threatens to exclude all alternatives. In *The Buribunks*, all conflict has been reduced to verbal disagreement; there is nothing outside the text – except unpersons. We have not reached that point in our culture, but it is easy to envision a future in which we are free to say and do anything, as long as we accept the hyperburibunkist paradigm; those who truly reject the paradigm will be doomed to become non-functional nobodies.[72]

To state these points in the terms of our critics of modern inauthenticity: as Kierkegaard might put it, we have created an omniscient 'public' that militates against any genuine, individual leap. Nietzsche might emphasise the need to forget the past in order to create something new – a forgetting that becomes nearly impossible in a world that records every moment with an extreme, indiscriminate antiquarianism. Heidegger would insist that authentic temporality originates in the future – but hyperburibunkism, as Schmitt would say, reduces the future to a dark rat-hole from which rat-nanoseconds emerge only to be absorbed into the ever-growing mountain of rat-terabytes.

Privacing and the public in the hyperburibunkist age

What are the prospects for politics in the age of hyperburibunkism? Can a more genuine community be restored? Can authentic discourse and action prevail in the public sphere?

None of the critics of modern inauthenticity we have examined was a leftist or a champion of liberal democracy. Most of them sympathised with the right-wing aspiration to restore authenticity by restricting liberty and imposing some

72 For a bitter extrapolation from our current condition, see Brooker (2011), in which one man's impassioned protest against a system of exploitation and entertainment is co-opted into becoming yet another form of entertainment within the system.

shared identity on a community. Nietzsche sneered at socialists and liberals, and admired Roman hardness. Both Schmitt and Heidegger supported National Socialism as a way to put an end to empty 'parliamentary' chatter and supposedly foster authentic, collective decisions. Instead of endless, ambiguous talk, the *Volk* would come to grips with its own being – to use the ontological discourse favoured by Heidegger and adopted by Schmitt in *The Concept of the Political*.[73]

In *The Buribunks*, Schmitt imagines a *reductio ad absurdum* of the liberal way of life, typified by free speech, free press and egalitarianism.[74] Buribunkism is the big-mouthed, infinite blather of ordinary persons – but it is a 'bounded infinity',[75] confined within impersonal bureaucracy and data management. Schmitt suggests that a restoration of depth would require a return to something like medieval Christianity,[76] with its hierarchy, its mysteries and its insistence on the transhuman significance of human life. Heidegger, too, expresses a certain nostalgia for the Middle Ages.[77]

However, authoritarianism cannot bring about authentic temporality; by diminishing individual liberty, it discourages the commitment and creativity of vigorous action. As Michael P.A. Murphy puts it, 'When we lose our freedom to *not* do something, our "choice" to do it is not an exercise of freedom at all.'[78] While such systems may inspire blind zeal in many, their enthusiasm comes at the expense of the 'enemies of the people' or 'malcontents', whose ability to act is crushed.

Furthermore, the caricature of liberalism as a realm of indecisive chatter underestimates the possibilities of public discourse, which can potentially inspire, arouse and unify people without the coercion and intimidation of authoritarian regimes. As Hannah Arendt argues, the public sphere can be a place for growth, initiative and the flourishing of action. To act, for Arendt, is to come into appearance – to disclose oneself and become oneself in a public space, 'to make articulate [one's own being] and call [it] into full existence'.[79]

In the face of the burgeoning, chattery public realm, we must find ways not to restrict liberty, but rather call it into full existence. Is there a way to deepen and enrich our freedom – a freedom that requires broad rights of self-expression using contemporary technology – while avoiding inauthentic temporality and its political manifestations?

73 The ontological language is less evident in the translation (Schmitt 2009) than in the original, where Schmitt describes enmity and national identity as *seinsmäßig* ('on the order of being'): Schmitt (1963), pp 27, 28, 29, 33, 39, 50.
74 For an alternative interpretation, see Tranter (2019), who takes the Buribunks as a fundamentally post-liberal and anti-liberal society.
75 Murphy (2019), p 162.
76 Chapter 2 of this volume, p 14 n 2.
77 Heidegger (2013), p 63.
78 Murphy (2019), p 171.
79 Arendt (1998), p 208.

I have no solution, but I suggest that the public cannot be renewed unless we reinforce the private. Arendt, while celebrating the potential of the public sphere, also credits modernity with discovering 'how rich and manifold the realm of the hidden can be under the conditions of intimacy'.[80] The function of privacy is 'to shelter the intimate'[81] – which may then serve as a source of some ideas, desires and feelings that one chooses to develop in public action. As Kierkegaard puts it, the problem with the predominance of public chatter is not that all publicity is wrong, but that 'the concealment and reserve of inwardness is not given time in which to conceive an essential mystery, which can then be made manifest'.[82] 'Only some one who knows how to remain essentially silent can really talk – and act essentially.'[83] Heidegger completes the thought by pointing out that, in turn, 'He who never says anything cannot keep silent at any given moment.'[84]

If this line of thought is correct, genuine discourse and action go hand in hand with silence; deep community requires deep intimacy with oneself. But, as Rebecca Solnit writes, our digitised experience inhabits 'a shallow between two deep zones, a safe spot between the dangers of contact with ourselves, with others'.[85] Constantly exchanging information with our accumulating 'friends', we drift away from both love and self-knowledge.

In a time when free, instant, global publishing is available to us all – when the default setting for our existence is public, so much so that the term 'publishing' has begun to sound obsolete – what we need is *privacing*: deliberate steps to create pockets of privacy in our hyperburibunkised lives.[86]

Most discussions of privacy do not go far enough. They emphasise the importance of ensuring that information does not fall into the wrong hands. But even if our information is in the 'right' hands, and we have nothing to be ashamed of, we have lost something when we behave in a way that is open to inspection. With the sense that our words and acts are under constant, automatic surveillance, we tend – consciously or not – to polish our persona, so our behaviour is defined in relation to how 'they' want us to behave. Whether we want to be perceived as harmless nobodies, as glamorous winners or as fearless rebels, our priority becomes to be seen, not to be.

Privacing is not just the protection of information, then, but the choice of being over seeming. It happens whenever we find occasions to have experiences that will be meaningful even if no one else ever learns of them, even if

80 Arendt (1998), p 72.
81 Arendt (1998), p 38.
82 Kierkegaard (1962), p 75.
83 Kierkegaard (1962), p 69.
84 Heidegger (2013), p 165.
85 Solnit (2013).
86 On the need for 'refuseniks' and 'negative space', see Rochford (2019), p 255. For an earlier version of my reflections on privacing see Polt (2017).

we take them with us to that place that so few secrets today survive long enough to reach: our grave.

Privacing can take the form of writing with a secure, non-digital tool,[87] writing that need not be seen by anyone. Privacing can consist in making music that is never recorded, sketching a scene and tearing up the sketch, or sinking into a novel that we read on that insensitive and oblivious old medium, paper. Privacing takes place when we explore an empty beach or a busy city without recording any 'diary' at all – only our memories, which we leave vulnerable to the natural process of purgation and sifting called forgetting. Privacing not only reacquaints us with ourselves, but also opens doors to intimacy, should we choose to mail a letter or tell someone about our walk on the beach. Privacing can serve as a source of ideas that we choose to make public in a deliberate and thoughtful way, restoring significance to the word 'publishing'.

What if a privacing movement began to subvert the hyperburibunkist system? Let us extrapolate and speculate …

> Your calendar keeps asking you to be more specific, but all you'll tell it is 'walk' for 2–4 pm this afternoon.
>
> Your apartment goes to sleep behind you, you disallow mapping and you set out on the sidewalk. Most people you meet are in your contacts – you nod to Jake, Yvonne, Karim.
>
> It was hard to memorise the address. The numbers wanted to slip away, seemed to beg you to entrust them to the Cloud.
>
> It was harder to get the money. It's only 100 an hour, but they only take cash, and it's been a long time since any was printed. You had to seek out little, independent shops that offer obsolete services like shoe repair and bookbinding, and convince them to part with some bills.
>
> It looks like an ordinary row house, but there's a person at a desk swathed in a scarf and wearing mirrored glasses. A sign instructs you to remove your contacts and watch. You haven't felt this naked in a long time. The person takes your devices and the cash in silence, and gestures to the staircase.
>
> The room upstairs houses dark, wooden cases of curios and books: an eighteenth-century edition of Homer, a small stuffed marsupial, an iridescent shell, a handwritten volume of poems. Immediately you double-tap your watch to upload images of these objects – then remember that it isn't there.
>
> There is a woman at a reading table – her face is slender and refined, her mouth is small, her hair put up – and you don't know her name. You instinctively blink twice to scan her and add her to your contacts – but they're downstairs. You'll have to try to remember her on the basis of glances.

87 Polt (2015).

Is there a pencil and paper? You could at least copy some of the poems, which have a strange rhythm all their own. You can't find a writing implement anywhere, though. In fact, there are no recording devices at all.

Finally you understand that nothing here – not the views out the dusty windowpanes, not the scent of leather and sage, not the colours of the prism on the mantelpiece – can be reproduced in any form.

A wall clock chimes. Your hour is up.

On the walk home you are lost in thought, troubled, oblivious to your notifications. You feel that you've been initiated into something new and old, something impossibly secret, something you cannot share with anyone except by telling them the address. But if you stay with your memories, you tell yourself – and you are not sure what you even mean by this – you may be able to share the secret with yourself.

In the age of hyperburibunkism, the threat of inauthenticity is ever more pressing. The practical, cultural and psychological obstacles to privacing are formidable. Overcoming them requires self-discipline, and may well call for political measures to weaken the techno-Tocquevillian 'tutelary powers' that surround us and the systems of surveillance in which we have embedded ourselves. But if we manage to pursue and encourage privacing, we may deepen our relations to ourselves and others, potentially enriching both private and public life. We may even manage to transform our streams of rat-seconds into coherent and meaningful lives and deaths.

References

Hannah Arendt (1998) *The Human Condition* (2nd ed.), University of Chicago Press.

Gordon Bell and Jim Gemmell (2009) *Total Recall: How the e-Memory Revolution Will Change Everything*, Dutton.

Charlie Brooker (dir.) (2011) 'Fifteen Million Merits', *Black Mirror*, Channel 4.

Miles Crawford (dir.) (2013) 'I Forgot My Phone', https://vimeo.com/73085316.

Dave Eggers (2014) *The Circle*, Vintage.

Attila Gyulai (2019) 'It's a Fact: The Buribunks are the Enemies of the Political' 28 *Griffith Law Review* 231.

Martin Heidegger (1953) *Sein und Zeit*, Niemeyer.

Martin Heidegger (2013) *Nature, History, State: 1933–34*, trans. Gregory Fried and Richard Polt, Athlone.

Søren Kierkegaard (1962) *The Present Age*, trans. Alexander Dru, Harper & Row.

Reinhart Koselleck (2002) *The Practice of Conceptual History: Timing History, Spacing Concepts* (trans. Todd Samuel Presner*et al.*), Stanford University Press.

Vittorio Lubrano (2019) 'On the Normality of Writing: Inscription/Description of Everyday Life' 28 *Griffith Law Review* 173.

Viktor Mayer-Schönberger (2009) *Delete: The Virtue of Forgetting in the Digital Age*, Princeton University Press.

Daniel McLoughlin (2019) 'The Biopolitics of the Buribunks: The Digital Archive and the End of History' 28 *Griffith Law Review* 137.

Evgeny Morozov (2013) *To Save Everything, Click Here*, PublicAffairs.

Michael P.A. Murphy (2019) 'What Does It Mean to be Anti-social? Potentiality and Political Ontology in The Buribunks' 28 *Griffith Law Review* 154.

Friedrich Nietzsche (1980) *On the Advantage and Disadvantage of History for Life* (trans. Peter Preuss), Hackett.

Richard Polt (2015) *The Typewriter Revolution: A Typist's Companion for the 21st Century*, Countryman Press.

Richard Polt (2017) 'On Privacing', in Michael Marder and Patrícia Vieira (eds), *The Philosophical Salon: Speculations, Reflections, Interventions*, Open Humanities Press, https://thephilosophicalsalon.com/on-privacing.

Francine Rochford (2019) 'Negative Space – the Paradox at the Heart of Buribunkology' 28 *Griffith Law Review* 247.

Carl Schmitt (1963) *Der Begriff des Politischen*, Duncker & Humblot.

Carl Schmitt (2009) *The Concept of the Political* (trans. George Schwab), University of Chicago Press.

Rebecca Solnit (2013) 'Diary: In the Day of the Postman' 35 *London Review of Books*, 29 August, www.lrb.co.uk/the-paper/v35/n16/rebecca-solnit/diary.

Astra Taylor (2015) *The People's Platform: Taking Back Power and Culture in the Digital Age*, Picador.

Alexis de Tocqueville (2000) *Democracy in America* (trans and ed Harvey C. Mansfield and Delba Winthrop), University of Chicago Press.

Kieran Tranter (2019) 'Die Buribunken as Science Fiction: The Self and Informational Existence' 28 *Griffith Law Review* 118.

Shoshana Zuboff (2015) 'Big Other: Surveillance Capitalism and the Prospects of an Information Civilization' 30 *Journal of Information Technology* 75.

Shoshana Zuboff (2020) *The Age of Surveillance Capitalism: The Fight for a Human Future at the New Frontier of Power*, PublicAffairs.

Chapter 7

Megarianism, emancipation and the (im)potentiality of political ontology

A commentary on freedom in Schmitt's dystopia

Michael P.A. Murphy

Introduction

> Outline of a philosophy of the Buribunks. I think, therefore I am; I speak, therefore I am; I write, therefore I am; I publish, therefore I am. This does not contain a contradiction, but is merely the ascending order of identities which develop beyond themselves according to the laws of logic. For the Buribunk, thinking is nothing other than soundless speech; speaking nothing but scriptless writing; writing nothing but anticipated publishing.[1]

Carl Schmitt's dystopian short story *The Buribunks* tells the tale of a people bound to the production of the written word. So strong a bond exists between being buribunkian and writing that the idea of not writing constitutes an ontological aberration. As with other dystopian fiction exploring themes of conformity and management, Schmitt describes a massive state apparatus that imposes the obligatory writing and monitors the continuation of writing for the individual. At the same time, however, as Buribunkdom openly enforces the practice of writing, there is a rhetoric of freedom grounded in the infinite potentiality to be written – that is to say, Buribunks are understood to be free because they can write anything. This tension between freedom to write anything and absolute enforcement of writing constitutes a central point of intrigue precisely because writing marks the definitive feature of buribunkian life.

In this chapter, I would like to explore the place of freedom in Schmitt's dystopia, to ground a broader reflection on the relationship between potentiality and political ontology. Drawing on the metaphysical reflections of Aristotle and Giorgio Agamben, I propose that there are three modalities of potentiality relevant to political ontology, each understanding the relationship between potentiality and actuality in different terms. Megarianism[2] subordinates all potentiality to actuality, such that only actual things matter. Emancipation

1 Chapter 2 of this volume, p 25.
2 Aristotle (2016), IX, 3, 1046b27–33.

DOI: 10.4324/9781003091066-9

subordinates actuality to impotentiality,[3] recognising that essence matters – whether potential or not – and that freedom to be is only truly free if it includes freedom to *not* be.[4] In between these two poles, the middle way is occupied by Aristotle, who recognises impotentiality and 'contrary capacity', but nevertheless privileges actuality over potentiality and impotentiality.[5] As I have argued elsewhere, paying attention to the place of potentiality within a political movement or system offers a set of new insights that assist in clarifying differences between alternative political ontologies.[6] To foreground the argument, the typical political mode of official Buribunkdom embraces a politically Megarian set of assumptions, while the 'anti-social Buribunks' seek out an emancipatory modality.

The first section of this chapter expands on the discussion of potentiality and freedom, contrasting Megarian and emancipatory modalities through Aristotle's *Metaphysics* and Agamben's commentary. The second section then places the question of potentiality in conversation with political ontology, discussing how a focus on the assumptions around potentiality can help in distinguishing different political forms of life. It is here that Agamben's political commentary on Aristotle returns to Schmitt, as Agamben's conceptualisations of constituent power and sovereignty[7] are indebted to Schmitt's.[8] Thus the ontologico-metaphysical conceptual apparatus developed is not so much an application of a radically unfamiliar framework as the folding back onto Schmitt's work of a framework already imbued with a strong Schmittian influence.[9] The third section explores Schmitt's discussion of *The Buribunks*, with particular attention to the comments on buribunkian life and the points where Megarian assumptions become visible in the story. The fourth section turns to the question of the 'anti-social Buribunks', suggesting that they pursue an emancipatory modality of political life within the context of the thoroughly Megarian Buribunkdom. The conclusion draws together the remarks on potentiality, political ontology and freedom with a commentary on the possibilities of emancipatory forms of life.

Potentiality and freedom

Aristotle's account of potentiality in the *Metaphysics* has served an important role for continental philosophers in the twentieth century. Specifically, the

3 See Murphy (2020b) for this distinction.
4 Agamben (1999), p 182; Agamben (2018b).
5 Aristotle (2016), IX, 9, 1051a3–11.
6 Murphy (2020a).
7 For example, Agamben (1998).
8 Schmitt (2014).
9 This is not to imply that Schmitt was unfamiliar with Aristotle. *Constitutional Theory* and *Legality and Legitimacy*, for example, both see Schmitt make passing references to Aristotle, referencing the typology of regimes discussed in the *Politics* rather than the *Metaphysics*, from which Agamben draws inspiration. See Schmitt (2004, 2008).

discussion of potentiality and actuality in Book Theta, which argues that since the essence of a thing is present in its potentiality and not only its actuality, every capacity to do something is simultaneously an incapacity. Agamben's argument to this point has consistently focused on the term of incapacity or impotentiality against Aristotle's ultimate prioritisation of actuality, and this metaphysics ultimately grounds his writings on political futures.[10]

Aristotle's *Metaphysics* confronts the belief that only actuality is relevant; negatively stated, this means that an unactualised potentiality is irrelevant. Aristotle lays out the argument in the third chapter of Book Theta: 'there are some people – for example, the Megarians – who say that a thing is capable of something only when actively doing it, and that when not actively doing it, it is not capable'.[11] This metaphysical position is compelling because it demands continual empirical proof; however, Aristotle argues by example that 'the consequences of this are absurd': 'For example, someone who is not building is not capable of building, but someone who is building is capable if and when he is building.'[12] Clearly, the builder able to build remains able when not building. In this sense, the potentiality exists outside of its actualisation. In other examples, Aristotle states that, 'for animals do not see in order that they may have sight, rather they have sight in order that they may see, and similarly too they have the craft of building in order that they may build'.[13] Potentiality continues beyond its actualisation, and appears to pre-exist it temporally, though elsewhere Aristotle dispels this belief.

It may appear from this discussion that Aristotle is willing to allow the capacity (or potentiality) to reign superior over the actuality. However, this is definitely not the case, following his second proposition: 'incapacity and being incapable are the lack that is contrary to this sort of capacity, so that every capacity is for the same thing in the same respect as the corresponding incapacity'.[14] Because every potentiality is also an impotentiality – a potentiality of the opposite – privileging the potentiality also entails privileging the impotentiality. Aristotle terms this 'the capacity for contraries' and, since in the state of potentiality 'to be capable of being healthy is also capable of being sick', he concludes that 'the activity is also better and more estimable than the excellent capacity'.[15] Thus, in Aristotle's response to the Megarians, we remain primarily metaphysically attuned to actuality, given the capacity for contraries, but we do not reduce existence to the actualised state.

Agamben's definitive contribution to metaphysics is undoubtedly his ongoing reflection on (im)potentiality, where he further develops Aristotle's notion of the capacity for contraries. Focusing on this superposition of capacity-to and

10 For a treatment of this relationship, see Backman (2017).
11 Aristotle (2016), IX, 3, 1046b27–29
12 Aristotle (2016), IX, 3, 1046b29–33.
13 Aristotle (2016), IX, 8, 1050b9–12.
14 Aristotle (2016), IX, 1, 1046b29–30.
15 Aristotle (2016), IX, 9, 1051a3–11.

capacity-not-to, Agamben restates the Aristotelian capacity for contraries with the emphasis placed not on potentiality over actuality but impotentiality over both:

> Every human power is *adynamia*, impotentiality; every human potentiality is in relation to its own privation. This is the origin (and the abyss) of human power, which is so violent and limitless with respect to other living beings. *Other living beings are capable only of their specific potentiality; they can only do this or that. But human beings are the animals who are capable of their own impotentiality. The greatness of human potentiality is measured by the abyss of human impotentiality.* [16]

The capacity for contraries is only freely a capacity – only truly possible – when the contrary is truly possible. Thus, for Agamben, potentiality is always (im) potentiality. Human freedom exists precisely because of the potential to not-be. Agamben reverses the implication of the capacity for contraries. While Aristotle privileges actuality precisely because the possibility of health entails the possibility of sickness, Agamben recognises that the true freedom of potentiality only exists if the actualisation of that potentiality is not predetermined – we are only free to do something if we are free not to do it.

As I have argued previously,[17] this Agambenian model is an emancipatory alternative to the Megarian model because it so strongly and directly counters its metaphysical assumptions. In place of a valuation of actuality alone, we find three modes of being, with actuality – surprisingly – in the place of least importance. Understood in political terms, whereas the Megarian model implies that only the actualised political decisions are relevant, Agamben's highlights that which cannot be, or that which is not forced to be. This broader scope of what counts has radical ramifications for a variety of topics, and indeed these factor into Agamben's explanations of modern statistics, guilt and human will, and elsewhere.[18] But what is most relevant for the present investigation is the specific relationship between politics and potentiality.

In Agamben, we find a clear relationship between metaphysics of potentiality and political ontology, from the very beginning. In fact, in *Homo Sacer* he begins with the discussion of life and political ontology reviewed above before turning to metaphysics as an analogy for the process of constituting a sovereign system: 'in the last analysis, the relation between constituting and constituted power … depends on how one thinks the existence and autonomy of potentiality'.[19] That is, if – as in the Megarians – all that matters is the actually existing system, then the power of the citizenry to constitute is irrelevant.[20] If,

16 Agamben (1999), p 182.
17 Murphy (2020b).
18 See Agamben (2018b), esp. pp 37–41; Agamben (2018a), esp. pp 29–31.
19 Agamben (1998), p 44.
20 On constitution and *pouvoir constituant*, see Murphy (2017).

instead, we recognise potentiality as existence, only then does our metaphysics grant the relevance of unactualised constituent power.

Potentiality and political ontology

Agamben's identification of Megarianism as a problematic modality for political structures is only one part of the onto-metaphysical story. Examining life in terms of emancipatory potentiality includes important insights ranging from individual to group, abstract to empirical, descriptive to prescriptive. In this section, I explore this relationship between potentiality and political ontology, recognising individual and structural elements.

First, we can turn to the philosophical investigation of life as a means of theorising political ontology. Discussions of politics that are founded on the definition of a particular form of political being, of a particular form of life, can be considered as a distinct form of political ontology. Both Giorgio Agamben[21] and Hannah Arendt[22] have drawn attention to Aristotle's division of life into two levels: one of existence and the other of living well. The political imaginaries of these thinkers rest upon their understandings of political ontology. Indeed, taking the example of Agamben, the tragedy of bare life is only possible once a fundamental division between *zoe* and *bios* has been established – we cannot understand why the reduction of *bios* to a bare form of life is a tragedy unless we first encounter a framework where life can be qualified at two levels.[23]

The discussion of life in Ancient Greece has long served as an important touchstone for political philosophers of the West, and received important attention beginning in the second half of the twentieth century. Hannah Arendt's *The Human Condition* discusses centrally the division between life of the home – mere existence of the *animal laborans* – and life of the city – where we find action and speech, 'out of which rises the realm of human affairs'.[24] Nearly half a century later, Giorgio Agamben's treatment of life in Ancient Greece again took up its divided nature in the introduction to the first volume of his Homo Sacer project.[25] Because Agamben's description more directly articulates the separation of the terms,[26] it is worth quoting his introductory passage at length:

21 See Agamben (1998).
22 See Arendt (1958).
23 See Agamben (1998).
24 Arendt (1958), p 25.
25 Following a convention suggested first by Adam Kotsko, I will capitalise Homo Sacer when referring to the project, italicise and capitalise *Homo Sacer* when referring to the work, and italicise *homo sacer* when referring to the figure of bare life. Kotsko (2016), p 123 n7.
26 It is worth noting, however, that these distinctions between *polis* and *oikos, bios* and *zoe*, have been challenged by Kotsko (2018), p 51ff and Derrida (2009), p. 315ff.

> The Greeks had no single term to express what we mean by the word 'life.' They used two terms that, although traceable to a common etymological root, are semantically and morphologically distinct: *zoe*, which expressed the simple fact of living common to all living beings (animals, men, or gods), and *bios*, which indicated the form or way of living proper to an individual or group. When Plato mentions three kinds of life in the *Philebus*, and when Aristotle distinguished the contemplative life of the philosopher (*bios theoretikos*) from the life of pleasure (*bios apolaustikos*) and the political life (*bios politikos*) in the *Nicomachean Ethics*, neither philosopher would have ever used the term *zoe* … This follows from the simple fact that what was at issue for both thinkers was not at all the simple natural life but rather a qualified life, a particular way of life.[27]

Agamben here disentangles life at two levels – *zoe*, which we might call existence, and *bios*, the form of life proper to the community in which individuals therein participate.[28] An individual in the Ancient *polis*, then, participated in *zoe* insofar as he was alive and breathing, as well as *bios* insofar as he took part in the activities of the specifically human community.

The two models of life discussed in this account all have clear linkages to the language of potentiality discussed above. The idea of *zoe*, a common and unspecified form of life common to many particular forms, describes life in terms of potentiality. *Zoe* is, indeed, full of potentiality precisely because it has not yet been formed one way or another but has a number of possibilities open. As *bios* emerges from *zoe*, we find one particular form of life actualised, such that life in that group prioritises the actualisation of a single form of living. Defining *bios* – and particularly defining one *bios* in contrast to others – is a matter of distinguishing key differences of a given actual form of life for a community.

Potentiality and political ontology intersect again at a higher level of analysis – the political community itself. Here, too, there are Megarian viewpoints,[29] which reduce the field of the political to actualised forms of power – for example, by rejecting the sovereignty of the people in favour of the authority of the executive. There are also a number of emancipatory political movements, seeking to break bonds in the name of freedom, and a full spectrum of political movements in between.[30] The specific political movement called for

27 Agamben (1998), p 1.

28 Elsewhere, the distinction has been separated as *bios* referring to the 'human-as-such' and *zoe* referring to 'life-as-such', common to anything that we say lives. Murphy (2017), p 91 n 2. Matthew Abbott frames this distinction as one between Being as such and ontic instances of political being, highlighting Agamben's debt to Heidegger. Abbott (2012), p 27.

29 See Agamben's critique: Agamben (1998), p 44.

30 For a typology of political protest and constituent power claims in terms of potentiality, see Murphy (2020a).

by Giorgio Agamben – *destituent potential* [31] – calls on individuals to withdraw from the process of political constitution by ceasing to participate in political structures. This vision of emancipatory politics – at the higher level of analysis – speaks to a vision of communities free from political domination, but proceeds at the individual level by an acceptance of *zoe* as such. That is to say, rather than call on a mass political movement to found a new *bios* that would be more just, this emancipatory ideal is for all *bioi* to be de-constituted by all individuals withdrawing from the *bios* of their community in favour of embracing the potentiality of *zoe*. The radicalism of Agamben's call lies precisely in that he does not seek to constitute anew, but to preserve the full freedom of constitution – only by individuals allowing their constituent potentiality to pass into impotentiality can they fully preserve their power.

Buribunkian life

The remainder of this chapter brings these conceptual discussions of potentiality and political ontology to bear upon Schmitt's tale of the Buribunks. Before conceptually contrasting the Megarian disposition of official Buribunkdom with the emancipatory form of life lived by the anti-social Buribunks, it is worthwhile reflecting on what counts as the common *bios* of the Buribunks. The question of what it means receives specific treatment in Schmitt's short story, and we can only glean that such a purposeful definition of the collective form of life should be significant for our metaphysical exploration.

One feature of Schmitt's reporting on the life of Buribunks that strikes the reader is his historical-journalistic style, approaching a fictive account as if he were writing any other academic treatise. He frames his project in precisely this light: 'Let's go *in media res*,' he entreats the reader, 'let's tackle the problem at its most burning, most interesting point: what is the criterion, the *differentia specifica*, the big distinctive feature?'[32] As he will do in precise definitions of political and juridical writings throughout his career, Schmitt approaches his short story with a purposeful eye to detail. What is particularly notable for our purposes is not only the practice of including precise descriptions in a work of fiction, but the extent to which his emphasises the definition of what the Buribunks *are*. Unpacking the descriptions and foundational assumptions of the form(s) of life of the Buribunks reveals the philosophical sophistication of this short story.

By searching for the distinctive feature that make a Buribunk's life buribunkian, Schmitt's definition can only be seen as a descriptor of *bios*. The two possible characteristics are that 'the Buribunks keep a diary' that they 'also have an enlarged mouth'.[33] The initial conclusion, it appears, is that the larger mouth is the *differentia specifica*; however, Schmitt nevertheless elects to focus his

31 Agamben (2016).
32 Chapter 2 of this volume, p 14.
33 Chapter 2 of this volume, p 14.

attention on the historical analysis of diary-writing development rather than the 'gradual enlargement of the mouth', which 'would require a more physiological-anatomical, in short a more medical, consideration'.[34]

That his focus is historical, social and ethical (rather than anatomical, physiological and medical) is also significant for the purposes of political ontology. The analysis of the physical body need not proceed in terms of *bios*, as we can analyse (and indeed in zoology often do) animals as living organisms, even as particular *kinds* of living organisms. However, as indicated by the etymology embedded in the term 'zoology', this remains an analysis of the existence rather than the elements of sociality in that animal's life – in short, this kind of physiological analysis takes as its object not *bios* but *zoe*. Diary writing, conversely, does not depend on a physiological-anatomical feature, notwithstanding Schmitt's speculation that a larger mouth leads to better diary writing, 'according to the theory of quantity becoming quality'.[35] Schmitt's conscious decision here to investigate *bios* over *zoe* entails a biology over a zoology,[36] a political ontology over a physiology.

This *differentia specifica* of diary-writing is found at both the collective and individual levels. At the collective level, 'every male and female Buribunk is obliged to keep a diary for every second of their existence'[37] – that is to say that the species sets this behaviour as necessary for participation in the group. Diary-writing then becomes – just like the social practices that emerged as species *Homo* differentiated from *Australopithecus* – definitive of the group.[38] We can tell that Buribunks are Buribunks because they behave in a buribunkian way, just as we can identify humans by their typically human practices – in both cases, there exists a *bios*.

While *bios* is defined with reference to the community, it is not limited to that larger level of analysis, but also can be interrogated at the individual level. Schmitt addresses the individual manifestations of buribunkian *bios* in terms of the attitude typical of a Buribunk: 'that attitude which distinguishes the Buribunk and which springs from the urge to preserve every second of one's own being for history – the creating and viewing oneself as a monument'.[39] In this statement, Schmitt identifies that the *bios* becomes a part of the individual as an attitude. Specifically, Schmitt calls this individualised and internalised disposition the 'buribunkian cinematic attitude'.[40] With the broad species normalising

34 Chapter 2 of this volume, p 15.
35 Chapter 2 of this volume, p 14 and *passim*.
36 Indeed, the rejection of zoology is even more important because – as Schmitt's translators note – the term used to refer to mouth, *Maul* rather than *Mund*, refers typically to an animal mouth rather than a human mouth. See Petersen and Reifarth (2019), p 114.
37 Chapter 2 of this volume, p 23.
38 Tomasello (1999).
39 Chapter 2 of this volume, p 16.
40 Chapter 2 of this volume, p 16.

and requiring the practice of diary keeping, and the individual internalising the practice at a deep psychological level, he can say that each individual Buribunk 'is nothing but a diary-keeper, he lives for the diary, he lives in and through the diary'.[41] In this sense, the *bios* of each Buribunk corresponds directly to the buribunkian *bios* as an abstraction.

Because the Buribunks see the world from the perspective of their diary-writing, there is a fundamental shift to the individual experience of the world: 'The diary-keeping Buribunk does not actually experience anything beforehand, but it is in the entry into the diary and its publication that constitutes the experience.'[42] The very experience of the world is mediated through the diary-writing process, just as our experience of the world is mediated through language. A phenomenology of the Buribunks is always, then, a buribunkological analysis of the written record of their diaries.

While there may be a physical characteristic of a larger mouth among the Buribunks, what socially sets the species apart from other beings is their practice of diary-writing, embedded at the level of the Buribunk and of Buribunkdom. Life-as-writing captures the *differentia specifica* of buribunkian *bios*.

As we saw in Agamben's account of life, while *zoe* begins immediately at the beginning of the animal's life, the human must adapt to a particular form of *bios*.[43] Just as Schmitt's discussion of the buribunkian form of life – namely, diary-writing – matches the Ancient Greek form of socially proper life, it also depends upon an initiation. Schmitt states that 'the ability to keep a diary gradually appears with the Buribunk-foetus',[44] though this is almost certainly a reference to the larger mouth, which he tells us is correlated with the heightened intelligence necessary for diary-writing.

What we might call the infancy[45] of buribunkian identity is that process of becoming-Buribunk, passing from the undifferentiated potentiality/*zoe* of the 'Buribunk-foetus' to the actualised/*bios* of the fully formed Buribunk. Recalling the double stakes of any form of life, bringing together both the individual living in a particular form of life and the community that determines that appropriate form, we find an important discussion in Schmitt's description of 'the specifically buribunkian state of mind', which 'gradually develops in its intensity over time'.[46] However, the fact that the process of becoming a Buribunk entails a gradual development does not mean that there are not

41 Chapter 2 of this volume, p 22.
42 Chapter 2 of this volume, p 16 n 3.
43 While this particular chapter draws on Agamben's reading, that is not the only possible source. Lubrano (2019), p 184, for example, draws on Rosa Bradiotti's reading of *zoe*.
44 Chapter 2 of this volume, p 25.
45 In my contribution to the special issue on *The Buribunks*, I explore in detail the philosophical stakes of buribunkian infancy and initiation. See Murphy (2019b).
46 Chapter 2 of this volume, p 20.

particularly salient threshold moments. Schmitt describes the moment of becoming-Buribunk in the clear language of birth:

> Only in the second in which the single letter leaves the senseless and meaningless indifference of the keyboard, and hits the lively connections on the white page, a historical reality is created; only this second is the birth hour of life.[47]

While the foetus may have the physiological predisposition to a greater intelligence over the smaller-mouthed foetuses of the lesser peoples, even the Buribunk is not truly or fully born *as Buribunk* until the second the diary-writing commences.

The individual practice of fully living as a Buribunk is intimately connected to the social structures that emerge and are constantly (re)produced in the buribunkian community. Each generation growing up in the buribunkian way of life not only confront the existing set of social practices as an objective reality,[48] but also confronts the developed state apparatuses of Buribunkdom, which penetrate into the core of buribunkian society. As mentioned above, 'every male and female Buribunk is obliged to keep a diary for every second of their existence'.[49] The language of obligation here delimits freedom harshly, and is enforced by a large buribunkological state apparatus. Indeed, Schmitt describes a significant governmental apparatus dedicated to the management of these diaries:

> The diaries thus arranged and inspected are submitted in regular monthly reports to the head of a Buribunk department who, in this way, has constant control over the course of psychological development in his province and he himself reports to a central agency, which creates master catalogues published them simultaneously in Esperanto, and is thus able to record buribunkologically all of Buribunkdom.[50]

While the Buribunks appear to truly be a 'society of control',[51] equipped with a powerful and managerial governmental apparatus, my focus is not on the analysis of this organisation but its implication – namely, that the diary-writing definitive of buribunkian *bios* is enforced.

This coercive element strikes a reader from a non-diary-writing species as highly controlling; however, Schmitt is careful to assert the freedom that exists within the

47 Chapter 2 of this volume, p 26.
48 Similar to the social theory of social construction in Berger and Luckmann (1967), ch 2.
49 Chapter 2 of this volume, p 23.
50 Chapter 2 of this volume, p 24.
51 I take this term from Deleuze (1992), although the data-doubles here are presumably paper rather than electronic. For a different exploration of the buribunkian data-doubles as informational existence, see Tranter (2019).

buribunkian diary-system. Indeed, we find this freedom precisely on the literal blank page of the diary, where 'no Buribunk is prevented in any way from freely creating his diary entries'.[52] There exists a seemingly unlimited sea of potentials here in what can be written. The Buribunk 'may he state that he lacks the intellectual strength for entries', or that 'only the sadness about this lack of strength gives him the necessary strength [to write]' – and indeed, this is a common enough entry that it 'is especially recognised and highly regarded'.[53] The diary entries are free to serve as a forum for rebellion and rejection of the very idea of the diary, and a Buribunk 'can also note, without having to fear even the slightest pressure, that he regards the diary as a pointless and burdensome institution, as a silly harassment, a laughable custom' using the very 'strongest expressions'.[54] In short, the Buribunks are guaranteed what Schmitt calls 'the unconstrained freedom of expression', supported from the highest levels of Buribunkdom, where they 'know very well that they would damage the nerve centre of their existence if they were to restrict' that freedom.[55] From this account, then, it seems that the very apparatus that earlier appeared as a harsh constraint and control is now a guarantor of freedom!

There is, then, a tension to be teased out between the controlling management and claims of freedom. On the surface, Schmitt's description of uncontrolled freedom within the constraints of mandatory writing makes it difficult to judge which element – freedom or control – is primary. What we must do in this case is turn to the assumptions at the foundation of buribunkian life, unpacking the political ontology and metaphysics of Schmitt's imagined beings. The freedom exists in the unconstrained nature of engaging with the practice of writing – 'we see true freedom' when 'we consciously submit ourselves to [the World Spirit] writing power'.[56] By taking on the task of writing the world history through the diary, the Buribunks shape their own destiny, acting in the creation of, rather than passing into, world history. In exercising this freedom, the Buribunks 'outwit the cunning of world history – writing it while it writes' them.[57] The limit to the freedom is found here in its most powerful expression: the Buribunks are free so long as they actualise their power. They can write as they please, but they cannot not-write as they please. To have any hope of freedom of expression, they must give up their greater freedom to write or to not-write. In this sense, we might say that the buribunkian freedom is a bounded infinity[58] – they experience infinite freedom of expression, but only within the confines and constraints of being forced to write.

52 Chapter 2 of this volume, p 24.
53 Chapter 2 of this volume, p 24.
54 Chapter 2 of this volume, p 24.
55 Chapter 2 of this volume, p 24.
56 Chapter 2 of this volume, p 27.
57 Chapter 2 of this volume, p 27.
58 The bounded infinity may be understood most simply in the fact that there are an infinite number of potential fractions in between 0 and 1, and therefore the set {1 … ½, ⅓, ¼ … 0} is both infinite insofar as it includes an infinite number of

How, then, might we summarise the life of the Buribunk? It seems as though there are two distinctive features and an accompanying philosophy. The Buribunks may be physiologically distinguished by their larger mouth and sociologically distinguished by their practices of diary-writing. The Buribunks write all things at all times, and have organised their society around the collection and systematisation of the diaries. This definitive practice is the buribunkian *bios* – to engage in this form of diary-writing is to be buribunkian. The Buribunks are free to write whatever they wish, including that they wish to not write, so long as they actually *do*.

Schmitt offers a philosophy of the Buribunks, a Cartesian riff followed by a series of questions: 'I write, therefore I am; I am, therefore I write. What do I write? I write myself. Who writes me? I myself write myself. What is the content of my writing? I write that I write myself.'[59] Perhaps the most significant question is the absent presence of a *why* question, the question that need not be asked by a Buribunk – and we should recall that Schmitt approaches the story as a Buribunk buribunkologist – because it is superfluous. The Buribunks write diaries because Buribunks are those who write diaries! No *why* question is necessary, because it begs a tautology. The freedom of the Buribunks is infinite within their *bios* – that is, within the fulfilment of their practices of writing. But what occurs beyond the threshold?

While the ontological argument exists only beneath the text, the dismissal of metaphysics is stated directly. The first mention occurs when reaffirming the factual disposition of buribunkology. Because of the vast collection of buribunkological material, all the daily diaries in addition to '400,000 dissertations' written on the topic, 'metaphysics no longer poses a danger' – that is, buribunkology 'is indeed more than a science, it is a fact'.[60] In this mention, Schmitt invokes metaphysics to stake an epistemological claim: that the physical data are so overwhelming that certainty does not demand reflexivity. The third reference to metaphysics is similarly uneventful. Speaking of the importance of diaries for remembering great events and individuals, Schmitt states that in the system of buribunkological record-keeping, a 'noble motive of human greatness is in this way relocated from the uncertain sphere of metaphysical illusion and returned to solid ground'.[61] Again, the term 'metaphysics' is invoked to prioritise the physical and the actual.

The second direct mention of metaphysics occurs in the end of the life of Ferker, and includes within it a second anti-Aristotelian metaphysical claim. When Ferker died, he was cremated, and his ashes were then used 'for the production of printing ink … from which a small part was sent to all printing

terms, but bounded insofar as none will be greater than 1 or less than 0. For an accessible introduction to the size of infinites, see Matson (2008).

59 Chapter 2 of this volume, p 26.

60 Chapter 2 of this volume, p 13.

61 Chapter 2 of this volume, p 28.

presses on earth'.[62] Then, as his diaries were disseminated and as others began their own record-keeping – to say nothing of the other uses of ink – Ferker's ashes spread:

> in every single one of the billions of letters, which the eye encounters over the years, there is an atom of the ashes of the immortal man. Thus the trace of his earthly days cannot disappear in aeons; through a grand, shall we say, antimetaphysical-positive gesture, he secured for himself (even in death a genius of actuality) his continued existence in the memory of humankind.[63]

To first elucidate the obvious mention, Schmitt calls Ferker's gesture of committing his ashes to the future ink of Buribunkdom an 'antimetaphysical-positive gesture'. Again, this is a rather epistemological framing of Ferker's work as emphasising the physical world: what matters in Ferker's gesture is its *materiality*, the tangible presence that he will continue to have. But in considering the place of metaphysics and potentiality, what is far more interesting is Schmitt's naming of Ferker as 'a genius of actuality'. Though he does not use the word, this is undoubtedly a metaphysical claim: Ferker's epistemological positivism – the positivism underlying buribunkology – depends solely on the actuality rather than the potentiality. This framing of actuality as the only consideration that matters is a firmly Megarian claim, following directly the precepts that drew Aristotle's criticism millennia ago. *Contra* the description of freedom in the unlimited subjects to be written about, this foundational Megarianism belies the metaphysical control inherent in Buribunkdom. But at this point of greatest demand of actuality, we are also able to find the strongest potential for rejection of buribunkian Megarianism, an emancipatory form of life lived out by the anti-social Buribunks. It is to their story that we must now turn.

Freedom, impotentiality and the anti-social Buribunks

Much attention above has been given to the Ancient Greek debates on metaphysics and the contemporary commentary on their way of life. The discussion of the anti-social Buribunks will prove no exception to this rule, as their story points to the important difference between renunciation and abjection from communal living. While the definitions of Agamben and Arendt discussed above may seem to describe a binary relation between *zoe* as an undifferentiated and generic form of life on the one hand, and *bios* as the communally specific form of life on the other, the dynamic clearly becomes more convoluted when we consider the possibility of politics when communal

62 Chapter 2 of this volume, p 19.
63 Chapter 2 of this volume, p 20.

membership is lost. Giorgio Agamben's work on the figure of the *homo sacer*[64] describes in detail the political-metaphysical stakes of the individual's experience of the exception. When the normal political situation is suspended by the sovereign, the individual's *bios* is stripped away, leaving only a bare form of life. While this form of life that has been stripped of communal specificity may appear to be *zoe*, it is in fact categorically distinct[65] – actuality that has been destroyed is not the same as unblemished potentiality, just as a field whose crops have been burned is not the same as fertile soil before seeding.

Agamben's critique of the Megarian impulses of contemporary society call attention to the ways in which the individual's *bios* is stripped away, and his strongest rejection of Megarian excesses comes in his embrace of an emancipatory form of life that renounces communal living. In so doing, the emancipatory alternative may *prima facie* appear similar to the *homo sacer* – being without membership in communal life – but the fact that this was taken on willingly as an embrace of undifferentiated potentiality rather than having choices and memberships forcibly and violently de-actualised means that the emancipatory alternative powerfully protects potentiality and freedom. This conceptual distinction is useful as it teases out how the story of the anti-social Buribunks who do not comply is important not only as a further demonstration of the Megarianism of Buribunkdom but also as a model for escaping that oppressive control.

Schmitt maintains that the Buribunks enjoy freedom, and for those who write, the freedom of expression afforded them is infinite. However, there is a boundary to this infinity, and beyond that threshold we find the figure of the anti-social creature. Just as the *bios* within the *polis* depends upon the boundary between the inside and outside, the relation between freedom within the bound and the anti-sociality beyond is fundamental. At what we might call an asymptote to the threshold, 'no Buribunk is prevented from writing in his diary that he refuses to keep a diary' – the 'apex', we are told, 'of these liberties' of expression.[66] However, the threshold between writing and not-writing is significant for the buribunkian society: 'Every entry of the refusal to keep a diary needs to be justified and described in detail' so that the 'freedom [of expression] must not become unrestrained anarchy'.[67] The freedom approaching the bound remains freedom, but entails an added responsibility.

But the refusal to write is an entirely different situation. Recalling the process of collection and systematisation of the diaries, it would be a relatively straightforward exercise for the officials of Buribunkdom to locate when a diary was not written. At this point, when a Buribunk, 'instead of writing that he

64 See Agamben (1998).
65 Agamben calls attention to the difference: Agamben (2016), p 263. Carlo Salzani (2015) also clarifies the difference between undifferentiated mere life and bare life.
66 Chapter 2 of this volume, p 24.
67 Chapter 2 of this volume, p 24.

refuses, really stops writing', he has transgressed the bound of freedom – or, in Schmitt's own words, he 'makes inappropriate use of the general freedom of mind' – the punishment is swift: that individual 'will be eliminated due to his anti-social disposition'.[68] This statement is striking because the offending Buribunk does not face censure for an act committed, but for the anti-sociality inherent in the refusal to fulfil an obligation.

It is imperative that we understand Schmitt's use of the verb 'eliminate' in describing the *bios* rather than the *zoe* of the offending Buribunk. The one who does not write is, like the *homo sacer* made famous in Agamben's political ontology, abjected[69] – not killed, but rendered such that his killing would not be murderous. Alienated from the writing of history, the anti-social Buribunk:

> will no longer be mentioned, he can therefore no longer make himself heard until he finally, sinking step by step, is forced into the lowest class, to help create the external conditions for the possibility of noble Buribunkdom, for example making by hand the paper on which the most valuable diaries are printed.[70]

The abjection of the individual is – like the initiation into *bios* – a process. As prior commentaries on Agamben have noted,[71] this political-ontological descent parallels the abjection of the proletarian in the early Marxist critique of industrial towns, and especially Engels's observations in *The Conditions of the Working Class of England*, where he differentiates slavery from capitalist oppression by the fact that the latter involves a piecemeal treading of the weaker underfoot.[72] Similar to the economic abjection seen in industrial capitalism, the individuals holding the very power that sustains the system – the buribunkian diary-writers for buribunkology and the proletariat for capitalism – are subject to abjection.[73] It is fitting that this parallel would share a sentence with the anti-social Buribunks being coerced into a material production process where the value of the products – the writing on the diaries – is alienated from the labourers who made them.

The effectiveness of abjecting portions of the population that do not follow the practice of diary-writing depends, again, upon the political-ontological connection between the diary-writing practices and the political being of the Buribunks. In this sense, there is something *natural* about eliminating the socially proper life of an individual who does not participate in the central

68 Chapter 2 of this volume, p 25.
69 Murphy (2017) has previously argued for understanding this relation as one of abjection, allowing for important parallels to be drawn between the work of Agamben on political relation and Marx on capitalism.
70 Chapter 2 of this volume, p 25.
71 De Boever (2009); Murphy (2017).
72 Engels (2009), pp 37, 91.
73 Murphy (2017), p 90.

communal practice. The buribunkological registers simply reflect that which is submitted, and when the diary ceases to be updated, 'eventually he vanishes from the screen of the monthly reports and ceases to exist'.[74] But why is this severity necessary? Here again, it is worthwhile to recall the relation between the individual disposition of *bios* and the community participation of *bios*. The buribunkological governmental apparatus is set up such that 'numerous adequate precautions see ... that the interest of the Buribunk in and of himself remains lively', so that the individual does not approach the bounds of infinite freedom by writing about refusal to write, but to ensure that 'they also prevent a detrimental and anti-social digression of this interest'.[75] If the anti-social disposition can be tramped down, 'we do not have to fear that the sublime rotation of this buribunkian world will ever come to an end'[76] – and conversely, if it cannot be controlled, then the rampant lack of writing will not only eliminate the individual-attitudinal *bios* but also fundamentally halt the communal *bios* in which other individuals participate.

Whereas the discussion of freedom above concluded with the image of a bounded infinity, the life of the anti-social Buribunk is hardly similar. The same analogy simply does not track onto a life whose *bios* is eliminated. In this exceptional case, we can see clearly the essence of the everyday.[77] In the abjection of the anti-social Buribunk, we see how writing becomes a necessity – to be buribunkian is to write, not merely to have the capacity for writing or to write at significant moments, but to actually write.

In the text of *The Buribunks*, Schmitt offers a number of fictional references and figures, but the most illustrative on this note is the Great Ferker. The first of the Buribunks, Ferker wrote a great deal of his life in a diary, but crucial moments are missing. Thus, while he is hailed as a great hero in the history of Buribunkdom, he is fallible because he neglected to fully actualise his Buribunk-*ness*, his writing. Whereas, in the time of Buribunkdom where Schmitt writes, everyone 'realises that one can turn the intellectual-spiritual struggles which hinder free creativity into an object of creativity', this was not the case in the life of the Great Ferker, who allowed moments to pass undocumented, as he 'had not yet recognised this urgently required rigour'.[78] The hero's fallibility is found within his failure to always actualise the writing-capacity. Phrased in terms of political ontology, the hero's moment of rupture with buribunkian being is found within his failure to actualise the writing capacity. This language of actualisation, however, does not come from political ontology but from metaphysics. It is through this metaphysical reflection that the significance of the political ontology that leaves no room for a failure to actualise will come into focus.

74 Chapter 2 of this volume, p 25.
75 Chapter 2 of this volume, p 24.
76 Chapter 2 of this volume, p 24.
77 Agamben (2002), p 48.
78 Chapter 2 of this volume, p 22.

From the point of view of Buribunkdom, the anti-social Buribunks are not complying with what it fundamentally means to be Buribunk. The elimination of the communal form of being for those individuals thus marks an attempt at the un-actualisation of their *bios*. But observed from the other perspective, examining the anti-social Buribunks' attitudes, we find a radically different view – one that directly embraces the undifferentiated potentiality of the word not written.

While Schmitt's philosophical methodology – especially in his works on sovereignty – calls careful attention to the subject position of power, examination of the anti-social Buribunks' actions from their own perspective requires attention instead to the objects of power. When focused on the activity of the subject, the objects are reduced to passivity; when we take seriously the agency and activity of the objects of power (in conventional narratives), we gain a whole new perspective.[79] Though his critique of sovereignty begins with Schmitt, Agamben is in fact at his most Foucauldian[80] when speaking of the objects of power, and the entire Homo Sacer project builds to a consideration of how objects of power can deconstruct the systems by which they are dominated.[81] Given Schmitt's methodology, we are not presented with the thought-process of the anti-social Buribunks. But with minimal consideration, we can reconstruct the calculation to not write.

The buribunkian perfectly abiding by the dictates of Buribunkdom follows the rules guiding their communal *bios* by meticulously keeping a diary. A second class of Buribunks, then, would be those who object to the practice of diary-keeping but nevertheless participate in the process by writing that they do not wish to write. This group holds the 'rebellious spirit',[82] and Schmitt notes that – while they do exist – this is an exceptional group. In kowtowing to Buribunkdom, written objections pose no real threat because by taking a highly visible and confessionary form, the rebellious spirit can be subjected to careful observation. Abiding this behavioural expectation, the rebellious Buribunks nevertheless willingly participate in buribunkian *bios*. The decision to not-write, on the other hand, is a (non-)act of rebellion at a much deeper level than that of the rebellious Buribunks. Rather than registering displeasure through continued participation, the anti-social Buribunks withdraw from both the activity of writing and the communal form of life associated with being-

79 A similar point has been made here by postcolonial security studies theorists. Barkawi and Laffey (2006) take the example of the dialogue between Athenian ambassadors and Melian people during the Peloponnesian War – conventionally written off as passive characters acted upon, their story is in fact important to the outcome of the war. 'Security studies', Barkawi and Laffey (2006, p 352) conclude, 'have a lot to gain by waking up to the significance of the Melians and their kin'.

80 For more on the Schmitt/Foucault synthesis in Agamben's work, see Murphy (2019a).

81 Agamben (2016).

82 Chapter 2 of this volume, p 24.

Buribunk. The rebellious Buribunks – like the social media activists today – are a hollow voice, as their actions remain complicit in the system that they claim a desire to reject. By *not* acting, the anti-social Buribunks are risking elimination from the social body because it is only under the shadow of that risk that freedom from buribunkian domination could ever be imaginable.

Conclusion: finding emancipation

Brought into discussion only recently, Schmitt's story of *The Buribunks* is a thought-provoking tale that can provoke new ideas through a philosophically sophisticated narrative that calls out elements of everyday life, past, present and future.[83] Indeed, our increasingly recorded society – where what is undocumented or 'un-tweeted' might as well have not happened – we might find in the Buribunks an example of how ridiculous hyperdocumentation is as a mode of life.[84] But the story also offers an example of how emancipation can proceed from moments of individual refusal. In a Megarian world, the emancipatory politics discussed by Giorgio Agamben and others might simply be a matter of ceasing our own diary-writing.

Freedom to do is only free when it includes its contrary capacity *to not do*. By identifying the place where only the products of doing matter – the Megarian focus on actuality – or where doing matters in relation to producing – as Agamben critiques Aristotle – then the moments of not-doing come into focus. A lesson of the Buribunks is that the key to these emancipatory forms of life may be found in those most directly targeted by the violence of Megarian social structures.

References

Matthew Abbott (2012) 'No Life is Bare, the Ordinary is Exceptional: Giorgio Agamben and the Question of Political Ontology' 14 *Parrhesia* 23.

Giorgio Agamben (1998) *Homo Sacer: Sovereign Power and Bare Life*, Stanford University Press.

Giorgio Agamben (1999) *Potentialities: Collected Essays in Philosophy*, Stanford University Press.

Giorgio Agamben (2002) *Remnants of Auschwitz: The Witness and the Archive*, Stanford University Press.

Giorgio Agamben (2016) *The Use of Bodies*, Stanford University Press.

Giorgio Agamben (2018a) *Karman: A Brief Treatise on Action, Guilt, and Gesture*, Stanford University Press.

Giorgio Agamben (2018b) *What is Real?*, Stanford University Press.

83 This hope is discussed in the editors' introduction to the special issue. See Bikundo and Tranter (2019), p 97.

84 In this light, Rochford's (2019) commentary on the right to be forgotten is especially thought-provoking.

Hannah Arendt (1958) *The Human Condition*, University of Chicago Press.

Aristotle (2016) *Metaphysics*, Hackett.

Jussi Backman (2017) 'Aristotle', in A. Kotsko and C. Salzani (eds), *Agamben's Philosophical Lineage*, Edinburgh University Press.

Tarak Barkawi and Mark Laffey (2006) 'The Postcolonial Moment in Security Studies' 32(2) *Review of International Studies* 329.

Peter L. Berger and Thomas Luckmann (1967) *The Social Construction of Reality: A Treatise in the Sociology of Knowledge*, Anchor Books.

Edwin Bikundo and Kieran Tranter (2019) 'The Buribunks: Carl Schmitt on Diaries, Modernity, and Future' 28 *Griffith Law Review* 95.

Arne De Boever (2009) 'Agamben and Marx: Sovereignty, Governmentality, Economy' 20 *Law and Critique* 259.

Gilles Deleuze (1992) 'Postscript on the Societies of Control' 59 *October* 3.

Jacques Derrida (2009) *The Beast and the Sovereign*, vol. I, University of Chicago Press.

Friedrich Engels (2009) *The Conditions of the Working Class of England*, Oxford University Press.

Adam Kotsko (2016) 'Agamben's Messianic Nihilism', in C. Dickinson and A. Kotsko (eds), *Agamben's Coming Philosophy: Finding a New Use for Theology*, Rowman & Littlefield.

Adam Kotsko (2018) *Neoliberalism's Demons: On the Political Theology of Late Capital*, Stanford University Press.

Vittorio Lubrano (2019) 'On the Normality of Writing: Inscription/Description of Everyday Life' 28 *Griffith Law Review* 173.

John Matson (2008) 'Does Infinity Come in Different Sizes?' 298(1) *Scientific American* 112.

Michael P.A. Murphy (2017) 'Pouvoir Constituant Betrayed: A Model of Abjection in Power Relations' 10(1) *Journal of Political Power* 85.

Michael P.A. Murphy (2019a) 'The Double Articulation of Sovereign Bordering: Spaces of Exception, Sovereign Vulnerability, and Agamben's Schmitt/Foucault Synthesis' *Journal of Borderlands Studies*, www.tandfonline.com/doi/abs/10.1080/08865655.2019.1683053.

Michael P.A. Murphy (2019b) 'What Does It Mean to Be Anti-Social? Potentiality and Political Ontology in The Buribanks' 28 *Griffith Law Review* 154.

Michael P.A. Murphy (2020a) 'Potentiality, Political Protest, and Constituent Power: A Response to the Special Issue' 16(3) *Journal of International Political Theory* 361.

Michael P.A. Murphy (2020b) 'The Rise, Fall, and Afterlife of Learning Styles: An Essay on Megarianism and Emancipation in Educational Potentiality' 39 *Studies in Philosophy of Education* 205.

Laura Petersen and Gert Reifarth (2019) 'The Buribunks: A Translators' Note' 28 *Griffith Law Review* 113.

Francine Rochford (2019) 'Negative Space – The Paradox at the Heart of Buribunkology' 28 *Griffith Law Review* 247.

Carlo Salzani (2015) 'From Benjamin's *bloßes Leben* to Agamben's *nuda vita*: A Genealogy', in B. Moran and C. Salzani (eds), *Toward the Critique of Violence: Walter Benjamin and Giorgio Agamben*, Bloomsbury, 109.

Carl Schmitt (2004) *Legality and Legitimacy*, Duke University Press.

Carl Schmitt (2008) *Constitutional Theory*, Duke University Press.

Carl Schmitt (2014) *Dictatorship: From the Origin of the Modern Concept of Sovereignty to Proletarian Class Struggle*, Polity Press.
Michael Tomasello (1999) *The Cultural Origins of Human Cognition*, Harvard University Press.
Kieran Tranter (2019) 'Die Buribunken as Science Fiction: The Self and Informational Existence' 28(2) *Griffith Law Review* 118.

Chapter 8

The challenges of anti-intellectual parody

Karen Petroski

Introduction

Carl Schmitt's *The Buribunks* is both prescient and nostalgic. To the early twenty-first century reader, it can seem like an uncanny anticipation of our pervasively mediated contemporary experiences of identity.[1] But *The Buribunks* does not unambiguously present the Buribunks as a welcome social or existential development. They seem, rather, to represent a hollowed-out form of existence, and in this regard the essay prompts nostalgia.[2] We can even read Schmitt's essay as an allegory of the kind of chaotic, ahistorical mode of existence that calls for an exceptional decision to become meaningful.[3]

This chapter will consider some additional ways in which *The Buribunks* is both a text of its time and place (post-World War I Germany) and part of a tradition of anti-intellectual discourse in Western culture. Anti-intellectualism might be of special concern now, a century after the writing and publication of *The Buribunks*. Information-technology developments foreseen in some (but not all) regards by 'C.S.' have modified the shape and sway of anti-intellectual discourse,[4] and the practical consequences of these developments have recently become more disturbing. Considering Schmitt's essay as, in part, a formal anticipation of these developments, the following pages examine a few specific aspects of anti-intellectual discourse: its relationships with its creators and audiences, as well as its self-reproduction through these relationships.

Critical accounts of the tradition of anti-intellectual discourse in the West have often focused only on parts of that tradition.[5] Such discourse takes a number of forms, distinguished partly by their targets and partly by their techniques. There is no one target of anti-intellectual discourse because 'the intellectual' is not a simple construct, even setting aside historical change in the construction and recognition of intellectuals as a social group. Intellectuals are

1 Rochford (2019), p 247; Tranter (2019), p 120.
2 See, for example, Balke (2019), p 633; Schultz (2019) pp 213–14.
3 Bredekamp (1999); Derrida (1998), pp 33–36.
4 For example, Hofstadter (1963); Jacoby (2008).
5 See, for example, Dewey (1910), p 477.

DOI: 10.4324/9781003091066-10

(and have long been) cast by their critics, variously, as provincial or self-absorbed elites;[6] as self-interested or politically compromised manipulators of trivial information;[7] and (in a mirror image of some self-identified intellectuals' self-image) as espousers of a minority and misguided orthodoxy who cast themselves, falsely, as critics of a destructive conventionalism.[8] These groups, which are partly created through criticism, do not fully overlap, and their different flaws suggest responsibility for different social ills, including but not limited to exploitation, simple waste or deceitful cover for oppression by others.

These different targets do share some features. In each form, the intellectual is a member of an identifiable social subgroup, seeking illegitimate domination and suffering some degree of closed-mindedness and bad faith. Each of these targets also has some relation to the ways self-identified intellectuals often conceive of themselves: as initiates into and protectors of an endangered tradition and/or as self-denying servants of the public good with access to insights not available to others.

Much of what differs between critical and positive views of intellectual activity is the degree of sincerity attributed to intellectuals' self-presentation. This self-presentation is fundamentally discursive and marked by particular formal features, such as allusion, citation, and structured argument. These features of intellectuals' self-presentation in turn generate another complexity in anti-intellectual discourse: such discourse can take a variety of forms. Different modes of anti-intellectual discourse embody different attitudes toward the characteristic formal markers of intellectual discourse, as well as towards what those markers might or might not signify.

One basic formal distinction in anti-intellectual discourse is between explicit critique of intellectual discourse and values on the one hand, and critiques that parrot intellectual discourse for ironic purposes on the other. Ironic critiques Alan Sokal's *Social Text* 'hoax' of 1996 is a prominent example – share some features with more direct criticism. Both seem to accuse some so-called intellectual discourse of self-absorption, impracticality and narrow-mindedness, while also endorsing classic intellectual virtues. Sokal's parody did not condemn all intellectual or academic work; the hoax involved an emperor's new clothes-style unveiling of one specific subset of such work, which (Sokal suggested) was itself untrue to intellectual values.[9] Such parroting of a particular mode of intellectual discourse as that performed by Sokal may also be used to very different ends, as when proponents of unorthodox, fringe or anti-rationalist notions adopt the trappings of academic discourse – citation, apparently reasoned analysis and so forth – to generate an 'alternative' to the established

6 For example, Jacoby (2008), pp 143, 153, 171; Houghton (1967) pp 110–35.
7 For example, Dewey (1910), pp 477–8; Houghton (1967) pp 110–35.
8 For example, Jacoby (2008), p 86.
9 See Sokal (2010).

intellectual discourse of a period or culture.[10] The generation of an ostensibly academic literature to be cited by climate-science sceptics is a good recent example of this phenomenon, which is not ironic in the way Sokal's text was.[11]

The Buribunks is a parody of academic discourse that, like Sokal's essay, depends on its readers' engagement with some conventions of intellectual discourse *and* with their familiar flaws.[12] Writing of this kind trains its readers to develop flexibility in both identifying as and criticising intellectuals as bad-faith actors.[13] Such writing can perpetuate distinctions between intellectuals and 'genuine' members of society; it tends to cast as insincere the intellectual's claim to have insights that might benefit others and presents intellectuals as voluntarily cutting themselves off from others' experiences. Such writing can suggest that intellectual self-presentation is entirely a pose, a mode of presenting any available informational content.

Anti-intellectual discourse has perhaps always been part of Western culture, even if it has flourished more in some periods than others. The next three sections of this chapter investigate, first, the techniques used by 'C.S.' in *The Buribunks* to parody academic and more broadly intellectual discourse; second, briefly, a few highlights of the Western tradition of anti-intellectual discourse; and third, the shape of contemporary (twenty-first century) manifestations of this tradition. Despite their longevity, these traditions might have been changing significantly in Schmitt's time and have changed even further since then.

Targets of *The Buribunks*

The Buribunks is an intricately structured artifact. Wouter Werner notes that the essay moves in its first half from theoretical to empirical registers before reversing and, in its second half, moving back from empirical to theoretical registers.[14] The account presented here will highlight a different aspect of the essay's structure: its movement through three separate parodies of (at least) three different forms of intellectual discourse. *The Buribunks* demarcates these separate rehearsals via subtitles, and this section will use that demarcation to consider each section of the essay in turn.

Although it can be reductive to characterise parody as a 'parasitic' form,[15] the parasite metaphor does capture some core features of parody. Parody depends on the existence – and reader recognition of – a prior 'host' text or discourse that is sent up by the subsequent 'parasitic' text.[16] Each of the three sections of

10 For example, Ringer (1963), pp 403, 446.
11 See Jacoby (2008), pp 61–80, 219–21; Oreskes and Conway (2019).
12 See Manderson & Bikundo (2019), p 191.
13 See Goodrich (2004), p 411 on the way satire characteristically exempts its readers from condemnation.
14 Werner (2019), p 260.
15 See, for example, Dentith (2000), p 189; Kiremidjian (1969), p 223.
16 See Dentith (2000), p 39.

The Buribunks appears to depend on a distinct 'host' discourse. It is possible to read these sections in sequence as implying a narrative, but it is also possible to imagine them re-sequenced, without introducing any fundamental incoherence into the essay. *The Buribunks* is as much a miscellany as it is a coherent whole. It juxtaposes different voices, styles and forms.

'Buribunkology as a science': the methodological target

The Buribunks begins by parroting the kinds of grandiose, sweeping claims often made in academic writing: 'It should be the ambition of every science to justify its existence through actual achievements and to ensure that an imposing body of work stands in the way of any subversive doubt regarding its potential as a science.'[17] The overblown confidence implied by the modifiers in this sentence ('any', 'actual', 'imposing') is deflated by the time the sentence concludes with expressions of barely veiled defensiveness ('any subversive doubt regarding its potential as a science'). A similar seesawing between inflation and vacuity marks the entire essay.[18]

C.S. encourages readers to read the essay ironically in other ways as well.[19] Twice, C.S. offers a logically flawed account of the relationship between academic study of the Buribunks and their existence outside of that study: 'it is self-evident that there would be no study of America if America had not been discovered, and no buribunkology if there were no buribunkologists,' C.S. writes.[20] The footnote at the end of this sentence doubles down on the point. Such reiterated confusion of presupposition with causation is a classic trope of 'pseudo-intellectual' or parroting anti-intellectual discourse,[21] here apparently presented self-consciously. C.S.'s reiteration of a flawed assertion in a footnote also communicates another characteristic fallacy of learned discourse: the confusion of quantity with quality. The text of the first section of *The Buribunks* also reiterates this scholarly mannerism via references to the 'more than 400,000 buribunkological dissertations'[22] in existence and the further institutional 'proof' of the Buribunks' existence in the form of weekly competitions resulting in prizes and grants.[23]

The upshot of these introductory remarks seems to be that academics create their own source material. But the circularity of intellectual work is not C.S.'s only formal target in this first part of the essay. *The Buribunks* also mocks the conventions of anticipating counter-arguments and claiming novelty for the

17 Chapter 2 of this volume, p 12.
18 See Schultz (2019), p 225
19 On Schmitt's reliance on irony more generally, see Manderson & Bikundo (2019), pp 189, 192.
20 Chapter 2 of this volume, p 12.
21 See Jacoby (2008), p 219.
22 Chapter 2 of this volume, p 13.
23 Chapter 2 of this volume, p 13.

approach presented: C.S. distinguishes buribunkology from 'scholasticism' and seems to align it with contemporary German academic neo-Hegelian vitalism,[24] concluding that 'it cannot be difficult for us to recognise the difference between today's buribunkology and obsolete scholasticism – it lies exactly in the essence, the spirit: buribunkology is alive, scholasticism is dead, the Buribunks live and the scholastics are long buried.'[25]

By the end of the short first section of *The Buribunks*, C.S. the methodologist appears exhausted, unable to sustain attention to fundamental distinctions in the essay's subject matter. The confusion of Buribunks and buribunkologists in the passage just quoted reappears in the next paragraph of the section, in which C. S. notes the similarities of the two groups: 'a similar spirit breathes life into both [buribunkology and Buribunkdom] and unites them in a harmonious marriage'.[26] The second footnote of the essay appears in this paragraph, only to introduce another referential confusion. The footnote chastises 'Schmitt' (mentioned nowhere else in the essay) for 'allowing himself [an] outright unbelievable statement' regarding the influence of Christianity on European culture. The footnote author (C.S.?) concludes: 'I reject this brazen statement in the strongest terms.'[27] If it were not already clear to readers that the essay is referentially complex, this footnote disorients readers into recognition of the essay's pervasive indirectness, if not its specific targets.

'The Buribunks': the sociological target

C.S.'s theoretical role has effectively consumed itself by the end of the methodological opening section of the essay. The second section of *The Buribunks* mimics not theoretical but sociological-historical writing.[28] This section of the essay has received much of the attention in other work on *The Buribunks*, perhaps because it is the longest part of the essay (longer than both of the other two sections combined) and the most clearly narrative. Instead of reviewing others' commentary fully here, I will just make a few brief observations.

This second section, like the essay as a whole, contains three distinct parts. The first two paragraphs of the section[29] suggest an anthropological model. The bulk of the section,[30] modelled on social-cultural history writing, discusses potential forebears of the Buribunks: Don Juan and Leporello, Ferker and Schnekke. And the last couple of pages present an ethnographic or sociological description of Buribunk society.[31] All three of these modes of academic

24 See Ringer (1963), pp 268, 402–3.
25 Chapter 2 of this volume, p 13.
26 Chapter 2 of this volume, p 13.
27 Chapter 2 of this volume, p 14 n 2.
28 See Ringer (1963), pp 169, 424.
29 Chapter 2 of this volume, p 14.
30 Chapter 2 of this volume, p 14–23.
31 Chapter 2 of this volume, pp 23–5.

discourse were subject to contestation, and still undergoing differentiation, in Schmitt's day.[32] C.S.'s amalgamation of these now more distinct discourses in the second part of *The Buribunks* mirrors this contemporary process of disciplinary individuation.

In the historical subsection of this part of the essay, Don Juan is a particularly interesting figure. Of the three proposed progenitors of the Buribunks, he is the only real (if fictional) figure. Don Juan was created by writing, but – unlike the Buribunks – not by his own writing, or by Schmitt's. Don Juan's status as a figure pre-existing C.S.'s essay, and thus in a way not belonging in the essay, is echoed by Don Juan's failure to keep his own diary and his resulting exclusion from full membership in the Buribunks' history. In this way, the 'historical' section of *The Buribunks* reiterates the themes of writing-into-being and its problematic circularity.

'Outline of a philosophy of **The Buribunks***': the manifesto target*

The third section of *The Buribunks*, sustaining these themes, opens with a mocking extrapolation of the discourse of Cartesian rationalism: 'I think, therefore I am; I speak, therefore I am; I write, therefore I am; I publish, therefore I am.'[33] This enactment of the discursive consequences of Descartes's self-founding assertion proposes the philosopher as an alternative founder of both academic professionalism and the Buribunks. In this way, the declaration repeats the suggestion of a kinship, if not an equivalency, between the two groups.

The balance of this final section of the essay moves beyond academic targets to mimic the discourse of the avant-garde. In the first few decades of the twentieth century, C.S. was not alone in mocking the discourse of modernism.[34] Several of the 'surreal' passages in the essay[35] channel this form of parodic discourse, mixing characteristics of the modernist avant-garde manifesto with a neo-Hegelian metaphysics: 'What do I write? I write myself. Who writes me? I myself write myself. What is the content of my writing? I write that I write myself. What is the big engine lifting me above this self-sufficient circle of I-ness? History!'[36]

This last section of the essay presents the Buribunks as having been written into existence and immerses us in their perspective, or the perspective of their representative. This perspective seems aligned not only with contemporary aesthetic discourse but also with the position of pure self-reference sought by many German intellectuals – both academic and otherwise – of the early

32 Ringer (1963), p 424.
33 Chapter 2 of this volume, p 25.
34 Diepeveen (2019), pp 63–79.
35 Bredekamp (1999), p 251 and n 15.
36 Chapter 2 of this volume, p 26.

twentieth century.[37] The tone of the closing section of the essay is playful, but like the earlier sections of the essay, these passages address a kind of discursive self-generation that seems to be flawed on its own terms, a symptom of a culture in chaotic disintegration. Read in this way, the essay as a whole hints that this cultural breakdown is a result of the self-absorption of writers who, in attempting to diagnose cultural malaise, have lost their distance from their surroundings as well as their own activity.

Traditions of anti-intellectual parroting

Like most parody, *The Buribunks* relies for its effect on its readers' awareness of 'targets' outside the text itself.[38] The essay alludes not just to early twentieth-century German discourses but also to traditions of parodic writing in Western culture. Two of these traditions will be the focus of this section.

Parody and anti-intellectualism

This essay has repeatedly characterised *The Buribunks* as a parody, and the previous section of the essay offered support for this characterisation. Parody typically 'seize[s] on particular aspects of a manner or a style and exaggerate[s] it to ludicrous effect', making the 'habit or mannerism … comically visible'.[39] Giorgio Agamben has described 'the two canonical features of parody' as 'the dependence on a preexistent model that is subsequently transformed from something serious into something comic, and the preservation of formal elements into which new and incongruous elements are introduced'.[40] Comprehension of a parodic text thus involves understanding not just its allusions to other texts or discourses (and especially their formal features), but also the parody's particular – often oppositional or critical, but sometimes playful – relation to those texts or discourses.

Parody is not inherently conservative or disruptive, but rather 'socially and politically multivalent.'[41] While some commentators argue that parody has an 'essentially subversive' effect, 'a strong alternative tradition … stresses the culturally conservative character of parody'.[42] On this view, 'parodies provide … a series of in-jokes … preserving a notion of the decorous or the "natural" by which the absurdities and extremities of writing can be measured'.[43]

37 Chapter 2 of this volume, p 27 n 13; see also Sauer (1972), pp 266, 283; Ringer (1963), pp 384–412.
38 See, for example, Diepeveen (2019) pp 78–9.
39 Dentith (2000), p 32.
40 Agamben (2007), p 39.
41 Dentith (2000), pp 19–20, 27–8.
42 Dentith (2000), pp 20, 25.
43 Dentith (2000), p 25.

To have either effect, a parodic text depends on its readers' recognition of the 'host' texts and on readers' willingness to entertain multiple attitudes toward those texts. Anti-academic or anti-intellectual parody, whether subversive or conservative in its aim, requires readers to both recognise the (formal) signs of academic discourse and to regard those signs as mere forms detachable from meaningful informational content. This kind of parody is almost as old as Western literary culture. The next two sections of this essay will focus on two traditions of particular relevance to *The Buribunks*: Menippean satire and the hoax.

Menippean satire and the anti-intellectual miscellany

In Chapter 14, Karen Schultz explores how *The Buribunks* mines and transforms traditions built on Latin verse satire.[44] The tradition of Menippean satire, in contrast, stems from Greek and Latin prose, especially that attributed to Lucian of Samosata (second century CE).[45] Often actually involving a 'mixture of prose and verse',[46] Menippean satire has always been characterised by formal variety rather than uniformity. It tends to target world-views or attitudes rather than specific individuals,[47] and traditionally has offered 'a learned parody of learning, or indeed a philosophical parody of philosophy, by means of a comic self-parodying mirror'.[48] Often produced by elites, Menippean satire has frequently taken aim at 'upstarts' or 'moderns' swimming against orthodoxy.[49]

Many esteemed works of European literature belong to the tradition of Menippean satire. Erasmus's *Praise of Folly* (1511), More's *Utopia* (1551) and Rabelais's *Gargantua* and *Pantagruel* (1532–64) are all classic and enduringly influential early modern Menippean satires.[50] Chapter 6 of *Pantagruel* (1532), for example, recounts 'How Pantagruel Met with a Limosin, Who Affected to Speak in Learned Phrase'.[51] Rabelais's 'Limosin' is reminiscent of the C.S. of

44 Schultz (2019).
45 For example, Gilmore (2018), pp 61, 83; Weinbrot (2005), pp 62–85.
46 Gilmore (2018), p 85.
47 See Lubrano (2019), p 175.
48 Dentith (2000), p 47. Goodrich (2004), p 410 offers a slightly different outline of Menippean satire in his history of satiric forms in Western legal scholarship; he characterises Menippean satire as fundamentally insurgent, rather than elitist. Still, the examples of Menippean-influenced satirical legal studies that Goodrich considers throughout his history were generated by authors with access to elite forums, even if those authors also used that access to provoke reconceptualisation of contemporary exclusionary hierarchies. Consistent with the account presented in this essay, Goodrich also acknowledges the kinship of Menippean satire with aesthetic avant-gardes since the nineteenth century: see Goodrich (2004), p 414 n 93.
49 Weinbrot (2005), pp 166–7, 223.
50 See Gilmore (2018), pp 83–5.
51 See Dentith (2000), p 79; see also Goodrich (2004), p 406, on the persistence of Rabelais's dice-throwing judge as a motif in legal scholarship.

the first section of *The Buribunks*, although Limosin is more blatantly pretentious in his translation of French words into 'quasi-Latin equivalents': 'We *transfretate* the *sequan* at the *dilucal* and *crepuscul*.'[52] *Gulliver's Travels* (1726) is a slightly later example of Menippean satire also influenced by Lucian and including some similar anti-intellectual targets, especially in Swift's account of the 'Academy of Lagado' in Part III.[53]

As these examples might suggest, Menippean satire is usually neither populist nor plain-spoken, despite its critique of learned discourse. John Gilmore has described 'one of the main problems of Menippean satire':

> Even [when] … it expresses sympathy with those who are not highly educated, it is very much a genre composed by intellectuals and dependent on verbal ingenuity and wordplay, literary allusions and the writers' assumption that their readers will appreciate in-jokes.[54]

Menippean satire 'can seem uncomfortably like a manifestation of intellectuals' disdain for those who do not share what they consider to be their superior education'.[55]

Although Menippean satire forms a recognisable tradition in Western literature, its target – learned discourse – has, of course, changed over the centuries. Menippean satire has had to change as well. Many contemporary instances of the tradition, for example, use media other than text; examples include the Monty Python films, online 'throwback' periodicals such as *McSweeney's* and many instances of contemporary political humour. *The Buribunks* falls somewhere between the magnum opus Menippean satires of early modern Europe and these more ephemeral forms. The essay flatters its readers' awareness of the discourse forms being parodied, as well as readers' implied critical distance from those forms. Despite its sharp tone, *The Buribunks* does not clearly offer a solution to the problems it identifies, and in this way too it is aligned with the classic 'severe' instances of Menippean satire.[56]

Around the time Schmitt's essay was published, the arts were experiencing a renovation we retrospectively call 'modernist'. Modernist art and its champions adopted several features of Menippean satire, such as generic mixing and a rejection of orthodoxies.[57] But in addition, works parodying the formal features of modernist discourse could become indistinguishable from their targets, and sometimes were apparently created with that effect in mind.[58]

52 Quoted in Dentith (2000), p 79.
53 See Gilmore (2018), p 101; Lubrano (2019), p 175.
54 Gilmore (2018), p 95; see also Goodrich (2004), p 411.
55 Gilmore (2018), p 98.
56 See Weinbrot (2005), pp. 17–18, 67, 85.
57 See Diepeveen (2019), pp 86, 109, 113, 134–6; see also Sauer (1972), pp 258, 266, 271, 283–4.
58 See Diepeveen (2019), p 78.

Hoaxes from the nineteenth century to the twentieth

A tradition of parasitic discourse distinct from parody – the hoax – was also flourishing around the time Schmitt produced *The Buribunks*. Hoaxes in the form of forgeries are certainly not a modern development, but the 'media hoax' addressed to a broad audience is arguably a product of the 'machine age' and its information technologies and structures.[59] *The Buribunks* participates in this modern hoax tradition in two ways: in its third section, the essay directly mimics a prominent contemporary hoax form, the faux avant-garde manifesto; in its overall structure, the essay may also be read as a commentary on the self-debunking qualities of Weimar-period German academic discourse, somewhat along the lines of Sokal's *Social Text* hoax.

Like parodies, hoaxes often highlight formal features of their target genres, but hoaxes usually mimic their targets less blatantly than parodies because a successful hoax requires readers *not* to recognise – at least not initially – that the hoax is mimicking another text. For a hoax to work as a hoax, its reader or viewer must initially be duped by the hoax into 'inhabit[ing] a different world from the world of a reader who "sees through" the hoax and reads it from a skeptic's perspective … [T]he whole raison d'être of the hoax is to embarrass its readership for its misapprehension of the "real" world.'[60] In this way, hoaxes arguably criticise their readers as much as they criticise any textual targets.[61] Still, the reader's position does change once the hoax is recognised or revealed. In the first phase of any hoax, there is only one 'insider', the author of the hoax. After the unveiling of the hoax, its attack is slightly blunted, but the circle of insiders is greatly expanded. A reader can at this point greet recognition of the trick with anger or laughter; laughter as a response 'can convert the shock of the experience to a reassertion of self-determination' by creating a 'gap' between the 'self that was duped and [the] … wiser self that can appreciate a good joke'[62] and belongs to a circle of knowing initiates.

Hoaxes of this kind probably originated in the eighteenth century. Jonathan Swift published a series of hoaxing letters and essays in 1708, and the *Oxford English Dictionary* dates the first use of the term 'hoax' to 1796.[63] The emergence of hoaxes in the industrialising West coincided with a proliferation of communicative technologies and institutional forms during the same period. Lynda Walsh has argued that nineteenth-century 'scientific hoaxes' (that is, journalistic pieces purporting to present non-existent scientific discoveries) 'could only occur in the … rhetorical opportunity … created when writers felt the need to interfere in the process of scientific truth becoming public truth'.[64]

59 Walsh (2006), p 220.
60 Walsh (2006), p 21.
61 Walsh (2006), pp 19–20.
62 Walsh (2006), p 167; see also p 119.
63 See Smith and Waugh (2019); Walsh (2006), pp 18, 220.
64 Walsh (2006), p 27; see also pp 31–2.

These hoaxes worked partly because their targets (popular journalistic accounts of actual scientific discoveries and advances) involved a specifically discursive partition of shared experience – as did the hoaxes themselves.

In Schmitt's day, hoaxes also targeted non-scientific discourses, including the aesthetic. In a recent book, Leonard Diepeveen has explained the emergence of a 'fraud discourse' in traditionalist criticism of modernist art. Critics using this discourse presented themselves as debunkers revealing the nonsensicality and pretentiousness of modernist art. Sometimes, such critics compared their efforts to the classic unveiling of a hoax, 'with the important difference that it is the intended *victims* [and not the creators of the hoax] who unveil modernism's fraud'.[65] Like Schmitt's essay and other anti-intellectual parody, this fraud discourse also included attacks on the spurious 'systems' underlying modernist art and criticism.[66]

A hoax seeks to convince its readers that 'no one could take not only itself, but the targeted work seriously'.[67] And it must scrupulously reproduce the formal features of its target in order to work. The hoax form has thus been naturally congenial to anti-intellectual messages. Alan Sokal's *Social Text* hoax illustrates both this congeniality and the limited shelf-life of hoaxes as such.[68] As a hoax, Sokal's essay points out the foibles of the *Social Text* editors and exposes them to ridicule. This aspect of the Sokal hoax criticised not academic discourse per se but a particular manifestation of it. The effectiveness of this attack, however, depended largely on Sokal's unveiling of the hoax; only this unveiling made clear the editors' gullibility and the vacuity of the targeted discourse. Arguably, Sokal's hoax then became a parody.[69]

Although it did not need unveiling, *The Buribunks* seems to be as much a part of this tradition as it is part of the tradition of Menippean satire. Much of Schmitt's mockery comes across as such, generating the 'frisson of pleasures and values shared between author and reader' that Diepeveen considers characteristic of modernist hoax-parody hybrids.[70] But – especially in its third section – *The Buribunks* also resembles classic media hoaxes in its attack on the broader, transhistorical phenomenon of mistaking discourse for reality. Even if we can recognise this attack as such today, it seems to have been aimed at targets very much of Schmitt's time. The writing of 'manifestos, demands, and plans' was widespread in German academia as well as in the aesthetic avant-garde at the time of Schmitt's writing.[71] Moreover, by the early 1920s, German academic discourse was moving towards a kind of 'escapis[m]' that could have made it –

65 Diepeveen (2019), p 13.
66 Diepeveen (2019), p 29; see also p 76.
67 Diepeveen (2019), p 75.
68 Sokal (1996).
69 See Walsh (2006), pp 236–7.
70 Diepeveen (2019), p 63.
71 Ringer (1963), p 309.

like Sokal's victims – a highly attractive parodic target in all its disciplinary manifestations.[72]

Contemporary anti-intellectual parroting

Anti-intellectualism might be an inevitable accompaniment of the presence of intellectuals in a culture. Learned discourse seems always to have had characteristics that attract mimicry and mockery: a set of quasi-ritualised formal features that (not unlike the similar formal signifiers of law) seek to stabilise an ambivalent relationship with social and physical power. The twenty-first century academy is no exception. It still occupies an uneasy social location, both too close to power and easily represented as ineffectual.[73]

Contemporary anti-intellectual discourse, like its earlier manifestations, appears in a variety of settings and forms. These settings include the US government and legal profession, as well as popular culture.[74] Elite-driven anti-intellectualism in the United States has often clothed the populist messages of more straightforward anti-intellectualism in the forms of academic-style discourse for the purpose of reallocating power within the elite. Anti-intellectual efforts along these lines are not always satirical or (by traditional definitions) hoaxing, but they do involve 'parroting' of the forms of traditional learning.

A number of recent studies, for example, have documented the long-term campaigns (largely but not exclusively based in the United States) to promote scepticism about scientific positions perceived as hostile to industry.[75] Steered by industrialists and 'market fundamentalist' politicians and figureheads, these campaigns have included the creation and funding of think tanks as well as 'newsletters, magazines, and journals – including journals with ostensible peer review – in which the results of industry-sponsored research could be reported, published, and then cited', producing 'a simulacrum of science, but not science itself'.[76] For more than a few audiences, these parroting products have, at least for the moment, discredited traditional scientific discourse – not by pointing out, even ironically, the elitism of that discourse, but by deploying the formal markers of such discourse as a vehicle for the authoritative presentation of disinformation.

Over the same period, a generations-long effort within the US legal academy and government has effectively shifted power from progressive to conservative lawyers and judges.[77] The so-called 'Powell Memo', drafted in 1971 for the US Chamber of Commerce by Lewis Powell (who was appointed to the US

72 Ringer (1963), p 403.
73 See, for example, Jacoby (2008), p xviii; see also pp 182, 242–78.
74 Jacoby (2008); Schlag (1996). On the American legal realists as Menippean satirists or cynics, see Goodrich (2004), pp 465–79.
75 See Oreskes and Conway (2019); Stahl (2016).
76 Oreskes and Conway (2019) p 244.
77 For example, Teles (2007).

Supreme Court soon thereafter), mapped out an ambitious, long-term plan for conservative promotion of pro-private enterprise principles in key US institutions, including the judiciary and academia.[78] The science simulacra described in the preceding paragraph are commonly regarded as one effect of the program Powell described. Legal academia and the judiciary experienced their own variant of this development between the 1980s and the 2010s, also consistent with Powell's program. In academic writing promoting such approaches as the economic analysis of legal policy, textualist approaches to statutory interpretation and constitutional originalism, conservative legal academics and judges such as Antonin Scalia and Richard Posner borrowed some of the formal markers of scholarly writing associated with the American legal realists' iconoclasm and the 'liberal consensus' that followed in mid-century. The borrowed features have included, for example, bold novelty claims, anti-establishment scepticism, critiques of orthodoxy and a preoccupation with quantification. Conservative academics adopted these forms to advance political, cultural and economic values quite different from those espoused by most of the realists and mid-century liberals.[79] The alternative legal discourse they created became a resource for like-minded scholars and aspiring public officials ready to populate public office when electoral results shifted their way.[80]

Peter Goodrich has demonstrated the possibility of reading some of the early conservative legal-academic products in this vein as satirical,[81] and indeed conservative rhetoric in US legal culture over the past half-century has depended heavily on its self-characterisation as insurgent and iconoclastic as well as restorationist. *The Buribunks* can be read as a document of elite-driven anti-intellectualism roughly in the vein of these more recent US legal-academic movements. Schmitt's essay, like these works, suggests the desirability of shifting institutional power away from those who have wrongfully come to occupy positions of academic prominence.

Anti-intellectualism in the twenty-first century is also taking other new forms – or at least forms to which our ancestors had no easy access. Both straightforward populist anti-intellectualism and anti-intellectual 'parroting' pervade contemporary electronic media. An example of such recent satirical 'parroting' in popular media is the Titania McGrath persona developed by comedian Andrew Doyle.[82] Doyle originally developed the persona as a Twitter account: McGrath was a vessel for absurdly hyperbolic mimicry of 'social justice warriors' and the 'woke'. McGrath's mockery is quite reminiscent of Sokal's and, in some ways, of Schmitt's. Her output mocks the solipsism of academic and aesthetic linguistic self-reference and self-creation,[83] revels in

78 See Stahl (2016), pp 59–63.
79 See, for example, Parker (2019).
80 See generally Stahl (2016); Teles (2007).
81 See Goodrich (2004) pp 434–54.
82 Smith and Waugh (2019); McGrath (2019).
83 For example, McGrath (2019), pp 3, 8, 17–18, 33, 37, 76, 87, 102–3, 104, 125, 130.

illogic and historical ignorance[84] and savages so-called elites while hypocritically presenting McGrath herself as a member of some ill-defined aesthetic avant-garde.[85]

Perhaps tellingly, however, the McGrath phenomenon does not seem poised to command lasting attention in the way Sokal's hoax did. Something has shifted since the 1990s. The shift has partly been due to technology, of course. The significance of 'publication' has fundamentally changed over the past several decades. Over the past generation, the glut of discursive material available to anyone with an Internet connection has yielded multiple parallel 'scholarly' traditions, marked as such mainly by superficial formal markers, and including those bad-faith traditions of science simulacra described above.[86] Thus the technological shift might also have ushered in a cultural shift: the more elite modes of 'parroting' described above have arguably diluted the comic and critical force of parody such as McGrath's, while also diluting the authority of the parroters' targets.

Shaken by economic, technological and political change, Weimar Germany was a similarly destabilising environment for intellectuals in particular.[87] *The Buribunks* can be read as an expression of that destabilisation. The relationship of the essay to its environment – perceived by contemporaries as chaotic to the point of ruin – might well explain some of the charm it has for us today. *The Buribunks* documents how the academic drive to order can be distorted into strange forms when it attempts to confront social and cultural upheaval. These forms, in turn, can attract mockery and derision as well as feverish appropriation, accelerating the discrediting of the discourse they were supposed to certify.

One lesson of *The Buribunks* for those committed to a viable academic culture concerns the importance of attention to the uses and misuses of formal markers of learning: the citation, the enumeration, the novelty claim and all the rest. This dimension of academic discourse might deserve more respect and study from mainstream academics and intellectuals than it tends to receive. To what extent is non-parodic intellectual discourse itself characterised by the parroting of formal markers at the expense of other values? A related lesson might be the inevitability of both parody and parroting of these formal markers of intellectual discourse. As this chapter has suggested, such recycling of the signs of intellectual discourse forms its own traditions, parallel to the traditions they imitate, and those parallel traditions might hold unique information about the shape of the learning they mirror and mock.

84 For example, McGrath (2019), pp 27, 28, 42, 61, 69, 83, 93, 115.
85 For example, McGrath (2019), pp 45, 100, 125, 133, 136, 148.
86 See Jacoby (2008), pp xi–xii, 219–31; Kaufman and Kaufman (2018).
87 See Ringer (1963), p 448.

References

Giorgio Agamben (2007) *Profanations* (trans Jeff Fort), Zone Books.

Friedrich Balke (2019) 'Carl Schmitt and Modernity', in Jens Meierhenrich and Oliver Simons (eds), *The Oxford Handbook of Carl Schmitt*, Oxford University Press, 629.

Horst Bredekamp (1999) 'From Walter Benjamin to Carl Schmitt, via Thomas Hobbes' (trans Melissa Thorson Hause and Jackson Bond), 25(2) *Critical Inquiry* 247.

Simon Dentith (2000) *Parody*, Routledge.

Jacques Derrida (1998) *Archive Fever: A Freudian Impression* (trans Eric Prenowitz), University of Chicago Press.

John Dewey (1910) 'Some Implications of Anti-Intellectualism' 7(18) *Journal of Philosophy, Psychology, & Scientific Methods* 477.

Leonard Diepeveen (2019) *Modernist Fraud: Hoax, Parody, Deception*, Oxford University Press.

John T. Gilmore (2018) *Satire*, Routledge.

Peter Goodrich (2004) 'Satirical Legal Studies: From the Legists to the "Lizard"' 103 *Michigan Law Review* 397.

Richard Hofstadter (1963) *Anti-Intellectualism in American Life*, Knopf.

Walter Houghton (1967) *The Victorian Frame of Mind: 1830–1870*, Yale University Press.

Susan Jacoby (2008) *The Age of American Unreason*, Pantheon.

Allison B. Kaufman and James C. Kaufman (eds) (2018) *Pseudoscience: The Conspiracy Against Science*, MIT Press.

G.D. Kiremidjian (1969) 'The Aesthetics of Parody' 28(2) *Journal of Aesthetics and Art Criticism* 231.

Vittorio Lubrano (2019) 'On the Normality of Writing: Inscription/Description of Everyday Life' 28 *Griffith Law Review* 173.

Desmond Manderson and Edwin Bikundo (2019) 'Forms of Irony in Carl Schmitt's Political Theology, The Buribunks, and Ex Captivitate Salvus' 28 *Griffith Law Review* 189.

Titania McGrath (2019) *Woke: A Guide to Social Justice*, Constable.

Naomi Oreskes and Erik M. Conway (2019) *Merchants of Doubt: How a Handful of Scientists Obscured the Truth on Issues from Tobacco Smoke to Climate Change* (rev ed), Bloomsbury.

Richard Parker (2019) 'The Faux Scholarship Foundations of the Regulatory Rollback Movement' 45 *Ecology Law Quarterly* 845.

Fritz K. Ringer (1963) *The Decline of the German Mandarins: The German Academic Community, 1890–1933*, Wesleyan University Press.

Francine Rochford (2019) 'Negative Space: The Paradox at the Heart of Buribunkology' 28 *Griffith Law Review* 247.

Wolfgang Sauer (1972) 'Weimar Culture: Experiments in Modernism' 39(2) *Social Research* 254.

Karen Schultz (2019) 'Schmitt's Satire in The Buribunks: Intertextual Links in Diary-Writing's Dystopia' 28 *Griffith Law Review* 206.

Pierre Schlag (1996) *Laying Down the Law: Mysticism, Fetishism, and the American Legal Mind*, New York University Press.

Adam J. Smith and Jo Waugh (2019) 'Titania McGrath: Twitter Parody of "Wokeness" Owes a Lot to Satirists of the 18th Century', *The Conversation*, 15 March, https://

theconversation.com/titania-mcgrath-twitter-parody-of-wokeness-owes-a-lot-to-satirists-of-the-18th-century-113312
Alan Sokal (1996) 'Transgressing the Boundaries: Toward a Transformative Hermeneutics of Quantum Gravity' 46/47 *Social Text* 217.
Alan Sokal (2010) *Beyond the Hoax: Science, Philosophy, and Culture*, Oxford University Press.
Jason Stahl (2016) *Right Moves: The Conservative Think Tank in American Political Culture Since 1945*, University of North Carolina Press.
Stephen Teles (2007) *The Rise of the Conservative Legal Movement: The Battle for Control of the Law*, Johns Hopkins University Press.
Kieran Tranter (2019) 'The Buribunks as Science Fiction: The Self and Informational Existence' 28 *Griffith Law Review* 118.
Lynda Walsh (2006) *Sins Against Science: The Scientific Media Hoaxes of Poe, Twain, and Others*, State University of New York Press.
Wouter G. Werner (2019) 'Buribunks and Foundational Paradoxes of International Law' 28 *Griffith Law Review* 259.
Howard Weinbrot (2005) *Menippean Satire Reconsidered: From Antiquity to the Eighteenth Century*, Johns Hopkins University Press.

Chapter 9

'Quantity turns into quality'

Breathing life into dead scholasticism

Francine Rochford

Introduction

The project of buribunkology has, as its essence, the process of diarisation – the consecration of every life-second 'on the altar in the light-filled temple of history'.[1] In this, the Buribunk records the unfolding of historical development, creating a 'homogeneous continuum',[2] demonstrating causal connections and contextualising incidents in their 'psychological, climatic, economic and sociological conditions'.[3] The *differentia specifica* noted in Schmitt's *The Buribunks* provide the 'historiographer' (if one may be allowed to use a scholarly term in reference to this most concrete of processes) with an outline of the 'big distinctive feature' of buribunkology. But why labour to provide this distinction? Are we not, in attempting to isolate the components of 'true' buribunkology, falling prey to the failures of scholarship and being lured into 'grey theories of speculation'?[4] Writing-as-action in buribunkology creates the record for the inquisition of futurity. The process of diarisation is not a futile indulgence, but an invitation to be read – or rather, it is a *demand* to be read. And if everyone is writing, who is reading? In this chapter, therefore, we will first consider the paradox of the unrequited gaze. The buribunkian orientation to the future is thwarted if the future is uninterested in considering, or unable to consider, the past because it is diarising the present. Second, we will consider the paradox of the loss of negative space in mature Buribunkdom – if everyone is recording, or diarising, the moment, who is experiencing that moment? Third, we will arrive at the conclusion to this conundrum – the inevitable march of history has provided the answer to the paradox in the enthusiastic adoption of oversight in the growing managerial classes. It is not for nothing that decades of investment in management theory and practice have resulted in tools of panoptic observation.

1 Chapter 2 of this volume, p 16.
2 Chapter 2 of this volume, p 17.
3 Chapter 2 of this volume, p 17.
4 Chapter 2 of this volume, p 14.

DOI: 10.4324/9781003091066-11

Next it is incumbent upon us to take a moment to consider the nature of facticity as a prerequisite to the activity of the Buribunks. Ferker's 'unflinching belief in nothing but the facts'[5] provides for us a fierce direction. But how are we preserve true records from the growing global library of recordings? Even in the individual diary of the most conscientious Buribunk, we can see an intermingling of the source stream of self-documentation with falsity. Perception is process, not product. This leads us to the current state of Buribunkdom and the millennial paradox – at the start of the new century, when we could argue that Buribunkdom has reached its inevitable zenith, are we instead experiencing an internal rot – a crisis of non-facticity? In this we do not mean, as one might think, the return of scholasticism or even speculation. Rather, what we are faced with is the good faith recording of *falsity* as *fact*. Fortunately, once again the march of history has provided us with the answer to this apparent conundrum. In the process of encoding, managerial direction can *convert* falsity into fact. There is no need to maintain the unnecessary distinction between falsity and fact; one may simply alter the conceptual parameters of the inquiry.

To illustrate the processes by which Buribunkdom has come to dominate the *Lebenswelt*, this analysis will focus most particularly on the university. The traditionalist may cavil at the adoption of the university as the modern manifestation of Buribunkdom in its mature form, given the great Schnekke's 'strong feeling of commonality'.[6] In fact, nothing is more natural than the gradual acceptance by the managerial classes of the university of the benefits of buribunkology and the adoption of 'indistinctive generality … a uniform lack of colour'[7] by the modern university. Once the practical disciplines of commerce, management and economics gained a foothold in the hitherto hidebound academy, the 'life-opposing'[8] spirit of the university was reformed. The modern university is an enlivened, thoroughly buribunkian institution, whose aim is to direct and store a solid mass of diarised moments, now triumphantly stable evidence of the passing of otherwise turgid lives. In universities we have a true 'realm of Buribunkdom'.[9]

The paradox of the unrequited gaze

The natural instinct is to begin with the process of writing. However, the essence of diarisation in buribunkology is that it is an invitation to read. Or rather, it is a demand to be read. In these final, mature stages of buribunkology, where everyone is writing, who is reading? If everyone is an author in everybody's diary, who is the audience? Is Foucault's account of the individualisation

5 Chapter 2 of this volume, p 21.
6 Chapter 2 of this volume, p 23.
7 Chapter 2 of this volume, p 23.
8 Chapter 2 of this volume, p 13.
9 Chapter 2 of this volume, p 19.

of authorship as a 'privileged moment'[10] time-stamped? Is authorship/readership now a collective, and diarisation a socialised event? Was 'intertextuality'[11] merely the precursor to the shared life, so that every autobiographical moment is simultaneously a biographical moment? A more compelling view is that we are seeing an 'evolution' of buribunkology. Every diarist is simultaneously an agent and reagent – both a voyeur of and sojourner in the lives of others. For life, *esse*, is now so much of a simultaneous looking into and reporting on the lives of others, and those others peering back, that there can no longer be said to be a purely autobiographical moment. Indeed, intertextuality itself has evolved. In the modern era:

> Texts on the computer monitors are said to be completely hyper textual links, that is, connections of combination that arrange texts as part of a simultaneous virtual network to constantly changing current textual formation which allows the processing of pictures, graphics. Even moving pictures and film on the same textual level could be a good example of this explanation because the system affords us opportunity to read texts, watch motion pictures, listen to audio reports, and even chat online.[12]

Moreover, we can consider more closely what it means to be 'read'. Perhaps, in making a demand to be 'read', all that is really required is that we be 'recorded'? A close analysis of Schmitt's account of buribunkology demonstrates that although the Buribunk may write with a latent view that what is written will be read, in fact reading does not bear a central place in the movement. It is sufficient that the moment is entered into history, and becomes 'historically present, in its concrete factual actuality and positivity'.[13] As we shall see *infra*, the modern diary is more likely, in fact, to be read – if, by reading, we can count those processes of coding, cross-indexing, referencing and linking as the modern manifestations of the verb 'to read'. As we know, the modern academic will write countless thousands of words with no expectation of being read,[14] but will still appear in indices, searches, databases and other encodings. We can put to rest the idea that 'reading' is a necessary corollary to the process of 'writing'.

Negative space in Buribunkdom

The concept of negative space in relation to Buribunkdom has two manifestations. One arises from the project itself; the cinematic attitude requires the

10 Foucault (1977), p 115.
11 Kristeva (1986).
12 Shakib (2013), p 4.
13 Chapter 2 of this volume, p 14.
14 Eveleth (2014); Evans (2008).

cinema audience. The 'negative space' is the passive optic into which the recorded word or image is projected. If viewed passively, the recorded word or image can only be diarised in retrospect. For the period – short or long – during which the diary is 'consumed', the Buribunk in the audience is not keeping a diary – thus breaking the cardinal rule of Buribunkdom. The second manifestation of negative space is the eventual inevitable loss of the active moment – the unrecorded space in which action *sans* word occurs. Without this primal space, the writings of the Buribunk diminish from experience into theory. This is the characteristic of scholarship, so cogently and accurately derided by Schmitt.

In answer to the first dimension of our paradox, we must look at the realities of modern diarisation. While possibilities of interaction inherent in the modern Buribunk deliver a significant challenge to authentic Buribunkdom, we can answer this challenge with the courageous assertion that the possibilities of modern diarisation are, in fact, a realisation of the essence of buribunkology. Simultaneously, we will see the resolution of several threads of analysis. We see that modern diarisation can create an *interactive* artefact.

But first we have to resolve the problem of the authorship. To state the problem inherent in modern buribunkology: how can it be said that the diarist is recording their lives for posterity when the authorial voice is a cacophony of action, reaction and interaction? As we observe the downcast eyes of the texter, the blogger, the Instagrammer, the Snapchatter, or the emailer, we can see the new architecture of the collective diary – Buribunkdom made manifest on a societal scale. This is a challenge for traditionalists looking for the single authorial voice – the diary as the projection of the 'I'. This process involves the I 'projecting itself into a tangible "You-World" [and streaming] back into the "World-I" with powerful rhythm, the highest harmony is reached through the absolute devotion of all powers to the inner self and its identity'.[15] Traditionalists, however, cannot avoid the march of history. Buribunkology is scientific fact – observed history – and the modern diarist is activated by the same World-Spirit as the great Schnekke. How do we deal with the example of Schnekke's 'distinct originality, his I which resonates in extreme autonomy'?[16] Does the interaction of the modern diarist remove it from the realms of Buribunkdom? Again, a resounding 'no' must follow this question! Schnekke's own 'strong feeling of commonality and ... universal instinct' mandate that we accept that 'I' is not the *esse* of 'diary'. The individual is a single cell of the 'collective organism'; the large-scale manifestation of the early surveys into the buribunkian form.

We are seeing neither Barthes's[17] *death* of the author nor the 'death of the reader'. We are experiencing the *rapprochement* of word and act, text and intertext, 'I' and 'we'. Barthes's now commonplace insight is that:

15 Chapter 2 of this volume, p 22.
16 Chapter 2 of this volume, p 23.
17 Barthes (1981).

> Any text is a new tissue of past citations. Bits of code, formulae, rhythmic models, fragments of social languages, etc. pass into the text and are redistributed within it, for there is always language before and around the text. Intertextuality, the condition of any text whatsoever, cannot, of course, be reduced to a problem of sources or influences; the intertext is a general field of anonymous formulae whose origin can scarcely ever be located; of unconscious or automatic quotations, given without quotation marks.[18]

Barthes's vision of the text as the product of the primordial swamp of generations of unconscious and preconscious iteration perfectly describes the intertemporal intertextuality of modern diarisation – a process of externalising intertextuality. The internet meme and the Facebook timeline post simultaneously draw upon the profane, the liturgical, the literary and the commercial heritage. They may draw upon both Shakespeare's novel vocabulary and a vibrant new vocabulary (relevantly topped by 'nomophobia', or the anxiety arising as a result of the lack of a phone)[19] without distinction. Intertextuality is an artefact in itself.

The touching devotion of the millennial and post-millennial to the process of diarisation is evidenced by their commitment to the constancy of posts, so they become a conscious stream. While psychologists recommend that people become more 'present' in their own lives,[20] they are undervaluing the process of constant diarisation, which is simultaneously reaching into the past for the indulgence of the future. A matter for another chapter or article is the reported loss of transactive memory as a result of reliance on constant engagement and interaction, but the existence of diary-record renders such a memory unnecessary. The 'common' diary both forms and informs the individual diary, just as the 'library matrix' is both 'a reference space for reading texts [and] a point of origin for works of literature'.[21] In our common diary, constantly replenished with comment, reply and counter-reply, we see history drawn into the present, and combined with immediate futurity. Diary becomes cosmos.

So what of our second problem – the problem of the action *sans* word? To a degree, this issue is defused by the simultaneity of modern media. If we accept that buribunkology has achieved its mature form – that of an intertextual, interactive collective diarisation – the action and the 'word' or recording of the action are simultaneous. The reader, or audience, is simultaneously the diarist. It is sufficient to leave that thought, as it is self-evident upon the most momentary reflection.

18 Barthes (1981), p 39.
19 Elmore (2014).
20 Atkinson and Hardey (2018).
21 Shakib (2013), p 4.

Heightened self-awareness and the great life

But we cannot leave the traditionalist view of buribunkology without considering the question of true consciousness. Is the 'phone zombie' a true Buribunk? What is the distinguishing mark of 'pure' buribunkology? When is a diary not a diary? We can see in Schmitt's careful analysis of Leporello's recording of the activities of Don Juan that it is not enough to consume experience without participation – or, rather, the recording of vicarious experience is not sufficient to be true Buribunkdom. Leporello 'lacks awareness of the writer's higher consciousness'.[22] He is not an 'independent writing personality'. In due course, Schmitt then castigates the meditations of Marcus Aurelius and the Confessions of Saint Augustine as 'sinking into decadence'.[23] The consolations of religion and philosophical self-denial move too far from reality to represent 'true' Buribunkdom. Applying this restriction *mutis mutandis* to the great number of later diary-writers, we find ourselves in an embarrassing position. Shall we be constrained to consider the recording of steps walked, calories consumed and six-minute work intervals as the only factual entries for the delight of our (auto)biographer?

Allow me to explain. In every writing there is so much of ideology in every tracing of cause to effect that a true Ferkian would be unable to recognise the point at which a true record of experience ends and the falsity of extrapolation and speculation begins. Moreover, a diarist with Ferkian discipline cannot rationally *experience* without simultaneously *diarising about experience* – thus creating a recursive spiral. Significantly, the heightened self-awareness required for *true* buribunkology is a process of selection and curation. Kuhn notes that 'narratives of identity are shaped as much by what is left out of the account – whether forgotten or repressed – as by what is actually told'.[24] Every recording of an event involves selection, organisation and excision and (perhaps) reordering. Kondo[25] cites the term 'self-interrogation' to describe the process of selection in 'tidying up', and Cardell applies this to the process of diarisation. She notes that

> 'making memories' is not simply a process of recuperating and preserving symbolic objects of the past, but is a future-orientated practice that positions the subject in a particular way. It provides an opportunity for self-conscious as well as discursive constructions of self as part of a process of editing and crafting a deliberate, intentional representation.[26]

22 Chapter 2 of this volume, p 17.
23 Chapter 2 of this volume, p 18.
24 Kuhn (2002), p 2.
25 Kondo (2016).
26 Cardell (2017), p 500.

If we return to the essence of true buribunkian observance, that 'spiritual region where the synthesis of … numerous contradictory elements' of 'contemporary religiosity', 'positivism and [nothing but the] facts'[27] exist, we can see that *externalisation* through publication as an object of creativity *necessarily involves* selection. However, that selection cannot abjure the ugly, perverted or deranged in our personality. It is not the process of *selection* per se that lures the diarist into the realms of speculation and false consciousness; rather, it is the rationale for selection. Do we curate in order to hide our intellectual or spiritual struggles, or do we curate to resolve them?

In this, the modern Buribunk has an advantage over less enlightened diarists. The labours of Schnekke to approach the *ideal* (if I may [mis]use the word) of buribunkology have borne fruit in the modern conditions for successful buribunkology – the 'harmonious perfection of buribunkian cosmos'.[28] The commonality and universality of the 'internet' are marked by both the autonomy of the diarist (with some exceptions) and the sacrificial intent to lay each individual open to the scrutiny of history. The 'world-changing idea of the modern corporation for human intellectual activity'[29] has, in the internet, achieved an unanticipated scope. More importantly, we see in the modern internet the progress towards 'leaving moral ideals behind'[30] that could only have been dreamt of in the early stages of Buribunkdom.

For the resolution of intellectual and spiritual struggles has become pleasingly (comparatively) acceptable. It has also provided a sort of training ground or apprenticeship for those approaching true Buribunkdom. The 'web log' or 'blog'[31] combines Schnekkian immediacy with a culture of openness and acceptance of the principle of amorality – at least in the traditional sense. Blogs are deployed with various curatorial approaches, ranging from the hesitant 'commentary' merely reporting on matters of interest to the 'blog as personal revelation'.[32] While even the most confessional blog will 'calibrate' content according to readership, with the example and training provided by the most experienced Buribunks, the constraints and self-censorship arising from archaic morality and its resultant internalised shame reaction fall away. The millennial blogger is an example to us all – exposing every life-second to the 'light-filled temple of history',[33] and the blog environment shows how far millennials have advanced from the (clearly traumatic) final days of Ferker, whose failure to disclose his shameful marriage demonstrates an unresolved neuropathology. A modern blogger has, by contrast 'a place to "shout," or express themselves by writing to an audience … [providing] both outlet and stimulus for working

27 Chapter 2 of this volume, p 21.
28 Chapter 2 of this volume, p 23.
29 Chapter 2 of this volume, p 21.
30 Chapter 2 of this volume, p 21.
31 Chen and He (2009).
32 Nardi et al. (2004).
33 Chapter 2 of this volume, p 16.

through personal issues. A blog often serves as a relief valve, a place to "get closure in writing".'[34]

In this estimable openness, the modern Buribunk casts off the thought of negative judgement in posterity and stares wide-eyed into the glare of futurity, facing off the triviality of false morality. The courage of the Buribunk spurs others into openness, as the 'knowledge sharing' beliefs of bloggers intersect with the 'reciprocal benefits' of the blog community.[35] In this motivation, we see the egoistic outcome of a modern society, untrammelled by archaic ritualised morality. Instead, we have an entirely transactional process – the true basis for the 'progress of humankind [which] can only be expected when everyone only thinks of themselves and lets everything else run its own course'.[36] The principle of voluntary exchange is the perfect process for the spread of buribunkology, and this is elegantly described in the reciprocity of the web blog. The 'ungovernability'[37] of the internet perfectly aligns with the 'run its own course'[38] ethic of buribunkology, despite regressive attempts to reverse this position.[39]

The blog-writer uses the writing medium, acknowledging buribunkian forebears. The modern buribunkian has even greater potential in other forms of recording. The potential of 'live-streaming', in particular, on the one hand *records* every moment of every day, and on the other creates the potential to actually have something interesting to record. More importantly, one can also see the effects of simultaneous recording and promulgation of the eventful diary. The escalation of the requirement of recordability – that is, having something interesting to record in the form of, say, base jumping, or engaging in parkour in a derelict building, is oddly juxtaposed with the uneventful but heavily subscribed videos of teenagers applying makeup or brushing their hair. The application of data analytics to the diarist creates a curious and self-reflexive phenomenon: the diarist, encouraged by the feedback of others, is prompted to escalate the behaviour that resulted in that feedback. We see *more of* everything – and nothing.

Facing the millennial paradox

The millennial paradox is the acute consciousness of 'embeddedness in the historical'.[40] The 'contemporary religiosity'[41] is created through the continuous projection of the self in the present for the future. Schmitt's description of

34 Nardi et al. (2004), p 44.
35 Hsu and Lin (2008).
36 Chapter 2 of this volume, p 21.
37 Weiser (2009).
38 Chapter 2 of this volume, p 21.
39 Downes (2018).
40 Chapter 2 of this volume, p 12.
41 Chapter 2 of this volume, p 21.

'pulsating projection of the "I" into the "You-World"'[42] is inescapably referable to the phenomenon of posting and re-posting all – even the most mundane aspects – of the inner self. The diarisation of each moment and voluntary submission of each entry to the World Wide Web is almost ubiquitous. Categorisation and cross-categorisation of each entry are virtually instantaneous, with the replacement of the card catalogue with the more efficient algorithmic device. It is evident that Buribunkdom has reached its zenith – a more mature and advanced form than even that described by Schmitt as represented by 'depictions of one another in photographs and films, constant traffic of diary exchanges [and] readings from diaries.'[43] As optimistic as Schmitt appeared in 1918 about the state of Buribunkdom, the limitations of silent movies and the temporal challenges of letter-writing could not hope to approach the capacities of modern video and instantaneous messaging. Twitter and Facebook have elevated the written and static diarisation process, and You Tube recording as a form of projection has itself become redundant. Twitch, YouTube Live and Periscope are some of the many (and increasing number of) livestreaming platforms enabling instantaneous recording and viewing of the virtual diary of the diarist.[44]

It is clear that, in the modern diarist, we can see the absolute manifestation of the Ferkian view that 'the progress of humankind can only be expected when everyone only thinks of themselves and lets everything else run its own course'.[45] The radical self-absorption of the millennial and post-millennial and the constant self-recording and posting of even the most mundane event create the highest form of self-reflection. The highest form, the 'Cam Girl',[46] is personified by 'JenniCam', the lifecam feed of Jennifer Ringley, which streamed from 1996 – or perhaps Danni Ashe's more 'pornographic' and arguably earlier equivalent.[47] Although theorists argue that there is a gendered dimension to the Cam Girl, and a lack of distance that 'threaten[s] to overwhelm the subject, to lead [the male viewer] to consume the object',[48] we must recall that the buribunkian eschews the theoretical and instead remember the injunction that the diarist thinks only of [her]self. That commentary takes its own course is well-understood in a millennial's interaction with the internet environment. The willingness of a netizen to invite satirical insult,[49] for example, is a demonstration that 'humour on social media is a hallmark of participatory culture; social media platforms promote public (humorous) interactions, in which practically everybody can not only receive but also produce online multimodal

42 Chapter 2 of this volume, p 22.
43 Chapter 2 of this volume, p 24.
44 Brown (2020).
45 Chapter 2 of this volume, p 21.
46 See, for instance, White (2003).
47 White (2003).
48 White (2003), p 21.
49 r\RoastMe, www.reddit.com/r/RoastMe

messages'.[50] More importantly, it is a demonstration that a communication on social media conveys to the recipient (who may be anywhere in the world) the agency to respond – a symbolic handing over of the 'conch'.[51] From that point, the conversation – the interactive diary-in-common – runs its course.

Finally, is diarisation a sufficiently distinctive feature to enrol the scores of diarists into the 'united front of buribunkologists'?[52] What, as Schmitt asks, is the *differentia specifica*? Are Twitchers and You Tubers the modern equivalent of Don Juan, with no interest in the past and as little in the future? I think not. In the attitude of the modern diarists we see the 'urge to preserve every single second of [their] own being for history: the creating and viewing of [themselves] as a monument'.[53] Twitchers and YouTubers, it could be said, have the 'buribunkian cinematic attitude'.[54] In the modern livestreamer, we see the fullest development of conscious archiving for the future.

The managerial gift: panoptic observation

Let us move from the ephemeral interactivity of the online environment to the solid insularity of the university. The university, so satisfied in a self-designated mission to carry the torch of knowledge into the future, has failed to adapt – until recently. With belated urgency, universities are subscribing to the Buribunk project. Scholars, rather than engaging in 'obsolete scholasticism',[55] must now find attitudes and mechanisms for engagement with contemporary communities. Whether this is the natural outcome of the increasing centrality of diarisation in the millennial Weltanschauung or the 'unstoppably forward-moving World Spirit'[56] that has overtaken academia, buribunkology has, by its 'secret weaving of the spirit',[57] enlivened the university. Through the controlling medium of university bureaucracy, academic scholarship has developed into a process resembling continuous diarisation. It is now important to revisit the role of consciousness in mature buribunkology and determine whether Ferker's early anti-intellectualism could not be wholly put aside and, *sine ira et studio*, academic discourse – even theory – be discovered as a new form of diarisation.

Few spheres can be said to have reached the level of unconscious buribunkology than the modern university. In no other space has the truth of the Hegelian insight that 'quantity turns into quality'[58] become more evident.

50 Dynel and Poppi (2019), pp 1–2.
51 Golding (1954).
52 Chapter 2 of this volume, p 14.
53 Chapter 2 of this volume, p 16.
54 Chapter 2 of this volume, p 16.
55 Chapter 2 of this volume, p 13.
56 Chapter 2 of this volume, p 13.
57 Chapter 2 of this volume, p 13.
58 Chapter 2 of this volume, p 12.

Commonly derided as encouraging a 'publish or perish' approach to intellectual activity,[59] the university has enabled a shift from the 'dead, life-opposing, formulaic mud of scholasticism' so derided in Schmitt's manifesto. Instead, the work of academia – even the most turgid scholarly text – is lifted into the ranks of buribunkology by the meticulous enumeration of the active moment – the 'diarisation' of academic life. Indeed, scholars are now pre-emptively required to allocate time to future output and are then audited and measured on the results. No doubt these strictures were necessary to draw the recumbent ranks of academics into the project and will be allowed to fall away as academics realise the self-evident value of the great life. At present we can only congratulate the prescience of the administrators of universities who can see the benefits of diarisation to the future.

Consider the measures taken by university bureaucracies to lift tedious scholarship to the standards of Buribunkdom – by requiring the scholar to be prostate before posterity:

> Academics can expect their publication output to be scrutinized annually during performance management reviews as a key indicator of job performance. Ramsden (1994) highlights the absolute necessity of prior publication if academics are to be successful in obtaining competitive research grants (which are another key performance and funding criterion). Creamer (1998) notes the use of publication productivity as an index of institutional or departmental prestige. Clearly it is in the best interests of both university employers and employees for staff to be publishing, and publishing often.[60]

Of course, this is not the only innovation that has drawn the scholar into Buribunkdom. Academic engagement is required of the previously cloistered scholar.[61] Academic engagement, involving the transfer of knowledge, is particularly demonstrated by the less hidebound universities, as 'faculty support for university–industry interaction is negatively influenced by the age of their university'.[62] The use of social media by academics to assist with teaching can potentially be regarded as a form of diarisation – both from the perspective of the student and that of the academic.[63] Stoner suggests that, 'There is a slow but steadily growing acceptance that social media effectively amplifies institutional communications'.[64] The use of social media invites the true essence of the Buribunk: 'through writing he gains the viewpoint of the absolute, understanding everything and also himself in his relativity'.[65] For the modern

59 McGrail, Rickard and Jones (2006).
60 McGrail, Rickard and Jones (2006), p 33.
61 Perkmann et al. (2013).
62 Perkmann et al. (2013), p 427.
63 Wilson (2013).
64 Stoner (2012).
65 Chapter 2 of this volume, p 28.

university, throwing off its other-worldly preoccupations, there is the recognition that 'social media, especially online social networking, are about revealing aspects of the self, whether authentic or counterfeit. Self-disclosure on Facebook, for example, can be communicated with irony, contain playful misrepresentations, or be characterized by earnestness.'[66] What could possibly go wrong with such a process? The great juggernaut of diarisation, now firmly established in society, is gaining ascendancy in academia and, in the process, stripping away the 'unworldliness'[67] from the academic form. The final, inevitable result of buribunkology is the democratisation of knowledge.

Adapting and adopting the insights of accounting

It is in the rituals and practices of accounting that we see the acceleration of the academic shift into accounting. Here we move our attention to an intertemporal analysis of diarisation pre-dating, but not pre-empting, the great Ferker. In the accounting traditions of the Benedictine monasteries we see an ironic mingling of facticity with superstition – ironic not only in the juxtaposition of the two, but also in the influence the *Regula Benedicti* and its sophisticated system of record-keeping has had upon the socialisation of the individual into the process of diarisation. Of course, the contribution of the Church to the ordering of the day cannot be understated. The observance of the canonical hours, together with appurtenances such as bells, signalling the call to duty, all pre-empt the type of ordered recording we see in diarisation. The ornament and idolatry of the ancient *Book of Hours* acted as an impressive tool for socialisation of the laity[68] into the technique of accounting for temporal units. The *Book of Hours* 'was to the laity what the breviary was to the clergy: a compendium of prayers mostly to be read at the eight canonical hours of the day'.[69] The influence of 'the affluent international elite – rulers, princes, and courtiers, high members of the clergy, and well-to-do merchants'[70] – is also evident in the creation of an example to the common people; Jeanne d'Évreux, Queen of France, and Queen Isabel of Spain possessed elaborate manuscripts guiding their devotions: 'the book of hours was the single most commonly produced book of the late middle ages.'[71] Through devices such as the ordered call to devotion and the creation of bespoke illustrated and illuminated devotional texts, discipline was attributed to temporal observance. Once this discipline had been introduced, it became a simple matter to, conversely, require ex post facto recording of the passage of time. Of course, the insights of Angelo Pietra in *Indirizza degri*

66 Martínez-Alemán (2014), p 16.
67 Chapter 2 of this volume, p 15.
68 Donovan (1991), p 27.
69 De Winter (1981), p 350.
70 De Winter (1981), p 342.
71 Reinburg (2012), p 20.

Economi [72] and the later work on double entry accounting in the Jesuit tradition by Ludovico Flori in 1636, *Trattato del modo di tenere il libro doppio domestico col suo esemplare,* [73] did not immediately align with the insights of Buribunkdom, but the kernel of truth was contained even in the language of the accounting discipline: the journal entry is a central concept in double entry accounting and through the conscientious application of the discipline of accounting a clear record is kept into the future. It is a happy coincidence that the prosecution of the disciplines of one technique will advance the disciplines of the other.

During the last decades of the twentieth century, the fusion of these traditions became inevitable due to the concentrated advances enabled by the disintegration of the private realm. Once the economies of the public have been applied to private activities (which then cease to be private), it is a simple matter to align the techniques of performance. The contribution of modernity is the capacity to simultaneously *do* and *diarise.* In production systems, transactions are monitored through various stages of production. In traditional employment, the individual is monitored and the results of that monitoring are recorded. In primitive manifestations, this may have occurred through physical oversight, requiring a managerial presence enabled in power and control by some equivalent of the 'invisible omnipresence'[74] of the panopticon.[75] As 'human resource management' systems take the benefits of modernity, the process of monitoring becomes simultaneously a process of recording. Workload allocation requires that a value be assigned to activity, the activity be recorded and then monitored as part of the process of maximising staff workload and thus minimising costs. The *Book of Hours* has evolved into the recording of work according to systematised uniform coding in specific time intervals. In place of the ornate illuminated passages, we have the elegant algorithm that apportions value. Billable hours record the meditations of professionals to the great capitalist world spirit. Short letters, telephone calls, client interviews – all are coded and recorded in a timesheet either manually, through 'automatic push-button devices designed to catch every working minute'[76] or even voice-based billing systems.[77]

In the university, we can see how the insights of business have been applied to academic workload to enable this crucial step towards Buribunkdom. As Graham notes, 'this is a legacy of the "audit explosion" …[through] which business models had been brought into the public sector during the 1980s and 1990s'.[78] The techniques of 'New Public Management', applied to the

72 Prieto et al. (2006), p 221.
73 Prieto et al. (2006), p 223.
74 Galič, Timan and Koops (2017), p 12.
75 Bentham (2010).
76 Darby (1978), p 39.
77 Ranjith et al. (2019).
78 Graham (2016), p 1052.

university, finally bring practicality to the dirge of academic life. An increasing 'specification of practice'[79] enables encoding into a systematic 'account of quantifiable performance'.[80] Through these mechanisms, a pre-emptive diarisation through encoding of individual activities occurs. Of course, the greatest benefit of this process is achieved through automation. Without automation, we would inevitably fall into the trap of the unrecorded moment. Automation, the 'administrative megatrend',[81] not only facilitates audit but also delivers additional impetus to the processes necessary for ongoing, consistent diarisation – numerical diarisation, encoding, recording, audit and storage. It is through this alone that we can deliver the promise of buribunkology. We see in this the magnificent mundanity of the encoding of the human workday. In this way, the various manifestations of university, ably steered by the market state, contains and transmits the very 'harmonious perfection of a buribunkian cosmos'.[82]

Modern sociological and technological advances have affected even that great academic vanity, the 'research' or publication component of the academic workload. Universities can now deploy the full 'range of control instruments of HR management, standardization of performance indicators and performance reviews, time management, workload management plans and other information systems regarding staff performance',[83] and can take advantage of 'NPM tools such as performance agreements and monitoring procedures'.[84] To be clear, these tools are buribunkology manifest. They ally the academic to the diarisation of every activity. Through automatic encoding, the activities can be preserved, audited and stored.

We may address at this point a parallel question: Is Buribunkdom capable of flourishing without the menial ministrations of the refuseniks? While the manifesto is attentive to the inevitable natural elimination of the refusenik, the traditional buribunkian schema fails to fully prosecute the idea. The refusenik who, with 'merciless inevitability … ceases to exist'[85] in the only way that matters, is in fact a necessary element of even mature Buribunkdom; yet

> No eye sees him, no ear hears him, and may his lament be ever so harrowing and drive him into madness, the iron law does not know mercy against the unworthy one who has excluded himself, in the same way as the fundamental laws of natural selection know no exception.[86]

79 Graham (2016), p 1056.
80 Ranson (2003), p 470.
81 Hood (1991); Graham (2016), p 1056.
82 Chapter 2 of this volume, p 23.
83 Leišyté (2016), p 830.
84 Leišyté (2016), p 836.
85 Chapter 2 of this volume, p 25.
86 Chapter 2 of this volume, p 25.

How do we visualise buribunkian society after the decline and eventual withering away of the refusenik class? One can imagine a vanishingly small proportion of the population who would willingly 'vanish' into obscurity. The anti-social, like the poor, will always with us.[87] But this is a small group, and the likely decline in the ranks of the *refusenik* leaves in its wake a serious threat to the state. If the attitudes and ethics of Buribunkdom will be soon absorbed in the womb, the maintenance of the 'external conditions' for the Buribunks to undertake their diarisation will be at risk. Already, 'knowledge workers' are beginning to outnumber those producing food or working in manual occupations.[88] Are the swelling ranks of the Buribunks, paradoxically, the death knell of buribunkology? We see the answer to this question in technology. Automation will provide simultaneous encoding, recording, audit and storage. We are, indeed, in peak Buribunkdom. The computer will take the role of the refusenik.

Resolving the crisis of non-facticity

Finally, how is the modern Buribunk ensuring facticity? As we have seen, the heightened self-awareness required for *true* buribunkology is a process of selection and curation. This can lead us to the charge that in selection and curation we have moved from absolute truthfulness – that there is no possibility of maintaining facticity. If we are resolute about the principle of 'nothing but the facts',[89] we can see the problem of the individual diary as a source of facts. The 'curation' of facts according to the preferred view of the author results in countless sources of error, deliberate and inadvertent. Indeed, even in the transmission of images between the retina and the brain there is fiction. Diarisation, moreover, is recollection, and recollection is reprocessing in intentional or unintentional glamours. The fictional but illuminating Binarily Augmented Retro Framing (BARF)[90] encapsulates the issue. We can readily comprehend the creation of the false recollection – and question the authenticity of our own memories.

The inevitable manifestation of modern Buribunkdom makes us easy on both of these points. As to the first, it has become clear that whatever tedious task is required for the maintenance of a mature Buribunk society, it can be incorporated into a simultaneous conscious diarisation. Even now, surveillance is integrated and reworked into intertextual diaries. As to the second, where the author is part of a reflexive community of diarists, the complex cross-referential archive triangulates each version of truth – each point of view. In this way, we

87 Matthew (26:11). The contested authorship of the Biblical texts may, perhaps, represent a primitive form of interactive Buribunkdom?
88 See, for instance, Yingshuai (2015) in the Chinese context.
89 Chapter 2 of this volume, p 21.
90 *Captain America: Civil War.*

see the benefits for the modern Buribunk of the digital space. The analyses of visual data playing out in real time demonstrate perfectly Kuhn's observation on 'narratives of identity' and the conscious or unconscious selection of data.[91] In the collective diarisation, consistent with the process of constant writing, recording becomes action and reaction.

One final warning point. It is the case that, disturbingly, the 'right to be forgotten' has assumed some momentum in the interconnected Buribunk world,[92] and the claim that 'Internet users must have effective control of what they put online and must be able to correct, withdraw or delete it at will'[93] threatens to disrupt the thread of recorded history-as-diary. What becomes of a reply to a diary entry when the original is deleted? Is this a real threat to mature Buribunkdom? Does it distort the course of history? Do we see the undermining of the key success of the modern, interactive diary? Once more, I choose to be optimistic. Perhaps the newest manifestation of buribunkology will be the careful curation of *absence*: like the postulated 'dark matter', existence can be calculated by careful observation of what is observed. In any event, there are strong grounds to be optimistic about a generation of people willing to share or to record to an amorphous 'Cloud' their smartwatch observations of heartbeat and blood oxygenation, their buying, viewing and activity preferences – even their genomic sequencing.[94]

Conclusion

The slightest glance will demonstrate that the post-millennial society has reached the pinnacle of Schnekkian recording, surveillance and reflection. In our exploration of the modern manifestations of buribunkology, we have seen that Schmitt's temple of history is filled with the eager recollections of the great masses of diarists and that the temple is, indeed, light-filled. The theoretical paradox arising from the great success of buribunkology – that the moment lived cannot be spent in recording – can be resolved by the modern mechanisms allowing instantaneous and interactive archiving. Here we see the full measure of the buribunkian cosmos and can look forward to the satisfactory resolution of what remains of the concerns of the traditionalist. We see also that, despite its early failures, the modern university is now a temple (if one may use a non-secular analogy) to the utopian buribunkian project. Only through the encoding and scrupulous audit of the life-second can we avoid the travails of the negative space at the heart of Buribunkdom. The tremendous capacity of modern technology enables the Buribunk to simultaneously experience facticity, narrate, record, code, cross-reference and store.

91 Kuhn (2002), p 2.
92 Bennett (2012).
93 Reding (2010).
94 Niemiec and Howard (2016).

We have only one final question: What of the reflective moment? Is there a time for creating the *Zeit zum Nachdenken*? Will this constant diarisation eventually diminish conscious Buribunkdom? I see two distinct problems. Reflection *sans* action is a metacognitive process necessary for learning;[95] what, then, results from the rush to put pen to paper (or keyboard to cursor)? It is beyond contention that 'a life without fame is a dance without music, a carousel without a street organ'.[96] But a life so bright, a fire so consuming, needs fuel. Can we speak without thinking? Can we write without reflection? Shu Paih-siang, quoted by Lin Yutang, noted that, 'idleness of time is like unoccupied floor space in a room … It is that unoccupied space which makes a room habitable, as it is our idle hours which make life endurable.'[97]

References

Rowland Atkinson and Mariann Hardey (2018) 'Three Things We Can All Learn from People Who Don't Use Smartphones or Social Media', *The Conversation*, 18 September.

Roland Barthes (1981) 'Theory of the Text', in Robert Young (ed), *Untying the Text: A Poststructuralist Reader*, Routledge, 31.

Steven C. Bennett (2012) 'The Right to Be Forgotten: Reconciling EU and US Perspectives' 30 *Berkeley Journal of International Law* 161.

J. Bentham (2010) *The Panopticon Writings*, ed M. Božovič, Verso.

Lionel Bently (1994) 'Copyright and the Death of the Author in Literature and Law' 57 *The Modern Law Review* 973.

Liza Brown (2020) '10 Best Live Streaming Platforms You Should Know', https://filmora.wondershare.com/live-streaming/10-best-live-streaming-platforms-you-should-know.html.

Kylie Cardell (2017) 'Modern Memory-Making: Marie Kondo, Online Journaling, and the Excavation, Curation and Control of Personal Digital Data' 32(3) *a/b: Auto/Biography Studies* 499.

Wenjiang Chen and Yijin He (2009) '*Little Web Log and Big Social Event: The Public Discourse of Internet*', 1st IEEE Symposium on Web Society, Lanzhou, 23–24 August.

D. Weston DarbyJr (1978) 'It's About Time' 4(3) *Legal Economics* 39.

Patrick M. De Winter (1981) 'A Book of Hours of Queen Isabel la Católica' 68(10) *The Bulletin of the Cleveland Museum of Art* 342.

Claire Donovan (1991) *The de Brailes Hours: Shaping the Book of Hours in Thirteenth-Century Oxford*, University of Toronto Press.

Larry Downes (2018) 'On Internet Regulation, the FCC Goes Back to the Future', *Forbes*, 12 March.

Marta Dynel and Fabio I.M Poppi (2019) 'Risum teneatis, amici?*: The Socio-pragmatics of RoastMe Humour' 139 *Journal of Pragmatics* 1.

Tim Elmore (2014) 'Nomophobia: A Rising Trend in Students', *Psychology Today*, 18 September.

95 Schön (1983), Eraut (1995).
96 Chapter 2 of this volume, p 27.
97 Yutang (1938).

Michael Eraut (1995) 'Schon Shock: A Case for Refraining Reflection-in-Action?' 1(1) *Teachers and Teaching* 9.

James A. Evans (2008) 'Electronic Publication and the Narrowing of Science and Scholarship' *Science*, 18 July, https://science.sciencemag.org/content/321/5887/395.

Rose Eveleth (2014) 'Academics Write Papers Arguing Over How Many People Read (and Cite) Their Papers', *Smithsonian Magazine*, 25 March, www.smithsonianmag.com/smart-news/half-academic-studies-are-never-read-more-three-people-180950222/?no-ist.

Michel Foucault (1977) 'What is an Author?' in *Language, Counter-Memory, Practice* (2nd edn), Cornell University Press.

Maša Galič, Tjerk Timan and Bert-Jaap Koops (2017) 'Bentham, Deleuze and Beyond: An Overview of Surveillance Theories from the Panopticon to Participation' 20(9) *Philosophy of Technology* 9.

William Golding (1954) *Lord of the Flies*, Faber and Faber.

Andrew T. Graham (2016) 'Role of Academic Managers in Workload and Performance Management of Academic Staff: A Case Study' 44(6) *Educational Management Administration & Leadership* 1042.

C. Hood (1991) 'A Public Management for All Seasons?' 69(1) *Public Administration* 3.

Chin-Lung Hsu and Judy Chuan-Chuan Lin (2008) 'Acceptance of Blog Usage: The Roles of Technology Acceptance, Social Influence and Knowledge Sharing Motivation' 45 *Information and Management* 65.

Marie Kondo (2016) *Spark Joy: An Illustrated Master Class on the Art of Organizing and Tidying Up*, Ten Speed.

Julia Kristeva (1986) *The Kristeva Reader* (ed Toril Moi), Blackwell.

Annette Kuhn (2002) *Family Secrets: Acts of Memory and Imagination*, Verso.

Liudvika Leišytė (2016) 'New Public Management and Research Productivity – a Precarious State of Affairs of Academic Work in the Netherlands' 41(5) *Studies in Higher Education* 828.

Ana M. Martínez-Alemán (2014) 'Social Media Go to College' 46(1) *Change: The Magazine of Higher Learning* 13.

Matthew R. McGrail, Claire M. Rickard and Rebecca Jones (2006) 'Publish or Perish: A Systematic Review of Interventions to Increase Academic Publication Rates' 25(1) *Higher Education Research & Development* 19.

Bonnie A. Nardi, Diane J. Schiano, Michelle Gumbrecht and Luke Swartz (2004) 'Why We Blog' 47(12) *Communications of the ACM* 41.

Emilia Niemiec and Heidi Carmen Howard (2016) 'Ethical Issues in Consumer Genome Sequencing: Use of Consumers' Samples and Data' 8 *Applied and Translational Genomics* 23.

Markus Perkmann*et al.* (2013) 'Academic Engagement and Commercialisation: A Review of the Literature on University–Industry Relations' 42 *Research Policy* 423.

Begoña Prieto, Lorenzo Maté and Jorge Tua (2006) 'The Accounting Records of the Monastery of Silos Throughout the Eighteenth Century: The Accumulation and Management of Its Patrimony in the Light of Its Accounts Books' 11(2) *Accounting History* 221.

D. Ranjith, G. Sruthi, S. Swathilakshmi and N. Vinotha (2019) 'Voice Based Billing System' 6(3) *International Research Journal of Engineering and Technology* 4269.

Stewart Ranson (2003) 'Public Accountability in the Age of Neo-liberal Governance' 18(5) *Journal of Education Policy* 459.

Viviane Reding (2010) 'Building Trust in Europe's Online Single Market', speech, http://europa.eu/rapid/pressReleasesAction.do?reference=SPEECH/10/327.
Virginia Reinburg (2012) *French Books of Hours: Making an Archive of Prayer, c.1400–1600*, Cambridge University Press.
Anthony Russo and Joe Russo (2016) *Captain America: Civil War*, Walt Disney Studios.
Donald Schön (1983) *The Reflective Practitioner: How Professionals Think in Action*, Basic Books.
Mohammad Khosravi Shakib (2013) 'Inevitability of Arts from Inter-textuality' 4(1) *International Journal of English and Literature* 1.
Michael Stoner (2012) 'Social Media and Advancement: A Report on Data from 2010–2012', 27 August, www.mstoner.com/blog/higher-ed/social-media-and-advancement-a-report-on-data-from-2010-2012.
Niraj Warikoo (2019) 'Native American Leader of Michigan: "Mob Mentality" in Students was "Scary"', *Detroit Free Press*, 20 January.
Scott Wartman (2019) 'Covington Catholic Student from Incident at the Indigenous Peoples March Issues Statement with His Side of the Story', *Cincinnati Enquirer*, 20 January.
Philip J. Weiser (2009) 'The Future of Internet Regulation' 43 *University of California Davis Law Review* 529.
Michele White (2003) 'Too Close to See: Men, Women and Webcams' 5(1) *New Media and Society* 7.
Cynthia D. Wilson (2013) 'Making Connections: Higher Education Meets Social Media' 45(4) *Change: The Magazine of Higher Learning* 51.
Sun Yingshuai (2015) '"Recurrence" and "Reconstitution": The Rise of "New Workers" and the Transition of China's Social Structure – Marxist Class Theory and the New Changes in the Contemporary Working Class' 5(2) *International Critical Thought* 148.
Lin Yutang (1938) *The Importance of Living*, William Morrow.

Part III

The Buribunks as writing

Chapter 10

On writing. Under control.

The Buribunks and the autographic society of control

Vittorio Lubrano

Introduction

> No clear chain of thought can stand up against the force of genuine, mythical images.
>
> Carl Schmitt, *The Leviathan in the State Theory of Thomas Hobbes* [1]

An entire century was not sufficient time to find a precise collocation for one of the most insidious works of Carl Schmitt: *The Buribunks*. Is it a parody of Schmitt's contemporary culture or virulent satire of '*Historismus und die Fortschrittsgläubigkeit*'? [2] Prophecy of a *société autophage* [3] still to come or witty exercise of style? Still, far from that 'sharp rationality'[4] that resounds in other classics, this Schmittian pamphlet holds the undisputed merit of surprising experts and amateurs alike because of its unique register, made of diffused irony and desecrating camouflages, dystopic expressivity and a caustic, critical attitude.

This chapter focuses on *The Buribunks* as a prismatic object that allows us to reflect indirectly on our present condition. In an attempt to produce an original interpretation of the text, this article's explicit aim is to actualise some of the pioneering intuitions within the text. Three complementary topics are intertwined in the following paragraphs: (1) Schmitt's idea of a society of control; (2) the activity of writing as a form of autobiography; and (3) the impressive convergence of dystopic reveries with contemporary phenomena.

The first topic, distributed particularly throughout the first and the last paragraphs, concerns the discreet but uncanny profile of a society of control, outlined despite the apparently facetious style of *The Buribunks*. Far from dualistic interpretations of control characterised by the haunting presence of the controller imposed on the controlled, Schmitt seems to predict the role that self-narration will play in upcoming societies: self-control, realised by means of a zealous autobiographic practice in each individual, will conflate the object

1 Schmitt (1996), p 81.
2 Koselleck (2000), pp 133, 141.
3 Jappe (2017).
4 Taubes (2013).

DOI: 10.4324/9781003091066-13

and subject of control into a perfect autographic machine. In this sense, the autobiography tends to circumscribe the *bíos* until its extinction, revealing a form of self-extractivism of data aimed at control and promotion, prediction and spectacularisation.

Life, re-programmed in the form of permanent interaction with one's own self-representation, is captured in this new *société du spectacle*, where the reference to the 'self' works as paranoid and isolating vector. This allows, in the conclusion, a possible conjuncture with one of the classical figurations of power: Thomas Hobbes's *Leviathan*.

The central section, mostly dedicated to the second topic, provides a careful reading of the text focused on the use of writing for cultural and political control. Schmitt understands that the civilising function promoted by modern intellectuals was a *Fata Morgana*, and qualities such as self-transparency, visibility/readability and encyclopedism could also transform it into a depersonalising praxis. Cultural activity, such as the writing of a Buribunk, extends its dominion until it literally *informs* life in its totality and becomes the only possible activity. Writing loses its classical positive connotations as a free and creative practice, a means of self-understanding, a formative process and a goal of cultural progress. In the last section, the essay focuses on the existential consequences for the Buribunk, the writing subject. This subject seems to disappear, leaving a norm – the imperative of (self-) writing – as the sole agent of an infinite narration. Thus, autobiographic practice paves the way to a form of standardised authoriality and exposes the contradictions of the Buribunks' subjectivation: a mortified existence, where creativity fuses with automatisation, resulting in depersonalised self-preservation from the very same activity that should cultivate self-consciousness and self-referential and introverted individuals simultaneously over-exposed to society.

The last paragraphs are entirely dedicated to re-actualising the text and extending beyond both a direct reading concerned with the witty criticisms of modernity and Koselleck's interpretation of buribunkology as an anticipation of totalitarianism on the basis of the paradigm of exclusion. The chapter thus argues that Schmitt, even in this allegedly minor work, reveals himself as an iconic precursor of contemporary tendencies that we only encounter in the most advanced sectors of post-human studies, ecological studies and contemporary biopolitics. Indeed, under the veil of apparent personalisation, life tends more and more to be *dispossessed by codes of automatic management*. It is *spectacularised*, furthermore, *in a self-referential form*, and missed in a very vain attempt to understand or exhibit it as self-evident. Similar to Schmitt's parodistic dystopia, it must conform to a complex, magnetic mechanism of information/representation that *extinguishes* other forms of life and the otherness of life itself, still impenetrable only few decades ago. The chapter concludes by reinterpreting the enigma that surrounds the Leviathan's face and defending the hypothesis that, after Buribunks, that captivating object of fascination can finally be interpreted as a screen for self-projection. The sovereignty of control therefore consists of the graphicisation of the self, a daily performance that pushes life towards annihilation, forcing it to the infinite task of constant re-description – auto(bio)graphy for life.

Under control: narrativity and control

There is no satisfying alternative to a lapidary *incipit* at the beginning of a text – the present *incipit* included. Those who approach Carl Schmitt – one of the most celebrated writers of lapidary incipits and author of *The Buribunks* – without indulging in a measure of irony and recursivity themselves risk misunderstanding the disruptive energy of a philosopher who pushes us to reflect even – or all the more so – while he is pretending to fool us.

Most readers will appreciate the seriousness of the question that dwells in this 'biting caricature'.[5] It is a *transpolitical*, perennial issue in politics, when politics is understood in terms of its *long durée*: how ought we to imagine political control? More specifically, how ought we to portray the specific structure of a power that meticulously reproduces a form of life without alternatives – a politics that depoliticises what is kept *under control*?

There are many examples of such figurations of control; with rare exceptions, they are far more effective when they involve a certain amount of impudent, figurative *rêverie*. Control can be exerted through the lens of a camera, as in *Peeping Tom*, where the visual fixation is animated by a ferocious eroticism capable of killing what it lays eyes on.[6] A further example is provided by the iconic force described by Tolkien,[7] in the form of the 'eye … that did not sleep', driven by 'a fierce eager will', 'almost like a finger', searching for someone. Such a gaze, which can both penetrate the hearth and poison it, stands out even more clearly in the overlapping of the dominant eye and the dominated eye in the *Hurin Saga*. [8] Of course, among modern representations it is imperative to mention Bentham's panopticon – an eye whose control over the field of visibility increases the less it is seen. Foucault was one of the first to reconsider the panopticon as an archetype for a new regime of *visibilité*, before other contemporary analyses reconceptualised it as the electronic panopticon[9] or superpanopticon,[10] the polyopticon[11] or the ban-opticon.[12] But also worth

5 Kennedy (2004), p 44.
6 Correspondingly, the Italian translation of the movie is *L'occhio che uccide* (*The Eye That Kills*).
7 Tolkien (2009), p. 401.
8 'Therefore with my eyes you shall see, and with my ears you shall hear, and nothing shall be hidden from you' are the words that Melkor addresses to Hurin. Tolkien (2007), ch 3.
9 Lyon (1994), especially chs 4, 10 and 12.
10 Poster (1989), p 122. See also Poster (1990), p 97.
11 Penley, Ross and Haraway (1990).
12 Han (2017), especially ch 7.

including in this pantheon of traceability is the technological apparatus that informs the universe of Orwell's *1984*. Capable of cutting the *revolutionary possibility* of love off at its roots,[13] it has become an exemplary model of a technophobic architecture of power – cameras and TV screens, inescapable projections and monitoring.

If we rely on the etymology of 'control' so as to trace it to the Anglo-French '*contreroller*' (derived from the Latin '*contrarotulus*': '*contra*', 'against' + '*rotulus*', 'little wheel/scroll') – that is, the act of 'comparison with a duplicate register' (rotulus)[14] – we become aware of the recurring topic of the interested gaze. The gaze that jumps from one *rotulus* to another in order to verify the perfect identity of the *seen* (rot. 2) and the fore-seen (rot. 1) has been transformed in many ways: the gaze that shadows political agencies; that which infiltrates them and superimposes their perspectives; the gaze that plays the role of sentinel of the outside and forager of the inside. At its best, and when intersecting with other gazes, such a gaze is able to tie them together and capture them so as to saturate any further imagination.

In this general framework, Schmitt's idea consists of drawing an incredibly sober figure of control: an autobiographer[15] (the Buribunk). Despite his at times grotesque descriptions, subtle ironies and meta-literary fictions, Schmitt outlines with great lucidity the narrative torsion of the contemporary bio-power[16] that has made self-narration (and therefore self-promotion, self-help techniques, self-motivation, self-analysis and so on) a fundamental part of our *life standard*. Today, the most unexpected form of control seems to be the hegemony of self-control, to which tireless autobiographical activity contributes. No longer the philosophical *virtus par excellence*,[17] self-control has become a technique for forcing the liveable into the visual, the anomalous into the predictable, possibility into readability. Whereas the eye of the Other, of Big Brother or the Dark Lord, once threatened the political scene as a barely noticed presence, intoxicating it with negative affections, the invisible eye that annihilates and destroys living beings now lies in the blind spot of our self-representation – taking the form of our very own eye, the eye that reads oneself. Still, an eye we cannot see[18] results in our conformity (a conformity that is not devoid of diversity) and in our gradual mortification. It is the eye that each of us feels is our own.

13 Despite Mark Fisher's attempt to relativise the predominance of Orwell's imaginary in order to understand the face of a new totalitarianism – 'capitalist realism' (Fisher 2009).
14 Already in the ordinances of Edward II of Caernarfon.
15 The Buribunk interacts constantly with his/her writing, which is available for public viewing. The eye, in this case, is the eye of the reader.
16 See also McLoughlin (2019).
17 See also De Carolis (1996), pp 41, 43.
18 In an extract from Valéry's *The Young Fate*, well known to Jacques Lacan, this impossibility was described in these terms: '*Je me voyais me voir*'.

On writing

Writing against modernity

In *The Buribunks,* control takes the form of an autobiographic ritual: the tireless production of a self-related text is offered for reading. It is the ultimate parody of an acerbic criticism that the 'intellectual potential who stands head and shoulders above all intellectual scribbling'[19] addresses against that optimistic look to the art of writing given by modern intellectuals.[20]

It has been noticed[21] that Schmitt probably took his cue from Kant's idea of text-sharing as a means for social progress,[22] with the aim of demolishing such a liberal myth.[23] The liberal ingenuity that imagined the individual as 'part of the [social] machine' and contributing with 'his writing' to the public discourse offers to Schmitt an especially perfect keystone for *détourner* these *aufgeklärten* intentions. Indeed, Buribunk society presents itself as a large 'collective organism' in which 'every male and female Buribunk is obliged to keep a diary for every second of their existence'.[24]

A surprising, embracing liberality surrounds this apparently progressive society, eager for scientificity; men devote themselves to producing 'entries'[25] on a vast array of topics from erotica to psychology, satire, politics, *otium* and so on. Massive amounts of data are collected with complete efficiency, catalogued in a functional way and exposed by means of exhaustive syntheses, while photo shoots, dedicated conferences, lectures and cinematographic exhibitions promulgate the praxis and analyse it further. Not a single detail is neglected, even if 'sociologically useful data'[26] are generally preferred, as they ensure a virtually infinite reuse of the material for new re-elaborations (with a gender, class or socio-psychological approach).

19 Taubes (2013).
20 Koselleck (2000, p 148) outlines a long list of possible references, far over the modern philosophy: Adam Smith, Hegel, Marx, Richard Wagner, Nietzsche, Lamprecht, Haeckel, Ostwald and possibly Lenin and Wilson too.
21 Accarino (1991), pp 391–404.
22 'But in so far as this or that individual who acts as part of the machine also considers himself as a member of a complete commonwealth or even of cosmopolitan society, and thence as a man of learning who may through his writings address a public in the truest sense of the word, he may indeed argue': Kant (2009), translated by H.B. Nisbet.
23 The relation between the act of writing and philosophy attracted the attention of Hadot (1995), pp 126–44, and Foucault, who found – especially in *Vita Antonii* by the Christian philosopher Athanasius of Alexandria – an elaboration of daily notes as a spiritual exercise capable of '*réduire le corps en servitude et déjouer les ruses de l'ennemi*' (Foucault 1983, pp 3–23). In contrast, buribunkology reverses the meaning of such disciplinary exercise, reducing it to dispossession and subjective dispersion.
24 Chapter 2 of this volume, p 24.
25 Chapter 2 of this volume, p 22.
26 Chapter 2 of this volume, p 17.

For the composition of the diary, a lack of censorship is also enforced: 'the highest respect for personal freedom' and 'a limitless, all-understanding, uncomplaining tolerance'[27] are granted to any kind of textual content. Furthermore, criticism[28] and insults (or rather, 'disgust and revulsion towards the whole enterprise')[29] are welcome. The *Wille zum Schreiben* is stimulated up to the paradoxical point where 'no Buribunk is prevented from writing in his diary that he refuses to keep a diary'.[30]

In spite of this 'magnificent, progressive destiny',[31] the moral obligation to rationality conflates with the social obligation to write at all costs, and the inward *Sollen* assumes a flavour both of increasing encyclopedism and of undisputable command. In such a realm – a sort of Paradise for writers – a blatant, inherent vice appears. Immediately, the contradiction between the obligation to report and the freedom of writing appears. In a society without any external sign of barbarity, which strives to increase self-consciousness and spread scientific developments, authoritarianism appears under the guise of a *coercion (into freedom) of writing*, even though it is an *obligation of writing in complete freedom*. 'Feel free to write whatever you want' becomes perfectly equivalent to its opposite, 'Feel forced to write whatever you want'. Wrapped with a rhetoric of liberality, such a request sounds extremely jeering and hypocritical.

A mere, caustic derision of liberal socio-constructivism and of a certain devotion to abstract, rational procedures would have been easy to target if it had not also included German Idealists who, in the nineteenth century, were already able to denote the emerging contradictions from the Age of Enlightenment. The Hegelian conceptual exertion to harmonise Reality and Rationality, individual freedom and social institutions had been the object of diffused mocking taunts. Moreover, the Buribunks' writing was a way to transcend the simple existential level of their life to thus reach a higher degree of science. In other words, life is transfigured or re-qualified (Hegel would say *aufgehoben*) through a permanent 'self-historicisation'.[32]

Every member of this peculiar population makes his own contribution to History – Schmitt, in a parody of the Hegelian jargon, calls it 'World Spirit'[33] or '*Weltgeschichte*' – in which each personal biography is reduced to 'an indistinctive generality'.[34] History as *Geschichte*, an unfolding of events, is here irreverently flattened as *Historie*, a specific branch of knowledge that reconstructs our past. Within this unusual context, the two distinct declinations of the term

27 Chapter 2 of this volume, p 24.
28 Criticisms have been here reduced from virtuous movers of social enhancement to simple plot devices, among others.
29 Chapter 2 of this volume, p 24.
30 Chapter 2 of this volume, p 24.
31 Leopardi (2013), XXXIV, verse 51.
32 Chapter 2 of this volume, p 15.
33 Chapter 2 of this volume, p 26.
34 Chapter 2 of this volume, p 23.

are driven to converge through a frenetic transcribing that reduces any distance between the two until they finally coincide completely and become indiscernible. Nothing happens outside historical memory or, in an astonishing balance between the two poles, what happens is immediately turned into historiographical report. The tension between a science of the totality of events and their complex and manifoldly related proceeding will never reach a moment of synthesis: it will remain just a haunting presence in the form of a promise – a perfect meta-autobiography still to be realised.

A biographixed population

In order to evaluate all the sophisticated implications of this original scientific command, of this science that is 'more than a science'[35] – which Schmitt reformulates in a Kantian register[36] – we have to take into account some of its indirect consequences. First, the act of writing ceases to be an *activity amongst others* and become *the* activity to which every other refers. We can easily grasp how such a priority establishes a very peculiar regime of truth[37] wherein, to be considered real, things have to be transcribed by Buribunkologists. Any omission is treated as a crime and sanctioned with social stigma.

Still, it would be wrong to linger on the effect of estrangement in a community that lives on tales. The focus on diaries indirectly suggests the presence of an original duplicity, of a dimension distinct from the historical one, which we can only reach through the implicit and virtual elements in the written text or, in some cases, by recalling the prehistory of buribunkology. It is the life world, the existence in its non-Hegelian concreteness, in its 'handgreifliche Inkommensurabilität', in its irreducibility to simple description; it is something that eludes the mechanism of reproduction-in-words, that rests on secrets, a dark background lightly touched by memory only in some parts. The world of history besieges exactly such a world: the transcription of life corrodes life.

Schmitt shows no remorse in illustrating the increasing expropriation of life in every respect. The uniqueness of birth – the coming to the world of future biographers – can now be controlled through the development of new techniques that allow the new foetus to 'keep a diary'[38] and even to 'inform each other'.[39] Craving for historicity overflows on proto-existence and forces it to confess: every chance or possibility is thus reduced to firm certainty within a collective biography. Needless to say, the very same dynamics works on post-existence as well.

35 Chapter 2 of this volume, p 14.
36 'Live so that every single one of your seconds can be recorded in your diary and fall into the hands of your biographer!' Chapter 2 of this volume, p 16.
37 Foucault (1971).
38 Chapter 2 of this volume, p 14.
39 Chapter 2 of this volume, p 25.

Death is one of the shameful *pudenda* of the Moses of Buribunkdom, Ferker, that venerable master and authentic pioneer of this science. And still, facing the enigma of the end of existence, of the final chapter of every personal story, even this first-born of buribunkology wavered. Fear, the pain of departure, mysteries of the afterlife have been reduced to the bare act of writing. Death is theoretically annihilated – perhaps as only Epicurus in his famous *Letter to Menoeceus* was able to do – and it turns into writing-no-more, mute word: we realise we are dead the moment the diary falls from our hands, when the pen turns quiet. Like the future, death in the end does not exist. Our life, which we perceive as belonging to us alone, fades away and we do not even preserve one element of singularity from our unrepeatable existence. If the report of life makes us existent, then our life means the act of writing passing through us, the Spirit writing on itself with our complicity. In this sense, our life survives beyond us. The Buribunk can embrace death 'smilingly'[40] because of the acknowledgement of being part of an immortal story where even the epilogue is one episode among others.

Deprived of origin and conclusion, life needs not to spill in any excess apart from the text, not even with regard to feelings. Pathos would scatter our interest towards other experiences than reporting on such experiences, and we would run the risk of feeling too much the life we are meant to transcribe. This is the case of Don Giovanni, who would be an ideal candidate for self-historicisation due to his extended record of conquests and the plethora of unrepeatable adventurous moments that he experienced. However, without a 'calm objectivity', an 'unemotional scientific endeavour', the 'murky depths of brutal hedonism'[41] impose a non-historical teleology: life for pleasure, *carpe diem*, cannot substitute life for biography (whence the unpleasant but incomplete task of Leporello, biographer indeed but still lacking in historicity). Things are not much different with Ferker, who 'secured for himself ... his continued existence in the memory of humankind'.[42] Beside the aforementioned fear of death, it was because of a forbidden love (a secret and undocumented passion for an 'illiterate person',[43] indeed one incapable of self-understanding) that such first cantor of the new science became the Adam of buribunkology – first buribunkologist but also the first to err. Fear of writing, emotional reactions, the deep folds of subjectivity have to become the object of writing and the sounding board of inner life.[44] The nefarious obligation to self-extroversion becomes even more manifest when seen from the perspective of a possible

40 Chapter 2 of this volume, p 28.
41 Chapter 2 of this volume, p 16.
42 Chapter 2 of this volume, p 20.
43 Chapter 2 of this volume, p 21.
44 There is a subtle and less evident coaction at work here, to which I will return in the next section. A Buribunk must either strive to publicise his inner voices or to eradicate them. An act of emotive violence that one is to embrace full-heartedly as well.

buribunkian psychology. Although discussed in a few passages under the label of 'psycho-pathological studies',[45] and without any mention of psychoanalysis – in 1918, the publication date of Schmitt's text, it had less than 10 years of formal international recognition[46] – we can draw some conclusion independently from the text. Our fascination with psychoanalysis and part of the charming complexity of the discipline rest on the asymmetry between patient and analyst. Precisely, this relation is twisted and confused by Schmitt: in a society in constant self-monitoring, the 'talking cure' is generalised and exceeds the limits of the couch of the psychoanalyst. The individual is in turn subject and object of analysis, and his diaries – from the most intimate note to the most mundane event – are at the mercy of future studies. The analyst's notebook, his symbolic privilege and burden as well, have been vulgarised and generalised. 'Torments' of the soul, 'intellectual-spiritual struggles'[47] – in brief, *das Unbewusstsein* itself – are exposed and put on stage. We are all patients of an interminable collective analysis.

From this analysis, we can see how the level of *Geschichtsphilosophie* has progressively absorbed and obscured the extra-textual, extra-biographical world (our psychological and biological existence, in a broad sense). Birth, death, pleasures, fears and dark sides of our personality have all been devoured by graphomania. Although analysed on an existential level only, the writing process is displayed not only as an activity among others, nor simply as a neutral activity. Schmitt understood very early on its political content and its problematic potential even when – or should we say *precisely when* – it is wrapped with a veil of scientificity, objectivity and reflexivity.

The author-actor

Before examining the *political content* in question, we need to insist on one further hidden aspect of the phenomenon of writing. A revealing question arises: What is left of the subject who writes?

We are very far from that *ethopoietic function* at work in Seneca's or Epictetus's works,[48] and recommended to disciples and friends in the very ritualistic moment of elaborating a script. For these authors, writing was a way to shape their own existence and, for a set of complex philosophico-meditative reasons, it gave the subject back to himself – an appropriation of the self against the frenetic developments of the world.

With the Buribunks, the diary also presents an apparently similar function. It is an instrument for becoming one's 'own master',[49] namely oneself. But it

45 Chapter 2 of this volume, p 23.
46 The International Psychoanalytical Association (IPA) was founded in 1910 by Sigmund Freud: Limentani (1996), pp 149–58.
47 Chapter 2 of this volume, p 22.
48 Foucault (1983) pp 3–23.
49 Chapter 2 of this volume, p 16.

would be a mistake to conflate this rhetoric with the classicist one. In fact, the former stems from the very modern subjectivity that Schmitt intends to destroy. The self-reflective technique of writing functions as a mediation between a starting situation (particular) and historical knowledge (universal). It thus blatantly involves a Hegelian *Aufhebung*, namely the dialectical process of sublating immediacy, while preserving, upgrading and conceptually understanding it. To transcribe oneself in writing is to transcend the existential horizon towards universal world history. The 'reward rests in the certainty of entering oneself into history and to be still quoted in aeons',[50] in turning into a vehicle of knowledge transmission so as to become ineradicable from the past. Consequently, writing appears as a *means* to realise oneself in a totality that implies us, a community of enlightened and self-conscious scientists.

On closer inspection, this function of writing reveals itself to only pertain to the dawn of buribunkology, to its elementary stage. A shift gradually takes place and the writing of the self is slowly revealed as the real *causa finalis* of existence. This is in line with note 4, dedicated to Marcus Aurelius's *Meditations*, in which the 'moralising auto-pedagogical constructions'[51] are condemned *prima facie* for being boring, but actually because they consider writing to be an activity with an extra-textual purpose – that takes life as a starting point for narrations and returns to it, restoring the fruits of this suspension from the world that remains but a temporary parenthesis. Yet the activity of writing cannot be reduced to a *means* in the service of life; it must be its *goal*, and any Buribunk has the duty to reinstate this priority.

Consequently, what initially operates as a report on the part of the living, as an instrument for self-clarification, degenerates into widespread obsession and generalised manipulation. Through the piling of information, the Buribunk thinks that he is expanding his – and the community's – self-consciousness, thereby making his own contribution to the proper functioning of society. In fact, self-historicisation becomes the reason to be, the unique anchor of a community in 'total mobilisation': subjectivity becomes completely extroverted, triggered by social thirst for factual evidence, and forced to publicly confess in an ever-renewed act of faith. As illustrated by Schnekke's encomium, tragically there will soon no longer be a *dehors du texte*. Such a paradoxical effect is amplified to an extreme peak of causticity, when the Schmittian irony mimics Descartes's introspection in order to expose its constitutive aporia:

> I think, therefore I am; I speak, therefore I am; I write, therefore I am; I publish, therefore I am … For the Buribunk, thinking is nothing other than soundless speech; speaking nothing but scriptless writing; writing nothing but anticipated publishing and publishing is thus identical with writing, with such minor differences that they may safely be disregarded.

50 Chapter 2 of this volume, p 13.
51 Chapter 2 of this volume, p 18 n 4.

> I write, therefore I am; I am, therefore I write. What do I write? I write myself. Who writes me? I myself write myself. What is the content of my writing? I write that I write myself. What is the big motivator lifting me above this self-sufficient circle of I-ness? History![52]

The ontological proof displayed here confirms that the certainty of existence derives from the obedience to a normed activity, which can easily be identified – beyond any nuance – with the act of writing. The absolute goal of life is to relive life by means of the memories it generated – to reduce it to *res gestae*. Through this duplication, the subject confronts his written self and recognises himself in it.

As already mentioned, the life-world tends to be submerged and distorted through the *editing procedures*. However, the aim of Schmitt is not to point out the risk of an alienated life. His subtle irony does not stop at the shifting point in which writing *as a means* (writing in order to live) ultimately reverses itself into *a goal* (living in order to write). The Schmittian intuition in *The Buribunks* goes beyond this classical trope and opens up an unexpected long-term outlook for a piece composed at the fall of the Second Reich.

We can venture a hypothesis that Schmitt himself does not develop in all its radicality, although he hints at it in short passages, moving in schizophrenic variations from explicit allusions to a more attenuated tone. Indeed, in some passages of the fable, a terminal stage of social progress emerges wherein the subject neither discards writing, nor relies further on it in an even greater self-reflection: he is simply lost in it.

In order to understand this underlying thesis, we need to put ourselves in the phase where this *Kultur durch Schreibung*[53] is fully deployed and try to reach using our imagination what Schmitt whispers in a few lines. We need to grasp the pure paradigm of subjectivity denounced here. A fully realised and ortho-regulated subjectivity, entirely devoted to text composition, is hardly capable of doing anything else, nor does it feel the need to do so. If the human being is still able to fill his diaries with some content, if he is still able to speak of what has happened to him, it is due to his concomitant and irremediable *extra-linguistic* condition. Following the logics of buribunkology to its extreme consequences, the simple fact that there is still something to write about bursts out as a miracle into the realm of linguistic self-referentiality. A virtuous Buribunk would not write of anything but his own writing, of pauses in his writing, of desire or boredom in doing it, of his good or bad writing, of his meta-reflection on the process … the 'extra' fades away. Subject and object of writing come in this way in a 'harmonious'[54] short-circuit.

52 Chapter 2 of this volume, pp 25–6.
53 That is, a form of civilisation by means of the writing activity.
54 Chapter 2 of this volume, p 23.

There is no need to chase heroes in order to fix their adventures 'for immortal fame' (Homer),[55] nor even to mirror oneself, as a hero of one's own time, in one's own spiritual testament (as Saint Augustine appears to have done, despite Schmitt's interpretative doubts). At the peak of theoretical paroxysm, caught in a purely onto-transformative mechanism where 'ideal and reality have melted into one in unheard-of perfection',[56] the writer becomes author-actor of a script (writing) that dominates and precedes him. Biographer and hero are conflated and collapse into an unrecognisable figure where the hero is no more an *other* to write on,[57] but a writer incapable of anything *other* (auto-actor or author-in-action).

The subject, no longer a creative author, no longer *fundamentum* of reality and knowledge, is reconfigured in an automatic mechanism of production of narrations. 'Writing' (*scribere* in Latin) – although the professional philologist would disagree – reveals here an unexpected co-implication. On the one hand, we observe the in*scrib*ing of a norm inwardly, so deeply that it becomes essential to the self – that is, it becomes what makes oneself what one is. On the other, we see the de*scrib*ing outwardly of the self, reduced to nothing but the application of the norm – even if it is called free becoming. Fluxes in opposite directions decompose subjectivity and recompose it in an uncanny, normalised form.

Unable to express himself otherwise than in writing (here we find the blinding, falsifying effect of the utopian community), the subject reveals himself in the text in a reversed form: deprived of himself, empty, a transparent shell always on the move, expropriated of the self and absolutely depersonalised. To assert subjectivity by means of description amounts to denying it while inscribing it in a transmedial circuit in which it sub-*scribes* to a subjecting norm. This obscured, cancelled 'sub' remains like a blank space in the writing-in-and-for-itself that we call buribunkology. 'Writing it while it writes us',[58] it condemns us to our own elimination. Beyond the muzzle of a conforming fanaticism that takes the Buribunk to be the one who 'is everything as he recognises all things in their reality',[59] we easily recognise that he is nothing as he does not experience any of them.

An interpretation of contemporaneity?

Pro-scritio, in-scritio, de-scritio

> To say everything essential in 10 pages is an extraordinary performance!
>
> Alexandre Kojève, letter to Carl Schmitt, Paris, 2 May 1955

55 Chapter 2 of this volume, p 27.
56 Chapter 2 of this volume, p 23.
57 'The progress of humankind can only be expected when everyone only thinks of themselves and lets everything else run its own course.'
58 Chapter 2 of this volume, p 27.
59 Chapter 2 of this volume, p 28.

We could reiterate the homage of the great Russian-French author and apply it even to this irreverent work. We would be left, though, with an open issue: How far does the 'essential' discovered by Schmitt still concern us – in other words, are there any temporal limits for a criticism *more utopico* published more than a century ago?

Without any doubt, the illusory certainties of modern philosophy are subtly revealed, so it is possible to highlight them without any further need for a deeper interpretation. The community trained at the school of Descartes, Kant and, above all, Hegel – the real Trinity of thought as reflecting subject – assumes the spectral form of a government of self-centred citizens, fragmented in introverted micro-worlds that are *at the same time* extroverted for scientific divulgation.

In this respect, *The Buribunks* works as a protest against the great philosophical currents before the twentieth century. In line with a certain way to interpret Schmitt's thought,[60] the text shows perfectly the aporias of modernity without being able to propose a sustainable alternative.[61] The modern mediation that establishes political order not on divine authority, but on an artificial, consensual and horizontal one, reorganised starting from the individual subjectivity, is first grasped and understood, then developed and derided. It does not matter whether such a mediation is declined in a positivist or Kantian, dialectical or historico-materialistic way. The impudence with which Schmitt levels off all these currents in a *pot pourri* – to the point where his references become inaccurate – implies here that they are but nuances of a unique paradigm.

Yet Reinhart Koselleck[62] highlights, within the lines of this text lies another minor thesis consisting of the possible anticipation of an oncoming regime where, on one side, the adherence to the norm guarantees social recognition (*Anerkennung*) and, on the other, any infraction of it condemns to downgrading, and ultimately to suppression. Indisputably, elements of racism are present in occasional passages[63] or even inherently.[64] But in the following

60 Galli (1996).

61 According to the illuminating interpretation that sees in Carl Schmitt the one who, in his interpretation of *the origin of politics*, was guilty of attempting to share with Nazism a *politics of the origin*. See Galli (1996), pp V–XXVI.

62 Koselleck (2000).

63 'The phosphorescence of African-European race mixing'; lesser peoples, Polynesians, Tierra del Fuegians, Baronga Negroes and other tribes incapable of an education' echo with a dark tone because of Schmitt's biographical choices after the rise to power of Hitler Chapter 2 of this volume, pp 18, 13.

64 The *differentia specifica* of Buribunks – to keep diaries – is challenged by an *equivalent physiological exceptionality* – a larger mouth – that makes this population unique among others. It could allow the mediation of the subject into World-History by means of evolution and *Historia Naturalis* without passing through a daily description of the self – although Schmitt seems sceptical about such hypothesis.

passage, an unexpected ruthlessness is rightly highlighted in the shaping of the social hierarchy:

> The wheel of progress passes silently over the silent one; he will no longer be mentioned, he can therefore no longer make himself heard until he finally, sinking step by step, is forced into the lowest class, to help create the external conditions for the possibility of noble Buribunkdom, for example making by hand the paper on which the most valuable diaries are printed … This is a strict but entirely natural selection of those who are better, as he who doesn't succeed in the intellectual struggle of the diaries, will fall behind progress and be absorbed by the masses who create those external conditions; as a result of these physical labours, menial services and so on, he is also no longer able to use every second of his life buribunkologically and thus his fate plays out with merciless inevitability. As he no longer writes, he can no longer defend himself against possible slurs regarding his person, he is no longer up to date, and eventually he vanishes from the screen of the monthly reports and ceases to exist.[65]

Koselleck's interpretation indicates an uncommon talent for pointing the finger to a brief fragment full of implications that cast a shadow on the whole text. The future society, wherein the shepherds of history dwell, is a society of exclusion that erects itself on an anonymous background, where those deprived of words are gradually reduced to silence.[66] The lower class, the class to which non-spiritual beings belong, is rejected and removed from both social memory and social space, through the very same forces that promote culture. The hypocrisy of liberal progressive egalitarianism could not be stated in a clearer form.[67] The elimination of those who fall behind has the same importance as an atmospheric variation and finds its justification in the accusation of human 'laziness and cowardice', driving directly to condemnation and social re-qualification. Hence, beyond sarcasm against nineteenth-century culture, this piece draws attention to that inclusion–exclusion mechanism that was realised in its most cruel and transparent form in totalitarian regimes.[68] While entertaining us with a caricature of the past, something '*schlimmer als parodiert*'[69] moves forward,

65 Chapter 2 of this volume, p 25.

66 The tendency to '*aufräumen*' – that is, to put in order – zealously cultivated by the entire society, resounds even in a secondary meaning of the term – literal and more polemic: to make room (*raum*) and in this sense to annihilate the existent, '*vernichten*'. See Benjamin (1928), p 43 and also Benjamin (2018). I thank Massimiliano 'Max' Carli for this brilliant insight. A proximity between barbarism and civil progress so acutely analysed by French and German authors after World War II.

67 See also Losurdo (2011).

68 Agamben (1998).

69 Koselleck (2000), p 149.

allowing us to glimpse through the contradictions of culture a rough image of its most extreme reversal.

What is even more extraordinary about this singular piece is that it seems to go even beyond the horizon of totalitarian regimes. What is in question here is not simply the capacity to mobilise an entire population according to a norm that pre-scribes while pro-scribing – that is, that requires obedience by the citizens while degrading and eliminating the non-citizens (those without homeland or history). A different biopolitics, with diverse objectives and techniques, becomes visible in some of the most radical aspects of the fable.

Schmitt was able to anticipate far in advance a tendency that is fully realised nowadays: the tendency to orient life coercively into the sphere of information, to extort from it every inner secret so as to dispose of it. A wide range of seemingly unconnected contemporary phenomena – Big Data, genome transcription, techniques for monitoring the affective capacity of bodies, data mining for the individuation of consumer profiles, widespread interaction by means of virtual interfaces, patenting of species – all these share a common techno-scientific root, development and process. Rosi Braidotti[70] and other authors in the last decade[71] have brilliantly pointed out how the whole spectrum of living matter, the so-called *zoé* – indeterminate life, shared horizontally with the whole multiplicity of living beings – is under siege by the very same forces that are trying to promote and value it. Among the emerging dynamics of our society, life is forced to speak in order to produce knowledge about and control over life itself. The prevailing rhetoric, on the other hand, speaks about enhancing and discovering life in its depths. However, it is a matter of appropriation of life for economic and political ends. What is unsaid, the element of falsity in the improvement of collective knowledge, is the destructive effect against life, the extinction of *zoé* because of a short-sighted biopolitics, which at the same time displays a ferocious form of necropolitics.[72]

In this regard, Schmitt's pages possess the undisputed merit to see through the crisis of modern subjectivity and to bring some of its echoes to us, who are striving for an alternative, in the aftermath of the enduring neoliberal *Kultur*.[73] Thus, in an apparently frivolous fable, some features of the contemporary tendency to transform *zoé* into information become visible.

The Buribunks are the paradigm of a new extraordinary society and of a culture of control. In order to administrate the living beings within the social sphere, these are inscribed in procedural practices, which have the accidental side-effect of extinguishing the life that is meant to be captured *transparently in all its forms.*

We witness on one side how life moves towards *automatisation*, namely through standardising practices (writing is the emblematic one) that bring down

70 Braidotti (2013).
71 Cooper (2008); Clough (2008), pp 1–22; Hardt and Negri (2000), p 215.
72 Mbembe (2003), pp 11–40.
73 De Carolis (2017).

its potential and reorganise it on the basis of criteria as predictability and immediate readability.

We find remarkable evidence of this in the moment in which the Buribunk embraces in himself the norm to which he refers his activity, inscribing it deeper than any inwardness. The act of writing plays the role of a constitutive imperative: it converts him to an algorithmic conduct of existence and transforms him into an automatic machine for production of stories. The projecting, symbolic, desiring horizon, for so long taken to be a peculiarity of the human being, is reconfigured into a unique procedure for the interpretation of the real ('to write on'); consequently, the Buribunk tends to become an *automaton*. Nevertheless, to stick to this aspect – despite its importance – is to only partially recognise the greatness of Schmitt's intuition.

For on the other side, the more life is projected externally and the more it is constantly described, the more control is exercised efficiently. In other words, life seems to reaffirm life, to promote and intensify it by means of description. Such a multiplying factor reveals itself ultimately as an actualised, ideological form of *spectacularisation*.[74] It is all about translating life as much as possible (quantitatively and qualitatively) into a fetish game with which we always interact. Thus, the entire social *spectrum* works in unison and unceasingly for the reproduction of a symbolic order made of images/narrations of virtualised existences, for the sake of entertainment or information. A further element of vivacity introduced by Schmitt comes from the *self-referentiality* of spectacularisation. In a perfected control society, each becomes responsible for his own social exposure and self-promotion.[75] Whence the sarcastic destiny of the Buribunk, who in order to duplicate himself in words does not leave any secret unsaid, including obscenities, monstrosities and mistakes. But the price he pays for this self-valorisation is the highest possible and sheds a cruel light – although only on the individual dimension – on the miserable outcome of the process. The more reproduction of life sticks to life itself and seems to correspond to it perfectly, the more such reproduction misses it, obscures it and slowly annihilates it. It is like a diaphanous screen that shows everything from the perceived real – except that, by doing so, it keeps it at a distance, thus altering our relation to it. This is illustrated in an exemplary way by the Buribunk, gathering all his spirit to write something but with nothing to write about apart from the norm he has become – his normality that tells us nothing.

74 Spectacle has to be understood according to the interpretation given by Debord in 1967, as an 'immense accumulation' of falsifying, ideological representations working as a pervasive instrument for structuring society and dismantling any revolutionary conflictuality. In this sense, 'The spectacle is not a collection of images; it is a social relation between people that is mediated by images' (Debord 1995, p 7).

75 The passage Koselleck analysed now assumes an additional meaning. It indicates the fate awaiting the non-competitors who refuse to follow the science of 'Advertising and Arrivistics' and any 'cinematic attitude' in order to create from the narration of the self a symbolic merchandise.

The subject extinguishes. But such *extinction* has to be intended as *a subjective declination* of a wider *mortification* of life. Not an animal,[76] not even a plant appears in the realm of Buribunks – surely a confirmation that any otherness before writing is doomed to fade away. Yet perhaps there is a further reason. As occurs with a single Buribunk life, it is not excluded that other living beings pass through a *mise par écrit*, although it is doubtful that they would find more benefits or peace therein. The picture Schmitt draws represents, in this sense, also the final stage of modern progress – a realised Anthropocene where, despite a massive amount of data, the human remains incapable of relating with his environment (the biological existence is forced into the biographical one, without any interest in ecological existence), even when the latter becomes an object for the sciences. Neither the rustle of leaves nor the roar of an animal makes its way in the daily routine of the describers[77] – an absence that testifies to the insensibility of a culture that annihilates while advancing. This opens for us a conclusive question.

Conclusion: the sovereignty of control, autographs on the *Leviathan*

It is no secret that Schmitt nourished a lifelong relationship of conflicting 'brotherhood' with Thomas Hobbes.[78] His meticulous analysis of Hobbes's 'baroque idea'[79] of representation, his thesis of the state as a *machina machinarum*[80] and his mythological polymorphism emanated from a *dispositif* marked by a tragic destiny[81] represent the most important legacy of his works as an interpreter of Hobbes. Yet a peculiar page of Hobbes's work drew the attention of Carl Schmitt above all: the frontispiece of *Leviathan* (Figure 10.1).

It was undoubtedly very clear to Schmitt that this sophisticated product of wit from the seventeenth century – an *assemblage* of geometric projection with royal symbolism – was 'fraught with inscrutable meaning'[82] far more astonishing than any anamorphosis.[83] Yet it must have been less clear to him how such a *politische Iconographie* [84] allowed, in a very specific place, a possible conjunction

76 Two apparent exceptions reveal in the end a rhetorical instrumentalisation of animals confirming the thesis: 'Apes and birds' are simply terms for comparison of racial physiognomies; while 'rats' are instead a metaphor for the incorporation of the future into history.
77 An uncanny coincidence: the ones deprived of terms (words), are *de facto* ex-terminated from such logocentred world.
78 Schmitt (2017), p 52.
79 Schmitt (1996), p 98.
80 Schmitt (1996), p 34.
81 'In other words, the dawn of a day when the great leviathan would be slaughtered was already visible.' Schmitt (1996), p 35; see also p 74.
82 Schmitt (1996), p 5.
83 See Malcolm (2002), pp 200–233.
84 Bredekamp (2012), pp 131–32.

Figure 10.1 The frontispiece of Leviathan
Source: Abraham Bosse, *Leviathan*, frontispiece from Thomas Hobbes's *Leviathan*, 1651, https://commons.wikimedia.org/wiki/File:Leviathan_by_Thomas_Hobbes.jpg

between the Hobbesian *artificium* and *The Buribunks* – where sovereignty intersects with autobiography and sovereign control becomes the sovereignty of control.

Inside the living flesh of the Leviathan, and more precisely *at its head*, dwells an enigma. In a great crowd, citizens who have been brought together, reunited, stand side by side without colliding. They turn their backs to the viewer and are held together within the clear-cut borders of the state body, staring in a single direction. They gaze in unison at a single face, indeed – but *what are they observing in it?*

Their gaze, averted from each other and exclusively directed at the face before them, turns out to be immersed in the contemplation of a figure who, although the object of concentrated attention, does not look (back) at them where they stand, as they are. History may complicate our quest for an answer: it may be the case that the visage was one of the *princeps* of the world – Charles II or Oliver Cromwell.[85] From the French Revolution on, the matter becomes far more slippery. According to Giacomo Marramao, the head was always the coming representative to be substituted following the beheading – a hidden archetype of the modern legitimation of power.[86] From the laborious exertion of buribunkology (an ahistorically historicist discipline), we can but sketch another answer and reconsider the meaning of the image as a whole.

The Buribunks allows us to apply a pinch of dystopian fantasy to this icon of political control and to realise that, more than being a particular, individual face – Sovereign Royalty – the crowned head is a framework with a specific function. Whereas we could once have imagined it as a symbol of the unity of the people – and therefore the cornerstone of 'protection and obedience' – in buribunkology it has a mirroring effect that involves the citizenry as a whole. This face mirrors each individual: here in this virtual space – the Sovereign Reality – each fills the *incognita facies* with a description of the self. In this visage, each admires a narcissistic projection of the self, an ego translated into an inflated configuration and made super- (literally 'sovereign').[87] Hence, only through the Buribunks is the person-alisation *dispositif* of modern power revealed in its most paradigmatic form: this face functions as an inter-face.[88] A new society reshaped through control and the spectacle of the (living) self entertains itself[89] with a never-ending (personal) text. In the face of the sovereign, each sees only moving images of him/herself, the narration of a life that has become a spectacle of everyone for everyone.

Besieged by tracks of the self, profiled with a stockpile of data, existence is entirely immersed in written and readable traces – what in ancient Greek could be translated as 'γράμμα' (*gramma*).[90] To constantly produce and reproduce a *gramma* of the self in order to hold it permanently before one's eyes as something to manage: this is the new form of control – life as pro-gramme (fore-gramme). It does not matter if the pro-gramme is a medical programme, an economic one, a TV programme or a programme for the future (those schedules that would fit perfectly with the archivistic logic of buribunkology). The paradigm of

85 Schmitt (1996), pp 31–6.
86 Marramao (2013) 311–29.
87 In this sense, we are already moving towards Freud's *Massenpsychologie und Ich-Analyse*.
88 In the compulsive autobiographisation of one's life, the head of the Leviathan works as a point of gathering and projecting autobiographical traces by which each of us is captivated. In this sense, the social order is secured from this conjuncture of mutual self-spectacularisation: the screen of today will hopefully become history.
89 From the Latin '*intra-tenere*', suggesting the idea of being entertained but also being captivated or even caught by something.
90 The word oscillates between the actual use of 'gram' (as small quantity), a trackable unity of measurement, and '-gram' or 'gram-' as the act of writing – usually as codified text – as in 'hologram', 'grammatic' and 'gramophone'.

contemporary control consists of producing the increasing transparency and immediate visibility of this self-programming activity,[91] which, as we see in Koselleck, can often imply more than one *Vernichtungsprogramm.*[92] The *gramma* that accompanies us stands before us as a visible anathema, as an omen for life.[93]

The autobiographical practice has lost its salvific or exemplary function because this cultural form has been intercepted by power,[94] becoming a protocol norm for social interaction. Nowadays, auto-bio-graphy tends to mortify and then to extinguish the vivacity of the *bíos*, which was once in constant tension with the two poles: (1) the *autos*, [95] and (2) the *graphic.* On the one hand, a line of tension opposed life to self-referentiality, namely the risk of degenerating from the dream of autonomy and self-determination into exclusive egotism and from vital forces beyond control into mere automatism. On the other hand, life was mediated/translated by means of dia-grams (aids for memorisation and explication) in order to be maximally understood. They worked as partial projections (according to the impossible task of watching us live while we are living) and were always exposed as being mendacious, misleading or improper – the graphic was a reflective mirror that always implied something deforming and enigmatic.

What remains of that *bíos* today tends to disappear. In the best case, it is reduced to biometry, to the continuous recalculation of the limits of our own life, so as to make of it a matter of fibres and the management of one's bowels. From the multiplication of data and of algorithmic correlations, we underestimate the risk of our body merely conforming to a mirage of the self.

Indeed, we risk forgetting that the self in the autobiographic genre was just a pre-text, not a lowest common denominator of the text to which the *bíos* must be reduced.[96] It emerged *automatically* – out of nowhere – in the middle of a practice of self-cultivation: writing on the trail of the supposed self, for instance. On the contrary, the contemporary idea of the self displays its centripetal function: as an inhibitor of life. This latter is flattened in our attempt to explain it, and therefore falls into cycles of affirming and promoting the self, leaving us unable to articulate any experience without reducing it to a (potentially paranoid) narrative *dispositif.*

91 Tiqqun (2020).
92 We nowadays understand this in terms of ecological collapse and the decreasing pluralism of forms of life.
93 To reply to Carl Schmitt's irony, it is possible to affirm that life as pro-gramme has become a unique political programme in late Western modernity.
94 *Reintegration* in Guy Debord's terminology (Debord 1995, p 47).
95 The ambiguity of this word is much more present in Romance languages, where in many cases it is perfectly coincident with the word 'self' – 'autocoscienza' as 'self-consciousness', for example. 'Autós' stands both for repetition and sameness and for identifying the self of someone/something.
96 Derrida seems to suggest something close to this in *Otobiographies* (Derrida 2005), p. 73: '*Il y a là une différance de l'autobiographie, une allo- et thanatographie*'.

Thus, the universal norm that drives our social control should properly be called an *autographic practice*. For philosophers, the *bíos* was still an element that, by means of words, could interact with the heterogeneous folds of existence – in relation to *theós* and *zoé, eros, techno* and *thánatos*. And still, this same concept was able – once mortified in a biological or biographical sense – to activate a need for insurrection with the promise of a (better) life still to come. In our present condition (characterised by automatisation, spectacularisation, self-referentiality, mortification/extinction), the *scriptor-lector*, or *autor-spectator*, is captured in a selfish story-telling,[97] in a mode of self-understanding that always takes the form of a graphic novel: no place for *bíos* on the verge of planetary extinction.

The autographic tendency has the merit of confusing the immediacy of the tracks related to our profilisation with life itself, and thus it reinforces, in both quantity and speed, forms of self-extractivism and sacrifice of the self to *read-ability*. Widespread and deeply rooted, the self-description of life has become the *Ur-norm* of our new norm-ality.[98] In this sense, Carl Schmitt's *fabula filosofica* seems to suggest to our present condition that control runs before and through our own eyes: we strive to focus (on) our representation of life, but we end up in a blunder, confined to a non-life that extorts streams of data and archives of notes. In accordance with Hobbes, the eye that does not diverge from a unique object of contemplation (a selfish self) risks no longer being able to see, 'it being almost all one for a man to be always sensible of one and the same thing, and not to be sensible at all of any thing'.[99]

References

Bruno Accarino (1991) 'Filosofia della storia: La parabola della modernità', in Carlo Galli (ed), *Logiche e crisi della modernità*, Il Mulino.

Giorgio Agamben (1998) *Homo Sacer: Sovereign Power and Bare Life*, Stanford University Press.

Walter Benjamin (1928) *Einbahnstrasse*, Ernst Rowohlt Verlag.

Walter Benjamin (2018) 'Der destruktive Charakter', in *Erfahrung und Zerstörung: Zwei Texte Walter Benjamins*, Verlag Vorwerk, 8.

Rosi Braidotti (2013) *The Posthuman*, Polity Press.

Horst Bredekamp (2012) *Thomas Hobbes – Der Leviathan. Das Urbild Des Modernen Staates Und Seine Gegenbilder*, Akademie Verlag.

97 It is not writing as such that is to blame as a radical evil before an uncontaminated life – that is, before the world of ineffability. This would be a case of political Romanticism, also criticised by Schmitt in a book published on *The Buribunks*. See Schmitt (1991).

98 This helps to explain the paradoxical experience of begging for an autograph from one who has made an art of self-promotion (the 'influencer'): the heroes of our present era and of buribunkology on full display.

99 Hobbes (1839), p 394.

Patricia Clough (2008) 'The Affective Turn: Political, Economy, Biomedia and Bodies' 25(1) *Theory, Culture & Society*1.

Melinda Cooper (2008) *Life as Surplus: Biotechnology & Capitalism in the Neoliberal Era*, University of Washington Press.

Guy Debord (1995) *The Society of the Spectacle*, Zone Books.

Massimo De Carolis (1996) 'Toward a Phenomenology of Opportunism', in Michael Hardt and Paulo Virno (eds), *Radical Thought in Italy: A Potential Politics*, University of Minnesota Press, 37.

Massimo De Carolis (2017) *Il Rovescio della Libertà*, Quodlibet.

Erik De Vries (2001) 'Alexandre Kojève – Carl Schmitt Correspondence and Alexandre Kojève "Colonialism from a European Perspective"' 29(1) *Interpretation* 115.

Jacques Derrida (2005) *Otobiographies*, Éditions Galilée.

Carlo Galli (1996) *Genealogia della Politica: Carl Schmitt e la Crisi del Pensiero Politico Moderno*, Il Mulino.

Mark Fisher (2009) *Capitalist Realism*, Zerobooks.

Michel Foucault (1971) *L'Ordre du Discours*, Gallimard.

Michel Foucault (1983) 'L'Écriture de Soi' 5 *Corps écrit* 3.

Michel Foucault (1994) *Dits and Écrits*, Gallimard.

Pierre Hadot (1995) *Philosophy as a Way of Life: Spiritual Exercises from Socrates to Foucault*, Blackwell.

Byung-Chul Han (2017) *Psychopolitics: Neoliberalism and New Technologies of Power*, Verso.

Donna Haraway (1985) 'A Manifesto for Cyborgs: Science, Technology, and Socialist Feminism in the 1980s' 5 *Socialist Review* 2.

Michael Hardt and Antonio Negri (2000) *Empire*, Harvard University Press.

Thomas Hobbes (1839) *The English Works of Thomas Hobbes of Malmesbury, Vol. I: Elements of Philosophy*, John Bohn.

Anselm Jappe (2017) *La Société Autophage. Capitalisme, Démesure et Autodestruction*, La Découverte.

Immanuel Kant (2009) *An Answer to the Question: What is Enlightenment?*, Penguin.

Ellen Kennedy (2004) *Constitutional Failure: Carl Schmitt in Weimar*, Duke University Press.

Reinhart Koselleck (2000) *Zeitschichten*, Suhrkamp Verlag.

Giacomo Leopardi (2013) 'Broom, or the Flower of the Desert', in *Canti* (trans Jonathan Galassi), Penguin.

Adam Limentani (1996) 'A Brief History of the International Psychoanalytical Association' 77(1) *The International Journal of Psychoanalysis* 149.

Domenico Losurdo (2011) *Liberalism. A Counter-History*, Verso.

David Lyon (1994) *The Electronic Eye: The Rise of Surveillance Society*, University of Minnesota Press.

Noel Malcolm (2002) *Aspects of Hobbes*, Oxford University Press.

Giacomo Marramao (2013) *Dopo il Leviatano. Individuo e Comunità*, Bollati Boringhieri.

Achille Mbembe (2003) 'Necropolitics' 15(1) *Public Culture* 11.

Daniel McLoughlin (2019) 'The Biopolitics of the Buribunks: The Digital Archive and the End of History' 28 *Griffith Law Review* 137.

Constance Penley, Andrew Ross and Donna Haraway (1990) 'Cyborgs at Large: Interview with Donna Haraway' 25/26 *Social Text* 8.

Mark Poster (1989) *Critical Theory and Poststructuralism: In Search of a Context*, Cornell University Press.

Mark Poster (1990) *The Mode of Information*, Polity Press.
Carl Schmitt (1991) *Political Romanticism*, MIT Press.
Carl Schmitt (1996) *The Leviathan in the State Theory of Thomas Hobbes: Meaning and Failure of a Political Symbol*, Greenwood Press.
Carl Schmitt (2017) *Ex Captivitate Salus*, Polity Press.
Jacob Taubes (2013) *To Carl Schmitt: Letters and Reflections*, Columbia University Press.
Tiqqun (2020) *The Cybernetic Hypothesis* (trans Robert Hurley), Semiotext(e).
J.R.R. Tolkien (2007) *The Children of Hurin*, HarperCollins.
J.R.R. Tolkien (2009) *The Lord of The Rings*, HarperCollins.

Chapter 11

Modernist life-writing and early cinema in Carl Schmitt's *The Buribunks*

Joseph Owen

Introduction

Conceived and written during a time of vast European avant-garde experimentation, *The Buribunks* is Carl Schmitt's most blatant attempt at creative modernist expression. Through literary devices common to modernist textual practices, Schmitt's idiosyncratic work functions as a satire of individual egoism, a parody of institutional bureaucracy and a warning against false forms of sovereign decision. His ironic revelation of modern selfhood is threefold: he shows how swiftly biography can slip into autobiography; how the privileging of human personality fuses with the privileging of human reason; and how the unlimited and undiscerning documentation of sense experience denies the true comprehension of history. On a literary level, Schmitt's preoccupation with the biographical mode was long-lasting and started in his early culture critiques, which are again receiving attention.[1] *The Buribunks*, the most mature work from his early period, has undergone renewed scholarly appraisal and a recent full translation in English.[2] In the text, the manifold critical targets include bohemians, positivists, rationalists and machine utopians. Together, these types constitute the Buribunks, who are bizarre figurations, transcribing written notes and submitting written entries to the extent that they are physically transformed, absorbing the tools of their labour. Pen and ink become body and blood. Each Buribunk is part of a collective entity but alienated from one another, insofar as each has a compromised identity in service of the whole. Schmitt's despair about both the modern sovereign subject and its depiction finds form in this speculative fiction, which confronts the modernist tendency to represent solitary interior consciousness as that which perceives and accounts for everything, all of the time.

Scholars variously describe *The Buribunks* as 'surrealistic', 'a dystopia', a mockery of 'the secular ritual of confession', 'a satire of detached intellectualism', an ironic 'world history of inscription', 'a critique of modern subjectivity'

1 Bikundo and Tranter (2019).
2 In this chapter, I use Gert Reifarth and Laura Petersen's English translation (Chapter 2 of this volume).

DOI: 10.4324/9781003091066-14

and a 'biting caricature of the boheme and of positivism'.[3] Such characterisations suggest and subvert its classification as a modernist text, hinting at modes and genres of modernism while remaining contemptuous of the putative aesthetic subjectivities modernism desired to represent. This provokes consideration of modernist attitudes to life-writing and early cinema, which bears on discussions of the text and Schmitt's wider political and legal thought. *The Buribunks* arrives, after all, on the cusp of Schmitt's decisive shift from a cultural to political thinker. Using techniques of extended irony and self-reflexive footnotes, Schmitt challenges the Wilhelmine culture that had failed to respond to a call for political clarity and visibility. He sought to critique an age that venerated rules and norms, celebrated scientific arrogance, idolised the podium of selfhood and valorised technological advance. As Ellen Kennedy notes:

> From an early discovery of modernism and expressionism, Schmitt created the figure of liberalism that guided his analysis of Weimar's institutions, a *Gestalt* and doctrine that was part romantic and part positivistic and that was the spirit of his age ... Schmitt's antiliberalism was literary and theological at its core.[4]

Schmitt uses the openings widened by aesthetic modernism against his enemy figure of liberalism. Many currents of contemporary modernism were likewise sceptical of the parliamentary tendency to accumulate details and endlessly discuss events. Although they favoured unfiltered access to individual experience, modernists tempered this access by acknowledging the fallibility of human perception and the associated implications for democracy. But whereas Schmitt sought the clarity of straight lines and visible decisions, modernists delved further into the confusion and multiplicity of experience to articulate the early twentieth-century epoch.

In 1918, the Wilhelmine *Kaiserreich* was on the verge of collapse. The existing political system had consisted of a tense hybrid of autocratic and popular rule. End-of-era anxiety is generally productive for intellectual output, and this period provided fertile ground for the artistic avant-garde and literary modernists in Germany – particularly in Berlin and Munich. It also encouraged Schmitt's intellectual musings: his diaries bear out concern about political disorder and cultural chaos. These anxieties constitute his melancholy creative method, which functions as a critique of biography, autobiography and diary in *The Buribunks*, deployed within a narrative that outlines the systemic failures of technological modernity and the inherent inadequacies of scientific progress. Despite its melancholy origins, the text itself is sardonic, witty and fundamentally exuberant, particularly in its portrait of the principles, methodology and

3 Bredekamp (1999), p 251; Balke (2017), pp 633, 644; Meierhenrich and Simons (2017), p 7; Kittler (1999), p 231; Mehring (2014), p 86; Kennedy (2004), p 44.
4 Kennedy (2004), p 40.

genealogy of Buribunkdom. This satire is born of Schmitt's historical moment. For Schmitt, the world of the Buribunks is one in which institutions are conspicuous and unwieldy, the practice of historicism is self-important and futile, and the individual is devitalised and detached from value. Although fictionalised diaries are common to literary dystopias, Reinhart Koselleck argues that these conditions of institutionalism, historicism and the cult of the individual form a 'negative utopia', in which the diary-keeping Buribunks represent 'the interior ... turned outward'. The public accumulation of interiority constitutes a project of surveillance, which he calls 'a mode of the performance of perfected terror'.[5] More accurately, *The Buribunks* is a twofold dissection, which argues that obsessive accumulation of details devalues the nature of interiority and that constant documentation of events obscures the experience of reality. Schmitt renders the mind as a hard surface, or as another unit of measurement, to critique the belief that selfhood can be understood, interrogated and articulated insofar as history can be mastered, coerced and anticipated.

This chapter demonstrates that through modernist means, Schmitt assaults what he views as a debased, inert and embedded institutional culture, one that indulges the individual through total, collective machinery. By manipulating voice and register, modernists 'challenge the established narrative practices' in their fictions.[6] By using their life experiences through variously ironic, sceptical and impersonal modes of distancing, they depict reality as it appears to the modern subject: as fractured, disorientated and uncertain. Through aesthetic self-creation and sensory fragmentation, modernism seeks to undermine the established values of realism. By reformulating experience, modernists see the 'rejection of modern reality [as] purely subjective'.[7] Realist presentations of experience are predicated on apparently objective detail, formal accuracy, rational Enlightenment thinking and an overarching monotheism. Modernists consider such predicates redundant among the discontinuities of the modern world and wish to reflect reality through its disconcerting effect on the individual consciousness. Concerned with developing and comprehending identity and the self, the modernist focus on selfhood indicates a deliberate refusal of the social and moral impositions of the time. Modernists are not compelled to present characters through the prism of social order, norms and customs; instead, the individual constitutes the prism through which to view the world. Whether tracing 'the growing emancipation of the expressive or creative individual from socially accepted forms of belief' or providing 'an intimate sense of a differing or dissentient identity', modernists arrest the narrative point of view from the stale conventions and moral certitude of yesteryear fiction.[8]

5 Koselleck (2002), p 93.
6 DiBattista and Wittman (2014), p xi.
7 Lukács (2005), p 403.
8 Butler, (2010), p 55.

Taking this general summary into account, I read *The Buribunks* through various modernist interpretations of biography, autobiography and diary in both literature and cinema. Given Schmitt's cultural appetite for the contemporary arts scene, this chapter draws on a wide range of sources for its analysis of *The Buribunks*, including Virginia Woolf's work on biography, Robert J. Flaherty's docufiction, Gertrude Stein's literary poetics and Carl Theodor Dreyer's *The Passion of Joan of Arc* (1928). The constituent elements of biography, autobiography and diary thus provide the headings within this chapter, organising my reading of Schmitt's playful and disquieting account of contemporaneous efforts to record human history. In his view, this mechanical, documentary process – one simultaneously fractured and consuming – had in the modern period come to prize unaccountable machinery and private self-obsession above all else. For Schmitt, if this tendency continued unchecked, it would drown populations in folly, inertia and limitless reflection, rendering intellectual and experiential life as a succession of fleeting, meaningless and self-involved moments, eternally glimpsed and remembered, without end or purpose.

Biography

Virginia Woolf wrote several essays on the nature of biography, which function as tempered manifestoes for a redesigned genre and new critical approach.[9] In modernist scholarship, Woolf's documentation of truth and reality has variously been theorised as 'the impossible art', 'this fictitious life', 'autobiografiction', 'life narrative' and 'life-writing'.[10] This preoccupation was partly fostered in negative opposition to her father, Sir Leslie Stephen, the first editor of the *Dictionary of National Biography*, whose intellectual and paternal influence on Woolf has been discussed widely.[11] Woolf writes in her essay 'The New Biography' (1927) that the character of Hamlet is the ideal figurative emblem for documenting the 'increasingly real … fictitious life' of the modern human subject. Consequently, the drama that contains Hamlet acts as the prime mover for private complexity, the influential origin story for contemporary biography. Multifaceted Hamlet is preferable to an unadorned archetype or cipher, which Woolf designates, a little dismissively, as 'John Smith of the Corn Exchange'. By this logic, the modern biographer should depict reality as derived from its subject's personality rather than through his or her actions. Truth, in this rendering, is more likely found among fraught individual subjectivities than upon a mere depository of names, items and dates. As Woolf summarises it, this mode of biography should complement the 'granite-like solidity' of fact with the 'rainbow-like intangibility' of imagination.[12]

9 Woolf, (2008), pp 99–123.
10 DiBattista and Wittman (2014), pp 55–66; Gualtieri (2000); Monk (2007); Riquelme (2013); Saunders (2010).
11 Bond (1986); Hill (1981).
12 Woolf (2008), p 95.

The instability of these oppositions means it is possible to indulge and lose both worlds – such is the delicate balance of truth and falsehood. Reality must be carefully sought amid the rubble of experience, in unfamiliar territories, through poetic abstractions, behind dark spots and across unending icy tundra. Woolf identifies the formal and sensual motivation for this search in her novel-length satire of biography, *Orlando* (1928), as a 'desire for distance, for music, for shadow, for space, [which] takes hold of us'.[13] Modernists sought the elusive character of the biographical subject and of the self-chronicling diarist. The modernist investigation into the nature of fictionality was predicated on the discovery of truths not accessible through scientific inquiry, realistic representation or statistical analysis – all of which seems to offer the infatuated biographer and its visual analogue, the documentarian, plenty of opportunities to 'be truthful; but fantastic'.[14]

The movement between biographical text and documentary vision appears obfuscating, but it is worth considering how Woolf's thoughts on biography and writing of *Orlando* developed with concurrent advances in the moving image.[15] Although Woolf was ambivalent about the ability of the cinematic form to adapt literary consciousness, she acknowledged how silent film could offer a fresh artistic perspective. In her 1926 article 'The Cinema', Woolf generously speculated on the overall possibilities of the medium; in her diaries, she sedulously noted down her viewing habits.[16] These included *Man of Aran* (1934), Robert J. Flaherty's partly fabricated study of inhabitants living in relative isolation off the west coast of Ireland.[17] Given that Woolf intended to depict the human subject both in its dizzying multitude and as a necessary product of modernity, Flaherty's nostalgic hankering for a primitivist, premodern existence must have supplied her with some form of jarring counterpoint. Not that they were without similarities in approach: both drew on ostensibly sympathetic colonial imaginaries to distinguish between western civilisation and what they reverentially deemed to be far-flung and exotic social orders. Mostly for comic purposes, Woolf provides a sketchily drawn Constantinople in chapter 4 of *Orlando*, while Flaherty, with apparent sincerity, captures arid plains of the Canadian Arctic as the setting for his dubious ethnographic study of Inuit peoples, *Nanook of the North* (1922). Flaherty's basic equipment and candid shooting techniques belied his Byzantine development process and calculated deception of the audience. After the initial filming, Flaherty dropped his cigarette, incinerating the original reels. With renewed focus, he returned to the Ungava Peninsula to fashion a narrative under more artificial conditions. This inevitably places the viewer, desirous of accurate representation, in an ethical and philosophical quandary.

13 Woolf (2003), p 103.
14 Woolf (1980), p 157.
15 Shail (2006).
16 Woolf (2008), pp 172–6.
17 Marie (2015), p 520.

Flaherty made the character of Nanook, the taciturn provider and patriarch of a tight-knit family, central to his new depiction. Among the acts of everyday survival, family members are shown hunting walruses, building igloos and, in a striking moment, emerging sequentially and impossibly out of a small kayak. One comic sequence has them meet jovially with 'the white man' at a trading post. The proceeding hijinks feature the children as they over-consume sea biscuit and lard, take remedy through castor oil and bite – apparently innocently – into a gramophone record. Although unspecified, these scenes come imbued with a knowing theatricality. Something is up. What if we learn that Nanook, in real life, was previously aware of the gramophone and its purpose; that he was already using rifles instead of spears for hunting; that his name was not even Nanook but Allakariallak; and that, rather than dying of starvation in the desert, he was likely at home succumbing to tuberculosis? What makes Flaherty's effacement of his Indigenous participants so galling today, but no less riveting in the cinematic instant, is the extent to which it allows the viewer to be morally complicit in their treatment. This is partly down to our fluctuating systems of knowledge. Recognition of subsequent postcolonial theory mitigates a broad appreciation of the film's technical and dramatic devices. Critiques of anthropology and ethnography weigh against its circumstances of production. These types of questions haunt documentary filmmakers, who are now often less coy and more self-reflexive than Flaherty.

'One often has to distort a thing in order to catch its true spirit,' Flaherty said in response to criticisms of his tendency to docudrama.[18] This thesis does not sound too dissimilar to Woolf's biographical manifesto, but it is fair to argue that Flaherty's embellishments in *Nanook* do not figure 'the fearless, lovable, happy go-lucky Eskimo' as Hamlet, Prince of Denmark.[19] Instead, Flaherty has scant desire for historical or psychoanalytic explanations; all things, including the human subjects, appear as hard and immediate surfaces, as extensions of natural habitat and subsistence labour. Truths of Allakariallak's internal life could be found in his various toils, in the barren terrain and in the heightened atmosphere of stoicism and melancholy. Yet, in Flaherty's subaltern translation of Woolf's dictum, *Nanook of the North* may as well be John Smith of the Corn Exchange, as defined only by his material existence. In *Nanook*, the viewer's melancholy is wrought from instabilities of fact, through Flaherty's condescending summaries and our knowledge of the participants' exploitation. The film has 'A Story of Life and Love in the Actual Arctic' as its subtitle, which draws attention to it as a work of fiction, although patterns of deceit regularly entwine following the colon. After all, Woolf's centuries-spanning fantasy *Orlando* is only, in some ways, 'A Biography'. Insistence on genre emphasises the essential deceptions of film and literature while seeking to conflate empirical modes of knowledge.

18 Gray (1950), p 47.
19 Flaherty (1922).

Schmitt flips the effect of fiction on reality around the other way. In his 1956 literary critique *Hamlet or Hecuba*, Schmitt identifies two mysteries in the play, labelling them 'the taboo of the queen' and 'the figure of the avenger'.[20] Because of these conundrums, Schmitt argues that the most famous drama of all could not be understood as fiction alone. Just as the gap between thought and action is unbridgeable for Hamlet, the riddle of truth and imagination within the play cannot be resolved. First, Schmitt could not accept the lack of clarity as to the guilt or innocence of Gertrude. As discussed in the opening act, Gertrude has married Claudius, who murdered her ex-husband, Hamlet's father and namesake. It is one of the play's dark areas, which only makes sense by acknowledging the historical intrusions that existed during its first performances: Mary Queen of Scots, deceased mother to the reigning King James I, had married her husband's murderer. For Schmitt, the power of the tragedy was located in its suggestion of reality, and not in Sigmund Freud's Oedipal interpretation.[21] The taboo, in this case, collapses the distinction between fact and fiction, combining the knowledge of trauma with the trauma of knowledge. Second, Hamlet's vengeful burden fuses with an introspection that amounts to indecision, which Schmitt calls the 'Hamletization' of the avenger, wherein 'the hero of the revenge play … suffers an internal distortion of his character and motivation'.[22] Hamlet, though not a 'copy' of James I, brings to light the circumstances of his 1603 accession to the English throne. These developments transform Hamlet from the traditional mythic hero into a necessarily tragic and modern one. With the taboo of the queen, this functions as one of several 'structurally determining, genuine intrusions', acquiring greater potency than mere mirrorings of and allusions to contemporary events.[23] For Schmitt, the dramatic and necessarily tragic effects conjured by Hamlet's psychological distortions are the product of true historical circumstances.

In *Hamlet or Hecuba*, Schmitt suggests that the potency of the historical situation transforms the pure play of theatre into what he terms tragedy, the fusion of reality and fiction in the context of a public dramatic spectacle.[24] This illustrates the spatial and temporal intersections central to his work. Hans-Georg Gadamer's acute critique of Schmitt, who reads *Hamlet* 'like a *roman à clef*', inverts Schmitt's belief that the time erupts within art, arguing instead that the play 'leaves an indefinite space around its real theme' and that, because of its 'open indeterminacy, myth is able to produce constant new invention from within itself'.[25] This underlines a fair appraisal of Schmitt: that he was a poor reader of literary texts whose refusal to recognise art's productive ambiguity

20 Schmitt (2009).
21 Schmitt (2009), p 7.
22 Schmitt (2009), p 21.
23 Schmitt (2009), pp 21–5.
24 Schmitt (2009).
25 Gadamer (2012), pp 498–500.

skewed his understanding of the relationship between politics and aesthetics, and of the difference between mere image and transcendent myth.

Flaherty and Woolf's diverse responses to the biographical form invert Schmitt's concept of tragedy in *Hamlet or Hecuba*; they also illuminate Schmitt's grappling with the genre in *The Buribunks*. Schmitt ironically employs the narrative device '*in medias res*' to place the reader immediately in his depiction of the Buribunks, who have two distinguishing features: constant diary keeping and large mouths. Repetitive actions and peculiar countenances define them. Schmitt suggests tackling 'the problem at its central, most interesting point', comparing the study of the Buribunks with popular contemporary anthropological assessments; his deliberately dubious narrator articulates, 'it is the intellect that designs the body', and by stating this, he blurs the mind/body distinction.[26] This emphasis on the relationship between interiority and corporeal imagery is one of the most insistent aspects of the text. 'It would therefore be careless, to say the least, to simply deem the diary to be the decisive fact in an intellectual sense rather than the enlarged mouth,' Schmitt writes,[27] before illustrating the correlation between intellect and physiognomy by using the example of tribes and employing a type of ironic racism. Given the anthropology of the period, in which large lips were taken as a serious indicator of primitiveness, it is not entirely clear if Schmitt, a notable future Nazi, is satirising forms of social Darwinism. The pompous narrator lists 'lesser peoples, Polynesians, Tierra del Fuegians, Baronga Negroes and other tribes incapable of an education, have a relatively small mouth, even though they are cannibals'. These characterisations initiate a probable 'close connection between the enlarged mouth and a higher intellect'.[28] This excerpt prefaces his writings in *Political Romanticism* (1919), published the following year:

> Primitive peoples – humanity as childlike – are also bearers of these unlimited possibilities. The contradiction between rational limitation and the irrational profusion of possibilities is romantically eliminated because another equally real but still unlimited reality is played off against limited reality: in opposition to the rationalistic, mechanized state, the childlike people; in opposition to the man already limited by his profession and accomplishments, the child who plays with all possibilities; in opposition to the clear line of the classical, the primitive in its infinity of meanings.[29]

Schmitt compares the plurality of meanings in Romanticism to a childlike primitivism, and consequently likens single linearity to a form of classical thinking. He traduces infinite possibilities and valorises the delimiting power of the

26 Chapter 2 of this volume, pp 14–5.
27 Chapter 2 of this volume, p 15.
28 Chapter 2 of this volume, p 14.
29 Schmitt (1991), p 69.

borderline. This amounts to using racial anthropology as dubious shorthand for illustrating his anxieties about lineal excess. In such literary techniques, Schmitt's racist thought emerges. These passages function as portents for his anti-Semitic characterisations of Jews in his 1938 book on the Leviathan and in texts such as *Land and Sea* (1942).

Buribunks undergo physiological changes because of their diary keeping. Consciousness alters their anatomical surfaces. The obsessive process of anticipation debilitates them. Through the Buribunks, Schmitt creates an alternative rendering of the human body, composed of transformed faces, creaturely habits and machine-like tendencies. The dread with which Buribunks view the future is described as 'the dark body' – imposing, fearful, racialised – which is precluded by an obsessive, anticipatory present.[30] Buribunks ignore the sovereign decision, as Schmitt understands it, in favour of the accumulative detail that generates outward order. This constitutes the manipulation of the material world from an institutionalised distance, which is disguised as the simple frictions of the collective good. The Buribunks are biophysically transformed through their vast data production and bureaucratic surveillance. Their deification of communal processes thwarts the pursuit of human meaningfulness. For Schmitt, the desire to produce excessive temporal proximity to history leads to psychological indulgence and physical deformity.

Schmitt's editorial footnotes bring into relief further aspects of the biographical form. They contain comments from an imagined interlocutor who criticises Schmitt in his guise as author of Buribunkian history. A supplementary fictional history plays out in the footer. Don Juan chooses not to dwell on his experiences, but the relentless activity of the Buribunks means, for reasons different from those of Don Juan, that they too have few opportunities to reflect. Deeper in the footnotes, Schmitt deploys numerous imagined references and citations to depict alleged scholarly agreement over one forerunner of the biographical method, Ferker, emphasising his capacity for psychological empathy. Schmitt jokingly refers to himself through the imagined interlocutor, doubting his methods of proof and his tendency to false conclusions, before outlining Ferker and his intellectual successor Schnekke, whose risible behaviour towards women presages the self-absorbed academic concerns of the neo-Buribunks. The final footnote suggests that fame after death is akin to the growing nails and hair of a corpse. Throughout the text, the footnotes provide the most outlandish examples of a satirical method, with which Schmitt undercuts tropes of biography and biographical fiction.

Autobiography

Woolf's *Orlando* questions the distinction between biography, autobiography and modernist fiction. It is many things: a satire of conventional Victorian

30 Chapter 2 of this volume, p 26.

biographies; a consciously indulgent portrayal of Woolf's lover, Vita Sackville-West; and a narrative that travels across genders, spaces and epochs. Beginning in the reign of Elizabeth I, the novel concludes on the book's supposed date of publication: 'Thursday the eleventh of October, Nineteen Hundred and Twenty-eight'.[31] These final lines are important to consider, given how Schmitt parodies the Buribunkian ideal of externalising and memorialising every lived instant: Buribunks literally publish each instant at the very moment it is experienced. Schmitt's early writing culminated in two works, *The Buribunks* and *Political Romanticism*. Both assault the obsession with autobiography as a mode of living and a basis from which to adopt a political identity. Buribunks are emblematic of the typical modern subject who turns life into autobiography; meanwhile, the political romantic is 'his own poet, his own philosopher, his own king, and his own master builder in the cathedral of his personality'.[32] Despite Schmitt's apparent disdain for autobiography, many of his exculpatory postwar works are noticeably autobiographical, while his diaries were consciously arranged in such a way as to restore his otherwise tarnished moral and intellectual legacy. Modernist interpretations of the autobiographical novel include the *Bildungsroman* sub-genre and the *Künstlerroman*, a novel wherein the protagonist undergoes personal growth, specifically about an artist's individual development towards intellectual and sensual maturity. This had an obvious appeal for modernists, who sought to supplant the dominance of moral and social codes through aesthetic regeneration. Rather than present a cohesive and autonomous picture of their lives, modernists used the form to interrogate the archaic moral traditions, which had shaped their upbringing, and to rearticulate private traumas in a manner that later defined war literature in the twentieth century.

Gertrude Stein offers a suggestive route into evaluating modernist biographical methods. Stein's literary portraiture is often bracketed into phases.[33] Ulla Haselstein notes that 'all of her portraits share the general tendency of avant-garde art to combine or fuse the modes of different media of words, sounds, and images'.[34] Stein's contribution to the genre of literary portraits is that of modernist reinvention, because 'she altogether refuses mimetic representation, but retains the most fundamental feature of the genre, namely its referentiality'.[35] For Stein, repetition is rather 'insistence',[36] which creates meaning through emphasis on word presentation in subtle, varying syntax. Stein's circular method of description tried to defy the temporalities of traditional literary forms. The restricted use of words and punctuation contributes to

31 Woolf (2003), p 162.
32 Schmitt (1991), p 20.
33 Hoffman (1965); Steiner (1978).
34 Haselstein (2003), p 724.
35 Haselstein (2003), p 727.
36 Stein (1957), pp 165–206.

the disorientating rhythms of her writing. Schmitt's 'outline of a philosophy of the Buribunken' is reminiscent of Stein's literary portraits:

> I write, therefore I am; I am, therefore I write. What do I write? I write myself. Who writes me? I myself write myself. What is the content of my writing? I write that I write myself. What is the big engine lifting me above this self-sufficient circle of I-ness? History!
>
> I am therefore a letter on the typewriter of history. I am a letter writing itself. But strictly speaking I do not write that I write myself but only the letter that I am. But, writing, the World Spirit captures itself in me – so that I, capturing myself, at the same time capture the World Spirit. In fact I do not capture myself and it through thinking, but writing – for in the beginning there is the deed and not the thought. That means: I am not only the reader of world history but also its writer.[37]

Neglecting the service of external portraiture, Buribunks are rather fixated with documenting the self. Schmitt focuses on those who value autobiography over reality because he was anxious that, for such a person, autobiography is, in fact, reality. Schmitt delineates this section of his critique by creating an imagined genealogy of biographers, beginning with Don Juan, who lives only in the moment, his servant Leporello, and the fictionalised Ferker and Schnekke – all failed portraitists – who developed the medium and paved the way for the ultimate biographers, the Buribunks.

The Buribunks is also a product of Schmitt's combined experiences as young man within the legal academy and under military command. The text offers an alternate society in which the desire to produce continual lines of information is held as the highest virtue, which is evidenced by a vast institutional framework. Organisations have lengthy and ludicrous initialisms, which constitute the populated landscape of the Buribunks. There are '400,000 buribunkological dissertations (20 divisions!)', the 'International Buribunkological Institute for Ferker and Related Research (IBIFERR)' and 'the Buribunk and Ferker Research Panel Commission (BAFREPAC)'. Schmitt creates a linear history of the Buribunks, which eventually leads to the supreme state of Buribunkdom, the purest realm of the Buribunks. He begins his visionary history with Leporello, who notes the sexual exploits of Don Juan, before tracing the dynasty of the Buribunks' forerunners, including the fictional creations of Ferker and Schnekke. These scholars' incipient, failed attempts at self-illustration lay the ground for the perfect world of accumulated knowledge. In this ultimate universe, the Buribunks give meaning to their existence by incessantly detailing it. Their concluding philosophy is one of inclusive and simultaneous 'I-ness'.[38] Such rampant officialdom, matched with unchecked egoism, fuels

37 Chapter 2 of this volume, pp 25–6.
38 Chapter 2 of this volume, p 13.

Schmitt's critique of liberal progress, particularly its emphasis on common laws and the modern individual as the central sovereign subject.

In short, the Buribunks' intellectual intensity produces a form of aesthetic self-awareness that connects mind and matter, which abolishes intellectual dualisms and creates a new form of philosophical idealism. Buribunkdom functions as the higher third, which reconciles oppositions that originate in the figure of Don Juan and continue, with differences, in Ferker: 'We see a wildly agitated life, filled with nerve-wracking experiences without Don Juan's mindless addiction to pleasure, in full awareness of its own wild agitation, I would even say of its own modernity and suitability for the theatre.' The biographical trajectory finds its end in 'the spiritual region where the synthesis of these numerous contradictory elements, of this tangle of negated negatives, takes place – the inexplicable, the absolute, the essence of every religiosity – is none other than the buribunkian'.[39] To locate the elusive character of human experience, Buribunks turn to a painstakingly manicured synthesis of information, in essence a technological equivalent of the Catholic Church. Schmitt wryly suggests that the remnants of theology persist, even within the vacuum of representative authority caused by the modern faith in technology.

Ferker is the 'Moses' in the history of the Buribunks, but not quite the hero, because he is struck down by the curse of anti-intellectualism. Schmitt illustrates this by noting the 'starkly alien elements circulating as foreign bodies in Ferker's otherwise pure blood; atavistic reminders still cast their shadows onto large periods of his life and cloud the pure image of autarkic noble Buribunkdom'. Either Ferker's marriage or clinical depression ends his attempts at the diary, because his 'psychological abnormality manifests itself in locking up the torments of his soul – instead of writing them down and externalising them in a publication – and allowing them to create poisonous dreams of an atavistic fear of death and of a moral sense of responsibility'. His intellectual successor, Schnekke, otherwise achieves a level of documentary purity because, strikingly, 'Genius fell from the tree of his own personality.' Schnekke is the diary, at the level of selfhood and historical context: 'On a level where the "I" projecting itself into a tangible "You-World" streams back into the "World-I" with powerful rhythm, the highest harmony is reached through the absolute devotion of all powers to the inner self and its identity.'[40] In a summary of Schmitt's critique of egoism, Schnekke's '"I" resonat[es] in extreme autonomy [and] rests in an indistinctive generality, in a uniform lack of colour, which is the result of the will to power at its most sacrificial'. The Buribunks have a universal instinct and collective diary because of Schnekke, who 'set and secured the external conditions for buribunkian interiority and elevated the resounding chaos of unconnected single Buribunkdom to the harmonious perfection of a buribunkian cosmos'.[41] Buribunks stand on the

39 Chapter 2 of this volume, p 21.
40 Chapter 2 of this volume, p 22.
41 Chapter 2 of this volume, p 23.

shoulders of private giants; their pursuit of shared autobiographical perfection owes its debt to their solitary and self-sufficient ancestors.

Schmitt sardonically expresses the over-saturated and falsely unifying nature of the Buribunks' project: 'What would all research be without the secret weaving of the spirit which fuses lifeless details into a living organism and aids empathic understanding by transforming every act of perception into a genuine internalisation of memory'.[42] Schmitt creates textual ambiguity in his use of 'organisator' in the original German because it can be translated as 'the secret weaving of the spirit which organises life-less details'. The study of scientific buribunkology forms the logical endgame for an academy obsessed with both organisation and transformation, which is inscribed through both quantitative and qualitative output. Schmitt remains sceptical of details that are rationalised, contextualised and historicised. He ironically scolds the inchoate and prototypical Leporello, who has 'less of an urge to gather reliable research into details – nowhere does he trace the deeper connections of the specific conquest'. As a sign of intellectual progress in scientific buribunkology, 'entries of an erotic, demonic, satirical, political and so on nature are grouped together (under the strictest observation of the copyright law pertaining to each entry)'.[43] Life is sterile, relative to the mode of scientific inquiry that seeks to understand it. Memory, otherwise clipped and intangible, is solidified and certified on repeat. This predates Schmitt's metaphor of the crusted mechanism, consisting of rules and norms that have grown torpid by repetition, which his exception seeks to overcome. Buribunkology concerns the present because it does not value memory as nostalgia for the past, nor does it provide a necessary archive for the future. For Schmitt, the Buribunks' non-relation to history is the ultimate way of not being political.

The defining message of *The Buribunks* is that to excessively quantify and repeat is to perpetually anticipate. This commitment to research means that the study of the Buribunks is valued more than the Buribunks themselves. Schmitt calls this mode of inquiry 'scientific buribunkology', which amounts to a chronically aware self-justifying meta-sphere of learning.[44] It is smug, circular, overly referential and ever inwardly expanding. This continued expansion leads to indelibility. To create, to manufacture and to multiply constitute success and supremacy. This economy functions at maximum output and at optimum delineation. This functioning holds innate value because quantity is made into quality by virtue of its facticity. This predates Schmitt's critique of liberalism, which he thinks 'discusses and negotiates every political detail … in the hope that the definitive dispute, the decisive bloody battle, can be transformed into a parliamentary debate and permit the decision to be suspended forever in everlasting discussion'.[45] Schmitt polemically dramatised parliamentary democracy

42 Chapter 2 of this volume, p 13.
43 Chapter 2 of this volume, p 23.
44 Chapter 2 of this volume, p 13.
45 Schmitt (2005), p 63

as a mode of government made up exclusively of discussion. His ironic appraisal of scientific buribunkology presages his diagnosis of the follies of political liberalism.

Schmitt complicates the self-proclaimed values of the liberal Enlightenment, which he would later taunt for its belief

> in a clear and simple upward line of human progress. Progress would above all result in the intellectual and moral perfection of humanity. The line moved between two points: from religious fanaticism to intellectual liberty, from dogma to criticism, from superstition to enlightenment, from darkness to light.[46]

He suggests that the Enlightenment was more accurately a part of the 'successive stages of the changing central domains [which] are conceived neither as a continuous line of "progress" upwards nor the opposite'.[47] In *The Buribunks*, constant documentation is a source of fact beyond mere science. This sense of superiority and of the supreme idea of fact makes scientific buribunkology the overwhelming and most conclusive sphere of knowledge and understanding, even 'more than theology, jurisprudence or philosophy'. Any refusal to keep a diary must be 'justified and described in detail'; the disobedient Buribunks will otherwise face elimination to the lowest class in the system. For them, elimination is a fate worse than death. With echoes of Samuel Beckett, Schmitt states that, 'The wheel of progress passes silently over the silent one.'[48] Such a punitive measure enforces a simple idea: that in this world, even nothing must be reproduced in detail.

Endless lines, details, repetitions, conversations and discussions: these constitute Schmitt's critique of the state of anticipation, which denies sovereignty and the political. Schmitt wishes to 'trace the outlines of [the] sociological architecture'. The central claim in the Buribunks' manifesto is that 'thinking is nothing other than soundless speech; speaking nothing but scriptless writing; writing nothing but anticipated publishing and therefore publishing is identical with writing, with such minor differences that they may safely be disregarded'.[49] The Buribunks write and publish simultaneously, and in doing so they distort notions of time and of the body. Through their extreme efforts to anticipate, they merge their commodity with their work. As Schmitt noted while in postwar detention, 'Our life acquires furrows and lines through our labors, through our productivity in work and profession.'[50] In the biophysical imperative to transform themselves, the Buribunks face a process that makes it

46 Schmitt (2007), p 53
47 Schmitt (2007), p 82
48 Chapter 2 of this volume, p 25.
49 Chapter 2 of this volume, p 25.
50 Schmitt (2017), p 46.

impossible to discern between I, the typewriter and history. Historical reality denotes the past, the midwife the present and the dark body the future.

This language precipitates Schmitt's full embrace of legal and political solutions to the problem of sovereignty. According to Schmitt, at unpredictable times 'the power of real life breaks through the crust of mechanism that has become torpid by repetition'.[51] This linguistic formulation, one of disputably Nietzschean provenance, does not preclude anticipation of the decisive event. The crusting of the mechanism, which suppresses or undoes some vital element of human life, functions as a dulled anticipatory image. Visible through its density and accumulation, the excess of rules and norms reveals the melancholy torpor of parliamentary liberalism. Within the mass of procedures, little can be discerned or clarified because of the surplus of lines. This is what the metaphor of the exception acts against: details, details, details. Schmitt craves the elimination of these details, which paradoxically articulates their visibility. To transpose these details into lines – into the torpid repetitions that reveal the crusted mechanism – is to anticipate, through the formation of a dense image, the apparently unanticipated exception. His satirically loose use of metaphor in *The Buribunks* illustrates his resistance to claims that a mere image could anticipate the exception. In *Political Theology* (1922), Schmitt resorts to the crusted mechanism and the torpor of repetition for his dulled anticipatory symbolism. His tendency to metaphor concedes to aesthetic sensibilities within his theory of sovereignty, and his cravings for the borderline produce a distorted silhouette, a phantasm of the immediate sovereign decision.

Diary

Schmitt had suspicions about the literary philosophy of romanticism, to which modernists were heirs. Søren Kierkegaard's 'The Seducer's Diary' contains one of the most striking illustrations of the romantic attitude.[52] Kierkegaard's story emphasises romanticism not as an identifiable collection of cultural objects, movements or legible styles, but as an attitude that necessarily treats individual experience as the primary mode of value and knowledge. It is about Johannes, a young man who chances upon a young girl and concocts a Byzantine and calculated amorous pursuit. These are components of a game, to be undertaken for his own amusement. Johannes passes it off as aesthetic experience, superficially stimulating, sensual and imaginative. Without concrete meaning or moral grounding, actions are defined by equivocation, fortune and caprice. This is the attitude Schmitt equates with romanticism. The romantic privileges his subjectivity above all else. There are no consequences, only the occasion upon which to perform. Scholars have identified Schmitt's critique of romanticism and advocacy of politics as itself a form of romanticism, which

51 Schmitt (2005), p 15.
52 Kierkegaard (1992), pp 243–376; Schmitt (1991), pp xiv–xx.

brings Schmitt into conversation not only with Kierkegaard but also foundational theorists such as Niccolò Machiavelli[53] – all of which is to suggest that Schmitt's political anthropology is necessarily a pessimistic one. Nonetheless, it is worth noting the strong relationship between irony and melancholy in Kierkegaard's work, which opens discussions between Schmitt and literary modernisms.[54] Schmitt's theory of sovereignty requires an analysis of modernist aesthetics to satisfactorily reconcile his ideas of irony and political decision.

Because of his legal studies, juridical placements and military service, Schmitt lived in a number of cities across imperial Germany. Berlin and Munich became the 'central places in his life' and he was broadly 'attracted by big cities'.[55] He was a precocious rural child thrown into the possibility and mania of city living. Schmitt's early diaries reveal he was both fascinated and repulsed by life in Germany's cities. His obvious intrigue in the urban setting is married to an anxiety about outsiderness. Of his early life in Berlin, he says he saw himself as:

> An obscure young man of modest origins … part neither of the governing elite nor of an opposition movement … that meant that, standing wholly in the dark, I looked from the darkness into a brightly lit room … the strong repulsion which I experienced left me no comfort with my role. The feeling of sadness which filled me, increased my distance and evoked distrust and alienation in others.[56]

Steadfastly provincial, Schmitt writes as if in permanent limbo and deploys darkness as a motif. In Müller's view, Berlin embodied for Schmitt 'a progressive, metropolitan synthesis of liberalism, Protestantism and assimilated Jewish culture'.[57] The Berlin of that time was 'not only North-German-Protestant but, at least in the popular imagination, in some way Jewish as well'. Despite his rising status in the capital, Schmitt always considered himself somewhat apart from 'the fin-de-siècle world of Berlin's elites'.[58] The city's diverse demographics, combined with a fear-fuelled anti-Semitism and anti-elitism, acutely affected Schmitt's perception of the capital.

The cultural life in Munich no less antagonised Schmitt, who did not identify with the 'aestheticised bellicosity' of the poets occupying the city's Left Bank during the war years.[59] In the 1910s, Schmitt was apparently neither warmonger nor jingoist, and remained sceptical about the heroic and literary value of *Fronterlebnis* ('front experience'), a poetic genre popularised by his

53 Ankersmit (1997), pp 125–30; Avanessian (2015), pp 199–220.
54 Khan (1985); Verstrynge (2006).
55 Mehring (2014), pp 9, 32.
56 Müller (2003), pp 17–18.
57 Müller (2003), p 19.
58 Balakrishnan (2000), p 13.
59 Balakrishnan (2000), p 17.

friend Ernst Jünger in works such as *Storm of Steel* (1920), which romanticised masculine camaraderie and conflict in battle.[60] Berlin had acted as the 'veritable antithesis of the world in which he had grown up'.[61] Munich, on the other hand, offered a patriotic and politically conventional poetic milieu. In both instances, Schmitt encountered metropolitan worlds founded on incoherence and contradiction. His response was one of confusion. He was ambivalent and anxious about the complex societies of the city. In the Weimar years, Schmitt often solicited sex workers in what Mehring calls his 'erotic state of exception'. Schmitt, as already made clear by his references in *The Buribunks*, had a lifelong fascination with Don Juan, whose literary motif he traced 'from Mozart to Grabbe's tragi-comical adaptation of the theme', through to Henry de Monthelant's tetralogy *The Young Girls* (1936–9). Mehring states that sex work was central to cultural depictions of urban life in Germany, citing novels by Stefan Zweig, Heinrich Mann and Erich Kästner in which 'the prostitute becomes the allegorical figure for the whole city'. He thinks particularly of Döblin's novel *Berlin Alexanderplatz* (1929) and notes Expressionist painters such as Ernst Ludwig Kirchner, Max Beckmann, Otto Dix and George Grosz 'presenting the milieu in garish colours'.[62] Schmitt was moved by Josef von Sternberg's erotically charged film *The Blue Angel* (1930), identifying with the professorial protagonist Immanuel Rath.[63] Overall, Schmitt had prurient, misogynistic and conflicted attitudes towards women.

Other developments in contemporary cinema caught Schmitt's attention.[64] He saw Carl Theodor Dreyer's *The Passion of Joan of Arc* (1928) more than ten times in six months, sometimes in the company of sex workers.[65] In the film, Dreyer depicts Joan's Passion – her short, final period of pain and sacrifice – during which she undergoes a procedural game of ensnarement and deception. As the opening card puts it, she is subject to a virulent 'band of blind theologians and skilled jurists'.[66] In efforts to appease their English masters, this over-educated set demand that Joan admits her heresy against the Church. Dreyer lights the actor Renée Jeanne Falconetti, who plays Joan, without make-up, so her face appears stark and unflattering. Ageing men grandstand and postulate, nose hair flaring, chins doubling and redoubling, heads dotted with warts and pious scalps. They constitute the carnival of grotesques. Their interrogations form Joan's suffering and endurance until death. In the chapel, where much of Joan's preliminary trial takes place, false logic is the enemy of the defendant. As used by the clerics, deductive reasoning functions as conniving wordplay.

60 Jünger (2004).
61 Balakrishnan (2000), p 13.
62 Mehring (2014), pp 210–2.
63 Bendersky (2017).
64 Scholars tentatively link Schmitt's political thought to cinematic aesthetics, see Miller (2009); Griffin (2009); Holtmeier (2016).
65 Mehring (2014), pp 210–12.
66 Dreyer (1928) *The Passion of Joan of Arc*. Antonin Artaud, avant-garde dramatist and proponent of 'the theatre of cruelty', features as a monk.

Endless discussion intends to debilitate the defendant. Tactics of staccato deliberation seek to deceive her. Prosecutorial feints conflate theology with law and law with politics. This results in a remarkable amount of talk for a silent film. Crucial dialogue appears in the intertitles, but the viewer creates assumptions through the actors' overt manners and expression. The civilised pretence of the captors masks the ever-present threat: to spit, shout down, admonish. To their devious challenges, Joan is the exception. She stands outside the accumulation of theological precedents. Her innocent responses function as paragons of pure articulation, which touch upon the sublime.

From his diaries, Schmitt was deeply impressed by this work of 'cinematic art'. His obsession was probably multifaceted. Circumstantially, the film reflected his difficult divorce, which the Catholic Church had initially refused him. It also had at its centre a figure of liberation who embodied many of his core political principles: an agent of sovereign exception able to transcend the vague, meaningless gestures of parliamentary performance. For him, the capacity to decide one's fate supplants the ability to discuss it. He further identified in St Joan, canonised in 1920, the archetype of an effective national myth:

> St Joan led her people out of a desperate military situation … Almost any sentence from the mouth of this saint is an answer that any nation may give itself. When this saint answered the question of whether she wanted to claim that God hated the English, saying that she did not know whether that was the case, but she knew that the English had to leave France, she thereby gave an answer that every people must give their oppressors and exploiters …[67]

Schmitt characterises Joan through both Dreyer's disjunctive presentation of the trial process, itself based on the 1431 court transcripts, and Falconetti's dramatic interpretation, which artfully combines expressions of bemusement and unanticipated clarity. Not only does Joan outwit the snare of state affiliation, complicated by the traitorous clerics' subservience to the English crown; she additionally reveals the pompous prurience of her adversaries. Joan functions as Schmitt's secularised God, as a potent avatar for political mythmaking. H.D., the modernist poet and contemporary critic, was sceptical of Dreyer's stylistic excesses.[68] Yet the director's rendition clearly affected Schmitt, who may have interpreted its commitment to subjective experience as that which most closely evokes the Passion. For him, the miracle in theology corresponds with the exception in politics. In art, the miracle is reproduced in Dreyer and Falconetti's experiential vision.

Schmitt was not persuaded by an environment that appropriated Freudian psychoanalysis to diagnose the ills of the age, and nor did he think that the

67 Mehring (2014), p 228.
68 Diepeveen (1984).

youth embodied, in Robert Wohl's words, the welcome 'agent of cultural renewal'.[69] Yet it seems inadequate, as suggested by many biographies, that Schmitt was more interested in opportunistically attaching himself to great painters, writers and composers of the generation for social advancement, rather than for his personal intellectual and artistic development. Such a concept reveals little of the nature of his cultural consumption during the period. As Wohl states, the German cohort of the widely cited generation of 1914 was the most likely to produce 'full-fledged social theories' in response to the innovations and problems of modernity.[70] It is possible to understand the allure for Schmitt of avant-garde works that combined such social theories, and to perceive his growing desire to counter bourgeois indulgence through and in response to these new media of intellectual expression. His post-war diaries, published as *Ex Captivitate Salus* (1950), bear out this appreciation:

> What the European impressionism of the nineteenth century, what futurism, cubism, and expressionism had broken open from many chaotic starting points found its unexpected fulfilment in the German language. The German poem became a new wonder work of sound, colour, and thought. It became a score whose tonal and coloristic plenitude is continuously intoned, interpreted, and conducted by the reader and hearer.[71]

Schmitt's nationalist summary considers the importance of the audience as much it does the performer. His expectations of early modernisms emphasise sound as music, colour as art and thought as philosophy. Chaos and disorder in language are the product of uncoordinated movements and unclear leadership in art. The 'German poem' brings together a variety of modes, encouraging the convergence of performance and word, which posits the value of fulfilment and the insufficiency of a starting point. For him, art requires a sense of a linear trajectory and of formal completion.

Throughout his life, Schmitt used his diary in part for the crude preservation of his reputation. He was acutely aware of cultivating his legacy. Jakob Norberg has written persuasively on Schmitt's tactical use of the form, traced from 'The Buribunks' through to his broader post-war criticisms of individual egoism and endless cultural conversation.[72] In *The Buribunks*, Schmitt imagines an 'obligatory collective diary', which Buribunks keep 'for every second of their existence'. As a literary device to represent the totalising and oppressive force of modern technology, the diary functions as a crude symbol, which Schmitt describes in great detail. First, the purpose of the diary is to immediately identify 'the respective circumstances of interest with regard to each

69 Wohl (1979), p 48.
70 Wohl (1979) p 3.
71 Schmitt (2017), p 40.
72 Norberg (2011); Norberg (2014).

individual' and to locate 'the smallest errors'. Second, it provides a disquieting textual resource for 'a psycho-pathologist [who] was interested in the dreams of a certain class of Buribunks during their puberty'. This person could have 'the relevant materials ... compiled in no time at all with the help of the card catalogues'.[73] The sinister, endless documentation is not just in service of self-obsession, but constitutes a broader society of observation, surveillance and control. Schmitt sees this type of state machine as a source of fear for its inhabitants, one that does not possess the vital energy to invigorate social life; instead, it facilitates a dehumanised society contributing, in Jeff Wallace's characterisation of the central modernist concern, 'the demise of the integrated humanist self'.[74]

Schmitt's writing of *The Buribunks* is informed not only by his attitudes towards the diary form but emerging styles of cinema. Together, these attitudes encouraged his interest in discontinuity as a way of interrogating truth, personality and anthropology. Friedrich Kittler includes a lengthy, translated extract of *The Buribunks* in his book *Gramophone, Film, Typewriter* (1999). Geoffrey Winthrop-Young notes that the pivotal issue of Kittler's broad theoretical stance is one of:

> discontinuity – a forceful, at times polemical emphasis on ruptures, breaks and caesuras designed to obliterate any attempt to infuse history with gradualist, progressive, teleological or dialectical notions. History is not smooth; it doesn't lead out of the cave of early illusions into the mature blaze of enlightenment; it does not exhibit any growing intelligibility; and it cannot be reduced to a fanciful relay of revolutionary subjects.[75]

Discontinuity is likewise crucial to understanding Schmitt's treatment of history in *The Buribunks*. The narrator dismisses the limited efforts of Leporello, Don Juan's servant, who lacks the ambition and ability to document his master's life in precise detail and perfect continuity. Leporello makes errors and omissions, possessing neither a methodological framework nor an obvious strategy because he has no interest in the demographic factors surrounding his subject. He fails to write about Don Juan in suitable context, offering few references to statistics, politics, law, economy or society. He lacks the tools and motivation for extended scientific inquiry and remains bereft of the chronic self-awareness required to project his own life onto the documentation of his subject. Schmitt ironically portrays the narrator's dismissiveness towards Leporello as a blind belief in the relentless meaning of historical record.[76] Schmitt's assessment of this complacency is central to his understanding of the question of sovereignty.

73 Chapter 2 of this volume, p 23.
74 Wallace (2011), p 15.
75 Winthrop-Young and Gane (2006), p 10.
76 Chapter 2 of this volume, pp 17–8.

First, to locate the origin of buribunkology, Schmitt finds 'planted in an unassuming primordial fashion the seed that now shades the earth as a powerful tree'. Starting with Don Juan, who is life-mocking and unscientific, Schmitt presents the ideal figure to represent the anti-elitist and anti-academic position. Don Juan sings, 'Ah, tomorrow morning | my list has to be increased by about ten', which shows that he at least understands the core value of documentation. Buribunkology is presented as a tool that co-opts individuality. The thrill of task completion and self-preservation is central to the Buribunks, who are scientific and unemotional, while Don Juan is a slave to passion. The sentiment of Buribunkian documentation can be traced in Don Juan, but not its manner, motivation or intention. Buribunks retain erotic thrill through task-completion and self-preservation, whereas Don Juan does not acknowledge the importance of situating himself within the context of history and has no 'Buribunkian cinematic attitude', which Schmitt likens to a form of holistic surveillance. Instead, Don Juan 'lived in the immediate present and his interest in the singular erotic experience did not contain anything in which we could glimpse the beginning of self-historisation'.[77]

Leporello, on the other hand, takes vicarious pleasure in recording and documenting Don Juan, who 'he drags … before the bench of world history, that means world court, to appear there as defender or prosecutor depending on the result of his observations and interpretations'. Leporello rejects autobiography and puts the subject ahead of himself. Ignorant of his breakthrough, Leporello remains subordinate to Don Juan and bereft of 'the writer's higher consciousness, the awareness of being the author of a piece of world history and therefore having become an associate judge of the world court'. A sorrowful, pale imitation of the Buribunk, Leporello is merely 'a superior manager who pulls the colourful marionette Don Juan on the strings of his superior business skills and intelligence. But instead of taking the quill into his fist, the poor devil clenches his fist in his pocket.' Leporello does not have the sense of self-awareness to project his own life onto proceedings and into his documentation, 'plac[ing] one photograph after the other, but nowhere is there an attempt to form a homogenous continuum out of the heterogeneous discontinuum of successive conquests – it is void of any intellectual connection or account of development'. That accounts for the story being called '*Don Juan, The Libertine Punished*, and not *Leporello's Tales*'.[78] His discontinuous method is only prototypical of the Buribunks.

Leporello's successor, Ferker, is the culmination of many ancestors, including Marc Aurel, Saint Augustine, Pliny the Elder and Richard Wagner. With faux-reverence, Schmitt lists the trajectory of documentarians, but Ferker is the first who knows to 'be history yourself!' and to insert himself into events. His story is one of innovation, canny ambition and social mobility, about a

77 Chapter 2 of this volume, p 15.
78 Chapter 2 of this volume, p 18.

figure whose devotion to self-documentation is unparalleled within his time. Upon Ferker's death, his ashes fuse with ink, 'from which a small part was sent to all printing presses on earth'. Subsequently, 'the whole of civilised humankind was educated about this event through leaflets and illuminated advertising and warned with unsurpassable intensity to always remember that in every single one of the billions of letters, which the eye encounters over the years, there is contained an atom of the ashes of the immortal man'. Ferker, 'in the midst of nerve-wracking events … cranks changing film images into his diary with cool calmness in order to incorporate them into history'.[79] Schmitt suggestively outlines the cinematic process as both an exacting documentary tool and a clear-eyed method for preserving facts, ossified through the lens and turned into historical record.

Conclusion

Schmitt uses techniques of modernism to broadly satirise and parody modernist efforts to depict individual consciousness. This tension finds its central site in *The Buribunks*, which takes a lively and critical attitude to myriad forms of biography, autobiography and diary. Through critical readings of modernist literature, philosophical modernism and developments in silent cinema, this chapter argues that Schmitt complicated genre forms and levels of narrative perspective to evaluate experimental literary styles and modernist aesthetics. Distinct from, although not unconnected to, the terseness that defines his major philosophical works, Schmitt employs circumlocutory and dense prose to satirise, in words borrowed from Virginia Woolf, 'the spirit of the age'.[80] The threat of political and social transformation at once focuses and distorts Schmitt's anxieties about modernist life-writing and early cinema, which is partly why the text brims with so many formal and thematic contradictions. As a result, Schmitt imitates the methods of documentary characteristic of modernist literary and cinematic approaches, which aim to capture life in all its ample length and detail, and to glimpse the fleeting moments from which meaning ultimately derives.

One in-text reference and its corresponding footnote exemplify Schmitt's multiplicitous approach, which outlines his paradoxical stance towards the contemporary cultural epoch. Schmitt's imagined interlocutor refers to a Buribunk named Pielenpiep, who published a 'still authoritative Ferker biography … in 200 volumes, a work of the noblest buribunkological observance'. This tome indicates the Buribunks' absurd, forlorn tendency to accumulate details and endlessly document events, the aesthetic perspective that must notice everything and therefore articulate everything. Schmitt nevertheless remains suspicious of artistic renderings that encourage only

79 Chapter 2 of this volume, p 20.
80 Woolf (2003), pp 116, 120, 121, 130, 131.

snapshots of reality and, by doing so, deliver discontinuous, decontextualised and deceitful images of documented life. The simultaneous wariness and excitement towards the modernist project thus pertain to a multitude of media, modes, forms, styles and approaches. This is emphasised in Schmitt's dual description of Ferker as a failed biographer of the elusive modern character and as the pitiful subject of Pielenpiep's comprehensive and stultifying biographical account. It is drily reported that Ferker, during his lifetime of multiple and various occupations, was once 'a cinema owner in Berlin'.[81]

References

Franklin Rudolf Ankersmit (1997) *Aesthetic Politics: Political Philosophy Beyond Fact and Value*, Stanford University Press.

Armen Avanessian (2015) 'Anti-Ironic Politics? The Fundamentalisms of Søren Kierkegaard and Carl Schmitt', in Armen Avanessian and Sophie Wennerscheid (eds), *Kierkegaard and Political Theory: Religion, Aesthetics, Politics and the Intervention of the Single Individual*, University of Chicago Press, 199.

Gopal Balakrishnan (2000) *The Enemy: An Intellectual Portrait of Carl Schmitt*, Verso.

Friedrich Balke (2017) 'Carl Schmitt and Modernity', in Jens Meierhenrich and Oliver Simons (eds), *The Oxford Handbook of Carl Schmitt*, Oxford University Press, 629.

Joseph W. Bendersky (2017) 'Schmitt's Diaries', in Jens Meierhenrich and Oliver Simons (eds), *The Oxford Handbook to Carl Schmitt*, Oxford University Press, 117.

Edwin Bikundo and Kieran Tranter (2019) 'Special Issue: Buribunks' 28 *Griffith Law Review*.

A.H. Bond (1986) 'Virginia Woolf and Leslie Stephen: A Father's Contribution to Psychosis and Genius' 14 *The Journal of the American Academy of Psychoanalysis* 507.

Horst Bredekamp, Melissa Thorson Hause and Jackson Bond (1999) 'From Walter Benjamin to Carl Schmitt, via Thomas Hobbes' 25 *Critical Inquiry* 247.

Christopher Butler (2010) *Modernism*, Oxford University Press.

Maria DiBattista and Emily O. Wittman (2014) *Modernism and Autobiography*, Cambridge University Press.

Leonard Diepeveen (1984) 'H.D. and the Film Arts' 18 *The Journal of Aesthetic Education* 57.

Carl Theodor Dreyer (dir) (1928) *The Passion of Joan of Arc*, Société Générale des Films.

Robert J. Flaherty (dir) (1922) *Nanook of the North: A Story of Life and Love in the Actual Arctic*, Pathé Exchange.

Hans-Georg Gadamer (2012) *Truth and Method*, Continuum.

Hugh Gray (1950) 'Robert Flaherty and the Naturalistic Documentary' 5 *Hollywood Quarterly* 41.

Jeff Griffin (2009) 'The State of Exception in Film: Cloverfield and 24' 18 *disClosure: A Journal of Social Theory* 75.

Elena Gualtieri (2000) 'The Impossible Art: Virginia Woolf on Modern Biography' 29 *The Cambridge Quarterly* 349.

Ulla Haselstein (2003) 'Gertrude Stein's Portraits of Matisse and Picasso' 34 *New Literary History* 723.

81 Chapter 2 of this volume, p 19.

Katherine C. Hill (1981) 'Virginia Woolf and Leslie Stephen: History and Literary Revolution' 96 *PMLA* 351.
Michael J. Hoffman (1965) 'Gertrude Stein's "Portraits"' 11 *Twentieth Century Literature* 115.
Matthew Holtmeier (2016) 'The Modern Political Cinema: From Third Cinema to Contemporary Networked Biopolitics' 20 *Film-Philosophy* 303.
Ernst Jünger (2004) *Storm of Steel*, Penguin.
Ellen Kennedy (2004) *Constitutional Failure: Carl Schmitt in Weimar*, Duke University Press.
Abrahim Khan (1985) 'Melancholy, Irony, and Kierkegaard' 17 *International Journal for Philosophy of Religion* 67.
Friedrich Kittler (1999) *Gramophone, Film, Typewriter*, Stanford University Press.
Søren Kierkegaard (1992) *Either/Or: A Fragment of Life*, Penguin.
Reinhart Koselleck (2002) *The Practice of Conceptual History: Timing History, Spacing Concepts*, Stanford University Press.
György Lukács (2005) 'The Ideology of Modernism', in Dorothy J. Hale (ed), *The Novel: An Anthology of Criticism and Theory 1900–2000*, John Wiley & Sons.
Caroline Marie (2015) 'Virginia Woolf's Cinegraphic Poetics in The Years' 52 *Comparative Literature Studies* 510.
Reinhard Mehring (2014) *Carl Schmitt: A Biography*, Polity Press.
Jens Meierhenrich and Oliver Simons (2017) '"A Fanatic of Order in an Epoch of Confusing Turmoil": The Political, Legal, and Cultural Thought of Carl Schmitt', in Jens Meierhenrich and Oliver Simons (eds), *The Oxford Handbook of Carl Schmitt*, Oxford University Press, 3.
Tyrus Miller (2009) *Singular Examples: Artistic Politics and the Neo-Avant-Garde*, Northwestern University Press.
Ray Monk (2007) 'This Fictitious Life: Virginia Woolf on Biography, Reality, and Character' 31 *Philosophy and Literature* 1.
Jan-Werner Müller (2003) *A Dangerous Mind: Carl Schmitt in Post-War European Thought*, Yale University Press.
Jakob Norberg (2011) 'Day-to-Day Politics: Carl Schmitt on the Diary' 157 *Telos* 21.
Jakob Norberg (2014) *Sociability and Its Enemies: German Political Theory After 1945*, Northwestern University Press.
John Paul Riquelme (2013) 'Modernist Transformations of Life Narrative: From Wilde and Woolf to Bechdel and Rushdie' 59 *Modern Fiction Studies* 461.
Max Saunders (2010) 'Woolf, Bloomsbury, the "New Biography", and the New Auto/biografiction', in *Self Impression: Life-Writing, Autobiografiction, and the Forms of Modern Literature*, Oxford University Press, 438.
Carl Schmitt (1991) *Political Romanticism*, MIT Press.
Carl Schmitt (2005) *Political Theology*, University of Chicago Press.
Carl Schmitt (2007) *The Concept of the Political*, University of Chicago Press.
Carl Schmitt (2009) *Hamlet or Hecuba: The Intrusion of the Time into the Play*, Telos Press.
Carl Schmitt (2017) *Ex Captivitate Salus*, Polity Press.
Andrew Shail (2006) '"She Looks Just Like One of We-All": British Cinema Culture and the Origins of Woolf's Orlando' 48 *Critical Quarterly* 45.
Gertrude Stein (1957) *Lectures in America*, Beacon Press.
Wendy Steiner (1978) *Exact Resemblance to Exact Resemblance: Literary Portraiture of Gertrude Stein*, Yale University Press.

Karl Verstrynge (2006) '"Over the Bridge of Sighs into Eternity": On Søren Kierkegaard's Prominent Role in the History of Melancholy' 4 *E-rea* 90.
Jeff Wallace (2011) *Beginning Modernism*, Manchester University Press.
Geoffrey Winthrop-Young and Nicholas Gane (2006) 'Friedrich Kittler: An Introduction' 23 *Theory, Culture & Society* 5.
Robert Wohl (1979) *The Generation of 1914*, Harvard University Press.
Virginia Woolf (1980) *The Diary of Virginia Woolf*, vol. 3, Harcourt Brace Jovanovich.
Virginia Woolf (2003) *Orlando: A Biography*, Wordsworth Editions.
Virginia Woolf (2008) *Selected Essays*, Oxford University Press.

Chapter 12

Die Buribunken – a pastiche

A mechanised modernity failing Hegel and Kierkegaard

Nour Benghellab

Introduction

In 1918, a short text, *The Buribunks*, signed by a certain C.S., behind which we find the eminent and controversial jurist Carl Schmitt, was published by the Catholic review *Summa*. The first puzzling thing for a reader is the narrative form of *The Buribunks*. It is written in the form of a scientific article following a classic scientific publication model. However, its title is intriguing to say the least, and it is supplemented by a subtitle that emphasises the uncanniness of the title: 'Ein geschichtsphilosophischer Versuch'. Along with this depiction of its philosophical nature, the author introduces the object of his study: the Buribunks. Thus the academic project, complying with the acknowledged rules of a scientific article, in particular with regard to the use of quotations (even though mocked by the use of *argumentum ad verecundiam*), as a serious contribution to the noble discipline of the philosophy of history, coexists with the non-serious, the parody and the fiction.

Indeed, the subject of C.S./Carl Schmitt's philosophical article is the Buribunks, fictional creatures described as the ultimate completion of human evolution. But how should this short text/article of non-fiction/fiction be read or understood? It seems that, almost unanimously, this text has been read as a work of fiction. In other words, most readers seem to think that the object of the text, the Buribunks, is the determining criterion for identifying the literary nature of *The Buribunks*. Thus, it is either a satirical fiction or science fiction, depending on whether the primacy for the classification is given to the tone of the text or to the scientist post-human world portrayed in it.[1] In addition to these tendencies, we propose to take the scientific narrative form of the text seriously and read it as a scientific contribution, since this is what its form suggests.

To this end, we will pay particular attention to its subtitle: 'Ein geschichtsphilosophischer Versuch'. The function of the subtitle is usually to specify the

1 See, among others, Bikundo and Tranter (2019); Kittler (1999), p 331; Koselleck (2002), pp 85–99; Tranter (2019).

DOI: 10.4324/9781003091066-15

object of a text or to situate it in some field of study. However, this subtitle, in German, can be understood in two ways that are reflected in its different translations. Following the official English translation of *The Buribunks*, it can be understood as 'An essay on the philosophy of history',[2] which indicates that the topic is the philosophy of history. However, it is also possible to understand it as a contribution to the disciplinary field of the philosophy of history. In this case, 'philosophy of history' is not its topic, but its nature. For example, Geoffrey Winthrop-Young and Michael Wutz, the two translators of *Gramophone, Film, Typewriter* by Friedrich A. Kittler, in which a part of *The Buribunks* is reproduced, translate the subtitle into 'A History-Philosophical Meditation'.[3] Similarly, Frédérique Vargas, in French, translates it into 'Un essai historico-philosophique'.[4] There is a tension between the subtitle and the content of *The Buribunks* regarding these two meanings. Here, we will accept the coexistence of those two meanings, because every contribution to the philosophy of history is always somehow a comment on the philosophy of history. In other words, *The Buribunks* will be read in the following as a commentary on different traditions of philosophy of history and as an attempt to set an alternative, new tradition in this field.[5]

More specifically, we will understand the essay as written by C.S.[6] and belonging to the science called buribunkology. In doing so, we will argue that this article is a pastiche by Schmitt in which one can see a sketch of his particular conception of decisionism. To this end, we will first situate the essay in the field to which it claims to contribute. We will then situate, within time and literature, the pastiche as a literary technique and sketch some of its main traits. In the fourth section, we will look at Schmitt's first engagements with this technique. In the three following sections, we will analyse closely how Schmitt, through C.S., uses the pastiche to lay the groundwork for his personal understanding of decisionism in *The Buribunks*. Finally, we will see how this article/novel cast light on the entanglement of questions of technicality, mechanisation, neutralisation and decisionism in Schmitt's works.

Preamble

The first part of the essay introduces us to buribunkology as a science. C.S. states from the outset that, 'before anything else, it should be the ambition of every science to justify its existence through actual achievements and to ensure that an imposing body of work stands in the way of any subversive doubt regarding its potential as a science'.[7] He explains then that Buribunks exist

2 Chapter 2 of this volume, p 12.
3 Kittler (1999), p 231.
4 Kittler (2018), p 379.
5 Lukács (1971, 2009).
6 The English translation is signed 'Carl Schmitt', but the German original 'C.S': C. S. (1918). Accordingly, we will assume that they are two different persons.
7 Chapter 2 of this volume, p 12.

because there is a science that studies them, as Americans exist since a science – American studies – studies them. Beyond this parodic tautology, one should notice that modern sciences do indeed often accept this relationship of 'self-fulfilling prophecy', a relation of co-construction vis-à-vis their objects.

Indeed, each science (at least in our modernity) will define its object and delimit its ontological borders. To this end, there is always some interaction between a science and its epistemology. These are the classical divisions between foundationalist and anti-foundationalist approaches, or between empirical-materialism and idealism.[8] Moreover, the a priori of epistemology used to delimit ontological boundaries is one of the main characteristics of modern sciences. It is the introduction of subjectivity in the definitional postures, especially since Descartes. In this sense, C.S. describes buribunkology as a science according to the post-Cartesian understanding of the word.

Indeed, with *cogito, ergo sum*, Descartes shifts the ordering between ontology and epistemology:

> Roughly speaking and admitting some exceptions … pre-Cartesian philosophy was definitely ontologically oriented, but post-Cartesian thought became largely preoccupied with epistemology. In this sense, Descartes is the father of modern philosophy. In fact, *cogito, ergo sum* … clearly suggests that an ontological statement (I am) is based on an epistemological datum (I think).[9]

In other words, since Descartes, knowledge (philosophy/sciences/buribunkology) antecedes the being (ontology/Buribunk). It is the thinking subject, the subjectivity, at the heart of the system who becomes the 'first cause', who founds knowledge. Descartes knows himself to be because he thinks and thinks of himself as being. Likewise, 'the existence of the Buribunks follows from the fact that buribunkology exists'[10] because 'there would be … no buribunkology if there were no buribunkologists'.[11] C.S., therefore, tells us that he is a Cartesian.

However, behind C.S. the modern Cartesian there seems to be someone else, someone who leads us to doubt C.S. and the seriousness of his business. It is this someone who seems to suggest that C.S.'s enterprise is laughable. With C.S. coexists a spirit 'who pulls the colourful marionette [C.S.] on the strings of his superior business skills and intelligence'.[12] *The Buribunks* has not one, but two authors. C.S. is neither Carl Schmitt's pseudonym nor his initials. He is an interlocutor and the target of the jurist's criticism. C.S. exists as the scriptor of

8 Blackburn (2005), p 118.
9 Woleński (2004), pp 4–5.
10 Chapter 2 of this volume, p 12 n 1.
11 Chapter 2 of this volume, p 12.
12 Chapter 2 of this volume, p 17.

The Buribunks. Here, Schmitt employs a literary technique that allows him to coexist as a critic, to be an invisible critical co-author (not so invisible since he appears in footnotes 2 and 13) of C.S., in order to lay the groundwork for his own thought.

Schmitt's technique to coexist as a challenger (and) co-author, which he had already mastered by the time of *The Buribunks*'s publication, is that of pastiche. Pastiche is often confused with parody or imitation, or even forgery. However, pastiche is dissimilar to these three in that it is neither a literary genre nor a usurpation. It is a technique that can be subsumed under multiple literary forms. Before continuing, as we address primarily an English-speaking audience, it is essential to precisely define pastiche as a literary technique given that a major debate, from which we will depart, has profoundly shaped (especially) the English understanding of this word.

The short long story of the pastiche as 'criticism in action'

As a matter of fact, major works on postmodernism and its intricate relation with, and deep rooting in, modernity and modernism understand pastiche as a genre opposed to parody. Indeed, 'as a formal game, pastiche in contemporary literature is often associated with postmodernism in its English-speaking meaning of gratuitous game or blank parody'.[13] According to Frederic Jameson, pastiche 'is to be sharply distinguished from the more readily received idea of parody'.[14] He explains:

> Pastiche is, like parody, the imitation of a peculiar or unique, idiosyncratic style, the wearing of a linguistic mask, speech in a dead language. But it is a neutral practice of such mimicry, without any of parody's ulterior motives, amputated of the satiric impulse, devoid of laughter and of any conviction that alongside the abnormal tongue you have momentarily borrowed, some healthy linguistic normality still exists. Pastiche is thus blank parody, a statue with blind eyeballs.[15]

In this sense, he asserts a 'formal' resemblance between parody and pastiche while emphasising their profound difference (motivated/political vs. neutral/apolitical). He then concludes that pastiche is disconnected from history. It is not a historical thing, but only a 'random cannibalization of all the styles of the past, [a] play of random stylistic allusion',[16] 'freed from [any] historical forces … Pastiche means style separated from history.'[17]

13 Bille Jørgensen (2012), p 106.
14 Jameson (2008), p 16.
15 Jameson (2008), p 17.
16 Jameson (2008), p 18.
17 Coyle (2015), p 199.

This understanding of pastiche as the empty style of an empty postmodernism is opposed to Linda Hutcheon's depiction of a parodic and ironic postmodernism. For her, 'postmodern fiction remains historical, precisely because it problematizes history through parody'.[18] She explains that, 'Parody – often called ironic quotation, pastiche, appropriation, or intertextuality – is usually considered central to postmodernism.'[19] For her, parody and pastiche are not distinct, as Jameson suggests. Pastiche is not the ahistorical and apolitical practice depicted by Jameson. She specifies:

> In objecting … to the relegation of the postmodern parodic to the ahistorical and empty realm of pastiche, I do not want to suggest that there is not a nostalgic, neoconservative recovery of past meaning going on in a lot of contemporary culture; I just want to draw a distinction between that practice and postmodernist parody.[20]

Indeed, she regards all productions during postmodernity, as a socio-economic period characterised by late capitalism, as not postmodern per se. She criticises Jameson's 'confusing [uses of] the word postmodernism for both the socio-economic periodization and the cultural designation'.[21] In other words, for her there is a specific critical practice of parody, pastiche being another 'name' for it, that characterises postmodernist cultural productions. It is in the context of this debate on postmodern that pastiche is discussed within contemporary English-speaking literature.

In this contribution, we will depart from this debate. First, we are here concerned with a text produced before postmodernism, understood as a 'socio-economic periodisation' or a 'cultural designation'. Second, the Hutcheon–Jameson debate coexists with a so-called 'socio-historical'[22] understanding of the pastiche that we will take on. This socio-historical approach does not oppose pastiche to parody, nor does it understand it as a synonym of parody. Moreover, this field's contributors do not approach pastiche as a postmodernist

18 Duvall (1999), p 272.
19 Hutcheon (2002), p 89.
20 Hutcheon (2002), p 94.
21 Hutcheon (2002), p 25.
22 Aron (2008); Bille Jørgensen (2012), p 105. In the same vein, Genette, who developed his theory of transtextuality in 1982, distinguishes parody and pastiche. For him, Parody is a playful transformation of a text and Pastiche a playful imitation, wherein transformation is the modification of the style without modification of the subject and imitation the modification of the subject without modification of the style. In this sense, Joyce's *Ulysses* is a parody and Proust's 'L'Affaire Lemoine' a pastiche. To arrive at this distinction, Genette uses a typology of five types of transtextuality to trace borders between the genre and its relation to the original text. Nevertheless, Genette warns that 'one must not view the five types of transtextuality as separate and absolute categories without any reciprocal contact or overlapping' (p. 7). Genette (1997).

specificity but as an older practice. For those scholars, 'Jameson is right … to distinguish pastiche from parody.'[23] Paul Aron, for example, insists on the fact that 'pastiche designates … the borrowing of a style to apply it to another object, while the parody transforms a singular text'.[24] Nonetheless, for them it is not 'that strange new thing [that] slowly comes to take [parody's] place'[25] in those times of cultural industries. On the contrary, it is an older practice that changed over time to become a strong critical practice during the inter-war period.[26]

In short, giving this 'socio-historical' approach, parody is understood as a literary genre and pastiche as a writing technique. In this respect, parody can sometimes have recourse to pastiche, but cannot be reduced to it. A parody can be written without any use of pastiche, and a piece using pastiches can be non-parodic (such as Proust's pastiches[27] or T.S. Eliot's *The Waste Land*).[28] Moreover, as a literary piece can employ different literary techniques, pastiche can be employed alongside other techniques, like irony is used alongside pastiche in *The Buribunks*. But as a critical practice, the use of pastiche aims to bring out another truth (a unique piece of work) made out of the truths it gathers (the 'pieces' from other pieces of work gathered). It is a stylistic practice aiming to produce a 'new truth' for diverse reasons, from homage to parody and mockery. In this sense, pastiche is 'neither original nor imitation'.[29] This critical and creative use of pastiche spread during the inter-war period among modernist productions as well as within conservative fringes.[30]

Indeed, as a stylistic exercise, pastiche dates back to antiquity. However, it was only at the end of the eighteenth century that, in French, the term *pastiche*, which previously had been used only for pictorial arts, began to describe a literary practice.[31] French borrowed it from Italian during the seventeenth century to describe a counterfeit,[32] but its meaning slowly changed to come to define an artistic technique that would take on a very particular meaning in literature.[33] It is the evolution, especially during the nineteenth and twentieth centuries, of the understanding of this technique that explains why we find it in a variety of literary genres often used for different, and contradictory, purposes, from the playful to literary and philosophical critique.[34]

23 Coyle (2015), p 123.
24 Aron (2009), p 15.
25 Jameson (2008), p 17.
26 Aron (2009); Coyle (2015).
27 Aron (2009), p 15.
28 Coyle (2015).
29 Hoesterey (2001), p 5.
30 Aron (2008); Coyle (2015).
31 Saint-Gérand (2006).
32 Hoesterey (2001), p 4.
33 Saint-Gérand (2006).
34 Aron (2008, 2009), p 16; Hoesterey (2001), pp 9–10.

In fact, during the eighteenth century, pastiche was used to describe the imitation of an author's style, a style '*à la*', which advertises itself as such – often for praise. However, from the *Ancien Régime* to World War I, the use of pastiche evolved and took various forms. It was associated with parody, especially in the performing arts. It was also used as a teaching method, as imitation was perceived as the best way to acquire a *distingué* writing style.[35] Hence, 'the school uses of pastiche … had … two major effects on the history of the genre'.[36] This systematic use made it possible to train a whole generation, the one of the turn of the twentieth century, including the future modernists, in the use of pastiche. It also enhanced its critical potential.[37]

As Michael Coyle puts it, 'before the modernist era, pastiche typically functioned either as homage or as instruction',[38] Pastiche was seen as an 'exercise apprentice artists undertake to achieve mastery of a tradition'.[39] But with modernism, the critical potential of pastiche was enhanced and exploited. In other words, pastiche began to be used as a tool of critique, and not only as one of teaching. Thus, for Gérard Genette, 'Proust says (and demonstrates) that a pastiche is "criticism in action".'[40] In short, over time the use of pastiche diversified until it established itself, during La Belle Époque, as a technique of literary criticism.[41] During the inter-war period, the golden age of modernism, the use of pastiche thrived. For Coyle, pastiche is a 'formal embodiment of history that … produces something new and models how "the past should be altered by the present as much as the present is directed by the past"'.[42]

This was the decisive moment when the term 'pastiche' entered English[43] and German (1871)[44] vocabulary to designate a practice of literary criticism. In English, the modern French understanding of the word will continue to coexist with the one inherited from the Italian '*pasticcio*', meaning hodgepodge, a blank agglomeration of disparate elements. In German, it is the modern French definition that will prevail in literary studies. Jan Erik Antonsen tells us:

35 Aron (2008, 2009).
36 Aron (2009), pp 21–2.
37 Aron (2008), pp 189–97.
38 Coyle (2015), p 123.
39 Coyle (2015), p 117.
40 Genette (1997), p 8.
41 Aron (2008), pp 186–9, 255–73; Aron (2009), p 22.
42 Coyle (2015), p 128.
43 The understanding of the word 'pastiche' as a critical technique is more recent in the English-speaking world. Indeed, 'as an evaluative term, its usage gradually acquired a hint of negative or dismissive connotation. The word implies a lack of originality or coherence, an imitative jumble. It was only in the latter half of the 20th C. – and most esp. in the context of theories of postmod. narrative – that pastiche acquired its current critical purchase.' Bowen (2012), p 1005; see also Aron (2008), p 14, esp. n 2.
44 Antonsen (2007), p 3.

> The 'Larousse du XIXe siècle' … already identifies two different meanings, both of which were in use in the 19th century: (a) the 'servile imitation' of another's style due to the author's inability to create an own individual style; and (b) the mimicking of another's style to emphasize one's own stylistic virtuosity, which may take the form of continuous parody. It is only in this second meaning that 'pastiche' emerges as a literary technical term.[45]

This second meaning would prevail among twentieth-century French and German litterateurs.

However, while the use of pastiche as a critical weapon in inter-war France is well documented, this was far from being the case on the other side of the Rhine. Antonsen identifies only a few uses of the pastiche in German literature besides the works of Clemens Brentano, Thomas Mann and Robert Neumann. He nuances, nonetheless, this absence and explains that German literature studies have tended to ignore this literary technique as an object of study, which may explain why so few German literary works can be identified with this technique.[46] Nevertheless, if pastiche did not have the same success in Germany as it did in France, there is no doubt that it was a technique in use among young litterateurs, including Schmitt.

In short, not being this postmodernist 'blank parody' that comes to replace the disruptive parody of modernism, pastiche is an oppugning practice that one can identify in some major modernist pieces. Accordingly, it is not the simple imitation of a forger but an artistic and literary technique. The pastiche, unlike imitation, does not seek to be confused with the original. It presents itself as being written 'in the manner of' an author, a style or an epoch, but its author does not renounce its authorship. He uses the style and words of others but asserts himself as a distinct author. He is not the forger who tries to impersonate. Nor is it a parody because, as a technique or a practice, one can utilise it in a non-parodic way.[47] In other words:

> pastiche is not so much to be considered as a genre that signals the object (author or work) pastiche, but as a practice allowing to explore the limits of [a] genre. This practice, as we shall see, takes the form of a game which, far from being empty, relies on the reader's engagement.[48]

The reader as paratext

At the turn of the twentieth century, the use of pastiche was a complex literary game. First, unlike counterfeits and imitations, the author of a pastiche often

45 Antonsen (2007), p 34.
46 Antonsen (2007), p 35.
47 Aron (2009); Bille Jørgensen (2012); Coyle (2015); Genette (1997).
48 Bille Jørgensen (2012), p 105.

displays the factitious nature of his work, either explicitly by announcing it in the preface or by explaining it in the afterword, or implicitly by including material (often puns and allusions) that does not fail to hint to readers about the nature of the piece. Similarly, the 'real' author of the text sometimes distances himself, creating a mirror effect, by making up a 'fictitious' author (signing the [real] published text), also named after puns or altered allusions to people or events. The use of pseudonyms was particularly widespread during the eighteenth and nineteenth centuries.[49] Those puns and allusions to the spurious nature of the text play on a relationship between the (real) author and his readership. It, in fact, 'relies on the reader's engagement'.[50]

The pastiche can then take several imitative forms: collage, quotation, plagiarism or '*dans le style de*'. 'Writing in the manner of', 'in the style of' and 'giving the genre (of)' are the most widespread pastiche practices.[51] These uses of the pastiche are common to writing willing to be eulogistic, and to those seeking to mock or highlight the gaps and defects of an author or a genre.[52] Further, pastiche makes sense only in a particular relationship between the author and his readership. This relationship is based on two elements: recontextualisation and recognition. 'Recontextualisation and recognition are thus the mechanisms through which the issues of the pastiche … are transferred to the second text.'[53] These are the mechanisms that allow us to understand what the pastiche itself is seriously telling us beyond its imitative dimension.

Recontextualisation is a reminder of the dual nature of the text. Thus, the pastiche is both a 'quoting and a quoted discourse'. It is a discourse that 'says' something (a to be quoted) while 'quoting' something else. Thus, 'some hints or conventions help the parody's recipient to remember that he is dealing with double discourse, quoting and quoted'.[54] Typically, contextual elements or topical tropes of the pastichised model are the hints used to signal the deception. Those hints inform the reader about the double discourse of the text, about the fact that something else is being said in it. Recognition is the 'election [the choice] of an audience able to understand and value recontextualization'.[55] In other words, the author of the pastiche writes for a specific audience, from whom he can anticipate a willed reaction: the recognition of the tropes he uses in his pastiche. Recognition is the appeal to the reader's engagement. Thus, recognition and recontextualisation are the two pillars of pastiche,

49 This is particularly evidenced by the high number of texts listed in Aron's study that are signed by pseudonyms. Nevertheless, the fact that pastiche was seen as minor, vulgar, genre or used mainly to mock largely explains this massive use of pen names. Aron (2008).
50 Bille Jørgensen (2012), p 105.
51 Hoesterey (2001), pp 9–15.
52 Aron (2008), p 6.
53 Aron (2009), p 9.
54 Aron (2009), p 18.
55 Aron (2009), p 18.

nourishing and reinforcing each other. Together, they ensure the characteristic features of the pastiche.

Out of this dynamic between the author and his reader, through the game of recognition and recontextualisation, the pastiche became more than a mere imitation. It is 'a preliminary study of the paradigm of iterative features common to one or several texts and the production of a novel text, according to idiolect imitated'.[56] It becomes an independent discourse, acquiring its independence as a text. It will say more than what the pastichised discourse actually says. Then, this overload of meaning, this semantic 'surplus-value', depending on the genre it takes, produces a specific discourse by the recycling of 'recognisable ingredients'.[57] This interplay between the author, his reader and the semantic added value of pastiche explains why one can encounter it in various literary forms, and which makes it a protean technique.

In this regard, the pastiche must always be taken seriously, as a saying discourse, as a discourse beyond the pastichised model. It is a positive or negative critique of a genre, a movement, a context, an era, an *air du temps*. In this sense, Roland Barthes wrote about Proust pastiches: 'What better testimony of fascination and demystification than the pastiche?' One can add, 'and what better way to prove one's value?' The pastiche is thus an exercise that allows one to both recognise and criticise, as well as to assert one's talent. We will then see that *The Buribunks* is a pastiche according to this understanding of it as a modernist oppugning practice and as a 'criticism in action'. However, it was not Schmitt's first pastiche.

Schmitt's silhouettes

We can already identify the characteristic features of the pastiche in *Schattenrisse*. This text, co-written by Fritz Eisler and published in 1913, is a series of portraits of cultural figures.[58] This satirical piece already announces Schmitt's antipathy for romanticism, positivism, neo-naturalism, ultra-scientism and the positivist cult of the so-called natural sciences. However, the satirical portraits are, in fact, pastiches:

> The form of the 'silhouettes', a gallery of portraits of contemporary cultural figures, was taken from Herbert Eulenberg, a successful contemporary author who was in charge of the 'matinees with poets and music poets' at the theater in Düsseldorf.[59]

Eulenberg had published under the title of *Schattenbilder* portraits of artists intending to ease access to masterpieces. In addition to Eulenberg, *Schattenrisse*

56 André Petitjean, quoted by Aron (2008), p 17.
57 Bowen (2012), p 1005.
58 Mehring (2014), p 38; Schmitt and Villinger (2015).
59 Mehring (2014), p 38.

is also inspired by Wilhelm Schäfer's *Anekdoten*. According to Reinhard Mehring, 'the ironic subversion of these models can be seen as the literary starting point of the *Schattenrisse* project, in which both Eulenberg and Schäfer are the object of satirical treatment'.[60] Thus, Schmitt and Eisler imitate the style of two authors at the forefront of the cultural scene.

In addition to stylistic borrowing, the preface to the piece is also edifying. We learn that the object of the silhouettes is to show that '"relativism" is not dead, and that "naturalism" is still alive'.[61] In this sense, the piece pastiches the entire pre-war literary debate. Accordingly, various actual authors, from Thomas Mann to Schäfer, are portrayed along fictional characters.[62] Eisler and Schmitt also employed numerous puns to forge names, starting with 'Johannes Negelinus', the official author. The pseudonym in itself is telling. Ingeborg Villinger explains that the name is a wink to Johannes Reuchlin, whose quarrel with the late scholastics was defended by Ulrich von Hutten. Von Hutten published *Dunkelmännerbriefe*, a series of pastiches attacking late scholasticism, under the name Magister Negelinus.[63] Hence, the two young men draw on this tradition, which uses pastiche to criticise the dominant dogma. In short, in 1913 Schmitt was already engaged with the pastiche as a form of criticism. And *The Buribunks* follows the same path of satirical writings. If, a priori, *The Buribunks* does not have the same form as *Schattenrisse*, it seems that it uses the same literary techniques, those of pastiche, to once again attack the dominant intellectual traditions on the eve of the 1920s.

'I is another': the semantic surplus-value of presence and absence

First, *The Buribunks* is a scientific article. For a semiology that is not concerned with the 'meaning' of words, but with the form as the only semiotic code to classify a text, there is no doubt that it is a scientific article. The first indication of the pastiche therefore lies in the literary form of the piece. It pastiches the scientific writing model. However, if the form is that of a scientific article, the title – a made-up word – sets the tone and suggests that the narrative form is subverted. Indeed, it is not a neologism – that scholarly invention of which our modern science, and especially the postmodern one, is so fond. On the contrary, the title is absurd. It does not refer to anything that the reader can recognise; indeed, it is quite the opposite of the very recognisable form. Thus, the contrast between the form – imitative (conform) – and the title – absurd –

60 Mehring (2014), p 38.
61 Mehring (2014), p 39; see the original in Schmitt and Villinger (2015), p 16.
62 The table of contents lists the following names: Wilhelm Ostwald, Walther Rathenau, Gottfried von Bouillon, Mein Bruder, Richard Dehmel, Herbert Eulenberg, Pipin der Kleine, Wilhelm Schäfer, Eberhardt Niegeburth, Anatole France, Thomas Mann, Fritz Mauthner. Schmitt and Villinger (2015), p 13.
63 Mehring (2014); Schmitt and Villinger (2015), p 69.

suggests to the reader that the scientific article is something else. It is more than it appears to be.

Moreover, sifting through the pages quickly, we do not fail to recognise the pundits of modern philosophy, chiefly of the philosophy of history. These easily recognisable names underprop the seriousness of the form that the title blurs. As a matter of fact, this quoting, quoted, quoting discourse is a typical manifestation of the pastiche. It uses diametrical signs to blur the line between real and fictitious discourse, and by doing so it betokens a double discourse. The second feature of the pastiche in *The Buribunks* is the presence/non-presence of the author. C.S. signs the essay, but footnotes 2 and 13 suggest that Carl Schmitt is other than the C.S. who signs the original version. There is, therefore, a *mise en abyme* that makes the 'I' another. The one who writes is not the author, but the one attacked/refuted by the author. Thus, the author is present in his non-presence and absent in his non-absence.

Roland Barthes says that 'writing is the destruction of every voice, of every point of origin. Writing is that neutral, composite, oblique space where our subject slips away, the negative where all identity is lost, starting with the very identity of the body writing.'[64] Indeed, the author's disappearance behind the scriptor participates in this distancing, which says that the discourse is double. This is because it is inhabited by the two personae. There is the author's shadow, his silhouette, which fades away, already passed, already past, not present. Nevertheless, there is also the present scriptor, this haunted presence, who is never anything but a here and now because he could not be anything else than the script he is scripting. He is what he scripts, what he is written to be. He is probably already a Buribunk: a non-presence (a non-being) outside the script he scripts.

The pastiche is ideal for creating, for ensuring, this non-absent absence, the author who is not there but always there, and this non-present presence, the scriptor who is present only in his non-presence. Even more, the pastiche is more than writing: it is a collage; it is multiple voices that can only exist in this space that the reader, who recontextualises and recognises, and constructs and gives meaning to the text, inhabits. Indeed, as the pastiche is the construction of a new with old ingredients, it constellates different styles, and 'quotes' by the same author or by several authors. By its creative imitation, out of 'plagiarism' the pastiche becomes more than what it assembles. From its textual accumulation and by its intertextual treatment, it becomes a semantic surplus-value.

In this perspective, *The Buribunks* fits this description. Indeed, we find this relationship between the scriptor, this non-present presence that replaces the author, this non-absent absence, in the ambiguous relationship we observe between C.S., who affixes his autograph, and Carl Schmitt, the phantom-author who only appears as an absence in footnotes 2 and 13. Additionally, *The*

64 Barthes (1984), p 61.

Buribunks is a collage of various voices: rationalism, romanticism, materialism and positivism. It is metaphysic and the enemy of metaphysic.

In the next sections, we will pay close attention to this collage because in it we can identify the core of the scientific contribution of *The Buribunks*. Indeed, as the pastiche is only a literary technique, it can be borrowed and used in different literary genres. In *The Buribunks*, Schmitt borrows and re-legitimises the pastiche as a technique of philosophical/scientific argumentation, a technique that had been relegated to parody, entertainment literature or political controversy. To this end, we will make extensive use of quotes to help us to see the proximity between Schmitt's writing and that of other authors.

However, let us mention before that, as a technique of philosophical critique, pastiche is old.[65] Likewise, the *Dunkelmännerbriefe* of the Magister Negelinus, at which *Schattenrisse* winks, certainly did not fail to inspire Schmitt. Indeed, Magister Negelinus's writing contribute to the late scholastic literature. However, von Hutten, who among others is behind the *Dunkelmännerbriefe*, pastiches scholastics in order to criticise their theses and especially their mode of reasoning. We can thus see in *The Buribunks* a similar attempt whereby Schmitt takes up von Hutten's critical method to attack his own scholastics, his own theoretical intellectual enemies.

For this purpose, Schmitt writes an article that takes up the codes and the theses of various theoretical movements. He criticises some by making visible their limits and aporias, and pays homage to others by denouncing the limited understanding that the state of the science of his time has of them. Often, homage and criticism come together and even merge. That said, given its density, we will explore only few aspects of the semantic surplus-value of *The Buribunks*. In particular, we will focus on what it tells us about positivism and Cartesianism through its laudatory and critical reading of Georg Wilhelm Friedrich Hegel and Søren Kierkegaard. We will then see how this scientific pastiche allows Schmitt to engage with the dominant theoretical currents of his time, mainly positivism and normativism, in the same way that Reuchlin, von Hutten and their co-authors did with the late scholastics. And we will see that it is indeed what it claims to be: a contribution to the philosophy of history; a contribution that sketches some of the elements that we will find in Schmitt's later work.

C.S.'s failure to turn quantity into quality

As already said, *The Buribunks* opens up on the question – apparently quickly dismissed – of the very reality of buribunkology as a science, and that of the Buribunks as empirical and historical reality. C.S. explains that there is a tautological relationship between buribunkology and its subject of study. Buribunkology exists because there are buribunkologists who produce literature in

65 Aron (2009), p 11.

this field. However, Buribunks also exist insofar as they are an a priori of buribunkology. Beyond the absurd, not so absurd, of this assertion, Schmitt engages C.S. head-on with a central, if not *the* central, question of modern philosophy: epistemology. Indeed, the question that opens *The Buribunks* is, 'How do I know what I know?' The first enterprise of C.S., then, is to prove that his knowledge, or the field of knowledge to which he is contributing, is valid scientific knowledge. Although he uses the rational tone of scientific argumentation, the tautological argument entangled with the absurd world 'Buribunk' hints about the attack that Schmitt intends to lead against Cartesian rationalism.

In fact, René Descartes's reflection on the foundation of knowledge led him to his *cogito, ergo sum*. Such a relationship between *cogito* and *sum* (being) implies that 'philosophy should and could find its starting point in epistemology'[66] and not in ontology – that is, not in the question of being. Descartes thus upsets the priorities of philosophy. This reversal of the starting point of philosophical meditations implies two elements discussed in *The Buribunks*. The first is the rejection of scholasticism by rationalism à la Descartes. The second, linked to the first, is the refocusing of philosophy on epistemology. This opening on the epistemological question is, in fact, the first charge against Descartes – or rather against his legacy – by the jurist. We will find the conclusion of this rebuke of Cartesianism in the third part of *The Buribunks.*

That said, it is worth noting that the central philosophical tradition in *The Buribunks* is Hegelianism. Seeking to complexify the evidence of buribunkology as a science, C.S. explains:

> There is a point where – to express it in Hegel's brilliant phrase – quantity turns into quality, then the discussion of the question of buribunkology as a science has to revolve around the cardinal point of whether the factual quantity of buribunkological actualities has reached such an extent that it is only sensitive to address it as a quality (which here means as a science).[67]

It follows, then, that several quantitative 'proofs' will allow, according to this 'law', to prove the 'quality' of buribunkology as a science. We learn that 400,000 theses have already been published in the field, that the 'International Buribunkological Institute for Ferker and Related Research (IBIFERR)' has won numerous prizes and praises, that buribunkology is one of the most prolific publishing industries and that the Buribunk and Ferker Research Panel Commission has an annual budget of several billions.[68] The ultimate proof of quantity turning into quality is this budget since, argues C.S., according to the words of the 'great philosopher of money' Simmel, 'it is money, in a

66 Woleński (2004), p 14.
67 Chapter 2 of this volume, pp 12–3.
68 Chapter 2 of this volume, p 13.

supreme sense, to which the transition from quantity into quality is most applicable'.[69]

Given the dual tone of the essay, Schmitt, by putting the relationship between quantity and quality under the pen of C.S., seeks to mock and criticise this relationship. Nevertheless, it is doubtful that he is scorning Hegel, one of the thinkers that he praised most along with Thomas Hobbes. On the contrary, Schmitt is charging the misuse and misunderstanding of the philosopher. In *Science of Logic*, Hegel deconstructs the simplistic conception of the relationship between quality and quantity. For him, this relationship must be understood in the complexity of its dialectical movement, not as a relationship of equivalence. For his demonstration, and unlike his predecessors – including Kant – Hegel takes quality, not quantity, as his starting point:[70]

> he observes that qualitative variation transforms the nature of reality. Therefore, the qualitative domain is that of differentiating determination: the only way for a qualitative being to change is to move into being-other and difference. We cannot go from red to blue without a jump. That is how quality manifests itself.[71]

The Swabian philosopher then addresses the question of quantity. He observes that, unlike qualitative variation, quantitative variation does not affect reality. It lets it be what it is: it is 'indifferent' to the nature of the real. Hegel concludes that variability is the very nature of the quantitative. Indeed, unlike quality – which dissolves and disappears, to be replaced by a being-other in the change – quantity is only a variation in the determination that does not affect reality or change the nature of the determination. In other words, when there is variation in quality, such as the change from red to blue, the change to blue implies the disappearance of red, a jump into another quality. On the contrary, variation in the quantity of red – red as determination – does not change the nature of the red as red. It stays red. Only its intensity, more or less red, varies. It is only as a variation that we perceive quantity.[72]

Quantity is, in short, the product of quality that exacerbates itself, the product of quality that surpasses itself in its 'self-movement'. It is, therefore, a variation in homogeneity: an indifferent difference. It is a multiplicity that is not a being-other, but an identity. Hegel concludes, then, that there is no quantity without quality. Indeed, as it is only a variation of a determination, it cannot be conceived in itself and for itself without reference to quality.[73] Thus,

69 Chapter 2 of this volume, p 13.
70 Hegel (2010), pp 45–336.
71 Quentin (2006), p 539; Hegel (2010), p 153.
72 Hegel (2010), pp 45–336.
73 Hegel (2010), pp 45–336.

for Hegel, one cannot reduce or deduce any quality from an aggregate of quantities by ignoring the relationship between quality and quantity.

The relationship between quantity and quality is therefore one of complexity that excludes a reduction to the same: 'Quality is implicitly quantity … and quantity is implicitly quality and in their dialectical development they "pass into each other".' Thus, an accumulation of quantities cannot be equivalent or identical to a quality. The philosopher explains that the quantification of quality is a first process, enabling the making of the 'material' intelligible. It is a measurement operation. However, 'measurement is a new form of quality, an internal regulation of quantity; measurement is constituted as the reintegration of quality into quantity'.[74] In short, the measure is the *Aufhebung* (sublation), the dialectical unit, of quality and quantity. In other words, it is the going beyond these two processes (quality and quality), since it is no longer one or the other, but contains, supposes, the one and the other.

However, measurement – this new qualified quality – is not an end to the system. Indeed, the theory of measurement constitutes the third part of the *Doctrine of Being*, the first part of the *Science of Logic*. The latter is the first part of the *Encyclopedia of Philosophical Sciences*. Thus, according to the Hegelian dialectic, this first 'stage' will *aufheben* (sublate): The *Doctrine of Being* is then *aufgehoben* in the *Doctrine of the Concept*, and the *Science of Logic* in the *Philosophy of Mind*.[75] Thus, even if we limit ourselves to the *Science of Logic*, Hegel's enterprise is not to reduce quality into quantity in a positivist logic – especially the positivism of his time. On the contrary, it is to criticise such an approach by showing that the relationship between quality and quantity is not a unilateral causality.

Furthermore, Hegel makes this 'empirical' relationship the starting point of the system, of the knowledge. In other words, science for Hegel cannot be reduced to experimentation or empirical accumulation. Yes, 'matter cannot be thought by the mind without the latter first passing through empirical reality and the constructions of the positive sciences'.[76] However, quality and quantity are properties of the being as *Dasein*. They are 'only the first moment of reality and truth, which finally absorb or retain a consciousness which has not yet emerged from it by the return to oneself of the reflection and the explanation of the concept'.[77] This relationship cannot, therefore, be an end in itself, nor the proof of any truth. The truth always emerges from a dialectical movement and not from a reduction of 'one to the other'. In short, we can say with Jean Theau that for Hegel, if the dialectical relationship between quality and quantity is reduced to the same, then there is no more science. And it is to this conclusion that Schmitt leads C.S.

74 Quentin (2006), p 541.
75 Hegel (2001).
76 Quentin (2006), p 550.
77 Theau (1975), p 12.

Indeed, if C.S. begins his demonstration with Hegel's 'famous' word, quantity as proof of quality leads him to a problem. Scholasticism, to which buribunkology in good positive science is opposed, meets the criteria of quantity, which allows it to claim the same quality as buribunkology. That, C.S. tells us, is absurd. He explains that scholasticism

> has long been negated by the unstoppably forward-moving World Spirit ... Therefore it cannot be difficult for us to recognize the difference between today's buribunkology and obsolete scholasticism – it lies exactly in the essence, the spirit: buribunkology is alive, scholasticism is dead, the Buribunks live and the scholastics are long buried.[78]

Certainly, C.S. admits that scholasticism was a necessary moment of development. He nevertheless affirms that 'a big effort [was] wasted foolishly, [and that] a nearly immoral waste of strength lured humankind from the green fields of secularity into the grey theories of speculation'.[79] On the contrary, C.S. reminds us that buribunkology is only about 'fact and fact again'.[80]

C.S.'s discredit of scholasticism pastiches Hegel's phrasing. Whether it is the negation of scholasticism by the World Spirit, the concreteness by the entry into history or the mandatory passage by scholasticism, we recognise the typical patterns of the Hegelian phrasing and dialectic. Nevertheless, C.S. still uses Hegel in an approximate, even fallacious, way. The Hegelian dialectic, specifically speculative, is brought back, reduced, to a positive positivity, to a mere fact, denying its metaphysical nature. However, despite all the trituration of C. S., he concludes by confirming the Hegelian theses that he misuses. Thus, he will unconsciously confirm that the reduction of science to empirical 'fact', to sensitive experiences, is not science. Indeed, he ends up by explaining: 'buribunkology is more than theology, jurisprudence or philosophy, it is indeed more than a science, it is a fact'.[81] Hence, if buribunkology is a fact, it denies itself as science. If buribunkology stays a fact, this means that it never leapt from quantity to quality. C.S. therefore fails in his project to convince us that buribunkology is science.

This permits Schmitt to show that his understanding (and critique) of positivism is similar to Hegel's. For both, the positivist representation of positivity stems from poor reasoning, from the reductionism of a complexity that can only be grasped dialectically to mere equivalence. The Hegelian understanding of the quality–quantity relationship is an illustration of this. And in *The Concept of the Political*, Schmitt got back to this misuse of Hegel's idea. Thus, he explains:

78 Chapter 2 of this volume, p 13.
79 Chapter 2 of this volume, p 14.
80 Chapter 2 of this volume, p 14.
81 Chapter 2 of this volume, p 14.

> The often-quoted sentence of quantity transforming into quality has a thoroughly political meaning. It is an expression of the recognition that from every domain the point of the political is reached and with it a new qualitative intensity of human groupings. The actual application of this sentence refers to the economic domain and becomes virulent in the nineteenth century. The process of such a transformation executes itself continuously in the autonomous, so-called politically neutral economic domain. The hitherto nonpolitical or pure matter of fact now turns political. When it reaches a certain quantity, economic property, for example, becomes obviously social (or more correctly, political) power, property turns into power, and what is at first only an economically motivated class antagonism turns into a class struggle of hostile groups.[82]

In short, Schmitt attacks the misunderstanding by positivist and apolitical economism of Hegel's famous phrase. He does the same in *The Buribunks*, only in the essay/novel he uses pastiche and caricature for his demonstration. Written by C.S., *The Buribunks* puts forward a naïve discourse reflecting a simplistic understanding of one of the most arid philosophies of the nineteenth century. Schmitt ushers C.S. to the point of absurdity: in seeking to assert buribunkology as science, C.S. comes to assert that it is not. And C.S., zealous scriptor, reports his reasoning candidly. By doing so, Schmitt, who addresses a readership that a priori understands the gap between Hegelian philosophy and C.S.'s understanding of it, pays homage to Hegel while rendering visible the shortcomings of the empiricist/positivist approaches.

This use of pastiche by Schmitt is similar to that found in the *Dunkelmännerbriefe*. In the latter, the writers are the scriptors of debates between the scholastic 'camp' (theirs) and the humanist one. They reproduce almost 'textually' their disputations with the challenging camp. However, scholastics, the scriptors, are depicted as using simplistic and vulgar Latin. Consequently, the scholastic posture is ridiculed and the humanists one elevated.[83]

In short, one might say that pastiche allows Schmitt to attack simplistic understandings of Hegelianism and to reaffirm, or even to co-opt, Hegelian thought into his own. It also permits him to highlight the limits of Hegelian thought. Indeed, as the pastiche draws partly on collage and the interlocking of several styles/thoughts, it is an ideal technique to visibilise gaps, aporias and shortcomings by contrasting multiple approaches. In the second part of the essay, we find such a use of the pastiche.

Towards the dead end of Hegelianism

The second part of the essay focuses, among other things, on reconstructing the genealogy of the Buribunks. To this end, C.S. considers several possible

82 Schmitt (2007), p 62.

83 For an analysis of the letters, see Becker (1981); see also von Hutten (2004).

ancestors to determine who was the first true Buribunk. C.S. explains that a 'moral feeling of responsibility forces upon us the question of which historical person we have to acknowledge as the predecessor of this glorious epoch – the dove which the World Spirit sent prior to its last and most advanced period',[84] the 'unknowing instrument of the World Spirit'.[85] After reviewing several candidates,[86] he identifies Schnekke as being the first true Buribunk. He is the hero of the Buribunkdom.

We recognise, once again, typical Hegelian phrasing and argumentative scheme. Indeed, like Hegel for Cesar, Alexander or Napoleon Bonaparte, C.S. argues that Schnekke, the instrument of the World Spirit, pursuing its project, its passion, makes history, makes his buribunkian way of life that of all of humanity. Thus, as in Hegel, we find that a heroic figure pursuing a personal ambition is at the origin of a particular social order, by the doing of the cunning of the reason. Schnekke founds a new normative order by rendering the object of his personal passion, writing a diary, a collective obligation.[87] By doing so – C.S. says – he realised the will of the World Spirit. Similarly, for Hegel, by invading Europe in the pursuit of his 'egoistic' ambition, Napoleon spread all around Europe the Spirit of the (French) Revolution, the Spirit of the *Aufklärung*, which will set the path for the accomplishment of the Spirit of the Mind.

However, before arriving at Schnekke, C.S. demonstrates that other personages are not real Buribunks. C.S.'s study of the Buribunks' ancestry starts with pastiching another famous passages in Hegelian philosophy: the master–slave dialectic. Don Juan is the first character he considers to be the ancestor of the Buribunks. Nonetheless, quickly (and we will come back to this), C.S. dismisses him as a potential candidate and turns to his valet, Leporello. C.S. explains that it was not Don Juan who initiated the accounting of the conquered women.[88] It was his valet, his slave, *sein Knecht*, who did this. Nevertheless, Leporello is also rejected as an ancestor; in doing so, Schmitt – who guides the scriptor's pen – steps aside from Hegel by challenging Leporello's buribunkness.

Indeed, C.S. explains that 'through an admirable ruse, [Leporello] rises above his master and even if he does not become Don Juan himself, he becomes more than that'.[89] Similarly, Hegel argues that the *Knecht* always ends up surpassing his master, another cunning of the reason. The master who makes things done by another and does nothing can only enjoy the immediacy of objects. He lives only in immediate enjoyment. On the contrary, the *Knecht*, who makes the object through his work, transforms nature. He thus has access to the active

84 Chapter 2 of this volume, p 15.
85 Chapter 2 of this volume, p 15.
86 Chapter 2 of this volume, pp 15–9.
87 Hegel (1975).
88 Chapter 2 of this volume, pp 15–7.
89 Blackburn (2005), p 103.

dimension of the object. For him, the object is not a simple 'passive object' to be enjoyed. For him, it is the result of active work. It is the result of the domination and transformation of nature. Thus, the domination relationship between the *Knecht* and the master is reversed. The master, by making the *Knecht* the one who does, and by being the one who only consumes, ultimately becomes the slave of his slave.[90] It is Leporello who makes Don Juan because it is he who keeps track of his conquests, and if he did not, there would be no Don Juan.

Moreover, *Aufhebung* obliges the slave to become more than his master through his mastering of nature. He no longer has a relationship of mere enjoyment of nature (of freedom). He transforms and dominates nature, writes history and therefore dominates more than the master does. He dominates nature and allows the master to exist in history, which the master – who only enjoys – cannot do by himself. For Hegel, the *Knecht* thus gains autonomy. On the contrary, C.S. does not recognise such autonomy to Leporello. Guided by Schmitt, C.S. affirms that Leporello cannot be a Buribunk because he is not his own master; he is not autonomous. Leporello is unaware of his contribution to writing history. He lacks the real Buribunk spirit. Thus, Schmitt rejects this thesis central to Hegelianism. For C.S., Leporello cannot be the ancestor of the Buribunks because he does not write his own (hi)story, but rather his master's. He does not see himself as a protagonist of history, but a simple spectator. To paraphrase Schmitt, Leporello has not made a decision, has not made history, and therefore is not sovereign. He is only the product of the march of time, a puppet of the World Spirit. For Schmitt, this absence of decision-making is one of the gaps in the Hegelian dialectic, a point to which we will return.

Finally, this critique of the master–slave dialectic enables Schmitt to inconspicuously introduce his critique of Hegelianism by contrasting Hegel's theses to those of the 'most anti-Hegelian' philosopher of the nineteenth century, Søren Kierkegaard. According to Mehring, Schmitt's 'encounter with Kierkegaard was highly important'.[91] He adds that 'with the help of Kierkegaard he finally left his religious pessimism behind. In 1915, he read the edition of Kierkegaard by Theodor Haecker'.[92] After this encounter, Kierkegaard entered Schmitt bibliographies, even if he always stayed in the shadows, alluded to but rarely quoted or mentioned by name.

Indeed, if we can find references to Hegel in Schmitt's first publications, we find no mention of Kierkegaard before 1916. In 1919, the year following the publication of *The Buribunks*, *Political Romanticism* was published. In it, we observe an increase in references to Hegel but also references to Kierkegaard. These mentions of the two philosophers were to be an enduring characteristic of Schmitt's work, although discreet, and both are referred to in the works that

90 Hegel (2013), p 520–43.
91 Mehring (2014), p 80.
92 Mehring (2014), p 80.

brought him fame, namely *Political Theology* and *The Concept of the Political.* If Hegel remains, after Hobbes, the most influential author in Schmittian thought, the encounter with Kierkegaard significantly contributed to Schmitt's reading of Hegelianism. This reading, which allows Schmitt to complement what he does not find in Hegel by Kierkegaard's thought, will be decisive in his critique of romanticism and his conception of decisionism.[93] In this regard, *The Buribunks* is one of the first texts in which one can find the very particular synthesis that Schmitt makes of Hegel and Kierkegaard.

The dialectic of the leap

Kierkegaard's introduction to the reader is made through the discussion of the master–slave dialectic. The initial candidate considered by C.S. as the first Buribunk is Don Juan, the seducer. He explains that the pride the seducer feels about his growing list of conquests resonates with 'a sentiment which frequently courses through the true buribunkologist when he considers ever-increasing extent or number of his publications'.[94] Moreover, glimpsing Kierkegaard, Schmitt makes C.S. introduce us to the famous womaniser through one of Mozart's Don Giovanni arias. Indeed, the opening excerpt of Kierkegaard's *Diary of a Seducer* is a quote from the same opera.[95] In this sense, the mere introduction of Kierkegaard is a play on pastiche. The anti-Hegelian Dane is brought up at the heart of a central Hegelian demonstration.

Nonetheless, C.S. immediately questions the buribunkological character of Don Juan:

> Don Juan had no interest whatsoever in the past, indeed just as little as in the future, which for him barely extended beyond his next rendezvous; he lived in the immediate present and his interest in the singular erotic experience did not contain anything in which we could glimpse the beginning of self-historicisation.[96]

Thus, this description meets Kierkegaard's view of the seducer, the 'esthetician', the romantic, an individual who only lives in immediacy. Don Juan is the seducer: the first stage of the Kierkegaardian dialectic. He is the aesthete, who lives only to satisfy his desires, to enjoy immediacy. Enjoyment is the only goal of his life. It is the stage of immediate being. For Kierkegaard, this stage is the one of 'the romantic, following Schlegel's conception, who does not suffer any yoke, who seeks pleasure, dissolves all reality into possibility and creates a

93 See among others, Kervégan (2005), pp 127–31; Mehring (2014), p 80.
94 Chapter 2 of this volume, p 15.
95 Kierkegaard (1987a).
96 Chapter 2 of this volume, p 15.

variegated series of moods, and ceaselessly goes towards new desires'.[97] He is the one who runs after change, change as accumulation, as quantity not as quality. In that respect, Mozart's Don Juan sings his long list of conquests – as Molière's Don Juan declaims, 'the whole pleasure of love lies in variety'.[98]

Running after immediate pleasures, 'the possibility … is more intense than the reality'[99] for the romantic. He lives outside time, outside history, outside concreteness. He seeks to extricate himself from all constraints, including those of time. According to Kierkegaard, in the romantic conception of life, of the ideal, there is 'no sense of activity and no sense of duration, and ultimately no content'.[100] For the Dane, 'the esthetician only lives in the possible and the past'.[101] Under this definition, he is also the romantic whom Schmitt attacks violently in *Political Romanticism*. In fact, he later explains that, 'in commonplace reality, the romantics could not play the role of the ego who creates the world. They preferred the state of eternal becoming and possibilities that are never consummated to the confines of concrete reality.'[102] He adds that the romantic uses 'the past as a negation of the present, as a way out of the prison of the reality that is concrete and present'.[103] Thus, for him, the real, the concrete, is solely a possibility, an *occasio*, for romanticisation, to exercise his romantic spirit. He is never in the moment, the past, the future. He never decides because 'a legal or a moral decision would … inevitably destroy romanticism. This is why the romantic is not in a position to deliberately take sides and make a decision.'[104]

In short, the romantic for Kierkegaard, as for Schmitt and C.S., lives outside time, history and concreteness. For this aesthete, the 'reality is empty, a realized possibility, a decision that has already been made'.[105] He is the aesthete whose political nullity for Schmitt (moral for Kierkegaard) cannot be expressed by concrete decisions. In this sense, C.S. is very Kierkegaardian and Schmittian in rejecting Don Juan as an ancestor. Here, the multiple voices of the pastiche

97 Wahl (1938), p 64. In this chapter, I rely on the reading of Kierkegaard by Jean Wahl for two reasons. First, Wahl relies, among others, on the same German translation of Kierkegaard that Schmitt read. Second, he bases his reading (mostly) on the German literature on Kierkegaard, the same available to Schmitt. Thus, using Wahl's reading allows us (partially) to account for how Kierkegaard was read and understood in Germany when Schmitt discovered him. In this sense, our object, here, is not to offer a (our) new reading/understanding of the Danish philosopher writings, but rather to give an account of how the latter was understood (and mobilised) by Schmitt in accordance with how he was understood (and used) in Germany during the first half of the twentieth century.
98 Molière (2001), p 15.
99 Wahl (1938), p 64.
100 Wahl (1938), p 63.
101 Wahl (1938), p 63.
102 Schmitt (2017), p 66.
103 Schmitt (2017), p 71.
104 Schmitt (2017), p 124.
105 Schmitt (2017), p 69.

express themselves loudly. These are three voices that do not want nor say the same thing, even if they are 'voiced' in the same discourse; three voices whose difference can only be perceived in the reader as a space of meaning. Their difference will only appear as C.S., naïf puppet, resumes his pursuit of an ancestor.

Having rejected Don Juan and Leporello as well as other potential candidates, the author C.S. finally concludes that 'only Ferker developed the diary into an ethical-historical possibility; he holds the rights of the first-born in the realm of Buribunkdom'.[106] Ferker came from a modest background. He went to the 'Latin-less school'. He pursued, successfully, numerous career paths, ultimately becoming a 'lecturer for Advertising and Arrivistics at the Business School in Alexandria'.[107] According to C.S., Ferker had a vibrant and diverse life, eventful and full of twists. A life that he carefully recorded in his diaries so that every second of it would become history.[108]

Ferker is the ideal type of bourgeois. He does not enjoy things in the way of the hedonist, the aesthete, the romantic. He is aware of himself, of the social elevation that has allowed him to reach the heights he has achieved. He knows that he is the master of his destiny. Above all, he makes this ultra-individualism the highest virtue and value. Indeed,

> not only was the human being Ferker ethically elevated, but also the most incredible scientific progress accomplished and a splendid example provided of the truth that the progress of humankind can only be expected when everyone only thinks of themselves and lets everything else run its own course.[109]

Ferker thus elevates self-centred individualism to a new religion. With Ferker, all metaphysical dualism is abolished. Ferker 'found (and that is the most essential aspect) a form of contemporary religiosity whilst strictly retaining an exclusive positivism and an unflinching belief in nothing but the facts'.[110] In other words, Ferker has taken a qualitative leap compared with Don Juan and Leporello. It is in Ferker that Kierkegaard faces Hegel. It is the confrontation that Schmitt made up, and that C.S. renders as the scriptors of the *Dunkelmännerbriefe* naively did with the humanists' arguments.

Jean Wahl explains that, for Kierkegaard, the synthetic, synthesised totality of Hegel remains deeply embedded in the aesthetic stage. It remains somehow romantic:

106 Chapter 2 of this volume, p 19.
107 Chapter 2 of this volume, p 19.
108 Chapter 2 of this volume, p 20.
109 Chapter 2 of this volume, p 21.
110 Chapter 2 of this volume, p 21.

> Would it not be a kind of Don Juanism, this will to exhaust all particular beauties to reach a total beauty, or even to gather all the particular truths, to integrate them … in a total truth? There is a qualitative logic quite distinct from this nonetheless quantitative cult of the whole in time and space.[111]

And the aesthete is never more than the one who accumulates beauties, thinking that this count will become quality according to the rule that quantity makes quality. On the contrary, for the Danish philosopher, dialectic is not continuous mediation. Dialectic, according to him, is qualitative leaps:

> For Kierkegaard, Wahl clarifies, continuity is an abstraction … The life of the spirit is made of stages, separated by an absolute clear-cut. We arrive at ethics by the suspension of aesthetics, and by the suspension of ethics we arrive at religion. There is here a qualitative dialectic, as opposed to the Hegelian dialectic, which suppresses the differences, which mixes the spheres.[112]

The negation of quality, then, cannot be quantity, but another quality. In this sense, the negation of aesthetics is Ferker's ethical stage, ignored by Hegel because there is no decision in his dialectic; it remains in the aesthetic stage.

Indeed, the ethical stage is when the individual chooses himself; it is the stage of choice, of individual choice. It is the 'citizen and married man'[113] stage. For the ethical man, time becomes a 'task', the task of carrying out oneself. Indeed,

> opposed to the aesthetic stage dominated by 'this as well as that'; opposed to Hegelianism dominated by the idea of 'up to a certain point', it will be the domain of choice, of the choice by which the individual assumes responsibility for himself, takes upon himself to be himself, and embraces his situation. It is the stage of the citizen and the married man. By ethical reaffirmation, a man swears loyalty to himself, dedicates himself to a task; for time has ceased to be an enemy to become a task.[114]

It is the stage where man roots in himself: 'The esthetic … is that in a person whereby he immediately is the person he is; the ethical is that whereby a person becomes what he becomes.'[115] And Ferker becomes. Indeed, from a modest background, and educated in the 'Latin-less school', he becomes the messiah of a new religion, a new world-view.

111 Wahl (1938), p 157.
112 Wahl (1938), p 57.
113 Wahl (1938), p 72.
114 Wahl (1938), p 72.
115 Kierkegaard (1987b).

Moreover, for Kierkegaard, the ethical stage is when a 'Man chooses himself in the ethical stage as an individual personality, but as an individual personality within a general, historical and social whole … He is transformed into the general.'[116] Similarly, C.S. describes Ferker:

> In full awareness of its own wild agitation, I would even say of its own modernity and suitability for the theatre; this self-awareness begins with abstaining from all ideology and still marvelling at the fact that life is (to speak in the crude tone of this time) a grand old thing. This knowledge of oneself as a subject of interest (artistic, scientific and historical interest), this heightened self-awareness, connected inextricably with completely dissolving into the community.[117]

In fact, the dissolution of Ferker into the general goes further, since even his physical person will 'become general'. After his death, he was cremated, and his ashes were mixed with the ink used all around the Buribunkdom. Thus, his person will imbue the Buribunkdom for several centuries.[118]

Ferker is the 'personification' of the ethical moment. More than dedicating his life to a task, writing his diary, more than embracing life as work, the few dozen careers that had been his, he compelled himself to a duty that negated the aesthete lifestyle: marriage being, according to Kierkegaard, the ultimate negation by the bourgeois (the achievement of the bourgeois stage) of the aesthete moment. Indeed, 'what Don Juan sought, vainly, in the multiplicity of beings, the knowledge of the human soul in all its richness, the husband acquires it by living in common with a woman who is his wife'.[119] And Ferker married his maid; it is this knowledge of the soul through marriage that Ferker undertook at the end of his life because 'marriage is the symbol of the ethical stage'.[120] In doing so, he completely embraced the ethical moment: he became Judge Wilhelm, the bourgeois.

However, laments C.S., more scandalous than this marriage, nothing about it is recorded in Ferker's diaries. Nowhere does he hint about the reasons that prompted him, 'shortly before his death … to enter a bourgeois Christian marriage [with] his own housekeeper'.[121] In addition, according to reliable sources of C.S., he feared death; and about this, also, nothing is recorded in the diaries.[122] This secret is to C.S. a grave nonfeasance. Like Kierkegaard, he thinks that secrets isolate from the general; keeping one outside the general keeps him apart from himself and apart from others.[123] By having secrets, then,

116 Walter Ruttenbeck, quoted and translated by Wahl (1938), pp 75–6.
117 Chapter 2 of this volume, p 20.
118 Chapter 2 of this volume, pp 19–20.
119 Wahl (1938), pp 76–7.
120 Wahl (1938), p 72.
121 Chapter 2 of this volume, p 21.
122 Chapter 2 of this volume, p 22.
123 Wahl (1938), p 78.

Ferker remained isolated from the general, stepped outside the Buribunkdom. He did not enter the Promised Land. So he is not the hero of the Buribunkdom, but its Moses – the one who saw the promised land but did not tread on its sacred soil.[124]

Ferker having failed, the founder of the Buribunkdom is yet to come. Another qualitative stage has to be attained: 'The individual [who] by his guilt [secret] has gone outside the universal … can return to it only by virtue of having come as the individual into an absolute relationship with the absolute.'[125] After the fall, the sin of secrecy, 'the ethical stage can only be a place of passage'.[126] Indeed, for Kierkegaard, the ethical stage is always somehow a stage of comic illusions and folly.[127] Then it has to be escaped, to be surpassed. In this sense, the folly of Ferker was only the ethical stage that failed to become, to be universal. Another qualitative leap is then necessary, one in which the 'absolute relationship with the absolute' is achieved. The individual who attained this absolute was Schnekke. He is the hero of the Buribunkdom. He realised, to the greatest extent, the Buribunkian ideal. He devoted his entire life to his diary: 'He is nothing but a diary-keeper, he lives for the diary, he lives in and through the diary – even though in the end he keeps a diary about the fact that he has run out of ideas about what he could write in the diary.'[128]

Schnekke chooses to devote himself absolutely to the absolute of the Buribunk world: writing his diary. Thus, if Ferker's life was 'sensational', Schnekke's is without individuality, without colours. Unlike Ferker, who in his ethics recognised himself and dissolved into the general, Schnekke became more than the general. He sacrificed himself for and through his subjectivity to the World Spirit. Schnekke gave up everything, everything that made Ferker's tumultuous life, to devote himself totally to the spirit of the world. Thus, 'the I projecting itself onto a tangible You-World streams back into the World-I with powerful rhythm, the highest harmony is reached through the absolute devotion of all powers to the inner self and its identity'.[129] Nevertheless, if Schnekke succeeded in attaining the stage of the I-ness of the absolute relationship to the absolute, he somehow failed this absoluteness. He refused the irrational Christian God.

Beyond Hegel and Kierkegaard: Prelude to Schmitt's philosophy of history

Thus, pushing Hegel and Kierkegaard to a dead end by pastichising them, Schmitt depicts his reading and conception of the philosophy of history. In *The*

124 Chapter 2 of this volume, p 21.
125 Kierkegaard (1994), pp 86–7.
126 Wahl (1938), p 79.
127 Wahl (1938), p 57.
128 Chapter 2 of this volume, p 22.
129 Chapter 2 of this volume, p 22.

Buribunks, we can see the first glimpses of what he would assert in *Political Romanticism, Political Theology* and *The Concept of the Political*, among others. Indeed, the year following the publication of *The Buribunks*, we read in *Political Romanticism*:

> Under the impression of Fichte's individualism, the romantics felt strong enough to play the role of the creator of the world themselves, and to bring forth reality out of themselves. At the same time, they were the heralds of the two new realities, community and history, to whose power they immediately succumbed.[130]

Schnekke, making the diary-keeping a collective obligation, created a new community, a new human 'race', a new world. From his subjectivism, 'its I-ness', a new world emerged. He became the creator of a new community and the initiator of a new historical era. Schnekke is then a rational romantic. In fact, Kierkegaard thinks that the religious stage retains something romantic at its core. And as we will see, for Schmitt any romantic afterglow is a renunciation of a real decision, which has to be political.

At first glance, it might seem paradoxical to start from Hegel and Kierkegaard and end up with a romantic ideal. But this follows from Schmitt's particular understanding of the two philosophers. On the one hand, according to him, 'there is an insuperable tension in the Hegelian dialectic. A contradictory tension which results from the fact that there is no decision in his dialectic. Only an unstoppable march of history.'[131] For Schmitt, this lack of decision is archetypal of the modern neutralised and depoliticised world. Neutralisation and depoliticisation are inherited from the romantic spirit. Against this indecision, 'in Kierkegaard, somehow he [Schmitt] finds the decision'.[132] For the Dane,

> Hegelianism is one of the most visible signs of the disease of the modern world, of softness and tepidness, which only wants 'to a certain degree' and obeys the *ne quid nimis*, of the lack of character, of the absence of choice, of the need that men have, not to see the real and not to live their thought.[133]

Nevertheless, for the jurist Schmitt, Kierkegaard remains romantic. Indeed, he describes him as 'the only great figure among the romantics'.[134] He adds that, 'in Kierkegaard, all the elements of the romantic were in force: irony; the

130 Schmitt (2017), p 64.
131 Kervégan (2005), p 45.
132 Kervégan (2005), p 45.
133 Wahl (1938), p 124.
134 Schmitt (2017), p 166 n 10.

aesthetic conception of the world; the antitheses of the possible and the real, the infinite and the finite; the feeling for the concrete moment'.[135] Moreover, Kierkegaard refused politics and, like Schnekke and Ferker, chose the subjective self. Unlike Hegel, who remained political despite the lack of decision, Kierkegaard did not embrace the objectivist stand that would allow him to reach the political moment.

Karl Löwith, criticising Schmitt's use of Kierkegaard, nonetheless agrees on this point. He explains that, 'Kierkegaard did not want to decide politically on the exceptional situation of 1848, he decided for Christian authority … whereas Schmitt played on the contrary, politically, the exception against the general.'[136] In other words, while Kierkegaard decided against the political, for the subjective, for private contemplation, Schmitt puts forward the political decision, the controversial decision, the objective decision. Schnekke would thus embed the absence of decision in Hegel's objective dialectic and the subjective Kierkegaardian decisionism. He symbolises the aporia between the Danish decision for a subjective concreteness and the Swabian indecision in the objective concreteness – an aporia that became an open door for the neutralised liberal man – the one who only seeks an absolute freedom to pursuit his private businesses and does not engage in any political enterprise.

In fact, C.S. describes a Schnekke who sets up a system in which only the neutralised liberal man is meant to be. He explains that in Buribunkdom, the freedom of the Buribunks is total in their private life. The only limit to this freedom concerns public, political decisions: Buribunks are not allowed to stop writing their diaries.[137] Therefore, they are not allowed to make a political decision to change the legal and political order. It goes without saying that in the pacified and neutralised world of the Buribunks, no 'physical' sanctions are taken against the one who decides to no longer be of the Buribunks' world, to refuse its political organisation. Instead, he will face a disappearance from history:

> The wheel of progress passes silently over the silent one; he will no longer be mentioned, he can therefore no longer make himself heard until he finally, sinking step by step, is forced into the lowest class, to help create the external conditions for the possibility of noble Buribunkdom.[138]

The Buribunk who no longer writes departs from history and time. He takes his leave of the Buribunkdom. Then simple 'homo sacer',[139] he is nothing more than a naked life, without content, a man without quality.[140] He will

135 Schmitt (2017), p 166.
136 Löwith (1991), p 21.
137 Chapter 2 of this volume, p 24.
138 Chapter 2 of this volume, p 25.
139 Agamben (1998).
140 Lambrow (2017).

become the Morlock who produces the necessary material conditions for the best sake of the Buribunkdom.

The real Buribunk, to the contrary, is the liberal ideal of the late nineteenth and early twentieth centuries (in the view of Schmitt). Indeed, in a world where 'everyone only thinks of themselves and lets everything else run its own course',[141] the Buribunk has no other task than to write himself, to make history through his personal story: 'What do I write? I write myself. Who writes me? I myself write myself. What is the content of my writing? I write that I write myself. What is the big engine lifting me above this self-sufficient circle of I-ness? History!'[142] From that moment in the essay, C.S. vanishes into the mass of Buribunks. He is no longer C.S., an individual addressing the reader, but a Buribunk, among others. He fades as individuality inside the whole, the general, the mass of Buribunks.

He will speak, from that moment onward, as a man-machine, among many others. Indeed, his voice – now the indistinct voice of any Buribunk – states, 'I am therefore a letter on the typewriter of history.'[143] Thus, the Buribunk describes himself as an automaton, a man-machine, the man a machine of Descartes, and Julien Jean Offroy de La Mettrie. His whole world is, in fact, a world of automatons, of human-machines. The essay then concludes with a description of a world whose philosophy is based on the mechanisation of its members' lives. This last section of the text, in particular, makes the essay read like a dystopia. Indeed, the modern reader can identify descriptions that one could ascribe to H.G. Wells.

However, if we read *The Buribunks* as it presents itself to us – that is to say, as a scientific article – the world of automatons proudly described to us by the Buribunk is no longer a dystopian universe, a future to come. On the contrary, it is the depoliticised and neutralised world that Schmitt would decry in the years following the essay/story's publication. Indeed, as already stated, the aporia resulting from the lack of decision of Hegelian dialectics and romantic subjectivism of Kierkegaard paved the way for the neutralised and depoliticised world inherited from the Enlightenment – or, more accurately, inherited from Descartes.

Indeed, for Schmitt, Descartes is the first to mechanise man. In 'Der Staat als Mechanismus bei Hobbes und Descartes', Schmitt writes that it is 'precisely through this philosopher [Descartes] that all human things were fundamentally changed in a revolutionary way, because he understood the human body as a mechanism. It was the prelude of the upcoming technical-Industrial Revolution'.[144] He continues: 'Compared to the mechanization of the human body, the mechanization of the state [by Hobbes] is secondary and less mediate. In

141 Chapter 2 of this volume, p 21.
142 Chapter 2 of this volume, p 26.
143 Chapter 2 of this volume, p 26.
144 Schmitt (1936), p 622.

itself, it is possible to conceive the state as an artificial mechanism without analogously mechanizing the human body.'[145] In other words, the state's mechanisation can remain a technological improvement – a technology in the hands of individuals, citizens, communities still taking political decisions. To the contrary, the mechanisation of man turns him into a machine. He is no longer the one who masters a technique. He becomes a technique, a technical tool, himself. Becoming technical, he is no longer a citizen. He is no longer political. He is the consumer, the bourgeois, the automaton.

For Schmitt, therefore, the mechanised world he observes is a consequence of Cartesian rationalism, which infuses and nourishes the positivism and normativism of his time, and which he intends to denounce. The mechanisation of the state, in Hobbes, is not responsible for the mechanisation of society.[146] On the contrary, it is the scientisation of society, the mechanisation of men by a thought that ignores the 'irrational', that man has become an automaton. Schmitt insists and concludes that 'the first metaphysical decision was taken by Descartes when the human body was thought of as a machine and the whole man, composed of a body and a soul, like an intellect on a machine'.[147] These words, printed in 1936–7, resonate strangely with the Buribunk philosophy. Indeed, Schmitt's ultimate description of the mechanised world of Buribunks is nothing more than an extension of Descartes's *cogito, ergo sum.*

In the last part of *The Buribunks*, outlining the philosophy of the Buribunks, C.S. explains, 'I think, therefore I am; I speak, therefore I am; I write, therefore I am; I publish, therefore I am.'[148] This pastiche of Descartes's most famous words introduces the description of a world in which the Buribunks are no longer 'human beings', but mechanised creatures. In other words, the human-machine, the 'man a machine', is not to be found only in a future to come that can only be observed by travelling with a Wellsian time machine. He is the man, the men Schmitt recognised in the liberal bourgeois – the contemporary fellows. For him, the mechanised man is history, something that has already happened; he is not a possible future, but an already made decision. *The Buribunks* is, therefore, one of the first attacks the jurist would undertake against the 'neutralisation and depoliticization'[149] of the modern secularised society.

Mehring suggests that Schmitt's experience in military administration during World War I inspired the human-machine world, the Buribunkdom. However, he adds that one can see a reversal in the way Schmitt perceives the

145 Schmitt (1936), p 622.
146 In the year following the publication of 'Der Staat als Mechanismus bei Hobbes und Descartes', Schmitt's opus on the Leviathan appeared, in which he denounced, with rare violence and anti-Semitism, the hijacking of Hobbesian thought and the murder of the Leviathan by scientist rationalism and positivism. Schmitt (2008).
147 Schmitt (1936), p 630.
148 Chapter 2 of this volume, p 25.
149 Schmitt (2007), pp 80–96.

present in this short text, 'from an orientation towards the past to an orientation towards the future'.[150] This change, still according to Mehring, would have a profound impact on the jurist's later works, leading him to 'denounce the position of positive law as a striving of security that takes its orientation from the past, and would liquidize legalism in the name of the political future'.[151] Yet this relation to time is linked in *The Buribunks*, as in other writings, to the issue of mechanisation.

Indeed, *The Buribunks* climaxes in a soliloquy about securing the future in the past, in history. More radically, the soliloquy states an overcoming, an elimination, of the future by its inscription in history. It is an elimination of time itself. By freezing the present, and the future that did not yet come, into history, in a mechanisation of time that admits no change, no political decision, it is time itself that disappears. In this sense, we find the parallel with the imprisonment of the political future in its inscription in positive law. This desire to keep the future on a leash is intimately linked to Schmitt's criticisms of the 'mechanisation' of law and the legislative apparatus resulting from the mechanisation of man.

In *The Crisis of Parliamentary Democracy*, as well as in 'Die Lage der europäischen Rechtswissenschaft', he would go on to denounce the reign of the 'motorized legislator'[152] of the twentieth century, for whom 'the decree, the ordinance, supplanted the law'.[153] Similarly, Schmitt argues in *The Crisis of Parliamentary Democracy* that there is a need to undo the confused thinking that does not distinguish the terms of the political debate (democracy, liberalism, individualism and rationalism). He argues that it is only at this price that it will be possible to break from the mechanical conception, from the technicalisation of parliamentarism, and to engage in a real debate of ideas on intellectual questions, to re-engage politically.[154] These critiques echo what can be found in 'Der Staat als Mechanismus bei Hobbes und Descartes', an article in which he blames Descartes for the human-machine, this 'Man a machine'.

In fact, according to Schmitt,

> the breakup [of] the dialogue [between Hegel and de Savigny] is, among other historical factors, one of the reasons for the legal unconsciousness which characterizes the 'motorized legislator' of the 20th century, for which the decree, the ordinance and the administrative circular have in fact replaced the general legal norm.[155]

In other words, Descartes's mechanised man's victory results from a lack of decision in the Hegelian dialectic and from Kierkegaard's subjective

150 Mehring (2014), p 83.
151 Mehring (2014), p 83.
152 Schmitt (1950), pp 18–21.
153 Schmitt (1950), p 18.
154 Schmitt (2000), pp 20–1, 33–50.
155 Kervégan (2005), p 144.

romanticism. The absence of dialogue between these two traditions is what, two decades later, seals for him 'the intellectual catastrophe of a generation, not to say an entire era of German idealistic philosophy and theology'.[156]

Schmitt's critique of the mechanisation and the importance of decision-making precede his publication of *The Buribunks* and the texts quoted in this chapter. What is unique about the text under consideration here is that it is the first to broaden the scope of this critique. Indeed, in his habilitation dissertation, *Gesetz und Urteil: eine Untersuchung zum Problem der Rechtspraxis*, Schmitt denounces the understanding of the role of the judge as a Subsumotionsautomat – that is, as 'a machine for subsuming individual cases under a presumed complete and coherent normative order'.[157] Thus, in 1912, we already find the theme of mechanisation here in the judicial decision, denounced for its fallaciousness. However, as Kervégan remarks, in *Gesetz und Urteil* Schmitt is still somehow 'shy', not entirely sure. He does not yet assert the decision as the founding moment of law, of the legal order. Schmitt, of course, insists on the relative autonomy of judicial decisions with regard to the norm, but he does not yet make of it *the* source of law.[158]

With *The Buribunks*, and *Political Romanticism* the following year, however, he asserts the decision as an element at the heart of the politico-legal system. In 1919, Schmitt attacked political romanticism. For him, it was an apolitical occasionalism, a politically neutralised movement, because it avoided any kind of (political) decision.[159] In *The Buribunks*, he tackles the same point, but from a different angle. He targets another responsible for the 'political neutralisation': mechanisation. The automaton denounced is no longer just the judge, but all the actors of society who are neutralised, mechanised. Through pastiche, Schmitt succeeds in making visible, better than through concepts, a universe that he sees in the modern society that is his own, the concrete effects of rationalists thought which had neutralised and depoliticised the entire social body to the point of reducing the individuals who compose it into simple automatons, human-machines.

In conclusion, *The Buribunks*, read as a pastiche, does not appear to be (only) a fiction – a science fiction. On the contrary, it is what claims to be: a scientific article, a piece of Schmitt's theoretical work and a reading of his time. Indeed, it embeds the seeds of the conception of the political and the legal, which will be Schmitt's trademark. On the one hand, Kierkegaard's contribution asserts itself there and paves the way for more assertive decisionism. On the other hand, his criticism of mechanisation's devastating effects encompasses the entire political order. It is no longer just an illusion, a fiction, which affects the judiciary decision. It becomes one of the central elements of depoliticisation and

156 Schmitt (1950), p 27.
157 Kervégan (2011), p 127.
158 Kervégan (2011), pp 129–30.
159 Schmitt (2017), pp 109–62.

neutralisation that undermines the socio-political body. *The Buribunks*, then, is an actual essay of philosophy of history, one of the first attempts by Schmitt to bring together Hegel and Kierkegaard, among many others, to tackle the mechanisation, neutralisation and depoliticisation of the social group.

References

Giorgio Agamben (1998) *Homo Sacer: Sovereign Power and Bare Life*, Stanford University Press.

Jan Erik Antonsen (2007) 'Pastiche', in Klaus Weimar, Harald Fricke and Jan-Dirk Müller (eds), *Reallexikon der deutschen Literaturwissenschaft: Neubearbeitung des Reallexikons der deutschen Literaturgeschichte*, de Gruyter.

Paul Aron (2008) *Histoire du pastiche: le pastiche littéraire français, de la Renaissance à nos jours*, Presses Universitaires de France.

Paul Aron (2009) 'Le pastiche comme objet d'étude littéraire. Quelques réflexions sur l'histoire du genre' XXX *Modèles linguistiques* 11.

Roland Barthes (1984) *Le bruissement de la langue*, Seuil.

Reinhard Paul Becker (1981) *A War of Fools: The Letters of Obscure Men. A Study of the Satire and the Satirized: Letters of Obscure Men – Study of the Satire and the Satirized*, Peter Lang.

Edwin Bikundo and Kieran Tranter (2019) 'The Buribunks: Carl Schmitt on Diaries, Modernity and Future' 28 *Griffith Law Review* 95.

Steen Bille Jørgensen (2012) 'Pastiche et poétique de l'œuvre. Stratégies de réécriture contemporaines' 112 *Revue d'histoire littéraire de la France* 105.

Simon Blackburn (2005) *The Oxford Dictionary of Philosophy* (2nd ed.), Oxford University Press.

Claire Bowen (2012) 'Pastiche', in Roland Greene*et al.* (eds), *The Princeton Encyclopedia of Poetry and Poetics* (4th ed), Princeton University Press.

Michael Coyle (2015) 'Doing Tradition in Different Voices: Pastiche in *The Waste Land*', in G. McIntire (ed), *The Cambridge Companion to The Waste Land*, Cambridge University Press, 116.

C.S. (1918) 'Die Buribunken' 4 *Summa* 89.

John N. Duvall (1999) 'Troping History: Modernist Residue in Fredric Jameson's Pastiche and Linda Hutcheon's Parody' 33 *Style* 372.

Gérard Genette (1997) *Palimpsests: Literature in the Second Degree*, University of Nebraska Press.

Georg Wilhelm Friedrich Hegel (1975) *Lectures on the Philosophy of World History: Introduction, Reason in History*, Cambridge University Press.

Georg Wilhelm Friedrich Hegel (2001) *Encyclopédie des sciences philosophiques en abrégé*, Gallimard.

Georg Wilhelm Friedrich Hegel (2010) *The Science of Logic*, Cambridge University Press.

Georg Wilhelm Friedrich Hegel (2013) *Phenomenology of Spirit*, Oxford University Press.

Ingeborg Hoesterey (2001) *Pastiche: Cultural Memory in Art, Film, Literature*, Indiana University Press.

Linda Hutcheon (2002) *The Politics of Postmodernism* (2nd ed), Routledge.

Jacques-Philippe Saint-Gérand (2006) 'Parodie et pastiche dans quelques dictionnaires français (1680–1890) ou destins dictionnairiques de la lexicographie?', in Catherine

Dousteyssier-Khoze and Floriane Place-Verghnes (eds), *Poétiques de la parodie et du pastiche de 1850 à nos jours*, Peter Lang.
Frederic Jameson (2008) *Postmodernism, or, the Cultural Logic of Late Capitalism*, Verso.
Jean-François Kervégan (2005) *Hegel, Carl Schmitt: le politique entre spéculation et positivité*, Presses Universitaire de France.
Jean-François Kervégan (2011) *Que faire de Carl Schmitt?*, Gallimard.
Søren Kierkegaard (1987a) *Either/or, Part I*, Princeton University Press.
Søren Kierkegaard (1987b) *Either/or, Part II*, Princeton University Press.
Søren Kierkegaard (1994) *Fear and Trembling, and, The Book on Adler*, Everyman's Library.
Friedrich A. Kittler (1999) *Gramophone, Film, Typewriter*, Stanford University Press.
Friedrich A. Kittler (2018) *Gramophone, Film, Typewriter*, Les Presses du réel.
Reinhart Koselleck (2002) *The Practice of Conceptual History: Timing History*, Spacing Concepts, Stanford University Press.
Alexander Lambrow (2017) '14 December 1930: Robert Musil Meets Carl Schmitt' 90 *The German Quarterly* 332–348.
Karl Löwith (1991) 'Le décisionnisme (occasionnel) de Carl Schmitt' 544 *Les Temps Modernes* 15.
Georg Lukács (1971) *The Theory of the Novel: A Historico-philosophical Essay on the Forms of Great Epic Literature*, MIT Press.
Georg Lukács (2009) *Die Theorie des Romans: Ein geschichtsphilosophischer Versuch über die Formen der großen Epik*, Aisthesis.
Reinnhart Mehring (2014) *Carl Schmitt: A Biography*, Polity.
Molière (2001) *Don Juan*, Houghton Mifflin Harcourt.
Bertrand Quentin (2006) 'Hegel et la matière: le philosophe allemand a-t-il encore quelque chose à nous dire?' 79 *Les Etudes philosophiques* 537.
Carl Schmitt (1936) 'Der Staat als Mechanismus bei Hobbes und Descartes' 30 *Archiv für Rechts- und Sozialphilosophie* 622.
Carl Schmitt (1950) *Die Lage der europäischen Rechtswissenschaft*, Internationaler Universitäts-Verlag.
Carl Schmitt (2000) *The Crisis of Parliamentary Democracy*, MIT Press.
Carl Schmitt (2007) *The Concept of the Political*, University of Chicago Press.
Carl Schmitt (2008) *The Leviathan in the State Theory of Thomas Hobbes: Meaning and Failure of a Political Symbol*, University of Chicago Press.
Carl Schmitt (2017) *Political Romanticism*, Routledge.
Carl Schmitt and Ingeborg Villinger (2015) *Carl Schmitts Kulturkritik der Moderne, Text, Kommentar und Analyse der 'Schattenrisse' des Johannes Negelinus*, De Gruyter.
Jean Theau (1975) 'Le rapport quantité-qualité chez Hegel et chez Bergson' 2 *Philosophiques* 3.
Kieran Tranter (2019) 'Die Buribunken as Science fiction: The Self and Informational Existence' 28 *Griffith Law Review* 118.
Ulrich von Hutten (2004) *Lettres des hommes obscurs*, Les Belles Lettres.
Jean André Wahl (1938) *Études Kierkegaardiennes*, Éditions Montaigne.
Jan Woleński (2004) 'The History of Epistemology', in Ilkka Niiniluoto, Matti Sintonen and Jan Woleński (eds), *Handbook of Epistemology*, Springer, 3.

Chapter 13

Sola scriptura

Doubling of life and critique of modernity in *The Buribunks*

Ernesto C. Sferrazza Papa

Introduction

> Life does not live.
>
> Ferdinand Kürnberger[1]

This chapter explores two main trajectories to understand Carl Schmitt's *The Buribunks*, a short '*philosophical fabula*'[2] that the famous, notorious, flawed, 30-year-old *Kronjurist* [3] published in 1918 in *Summa*, the well-known journal of the German intelligentsia published by Franz Blei. First, the chapter argues that *The Buribunks* is a relevant moment in twentieth-century currents of documentality and hyper-medialisation of society. Second, it suggests that *The Buribunks* should be understood in parallel with other paradoxical moments of ironisation of culture in order to deploy the Schmittean radical criticism against modernity and its bishops – Descartes and Hegel above all.

Specialised literature, even the most vigilant, has always neglected this fulminating Schmittean satire, whose taunting and irreverent tone – albeit far from the conceptual depth of his contemporary works – is not completely alien to young Schmitt's stylistic register. With the significant exception of Koselleck, who dedicated to *The Buribunks* some more structured reflections on the relationship between utopian imagination and temporality,[4] critics showed a substantial lack of interest in this negative Utopia. Despite some sporadic exceptions – in addition to the aforementioned Koselleck, one may mention Bruno Accarino,[5] Carlo Galli[6] and Friedrich Balke[7] – *The Buribunks* has been relegated to the rank of *divertissement*. Only in recent years has a structured

1 *Exergue* to Adorno (1999), p 19.
2 Lubrano (2019), p 175.
3 Bendersky (1983).
4 Koselleck (2002), pp 93–9.
5 Accarino (1991).
6 Galli (1996a).
7 Balke (2017).

DOI: 10.4324/9781003091066-16

reflection on *The Buribunks* threaded its way through the international academic debate.

This renewed interest does not just translate in the act of rediscovering silenced or forgotten texts, which is typical of a certain academic mannerism. *The Buribunks* is not a simple opportunity to expand the criticism database on Schmitt – a point of interest only for insiders; rather, it is a text whose implications and themes are paradoxically on the agenda. There is a scientific and political urgency to rediscover *The Buribunks*. There is no doubt that in this text, which ironically and literally depicts a critique of modern philosophy that will find conceptual solidness in texts such as *Political Romanticism* (1919),[8] *Dictatorship* (1921),[9] *Political Theology* (1922)[10] and *The Concept of the Political* (1927),[11] Schmitt has prophetically reflected on dynamics that are fully deployed today. I do not believe that starting from *The Buribunks* will pave the way towards a more refined analysis of Schmitt's oeuvre than those carried out thus far; nevertheless, it is quite striking to find issues in this text firing up the early twenty-first century philosophical, critical and political debate. Besides, seeing how some issues crucial to Schmitt's critical analysis of modernity and modern philosophical rationalism are articulated in *The Buribunks* could be of interest to the scientific research on this author. In short, the time is now ripe to dedicate to *The Buribunks* the scientific analysis it deserves.

The written life

Reinhart Koselleck defined *The Buribunks* as 'an extravagant parody of historicism and the belief in progress, as expressed in the agenda of the scientific and social organization of the time'.[12] We are therefore faced with a conceptual commitment, which is proportionally inverse to the stylistic lightness used by the author. *The Buribunks* represents the parodic, caricatural, light side of the heavy philosophical-academic conceptuality of the writings of those years. In his works published at the turn of the 1920s, Schmitt will lay the foundations for the entirety of his work: the great juridical-political issues (the origin of law and politics, the relationship between these two dimensions, the critique of technology, the political theology) will be the focal points that will determine his intellectual stature. I intend now to analyse some strictly philosophical issues raised by this *fabula*, starting with the form of life that is at the centre of *The Buribunks*. Who are the Buribunks? What form does the Buribunks' life take?

Schmitt dispels doubt about the existence of this world from the very beginning of his essay. We are sure of the existence of Buribunkdom by the

8 Schmitt (1986).
9 Schmitt (2013).
10 Schmitt (1985).
11 Schmitt (2007).
12 Koselleck (2002), p 93.

fact that one can find a wide range of studies on it. Scientific discourse is not a re-translation of the world of life, but represents the place of production and verification of it. The primacy of writing is enshrined from the first lines of the *fabula*, and this primacy is the critical leitmotif of the entire text. The existence of reality as described by science is testified by the very fact that science makes it the object of its analysis:

> before anything else, it should be the ambition of every science to justify its existence through actual achievements and to ensure that an imposing body of work stands in the way of any subversive doubt regarding its potential as a science. If the value of any methodological discussion about the scientific nature of human intellectual activity lies only in reflecting upon the intellectual methods and aims of the work, then this presupposes a body of work in the first place – in the same way, it is self-evident that there would be no study of America if America had not been discovered, and no buribunkology if there were no buribunkologists.[13]

The Buribunks' reign and inhabitants can be described in a few lines. The only physical characteristic we are aware of is their wide mouth. As for the rest, these sexed individuals are entirely defined by the peculiar activity with which they occupy and resolve their lives: 'every male and female Buribunk is obliged to keep a diary for every second of their existence'.[14] The underlying philosophical question concerns a way of life that is entirely limited to its discursiveness, an existence that is '*sola scriptura*'.

From the point of view of the so-called history of ideas, we can inscribe *The Buribunks* in that strand of texts recounting the explosion of writing that will materially mark the course of the twentieth century, and that Derrida, starting from his *Introduction à la Origin de la Géométrie de Husserl* (1962), will report as one of the epochal events in the history of philosophy. One of the consequences of this multiplication and documentary accumulation is the acknowledgement that entering history ultimately means entering the discourse and being subject to an inscription on a medium that, while recording, allows reiteration, and therefore permits memory. As Derrida puts it in *On Grammatology*, this complex movement of inscription-registration is summed up in the formula '*Il n'y a pas de hors-texte*';[15] as Maurizio Ferraris points out, this textual dimension is to be radically interpreted as a question of writing, so that we could say there is nothing social or historical outside of writing.[16] Thus, Schmitt's tale must be understood as an excerpt in this philosophical genealogy of documentality.

13 Chapter 2 of this volume, p 12.
14 Chapter 2 of this volume, p 23.
15 Derrida (1997).
16 Ferraris (2013).

Buribunks live what Gianni Vattimo – the noble father of weak thought, the philosophical variant of postmodernism – defines as 'mediatisation of existence'[17] in *The Transparent Society*; this implies radical transformations of subjectivity, produced by the infiltration of media in every ravine of life. Wherever the *medium* imposes itself on life, the truth of existence is embodied in the filter, which at the same time testifies to it and makes it truly possible as a moment in historical time. In Vattimo's analysis, this process gives rise to a progressive derealisation of reality; postmodernity responds to the solidity of the modern being with the 'oscillation, plurality, and ultimately the erosion of the same principle of reality',[18] as if the possibility of a discursive multiplication of life coincided with the extinction of the solidity of life itself, which is now distanced from the reality principle. In Vattimo's view, the 'derealisation process inaugurated by the mass media society'[19] can have an outcome, or at least a horizon, of emancipation. Namely, he sees such a horizon in the 'liberation of the plurality of interpretations'[20] – that is, in actualising Nietzschean doctrine according to which there are no facts, only interpretations.

The complete mediatisation of life, recorded by Vattimo at the end of the last century, is already fully anticipated in *The Buribunks*. Critics have unanimously recognised that Schmitt's writing is a sensational anticipation of the logic of contemporary media and social networks, and this is probably the reason for the profound interest in this dazzling Schmittean satire. *The Buribunks* would grasp, in an almost prophetic way, the characteristic essence of our era, representing one of its most precise anticipations.

However, unlike the society of transparency described by Vattimo, which is marked by chaos, complexity and a plurality of truths, the Buribunk world is a perfectly organised one, where chaos is put-into-shape, brought back to the technologies of the archive. Once the diary is completed, it is sorted and catalogued, thus becoming a segment of history: 'copies of all diary entries are submitted daily and collated by local councils'.[21] And this is a profoundly modern trait of the world imagined by Schmitt, who shares with the adventures of modern rationalism the attempt to shape the chaos of rebellious existences. This compulsion to the form-of-archive is revealed in *The Buribunks* as the prelude to the totalitarian control of lives. In the Buribunk world, not only is everyone forced to write, but even the refusal of writing is akin to the same modalities of its acceptance. This totalitarianism brings every moment back into the same system that was built precisely to deny it from the beginning. Indeed, anyone who does not want to write doesn't have to, but instead must carefully write his motives and every useful detail to illustrate his reasons for it in his

17 Vattimo (2000), p 3.
18 Vattimo (2000), p 14.
19 Vattimo (2000), p 117.
20 Vattimo (2000), p 118.
21 Chapter 2 of this volume, p 23.

diary. And this is a typical movement of a liberal society – which is the real polemical target of Schmitt's entire work: foreseeing dissent while building the tools to silence it, leading it back to the dominant logic:

> a rebellious spirit, however, also expresses itself here, albeit rarely. But it needs to be taken into account that in the realm of the Buribunks there rules a limitless, all-understanding, uncomplaining tolerance and the highest respect for personal freedom. No Buribunk is prevented in any way from freely creating his diary entries; not only may he state that he lacks the intellectual strength for entries and that only the sadness about this lack of strength gives him the necessary strength – this is even a very popular type of entry that is especially recognised and highly regarded. He can also note, without having to fear even the slightest pressure, that he regards the diary as a pointless and burdensome institution, as a silly harassment, as a laughable custom; in short, he is not barred from using the strongest expressions.[22]

Thus, the linking of every fragment of life to the obligation of writing produces a totalisation of Buribunks' existence, a real biopolitical system in which each Buribunk is the docile agent of his own surveillance. From this point of view, there is no doubt that Foucault would have benefited, during the drafting of *Discipline and Punish*, from reading the Schmittean *fabula*.[23]

22 Chapter 2 of this volume, p 24.
23 This might seem as a curious juxtaposition, as Carl Schmitt and Michel Foucault represent two diverging traditions of philosophical thought. However, the correlation between them is conceptually reasonable, and it has already been traced. Matthew Hannah (2011), p 227, for instance, underlines a 'quasi-biopolitical dimension of political order' in Schmitt's political philosophy; Peter Rogers (20111), p 183, investigating a parallel between Schmitt and Foucault, insists on 'the role of space in creating order'; Giorgio Agamben's political philosophy should be understood as a synthesis of Schmitt's political theology and Foucault's biopolitics of the population: see Luisetti (2011). Clearly, and especially concerning the biopolitical aspects of Schmitt's text, substantial differences remain. While Foucault is more interested in the analysis of the effects of disciplinary power on the body, Schmitt's *The Buribunks* deals mostly with the *dispositif* of textuality. In *Discipline and Punish*, the coercive apparatus of power aims at producing an orthopaedisation of bodies, a *dressage*: 'the classical age discovered the body as object and target of power. It is easy enough to find signs of the attention then paid to the body – to the body that is manipulated, shaped, trained, which obeys, responds, becomes skilful and increases its forces' (Foucault 1995, p. 136). In *The Buribunks*, discipline is obtained through the medialisation of the entire society, and the central role of the body is replaced with the social compulsion to be visible through the continuous written recording of life. Even though this crucial difference must be recognised, I agree with Daniel McLoughlin (2019), p 144, who argues that 'the diary keeping system not only permits the biopolitical management of the population, but also, the disciplinary control of individual Buribunks'.

History and death

The philosophy of history dominating Buribunkdom is marked by an exclusionary logic. If writing means becoming a piece of world history, not writing means being excluded from it: 'whoever, instead of writing that he refuses, really stops writing, makes inappropriate use of the general freedom of mind and will be eliminated due to his anti-social disposition'.[24] However, this exclusion is not physical: Buribunks replace the exemplary punishment of the death of the body with an historical and social death. In Buribunk society, those refusing to write their diary are destined to be excluded from history and socially marginalised:

> the wheel of progress passes silently over the silent one; he will no longer be mentioned, he can therefore no longer make himself heard until he finally, sinking step by step, is forced into the lowest class, to help create the external conditions for the possibility of noble Buribunkdom, for example making by hand the paper on which the most valuable diaries are printed.[25]

Any society, even at its utopian peak, and perhaps precisely at its utopian peak, needs the excluded ones, the 'wasted lives', since they support it and make it materially possible; any construction of order involves the production of scraps, slag, waste, just as the sculptor inevitably produces scraps in his artistic making.[26]

However, it is precisely the philosophy of history and its methodical rationalism that defines Buribunk society, and Schmitt's analysis is to validate these forms of exclusion of rebel bodies. Indeed, the fundamental principles of this philosophy of history are the parodic transposition of the Cartesian formula *cogito ergo sum*. Through this form, which summarised a methodically and rigorously conducted reasoning that followed the *regulae ad directionem ingenii*, the Cartesian subject founded the certainty of existence in the evidence of thought. From doubt to certainty. Even in *Political Theology*, Schmitt will criticise Descartes's *Discourse on Method* – albeit acknowledging its greatness – since he will see in it 'a document of the new rationalist spirit. In the depth of doubt, it finds consolation by using reason unswervingly'.[27]

Part IV of the *Discourse on Method* is the well-known, capital place of modern philosophy where the cogito makes its appearance. It is useful to report it here to compare it with Schmitt's impression. Descartes:

24 Chapter 2 of this volume, p 25.
25 Chapter 2 of this volume, p 25.
26 Bauman (2004); Cuozzo (2020).
27 Schmitt (1985), p 47.

> I resolved to assume that everything that ever entered into my mind was no more true than the illusions of my dreams. But immediately afterwards I notice that whilst I thus wished to think all things false, it was absolutely essential that the 'I' who thought this should be somewhat, and remarking that this truth '*I think, therefore I am*' was so certain and so assured that all the most extravagant suppositions brought forward by the sceptics were incapable of shaking it, I came to the conclusion that I could receive it without scruple as the first principle of the Philosophy for which I was seeking.[28]

Schmitt:

> I think, therefore I am; I speak, therefore I am; I write, therefore I am; I publish, therefore I am. This does not contain a contradiction, but is merely the ascending order of identities which develop beyond themselves according to the law of logic. For the Buribunk, thinking is nothing other than soundless speech; speaking nothing but scriptless writing; writing nothing but anticipated publishing and therefore publishing is identical with writing, with such minor differences that they may safely be disregarded. I write, therefore I am; I am, therefore I write. What do I write? I write myself. Who writes me? I myself write myself. What is the content of my writing? I write that I write myself. What is the big engine lifting me above this self-sufficient circle of I-ness? History![29]

This dense passage deserves a close analysis. The formula of the Cartesian cogito is parodied by means of an involution of being on writing. Through a series of deductions conforming to logical laws, being and writing end up collapsing on each other. But if being and writing are the same, and if a Buribunk has to write about himself, then his writing will necessarily consist of the very fact that he is writing. Life will then be reduced entirely to writing that one is writing. Schmitt forces the Buribunks into that paradoxical point where the doubling of life, allowed and imposed by the act of writing, is reversed in the cancellation of life itself. Despite Schmitt's aversion to Nietzsche's philosophy, a controversial target throughout the entire *Glossarium*,[30] it can be suggested boldly that among the sources of *The Buribunks*, there would be a passage from the second of the *Untimely Meditations* – that is, *On the Uses and Disadvantages of History for Life*. In this passage, Nietzsche seems to anticipate the traits of Borges's hero, Ireneo Funes, the character who is unable to live because he remembers every single moment of his life. Nietzsche:

28 Descartes (2003), p 23.
29 Chapter 2 of this volume, p 25.
30 See Galli (2014).

> Imagine the extremest possible example of a man who did not possess the power of forgetting at all and who was thus condemned to see everywhere a state of becoming: such a man would no longer believe in his own being, would no longer believe in himself, would see everything flowing asunder in moving points and would lose himself in the stream of becoming: like a true pupil of Heraclitus, he would in the end hardly dare to raise his finger.[31]

Borges:

> With one quick look, you and I perceive three wineglasses on a table; Funes perceived every grape that had been pressed into the wine and all the stalks and tendrils of its vineyard. He knew the forms of the clouds in the southern sky on the morning of April 30, 1882, and he could compare them in his memory with the veins in the marbled binding of a book he had seen only once, or with the feathers of spray lifted by an oar on the Rio Negro on the eve of the Battle of Quebracho. Nor were those memories simple – every visual inlage was linked to muscular sensations, thermal sensations, and so on. He was able to reconstruct every dream, every daydream he had ever had. Two or three times he had reconstructed an entire day; he had never once erred or faltered, but each reconstruction had itself taken an entire day. 'I, myself, alone, have more memories than all mankind since the world began,' he said to me. And also: 'My dreams are like other people's waking hours.' And again, toward dawn: 'My memory, sir, is like a garbage heap.' A circle drawn on a blackboard, a right triangle, a rhombus – all these are forms we can fully intuit; Ireneo could do the same with the stormy mane of a young colt, a small herd of cattle on a mountain side, a flickering fire and its uncountable ashes, and the many faces of a dead man at a wake. I have no idea how many stars he saw in the sky.[32]

The critiques of Nietzsche's antiquarian history and Borges's total memory thematise a fundamental point. Only in the possibility of oblivion – that is, in the gap, in the surplus, in the transcendence with respect to the datum – is found the authentic possibility of history, life and knowledge. This possibility must be identified in a knowledge and in a form of existence that, by placing its logics outside any form of idealism, does not allow the subject and the object to merge and become indiscernible. Conversely, the absolute immanence of Buribunkdom, despite being narrated as absolutely 'transparent', does not allow *ipso facto* to think about the liveability of life. Object and subject coincide point by point: the Buribunk 'understands himself as a history's

31 Nietzsche (1997), p 62
32 Borges (1998), p 135.

subject-object, in which the World Soul has become action through writing itself'.[33]

The same temporality is abolished and concentrated upon in the immobile present of writing, as Schmitt himself points out: 'What does, ethically speaking, the Buribunk do who keeps a diary every second of his life? He wrests every second from the future in order to incorporate it into history.'[34] And, in this life that 'does not live', even death comes without fear, and has the shape of a pen that ceases to write:

> the death of the individual is also merely such a rat-second; it does not carry within itself its content – happy or sad – but only receives it through the writing of history. In the rat-second of my death, however, quill and diary fall from my hand and I seem to be no longer actively involved in this writing of history; the essence of diary-keeping, the will to power over history fades and makes room for a foreign will.[35]

Not only does this philosophy of identity produce the coincidence between life and writing; it also produces the coincidence between history and diaristic accumulation. The two dimensions are intertwined, and the writer becomes 'a letter on the typewriter of history'.[36] In this dystopian universe, becoming *geschichtsfähig* is possible only by writing and recording every moment. As a consequence, history 'is realised only if and to the extent in which it is written down'.[37] From this point of view, then, the marginalisation and exclusion of those refusing the diary-writing is the logical result of the structure of history and its temporality. But the very negation of the subject is obtained precisely through the historical dimension created by buribunkology. Ultimately, Buribunk existence is marked by a powerful nihilism, which is the ultimate outcome of the structures of the modern and of the attempt, which is circularly pursued by Buribunkdom and conceptualised by Hegel, 'of the alleged ability to operate the *Aufhebung* of every contradiction'.[38]

Therefore, the crisis of the subject is at the same time a crisis of temporality, the different phases of which are collapsing at the moment of writing. Thus, the mediatisation of life is accompanied by a 'reduction of history on the level of simultaneity',[39] by a form of 'chronicle' in which the real dissolves entirely in its narration. In this sense, the insertion of reality into discourse tends to invert the parts and replace speech with reality just as in Orson Welles's social experiment. The paranoid and obsessive duplication of the real, whose example *par excellence* is the compulsive diary-writing, gives shape to a reality that is not

33 Chapter 2 of this volume, p 16.
34 Chapter 2 of this volume, p 26.
35 Chapter 2 of this volume, p 26.
36 Chapter 2 of this volume, p 26.
37 Accarino (1991), p 401.
38 Galli (1996b), p 190.
39 Vattimo (2000), p 27.

revealed in the immediacy of the event, nor in the course of history, but in the mediation of words.

The last romantics

The explicit and implicit references that can be spotted in *Die Buribunken* are not uninteresting, as they immediately highlight the polemical targets of Schmitt's philosophical reflection. As Koselleck wrote, Schmitt 'calls upon a wealth of silent testimonies, often only able to be gleaned from allusions'.[40] Among these silent witnesses, Koselleck includes Descartes, Adam Smith, Hegel, Marx, Wagner, Nietzsche, Lamprecht, Haeckel, Ostwald and Lenin. The Schmittean *fabula* is studded with crypto-citations condensing an entire galaxy of philosophical controversy.

Daniel McLoughlin legitimately identifies *The Buribunks*'s main polemical target in 'the Hegelian philosophy of history',[41] particularly in Hegel's claim – an unfounded claim, in Schmitt's opinion – that the real and the rational may coincide. That is to say that the 'sense' of reality does not lie in the relationship with transcendence as a 'Catholic' approach would require, but in its mere and positivistic actuality. Indeed, Hegelian idealism is called directly into question even from the subtitle, which refers to the philosophy of history animating Buribunk society. In *Political Theology*, Schmitt also states that 'the immanence philosophy found its greatest systematic architect in Hegel';[42] Hegel is 'blamed' for having developed a dialectical system presuming to 'reabsorb' the negative in the rational development of the historical process, with the consequence that historical development is self-explanatory. It does not need to resort to a transcendent horizon to justify itself. But it is equally true that Hegel is only the centre of a larger target. He is the point of arrival where modern rationalism – the noble father of which is Descartes, with his *Discourse on Method* – is expressed and realised in all its power. While hitting out Hegel, Schmitt hits out the modern, its rationalism, as well as the claim to reduce the scientific enterprise to the exhaustiveness of the method.

Buribunk biographism shares a tendency towards mechanism and abstractionism with Cartesian rationalism. Mechanical, because the rules of the method closely resemble the regulation imposed on the Buribunks for remaining within the social pact – that is, the compulsion to write the diary continuously and obsessively; abstract, because the existence of each Buribunk is dissolved in the buribunkological archive just as the Cartesian subject, founding in itself the possibility of existence through the acknowledgement of the immediacy of the *cogito*, is extruded from history. When life takes the form of *sola scriptura*, it becomes impossible. A point of transcendence with respect to

40 Koselleck (2002), p 98.
41 McLoughlin (2019), p 137.
42 Schmitt (1985), p 50.

writing, a hiatus, an element escaping its mediatisation must all be preserved. When this escape-line is missing, society takes on a totalitarian form and life is unthinkable. More generally, *The Buribunks*'s critical scheme is that between immanence and transcendence, which finds a crucial place in the analysis of romanticism.

I suggest that the structure of modernity is Schmitt's polemical target, and this appears clearly in his caricatures of the Cartesian and Hegelian formulas. *The Buribunks* criticises both the cogito and universal history – that is, respectively, the possibility of a self-foundation of the subject and the reconversion of all singularities into a totality – the World Spirit – that annihilates them. But in *The Buribunks* there is also a critique of the romantic attitude, albeit in a veiled manner. A deeper critique of this attitude is at the heart of Schmitt's 1919 essay, *Political Romanticism*. In this text, the romantic attitude is deconstructed and related to a form of occasionalism – that is, to an aestheticising dimension, in which 'discourses as well as institutions become subject to a contingency pressure never known before'.[43] This criticism is also present in *The Buribunks*, albeit in a different form.

In the chapter of *Political Romanticism* dedicated to *La recherche de la réalité*, Schmitt thematises the structural parallelism between political romanticism and Cartesian rationalism, both analysed as the places in which the subject–object opposition is aesthetically resolved. As Balke points out, in this negotiation with the world, 'its truthfulness, authenticity, or ontologicalness'[44] is no longer guaranteed. Thus, the satire of a life conceived as *sola scriptura* is connected with Schmitt's conceptual critique of German science and culture of the time, which were both guilty of being caught in 'ambiguities and verbal disputes',[45] in an 'endless conversation and a fruitless discourse',[46] with the claim of transforming this confused verbiage into an 'objective clarification'.[47] Not only does the life continuously narrated by the Buribunk follow the ridiculous eternal dialogue of the romantics, but the circularity between the Buribunk and buribunkology reflects the circularity between subject and object, which is proper to the romantic philosophy of identity.

Romanticism consists of an attitude, not the search for a properly romantic object, therefore all the precariousness of modern subjectivist experience is reflected in it. This modern subjectivist experience claims to base the objectivity of the real on the subject and on his inexhaustible search for reality. Just as the Buribunks must keep a diary of every moment of their existence in order to become part of the World Spirit, for the romantic mentality, everything that happens 'is the work of the World Spirit that produces itself historically'.[48] This

43 Balke (2017), p 635.
44 Balke (2017), p 636.
45 Schmitt (1986), p 1.
46 Schmitt (1986), p 1.
47 Schmitt (1986), p 1.
48 Schmitt, (1986), p 62.

renders it satisfactory, *ipso facto*. From this point of view, Buribunks are the epigones of the romantic attitude (which in turn is, for Schmitt, an offshoot of modern rationalism). Indeed, in romantic subjectivism, 'reality itself was not to be gained in a subjectivistic fashion. In consequence, something else was substituted for it, something apparently even more vast: totality.'[49]

Just like the romantics described by Schmitt in *Political Romanticism*, the Buribunks transform 'every instant into a historical moment'[50] with their diary-writing. But the infinite dialogicity in which the romantic subject is lost, as well as the *sola scriptura* in which the concreteness of Buribunk existence flows, reveal themselves as 'a small figure of art'.[51] The adventure of the search for reality, inaugurated by Descartes with his radical doubt, 'ended in the will to appearance'.[52] The lives of the Buribunks, in their constitutive impossibility, are the ripe fruit of this modest result. Once transcendence has been eliminated from the horizon of meaning of existence, the subject does not remain. In its place is only its phantasmagorical image, the claim that life is entirely knowable by discursive means.

Conclusions: three uses of *The Buribunks*

The Buribunks brings together in an ironic way themes that will be central to all of Schmitt's oeuvre. Starting from these pages, and in the light of the critical literature that is finally, albeit slowly, developing around this philosophical fabula, I believe three possible lines of research can be traced.

First of all – and this is the most classical perspective animating these pages – it is possible to consider *The Buribunks* as a coherent text within Schmitt's critical-philosophical production, and not as a mere literary *divertissement*. With this in mind, it is a question of analysing the way in which the themes dealt with in *The Buribunks* mark the 1920s of Schmitt's production, albeit in a light-hearted manner. Then critics should investigate the way in which this text intertwines both with Schmitt's coeval production and, ultimately, with his entire oeuvre.

Second, in the *negative Utopie* depicted by Schmitt, it is possible to spot the prophecy of the processes of mediatisation of the real, as well as their biopolitical consequences, which are fully deployed in our days. From this perspective, *The Buribunks* can be understood as a passage from a proto-biopolitics of digital surveillance;[53] in the Buribunk world, as well as in the current biopolitics of digital surveillance, the writing of life 'becomes a prerequisite for effective surveillance'.[54] Buribunks' reports converge in a gigantic archive representing the

49 Schmitt (1986), p 73.
50 Schmitt (1986), p 74.
51 Schmitt (1986), p 78.
52 Schmitt (1986), p 78
53 Lyon (1994, 2001, 2018).
54 Koselleck (2002), p 97.

analogue version of today's digital archives, which draw a map of surveillance and control that is all but free of hardship.[55] The Buribunks gain social recognition and become part of the historical process only through their diary-writing. Therefore, their obsessive activity is the analogue of the mediatisation of existence that today the various social networks prescribe as the only means to appear and be recognised. We should ask ourselves whether a Buribunk diary is really so different from any Facebook wall.[56] And we should also ask ourselves about the extent to which the digital biopolitics of our contemporary culture is based on dynamics similar to those described by Schmitt, since 'the contemporary target of digital surveillance does constitute themselves as a subject through their social media profile'.[57]

A third line of research still seems unexplored to me, and I hope critics will decide to follow it further. By implicitly attacking German science and culture of the time, Schmitt organises a critique *in nuce* of the scientific and academic procedures that will mark the twentieth century, and that are still active today. Yet the critique of a kind of science that is disjointed from life and coincides entirely with its methodology is not the only aspect in question. There is also a powerful critique of academic and scientific autoreferentiality, a subtle controversy with the system of scientific publications. Such system is parodied mainly in the notes of the text, where we are comically referred to the 200 volumes of Ferker's biography compiled by Pielenpiep, and more generally to all buribunkological studies. Given the initially declared circularity according to which 'every buribunkological publication is in turn part of buribunkology', these studies give substance to the very existence of their object.[58] The result is the literally unrestrainable multiplication of scientific publications, which shows the incongruity of the Hegelian maxim recalled by Schmitt, according to which 'there is a point where … quantity turns into quality'.[59] Today's mass of publications makes scientific knowledge – and I am referring here to a knowledge that is not a technicality increasingly focused on detail and minutia – more and more problematic, due to a sort of contradiction immanent in its development. It is the analogue of the ridiculous academic buribunkology:

> the discussion of the question of buribunkology as a science has to resolve around the cardinal point of whether the factual quantity of buribunkological actualities has reached such an extent that is only sensible to address it as a quality (which here means as a science). In response we would therefore have to supply a bibliography of buribunkological research. However, we restrict ourselves to mentioning that already more

55 Tello (2018).
56 Tranter (2019).
57 McLoughlin (2019), p 151.
58 Chapter 2 of this volume, p 12.
59 Chapter 2 of this volume, p 12.

than 400,000 buribunkological dissertations (20 divisions!) have been published and for years the weekly competitions of the International Buribunkological Institute for Ferker and Related Research (IBIFERR) have always culminated in numerous prizes and laudatory recognition.[60]

The same scientific hyper-productivity endured by the Buribunk society, which was ridiculed by Schmitt, affects academic research in the current era of *publish or perish*.[61] In the dystopia imagined by Schmitt, the time of life is entirely occupied by the writing of life; similarly, today's academic politics is dangerously inclined to a modality of scientific research that ends up as *sola scriptura*. The Cartesian formula can also be paraphrased in the context of the current academic system, whereby the individual researcher docilely introjects the imperative to publish compulsively. This implicates a process of subjectivation constructed in the form of 'I publish, therefore I am'. The hyper-productivity of the academic system, which critics report as one of the crucial issues for a renewed policy of scientific research, finds in Schmitt's satire an initial alarm bell that is still ringing.

References

Bruno Accarino (1991) 'Filosofia della storia: La parabola della modernità', in Carlo Galli (ed), *Logiche e crisi della modernità*, Il Mulino.

Theodor Adorno (1999) *Minima Moralia: Reflections on a Damaged Life*, Verso.

Friedrich Balke (2017) 'Carl Schmitt and Modernity', in Jens Meierhenrich and Oliver Simons (eds), *The Oxford Handbook of Carl Schmitt*, Oxford University Press, 629.

Zygmunt Bauman (2004) *Wasted Lives: Modernity and its Outcasts*, Polity Press.

Joseph J. Bendersky (1983) *Carl Schmitt: Theorist for the Reich*, Princeton University Press.

Jorge Luis Borges (1998) *Collected Fictions*, Penguin.

Gianluca Cuozzo (2020) 'New Wastes: Nature is Not an Unlimited Station', in Luca Valera and Juan Carlos Castilla (eds), *Global Changes: Ethics, Politics and Environment in the Contemporary Technological World*, Springer Verlag.

Hendrik P. van Dalen and Kène Henkens (2012) 'Intended and Unintended Consequences of a Publish-or-Perish Culture: A Worldwide Survey' 63 *Journal of the American Society for Information Science and Technology* 7.

Jacques Derrida (1997) *Of Grammatology*, Johns Hopkins University Press.

René Descartes (2003) *Discourse on Method and Meditations*, Dover.

Maurizio Ferraris (2013) *Documentality: Why It is Necessary to Leave Traces*, Fordham University Press.

Michel Foucault (1995) *Discipline and Punish: The Birth of the Prison*, Vintage Books.

Carlo Galli (1996a) 'Carl Schmitt fra i Buribunki' 3 *L'informazione Bibliografica* 371.

Carlo Galli (1996b) *Genealogia della politica: Carl Schmitt e la crisi del pensiero politico moderno*, Il Mulino.

Carlo Galli (2014) 'Nichilismi a confronto: Nietzsche e Schmitt' 1 *Filosofia politica* 99.

60 Chapter 2 of this volume, p 13.

61 Dalen and Henkens (2012); Grimes, Bauch and Ioannidis (2018).

David Robert Grimes, Chris T. Bauch and John P.A. Ioannidis (2018) 'Modelling Science Trustworthiness Under Publish or Perish Pressure' 5 *Royal Society Open Science* 1.

Matthew Hannah (2011) 'Pastoral Power', in Stephen Legg (ed), *Spatality, Sovereignty and Carl Schmitt: Geographies of the Nomos*, Routledge, 124.

Reinhart Koselleck (2002) *The Practice of Conceptual History: Timing History, Spacing Concepts*, Stanford University Press.

Vittorio Lubrano (2019) 'On the Normativity of Writing: Inscription/Description of Everyday Life' 28(2) *Griffith Law Review* 99.

Federico Luisetti (2011) 'Carl Schmitt and Giorgio Agamben: From Biopolitics to Political Romanticism' 1 *Journal of Philosophy of Life* 1.

David Lyon (1994) *The Electronic Eye: The Rise of Surveillance Society*, University of Minnesota Press.

David Lyon (2001) *Surveillance Society: Monitoring Everyday Life*, Open University Press.

David Lyon (2018) *The Culture of Surveillance: Watching as a Way of Life*, Polity Press.

Daniel McLoughlin (2019) 'The Biopolitics of the Buribunks: The Digital Archive and the End of History' 28 *Griffith Law Review* 99.

Friedrich Nietzsche (1997) *Untimely Meditations*, Cambridge University Press.

Peter Rogers (2011) 'Between Nomos and Everyday Life: Securing the Spatial Order of Foucault and Schmitt', in Stephen Legg (ed), *Spatality, Sovereignty and Carl Schmitt: Geographies of the Nomos*, Routledge, ch 11.

Carl Schmitt (1985) *Political Theology: Four Chapters on the Concept of Sovereignty*, MIT Press.

Carl Schmitt (1986) *Political Romanticism*, MIT Press.

Carl Schmitt (2007) *The Concept of the Political*, University of Chicago Press.

Carl Schmitt (2013) *Dictatorship*, Polity Press.

Andrés Maximiliano Tello (2018) *Anarchivismo: Tecnologías políticas del archivo*, La Cebra.

Kieran Tranter (2019) 'Die Buribunken as Science Fiction: The Self and Informational Existence' 28(2) *Griffith Law Review* 99.

Gianni Vattimo (2000) *La società trasparente*, Garzanti.

Chapter 14

Schmitt's Roman links in *The Buribunks*

Enriching the satire

Karen Schultz

Introduction

Carl Schmitt's *The Buribunks*,[1] published in 1918 and sub-titled 'An essay on the philosophy of history', has been described as a satire. Koselleck succinctly observes of this 'extravagant parody of historicism and the belief in progress' that 'In genre-historical terms, it was a satire.'[2] An early literary, fictional work in Schmitt's canon, *The Buribunks* manipulates oppositions that Schmitt considered in his analytical works. Narrated by a self-deluded persona (the narrator) concerning a fictitious society and philosophical system, *The Buribunks* satirises the ideology of 'buribunkology as science'.[3] The fictional narrator's 'literal' positions and arguments are subverted by assumed audience knowledge and evident parody,[4] or by actual audience knowledge and identification with Schmitt's thought. Carefully reading *The Buribunks* with an eye to its multiple levels of meaning exposes a satiric double voice – satire's meaning and message depend on interpreting its transgression, subversion and 'political stance'.[5] Recognising the 'political' as a concept and defining category was integral to Schmitt's thought.

Schmitt deploys satire and irony in *The Buribunks* to sabotage Buribunkdom's realm of technocratic, self-archiving diarists and their automated diary-writing; the Buribunks are 'both the drivers and products of a self-created history'.[6] In satirising buribunkology's conflation of 'history's subject-object',[7] Schmitt harnesses tensions to devastating effect, including fiction/reality, subject/object, writing/thinking, visibility/invisibility and form/substance. The result is the destabilisation of three conceptually distinct, but interlinked, satiric targets: romantic occasionalist diary-writing, progressivist philosophy of history and

1 Chapter 2 of this volume.
2 Koselleck (2002), p 84.
3 Chapter 2 of this volume, p 12.
4 Uden (2015), p 25 and Ch 1.
5 O'Gorman (2000), p 12.
6 Werner (2019), p 4.
7 Chapter 2 of this volume, p 16.

DOI: 10.4324/9781003091066-17

positivist social science. For Schmitt abrades diary-writing's romantic occasionalist subjectivism, limitless conversation and vanity; he challenges historical progressivist philosophy's repetition and utopian thinking; and he deprecates positivist social science's socio-technical justifications and empty form. *The Buribunks* adopts the rationales of *Political Romanticism* to reject the construction of the romantic subject and romanticism as 'subjectified occasionalism'[8] – Schmitt's polemic against diarists and diary-writing illustrates his antipathy to political romanticism's passivity and sterility.[9] This polemic has cinematic effect[10] in *The Buribunks*'s surreal world of machine-like diarists, but that is not the focus of this chapter.

Instead, this chapter seeks to underline how *The Buribunks*'s multilayered satire and irony are enriched by its express or implicit inspiration from its Roman links to Tacitus and Juvenal. The Roman links can be understood to contribute to *The Buribunks*'s heterogeneous inspiration. In *The Buribunks*, a quotation extracted from Tacitus's *Annales* – '*sine ira et studio*'[11] – appears to elevate Buribunk integrity by identifying the narrator's 'impartial' role. In fact, the phrase ironically underlines buribunkology's partialities. Equally, a quotation extracted from Juvenal's *Satire* 7 – '*cum desertis Aganippes / vallibus esuriens migraret in atria Clio*'[12] – concludes Schmitt's 'Preliminary Remarks' to *Dictatorship*,[13] and could be considered to be of only cursory relevance. Yet the quotation can be understood to flag the implicit inspiration that Juvenal's *Satire* 7 offers to *The Buribunks*.

Specifically, this chapter considers Schmitt's Roman links in *The Buribunks* (1918) and how they enrich the satire. Broadly, it examines Schmitt's background in the classics and satire, and focuses on *The Buribunks*'s satiric toolkit and its connections, explicit or implicit, with two Roman authors – Tacitus and Juvenal. Their Latin texts – Tacitus's *Annales* and Juvenal's *Satire* 7 – are expressly referenced in Schmitt's early scholarly text, *Dictatorship* (1921). These intertextual links enrich Schmitt's critique of diary-writing and the philosophy of history in this fantastical world. To illustrate this, Schmitt's background and early texts – his early familiarity with the classics and satire, and the relevant Roman links in his early text, *Dictatorship* – are first sketched. Second, key aspects of satire and irony are canvassed and applied to *The Buribunks*. Third, *The Buribunks*'s links with Tacitus's irony are considered – the narrator's seeming lack of understanding of the implications of Tacitus's phrase '*sine ira et studio*' casts doubt on the narrator's reliability. Fourth, *The Buribunks*'s links with Juvenal's satire are explored – Juvenal's satire targets, and likely pillories, the

8 Schmitt (1986), p 17, 'Preface'. See Mehring (2014), p 101.
9 Schultz (2019).
10 Chapter 2 of this volume, p 16.
11 Tacitus (1876) or Tacitus (2004) – 'Without anger or partiality' (my translation).
12 Juvenal (1918) or Juvenal (2011) – 'As starving Clio abandons the vales of Aganippe and flees to the auction rooms' (my translation).
13 Schmitt (2014a), p xlv, quoting Juvenal, *Satire* 7, lines 6–7.

plight of intellectuals, including historians. Finally, it is proposed that the admonitory implications of this fictional text's dystopia sharpen Schmitt's satire in *The Buribunks*.

Schmitt's background, the classics and early texts

Franz Blei, the editor of the heterogeneous journal *Summa* where *The Buribunks* was published in 1918,[14] identified Schmitt as a 'classicist' who was antipathetic to the 'Romantic' as a defining category.[15] Clearly, Schmitt's early classical education and continuing attraction to literature and the classics were red threads within his corpus of work. His classical education facilitated his familiarity with satire; his early texts deploy satire or literary jokes. Schmitt's background and early texts – including *Dictatorship* and its reference to two Roman links that inspired Schmitt in *The Buribunks* – are sketched next.

Schmitt's classical education and philological interests have been outlined in biographies and biographical notes.[16] The secondary school curriculum of his public humanistic gymnasium at Attendorn focused on classical languages, with a major emphasis on Latin and then Ancient Greek.[17] From the age of 11,[18] Schmitt was enveloped in the internationally acclaimed German classical education. It was so acclaimed because of its broad approach to the development of *'Alterthumswissenschaft'*, or antiquity – that is, of 'knowledge of the spirit and power of Greek and Roman antiquity learned from its original works'.[19] Schmitt's classical education would have identified the roots of satire and irony in classical Roman authors, including Juvenal and Tacitus. In 1907, when deciding on tertiary studies, Schmitt so valued the classics and classical languages that he intended to commence philology studies.[20] But this direction was challenged by his uncle's preference for law and, ultimately, Schmitt detoured from philology – when entering Friedrich Wilhelm University (renamed Humboldt University) in Berlin, the Faculty of Law's signage prompted his literal detour to enter and register for law instead.[21] Yet the law curriculum's emphasis on Roman law effectively resolved any quandary as to whether

14 Lambrow (2017), p 332.
15 Kennedy (2004), p 72.
16 Balakrishnan (2000), p 12: Schmitt was fluent in French, and studied modern languages including Spanish and Italian. See Kennedy (2004), p 72, regarding Schmitt's 'tendency to antiquity, [and] Latin'. See Hoelzl and Ward (2014), p xxi, regarding Schmitt's interest in philology. See Mehring (2014), pp 5–9.
17 Bendersky (1983), p 6; Mehring (2014), p 6.
18 Mehring (2014), p 5.
19 Rapple (1997), p 173, quoting the classicist Matthew Arnold writing during the nineteenth century: Arnold (1960–77), p 294.
20 Mehring (2014), p 7.
21 Bendersky (1983), p 8.

philology or law was the better direction – 'philology was useful for law'[22] and Schmitt 'became thoroughly fascinated by jurisprudence'.[23]

Equally, Schmitt's early literary and cultural work[24] anticipated *The Buribunks*'s satiric toolkit. His early texts flag both the interdisciplinary nature of his later cultural critique and political theory,[25] and his experimentation with genres. Schmitt had frequented the café-literati society where satire had flourished;[26] he was drawn to poetry and expressionist, avant-garde art.[27] In relation to poetry, he authored major literary criticism of the expressionist Theodor Däubler's *Das Nordlicht*, arguing that this epic poem counterbalanced mechanistic modern society – 'a society of circulation, technique and organisation, a "Betrieb" devoid of spirit'.[28] Equally, in relation to early experimentation with genres, while Schmitt did not complete his proposed 'literary joke' of a 'Schnekkeroman' – 'literally, "snail novel"' – he did co-author *Schattenrisse* (1913) with his long-term friend Eisler,[29] using the pseudonym Johannes Negelinus.[30] *Schattenrisse* was published as a portrait gallery of parodies – ironic silhouettes – of German cultural and intellectual figures.[31] The text deploys 'vulgar and hypertrophic language' and obscure references in its caricature of modernist culture and the 'perceived nonsensical nature of contemporary politics, literature and science'.[32] As 'text and genre', *Schattenrisse* and *The Buribunks* are 'not dissimilar'.[33] However, these early, lighter, ironic or satiric flights were displaced by Schmitt's scholarly and exegetical texts and their dark potential. This dark potential was itself prefigured in what Koselleck describes as *The Buribunks*'s 'admonitory function'.[34]

Schmitt's early texts signal the transformation of his perspectives as his 'Zeitdiagnosen'[35] developed, and as his intellectual and conceptual apparatus evolved. In relation to his 'Zeitdiagnosen' or analysis of the times, Schmitt's perspectives were affected by contemporary events and contextual shifts,

22 Mehring (2014), p 7; see pp 7–9 for greater detail.
23 Bendersky (1983), p 8.
24 Kennedy (2004), pp 42ff; Balke (2016), p 634, briefly gesturing to Schmitt's 'early publications'; Rogers (2016).
25 Kennedy (2004), p 43.
26 Balakrishnan (2000), pp 16–17; Kennedy (2004), p 39.
27 On poetry: Turk (2016), p 762, outlining the influence of Däubler's 'Das Nordlicht', and Schmitt's early text of literary criticism, *Theodor Däubler's 'The Northern Light'*. On expressionist art: Turk (2016), p 761; Mehring (2014), p 6, sketching Schmitt's friendship with Kluxen.
28 Turk (2016), pp 767–8. The sense of an operation – Betrieb – is telling.
29 Mehring (2014), pp 23 and 26, for 'Schnekkeroman'.
30 Turk (2016), p 761 and n 8.
31 Mehring (2014), pp 38–40, 67 and 115.
32 Turk (2016), p 762.
33 Meierhenrich and Simons (2016), p 40. See Mehring (2014), pp 40, 92–3. Note, however, the degree of 'vulgar' language as a point of contrast.
34 Koselleck (2002), p 99.
35 Wolin (1992), p 428.

including the German military loss in World War I, the disintegration of Wilhelmine Germany, the Weimar Republic's emergence, and the Nazi destruction of the 'Weimar experiment'.[36] Commentators have problematised the timing and cohesion of Schmitt's 'right-wing crystallization'[37] in his transformation from a 'semi-Bohemian Catholic anti-modernist military functionary working for the martial law administration'.[38] For Schmitt's early journals display an antagonism to 'militarism and authoritarianism' – that is, an early 'visceral antiauthoritarianism and concern for decidedly liberal ideals'.[39] In relation to the evolution of Schmitt's intellectual and conceptual apparatus, his embrace and then critique of neo-Kantianism is particularly interesting, given the prominence of 'history's subject-object' to *The Buribunks*. Schmitt's 'neo-Kantian reappraisal of the deficiencies inherent in the sharp subjective/objective distinction' transformed in his 'post-1918 anti-Kantian literature'.[40] Commentators have recognised that Schmitt's abandonment of neo-Kantianism reflects criticism that 'the Kantian tendency to exclude vital, historical and metaphysical contents from its account of necessary order impoverishes human freedom by defining it merely as a formal capacity for obtaining and validating laws'.[41] For Schmitt was antipathetic to 'higher law' that misinterpreted the state and human freedom.

Schmitt's early texts include *Dictatorship* and its Roman links. *Dictatorship*'s development from 1916 during World War I, and its first publication in 1921,[42] bookended *The Buribunks*'s publication in 1918. It was a 'groundbreaking text'[43] – a 'historical, sociological and genealogical'[44] analysis, and Schmitt's most scholarly work,[45] with 'complex roots' in classical Roman

36 McCormick (2010), p 396, regarding World War I; McElligott (2013), pp 9, 28, regarding the Wilhelmine disintegration and Weimar emergence; Fink (1996), p 80, regarding the Nazi destruction.
37 Balakrishnan (2000), pp 17, 32 (Schmitt's 'abrupt shift to the right'); Scheuerman (1999), p 24 (Schmitt's 'Nazi period makeover'); Rogers (2016), pp 124ff. See Mehring (2014), pp 136, 144.
38 Balakrishnan (2000), p 17. See Mehring (2014), pp 61ff; Rogers (2016), p 123; Tuori (2016), p 95.
39 Rogers (2016), pp 123, 125 and 124 respectively. See Mehring (2014), pp 73 and 92–3, regarding Schmitt's lack of adherence to the '"ideas of 1914" of the authoritarian military state'.
40 McCormick (2010), p 211, regarding the neo-Kantian reappraisal, and p 36, regarding Schmitt's neo-Kantian critique; Seitzer and Thornhill (2008), p 9, regarding the anti-Kantian literature. See Mehring (2014), pp 28–9, 86, 145.
41 Seitzer and Thornhill (2008), p 9.
42 Mehring (2014), pp 102–3; Rogers (2016), p 123 and n 1, noting that the 1921 text of *Dictatorship* had a brief predecessor in Schmitt's 'Diktatur und Belagerungszustand: Eine staatsrechtliche Studie' (1916). Note too 'Die Einwirkungen des Kriegszunstandes auf das ordentliche strafprozessuale Verfahren' (1917): Hoelzl and Ward (2014), p xi.
43 Hoelzl and Ward (2014), p xi.
44 Hoelzl and Ward (2014), p xiv.
45 Schmitt (2014b), Polity hard-copy back cover, para 3; Boucher (2018), p 93.

thought and receptions.[46] Here, Schmitt traces the chronological transition of dictatorship models, from classical Roman commissary dictatorships to sovereign or revolutionary dictatorships. Equally, *Dictatorship* is a 'Janus-faced book':[47] it is forward-looking in laying the groundwork for Schmitt's future conceptual preferences for dictatorship, but it is backward-looking in favouring classical dictatorship models and temporary limited commissarial dictatorship (as opposed to sovereign dictatorship) with its legally prescribed 'time- or task-related limits' that Schmitt had first endorsed.[48] McCormick warns against reading Schmitt's early work in terms of '[his] later more extreme authoritarianism'.[49] For, when writing *The Buribunks*, Schmitt's intellectual trajectories and arguments were continuing to evolve – he was not yet wedded to a fully charged version of the sovereign leader and their 'decision', as was to occur in the 'puzzle of *Political Theology*'.[50] Notwithstanding this, *Dictatorship*'s focus on dictatorship models prefigures the risk of totalitarianism that crystallises, and is explored, in *The Buribunks*.

Equally, *Dictatorship* references both Tacitus and Juvenal, two authors who coincidentally offer inspiration for *The Buribunks*. Tacitus's *Annales* is significant to *Dictatorship* – it facilitates Schmitt's analysis of the governance structures of the Augustan emperors and the construction of Roman dictatorship models. *Dictatorship*'s first paragraph mentions Tacitus within its historical sweep of classical authors; its second paragraph conflates Tacitus's basic cleavage between the 'older republican dictatorships and the later ones of Sulla and Caesar'.[51] Later, Schmitt refers to Tacitus's use of the *Annales* to 'describe the clever politics of Tiberius', and to recognise that the State requires necessary events 'that conjure the impression of freedom, simulacra, or decorative occasions designed to pacify the population'.[52] In addition, Schmitt's 'Preliminary Remarks' to the 1921 edition of *Dictatorship* extract a quotation from Juvenal's *Satire* 7 as a coda. In these 'Preliminary Remarks', Schmitt identifies the trigger for writing *Dictatorship* – it was not the 'current discussions on "dictatorship, violence and terror"', but the question of the 'legal value of the decision'.[53] His awareness of these 'current discussions' is flagged when he extracts *Satire* 7's two-line sketch of Clio, the Roman Muse of history, being driven from the mythic springs of artistic inspiration to the auction rooms – '*cum desertis*

46 Tuori (2016), p 95.
47 Scheuerman (1999), p 32.
48 McCormick (1997), p 134.
49 McCormick (1997), p 127 n 9: this is McCormick's query on Caldwell's reading of the early work 'Diktatur und Belagerungszustand'.
50 McCormick (1997), p 136.
51 Schmitt (2014b), p 2: Tacitus counterposes the temporary expedient (decemviral office; military tribune's consular authority) with dictatorship as a non-lasting despotism. Note that the *Annales* is not directly referenced here.
52 Schmitt (2014b), p 11, referencing Tacitus, *Annales* 1.2.
53 Schmitt (2014a), p xlv, instancing *Gesetz und Urteil* (1912) as his previous emphasis of the 'legal value of the decision'.

Aganippes / vallibus esuriens migraret in atria Clio'.[54] Like Clio, Schmitt experienced the disjointedness of the 'unfavourable external circumstances of our time'.[55] He was likely referencing Munich's turmoil during his administrative military service up to 1919,[56] as instanced in *Dictatorship*'s 'fleeting references' to chaos and violent political struggles accompanying Munich's political reconstruction and new constitution.[57] Equally, Schmitt was perhaps referencing his military experience in a 'war effort he detested'.[58] That Juvenal could be so applied evidences Schmitt's scholarly scope; like Tacitus, Juvenal is a 'notoriously difficult' writer.[59]

Yet it is not claimed here that Juvenal's or Tacitus's texts were direct models for *The Buribunks*. Juvenal's satire differs formally from Schmitt's – Juvenal's tradition was the Latin verse satire with its associated rhetorical topics and techniques,[60] although Juvenal's innovations frequently exploded the style. Moreover, Tacitus's text differs formally from Schmitt's surreal narrator's fulsome, parodic voice – Tacitus's aphoristic style and overtly historical focus target the real Augustan emperors. Instead, this chapter claims that Juvenal's and Tacitus's texts offered relevant satiric or ironic method, and even substance. Given Schmitt's familiarity with these texts and their points of broad similarity to *The Buribunks*, they may be included among *The Buribunks*'s grab-bag of sources of inspiration: Juvenal's *Satire* 7 satirises Roman historians, intellectuals and patrons; Tacitus's *Annales* problematises historians and history-writing. Admittedly, Schmitt only extracts a sliver of text from *Satire* 7 and references it in *Dictatorship*, but his facility with Latin, his scholarly appetite for the classics and his lifelong fascination with the 'expressive potentials and limitations of different languages'[61] bolster the case for presuming his familiarity with *Satire* 7 as a whole. Like Juvenal, then,[62] Schmitt appears to be 'creatively exploiting'[63] the ideas featured in various literary texts.

The Buribunks and satire

Genres for Schmitt are 'never neutral media or convenient vehicles for messages' – writing within a genre is itself a 'politically inflected practice'.[64] In this

54 'As starving Clio abandons the vales of Aganippe and flees to the auction rooms' (my translation).
55 Schmitt (2014a), p xlv.
56 Hoelzl and Ward (2014), p xii; Mehring (2014), pp 97–8.
57 Hoelzl and Ward (2014), p xvi and n 9.
58 Bendersky (2016), p 126.
59 Green (1989), p 176.
60 Keane (2015), pp 26ff, particularly pp 26–9, 37.
61 Balakrishnan (2000), p 12.
62 Braund (2007), p 45, citing Juvenal's use of Suetonius and his list of five intellectuals.
63 Keane (2015), p 13.
64 Norberg (2011), p 22.

vein, *The Buribunks*'s satiric project has been identified as a 'caustic essay on diary writing and the value commitments implicit in the practice',[65] a 'merciless parody of the modern conception of historical progress as both surveyed and prosecuted by men'[66] and 'a biting caricature of boheme and positivism'.[67] For Schmitt, satire's melting-pot would have included the satire and irony of the classical Roman authors, Western literary tradition and German café-literati society.

Next, the satiric toolkit will be canvassed, followed by satiric conventions, including assumed audience knowledge and the double voice.

The satiric toolkit

The Western tradition of literary satire displays a complex cross-fertilisation and evolution – satire lacks a pigeonhole or 'omnibus definition'.[68] Broadly, the satiric toolkit incorporates literary tools of inversion, reversal and deflation to present an upside-down world; exaggeration and minimisation[69] are deployed to signal pretensions to be pilloried, promotions to be deflated or delusions to be destroyed. Schmitt's 'penchant for binaries'[70] accommodates this particularly well. Satirists use comic relief tools – for instance, humour, wit, parody, caricature, irony, ridicule, and invective – as weapons for fashioning, and then attacking, a distorted, disjointed or disturbed world. Yet satire is not simply 'visceral laughter or corrosive spite',[71] for its purpose is critical. Satiric purpose reveals or problematises deficiencies, or exposes shortcomings, in the contexts, rationales, norms or world-views being attacked. It operates against a standard, and hence is derisive and perhaps divisive, but serious. The satirist, however, is not duty-bound to resolve 'what is perceived as a problem or replace what is satirically disassembled or unmasked with a solution'[72] – satire requires interpretation by its audiences. Nor will the unmasking necessarily be unambiguous, particularly where satire (as a literary genre) depends on the master-trope of irony (as a literary device). For irony itself depends on the 'divergence in sense between utterance (*quae dicuntur*) and the unsaid (*quae sentias*)' – 'the nature of the unsaid is indeterminable'.[73] Put differently, irony is a 'function of language operating on two levels, of a voice divided from itself',[74] and the verbal play

65 Norberg (2011), p 22.
66 Norberg (2011), p 22 n 4, describing Koselleck.
67 Kennedy (2004), p 44.
68 Quintero (2007), p 9.
69 Fife (2016), p 326.
70 Meierhenrich and Simons (2016), p 18.
71 Quintero (2007), p 3.
72 Quintero (2007), p 3.
73 O'Gorman (2000), p 11.
74 Haynes (2012), p 293.

may increase the variability of the interpretation. Needless to say, Schmitt, with his facility for word-play, had a 'deep attraction to the force of irony'.[75]

Specifically, Schmitt deploys satiric and comic relief tools in the branding of each Buribunk with two essential characteristics or 'facts' – the facts of being both large-mouthed and compulsive diarists. The question of the 'more meaningful fact' is expressly problematised.[76] As the first fact, each Buribunk is recognised by their '*erweitertes Maul*'. The German noun, in referencing animals' mouths and name-calling, has derisive or derogatory connotations when applied to humans. But the narrator positively correlates this exaggerated, 'broad-mouthed'[77] characteristic to a larger, 'particularly productive intellect' – both the narrator and the Buribunk accept the 'intellectual importance of the enlarged mouth'.[78] Not only is this comparison incredible and farcical, but the text ironically subverts it – to be 'broad-mouthed' clearly does not *per se* impel quality outputs, creativity of thought or freedom of speech. For, in Buribunkdom, only the *quantity* of outputs as dissertations and publications is remarkable (to the point of being absolutely extreme);[79] only the *production* and performance of diary-entries are valued (to the point of eclipsing their content) and only the *practice* of repetitive diarising is allowed (to the point of negating the freedom to abstain from diarising). But these exaggerated aspects yield a dark undercurrent. Disturbingly, a Buribunk directive prescribes that if an individual Buribunk perceives diarising 'as a pointless and burdensome institution, as a silly harassment, as a "laughable custom"', they are compelled to record this – hence, in a reversal, this obligation[80] is cast by buribunkology as a 'freedom'![81] Moreover, a 'rebellious spirit'[82] is perceived not by their actual failure to diarise (an authentic rejection of diarising), but by their formal diarising of their failure to diarise (a formal recording of a rejection of diarising). The Buribunks are attempting to oppressively 'perfect' and control thought, and to conflate thought and action – that is, to achieve a total mind-control and mechanical uniformity that appears to perform the acceptance or internalisation of diary-writing. The cost of ignoring quality, authenticity and freedom, however, is superficial quantity, shallowness and coercion.

Expanding this first 'fact' of Buribunk identity, the text illustrates how Buribunk evolution deflates and dehumanises by again employing the device of associating humans with animal attributes. Buribunkology's 'heroes' have names with animalistic connotations – Ferker (German *ferkel*, a piglet), and Schnekke (German *schnecke*, a snail). Parodically, neither diminutive name projects these

75 Manderson and Bikundo (2019), pp 191.
76 Chapter 2 of this volume, p 14.
77 Koselleck (2002), p 97.
78 Chapter 2 of this volume, p 14.
79 Chapter 2 of this volume, p 13.
80 Werner (2019), pp 4–5.
81 Chapter 2 of this volume, p 24.
82 Chapter 2 of this volume, p 24.

proto-Buribunks' reputed greatness. Later, each Buribunk's existence *en masse* is associated with rat-seconds – the Buribunks are obsessed with wresting each rat-second from the 'dark rat hole of the future' to incorporate it within the 'reality of the historical'.[83] Diarising is the vehicle for this rearguard action to prevent the present and future from fleeing the past. The Buribunks attempt to conflate the past and future to control time, and so to defeat the notion of '*festum breve gloria mundi*'[84] – that is, that 'worldly fame is a brief joy'. For the Buribunk goal is to convert fleeting rat-seconds to a 'forever' fame! Hence, the narrator attempts to distinguish the Buribunks and their 'enlarged mouth and a higher intellect'[85] from the 'mindless human beings' who are directly identified with 'millions and billions of rats' streaming to the past.[86] But the irony is apparent – the large-mouthed Buribunks, existing only to record/diarise in a society that distinguishes writing from thinking, are clearly mindless and deluded. Their unity of a conflated past, present and future is bleak.

As the second 'fact' of Buribunk identity, each Buribunk's definition as a compulsive diarist brands their historical existence with a technological, machine-like character – each Buribunk is a 'letter on the typewriter of history'.[87] This mechanised life is the result of the Buribunks being tethered to, and enslaved by, their diaries. It is a life of 'interiorised submission'[88] – not only do the Buribunks submit their diarised records to local councils for the conveyer-belt construction of buribunkian profiles,[89] but they submit totally to the centralised, 'totalitarian' surveillance[90] that determines everything buribunkian. Writing has trumped thinking: 'For the Buribunk, thinking is nothing [but] soundless speech; speaking nothing but scriptless writing; writing nothing but anticipated publishing and therefore publishing is identical with writing.'[91] This self-referential series of negations is grim. Ultimately, the Buribunks' humanity is erased in their continual, daily self-notation or self-archiving, rendering each one 'a key in the typewriter of history', a 'continuous chronicle'.[92] The narrator actually perceives this practice to be a pathway to immortality – diaries, in the service of posterity, effectively incorporate each future second within history.[93] But this 'rigorously temporalised utopia'[94] begets an 'absolute servitude in the name of science and tolerance'.[95] The defining category or imperative

83 Chapter 2 of this volume, p 26.
84 Chapter 2 of this volume, p 27.
85 Chapter 2 of this volume, p 14.
86 Chapter 2 of this volume, p 26.
87 Chapter 2 of this volume, p 26.
88 Tihanov (2007), p 125.
89 Chapter 2 of this volume, p 23.
90 Werner (2019), p 4.
91 Chapter 2 of this volume, p 25.
92 Kittler (1999), p 241 (their translation).
93 Chapter 2 of this volume, p 26.
94 Koselleck (2002), p 97.
95 Koselleck (2002), p 98.

here is not value but form, not quality but quantity – significant numbers of diaries are rigorously collated, catalogued, cross-referenced and publicised without questioning the triviality of their contents. From this solipsistic record-keeping and accumulation of facts, the Buribunks' fervent hope is that 'meaning will emerge immanently', and the World Spirit will be graspable, even to itself.[96] Yet, at *The Buribunks*'s conclusion, the narrator unwittingly undercuts each Buribunk's seeming elevation of identification with the World Spirit: 'He is the World Spirit writing itself, perpetuating itself, outwitting itself in its immediate irrefutable factuality.'[97] For the fact of 'outwitting' the World Spirit's experience of its own 'factuality' casts the World Spirit as clueless.

Satiric conventions

Key satiric conventions include assumed audience knowledge and the double voice. In terms of assumed audience knowledge, satiric audiences and targets are never homogeneous or unitary. Satirists implicitly address both 'the enemies of society … and the custodians of society's laws' – satirists and audiences are both 'embedded in an ideological matrix', and the issue of 'for whom and against whom the satire is written' is critical to the 'satirist's purpose and strategy'.[98] Moreover, historical context is not simply an 'inert background', but a milieu that produces the satire, satirist, historical audiences and 'the historical world it conjures up'.[99] Effectively, the 'production' of an assumed audience knowledge or '"active" readerly hermeneutic'[100] understands a text's 'vague satiric targets as interpretive "gaps"', allows contemporary audiences to furnish various interpretations, and recognises that a 'multiplicity of interpretations' may be conveyed.[101] Hence, assumed audience knowledge overlaps with satiric 'doublespeak' that, in its broadest sense, signals text that 'enact[s]' 'different meanings for different audiences'.[102]

In terms of a satiric double voice, a fictive author, persona or narrator is deployed in *The Buribunks* and relegates the actual author to an 'invisible satirist'. This structure usually insulates the narrator's arguments from direct attack while allowing the actual author to undercut these arguments; this additionally allows the subversive 'staging' of the narrator's 'decoy message[s]'.[103] Hence, the satiric text conveys positions that appeal to, or resonate with, diverse audiences, and that may be articulated in diverse degrees of assertiveness or clarity –

96 Schupmann (2016), p 320.
97 Chapter 2 of this volume, p 28.
98 Griffin (2015), p 188.
99 Griffin (2015), p 188.
100 Uden (2015), p 25 and Ch 1; Bartsch (1994), pp 101, 169, outlining doublespeak.
101 Uden (2015), pp 25, 39.
102 Bartsch (1994), pp 145–6; see pp 100–1, 115–16, for a wider appraisal of doublespeak.
103 Bartsch (1994), p 115.

the scale runs from subtle 'light' touches to aggressive 'hard hits'. But whatever the impact, satire is meant to convey a message and to persuade. *The Buribunks*'s adoption of a narrator and double voice[104] introduces a degree of interpretative ambiguity evidently lacking in *Dictatorship*. For *The Buribunks*'s 'authors' – Schmitt and the narrator – exhibit various levels of invisibility. In terms of the ostensibly *visible* narrator, the narrator should actually be *invisible* if he/she truly identifies with the Buribunk cogs swallowed up in buribunkology's fictive science. By contrast, in terms of the actual author or satirist – Schmitt – at least two invisibilities are operating. First, Schmitt is predominantly an 'invisible satirist' in the sense of disappearing behind a role, similar to Juvenal's vanishing in certain later satires.[105] Contemporary readers were mystified[106] that the text lacked any attribution of authorship, except for the cryptic concluding initials, 'C.S.'. They were unaware that Schmitt was the actual author, not least as he is expressly referenced and indignantly castigated by the narrator in two footnotes.[107] Second, Schmitt continues to be an 'invisible satirist' despite the express reference in these two footnotes. When the narrator – buribunkology's acolyte and apologist – attempts unsuccessfully to debunk Schmitt's views, Schmitt is cast as an actual subversive voice to the narration. Recently, however, there has been a twist on *The Buribunks*'s 'invisible satirist' device. Although Schmitt could be understood to be subverting racial eugenics when referring to the listed 'lesser peoples',[108] Manderson and Bikundo identify this as a 'double-bluff' of irony – it accords 'Schmitt permission to insinuate views' and, hence, the text's ambiguity may mask a racially discriminatory attitude.[109] Again, a dark undercurrent appears in Schmitt's texts.

Satire's ambiguity, then, can mask diverse personas. The persona or narrator of history-writing is particularly underlined in the next consideration – *The Buribunks*'s intersection with Tacitus's *Annales*.

The Buribunks and Tacitus's *Annales*

The Buribunks's use of the phrase '*sine ira et studio*' from Tacitus's *Annales* signposts the issue of the historian's or narrator's freedom from bias. Tacitus, the 'politician, orator, historian',[110] with his nostalgia for the Roman Republic, remained an author of interest for Schmitt – he was a fellow conservative intellectual who 'portrayed the sinking ship of state realistically'.[111] He has been

104 Bartsch (1994), Ch 4.
105 Uden (2015), p 51 and ch 2; Braund (2007), p 25.
106 Lambrow (2017), p 332; Tihanov (2007), p 124 and n 22.
107 Chapter 2 of this volume, pp 14 n 2 and p 27 n 13.
108 Chapter 2 of this volume, p 14.
109 Manderson and Bikundo (2019), pp 191–2.
110 O'Gorman (2018), p 9.
111 Beebee (2011), p 201; see pp 200–1, regarding Schmitt's later recollections in his diaries and letters.

described as a compound historian-poet – for Mellor, 'Tacitus is the tragic poet of lost liberty'.[112] For the purposes of this chapter, Tacitus's *Annales* is of relevance not for its historiographical treatment of the post-Augustan, Julio-Claudian dynasty, but for its enigmatic, ironic style that has triggered countless interpretive debates. In the *Annales*'s introductory paragraphs, Tacitus traces 'successive power blocs' in a 'double sequence':[113] first, the sweep of Roman kings/dictators up to Augustus, then, the Julio-Claudian emperors from Tiberius to Nero, shadowed by the history-writers of progressively degenerating imperial histories. Admitting that 'famous writers', as 'geniuses' or 'intellects of distinction', had documented the Roman Commonwealth/Augustan age, the Tacitean narrator reports the production of fictitious or biased imperial 'histories' – histories produced from fear, sycophancy or loathing of an emperor.[114] Seeking to depart from these histories, and to pre-emptively counter allegations of fiction or bias, the Tacitean narrator deploys the phrase '*sine ira et studio*'.[115] He proclaims that his history-writing lacks pretension or partiality, at least within ancient perspectives of bias.

Ancient and modern perspectives of bias are not coterminous. For Luce, the 'immortal phrase'[116] and ancient declaration '*sine ira et studio*' is 'the most memorable claim by an ancient historian' of their freedom from bias.[117] This phrase signals the ancient historian's distance from the 'figures whose history he is narrating'[118] – a distance configured as remoteness-in-time and temporal distance, or an 'absence of favouritism or hatred'.[119] But this phrase evidently fails to convey the modern sense of 'freedom from bias' that rejects personal opinion infecting one's judgement; hence, it offers a 'puzzlingly narrow and incomplete' definition of bias when compared with modern perspectives of objectivity and impartiality.[120] Weber's 1919 lecture, 'Politics as a Vocation',[121] exemplifies the modern deployment of the phrase.

However, the phrase '*sine ira et studio*' does not absolve the ancient historian from judging the historical figure's character – it underlines instead that the historian's 'opinions will result from a personal involvement with the characters and events'.[122] The ancient historian can combine a 'highly opinionated manner' with 'this expression of high-minded detachment'.[123] Yet the Tacitean

112 Mellor (1999), p 108.
113 Henderson (1998), p 257.
114 Tacitus (2004), p 49, *Annales* 1.1.2.
115 Tacitus (2004), p 49, *Annales* 1.1.3: 'without anger or partiality' (my translation).
116 Tacitus (2004), p 100 (Goodyear's commentary).
117 Luce (1989), p 16.
118 Fox (2007), p 167.
119 Luce (1989), p 17.
120 Luce (1989), p 31.
121 Weber (1994), p 330. Note that Schmitt had attended this lecture in 1919 (post-dating *The Buribunks*'s 1918 publication). See Mehring (2014), p 101.
122 Fox (2007), pp 167–8.
123 Fox (2007), p 168.

narrator's persistent failure to satisfy the phrase '*sine ira et studio*' has promoted continued debate. For instance, does this failure flag a conscious or unconscious preference for a senatorial view?[124] Is this Tacitus's personal reaction to Domitian's oppressive reign,[125] or a calculated use of irony?[126] Explaining the *Annales*'s introductory paragraphs, Henderson observes that, while the 'historian (impossibly) exorcises warped passions' by disclaiming bias, his 'dispassion does not last a sentence'![127] This is calculated irony – it is Tacitus advertising that he is ironising his text.[128] For in the next paragraph, the Tacitean narrator outlines Augustus's procession to power in a double sequence: first, Augustus's acquisition of institutional roles for the 'protection of the people'; then, Augustus's gladhanding of the populace ('gifts', 'cheap corn', 'sweets of repose').[129] The trenchant listing of ploys to attain power engages or implicates O'Gorman's 'sceptical reader' in producing the text – as O'Gorman explains, Tacitus imposes responsibility on the 'sceptical reader' to scrutinise the 'successive modes of power as progress, decline or cycle'.[130] For the purposes of this chapter, the key takeaways from Tacitus's *Annales* are that Tacitus 'situates himself in a tradition of sceptical historiography',[131] and that the phrase '*sine ira et studio*' was understood to contribute to fashioning a narrator's persona.

Turning to *The Buribunks*, the narrator claims that the Buribunks are reporting history '*sine ira et studio*'.[132] This disclaimer of bias is intended to assist the Buribunks' reputation, but the phrase is double-edged – it measures the narrator's and Buribunks' reliability (or unreliability) relative to how their truth claims are understood to be supported (or destroyed) in the text. For instance, the narrator is constructed as unreliable when his sweeping, insubstantial straw-claim that Ferker is a 'hero' is subverted by both the footnoted revelation of 78,029 Buribunk 'Intellectual Heroes', and the ludibrious slide of the footnote's additional examples.[133] Hence, the phrase '*sine ira et studio*' underlines the lack of insight of both the narrator and the Buribunks, and intensifies buribunkology's anomalies.

It is instructive to examine *The Buribunks*'s lead-up to, and actual deployment of, the phrase. The lead-up focuses on the first Buribunk leader, Ferker. After describing the great Ferker's glories, the narrator sheepishly reveals Ferker's perceived failings, and ultimately prevaricates regarding Ferker's status as a 'hero'. In this progression, Ferker is first labelled a 'hero' in the text with

124 O'Gorman (2000), pp 2, 42.
125 Sullivan (1976), p 326.
126 O'Gorman (2000), p 2.
127 Henderson (1998), p 257; original italics.
128 Henderson (1998), p 260.
129 Tacitus (1876), *Annales* 1.2 (Church and Brodribb translation).
130 O'Gorman (2000), pp 8–10.
131 O'Gorman (2000), p 14.
132 Chapter 2 of this volume, p 22.
133 Chapter 2 of this volume, p 20 n 8.

repeated affirmations of his ethics and greatness,[134] but then faces allegations of 'perversions' – relevantly, an illicit marriage, fear of death and absence of dia-rising. Admitting that these perversions militate against Ferker being an entitled 'hero of Buribunkdom', the narrator then reports Ferker's re-designation as a 'Moses'.[135] Ironically, the increasing mechanisation and massification of Buribunk labour and production mean that any metaphoric exodus to future Buribunkdom's 'Promised Land' would result in the Buribunks' greater enslavement and lesser humanity! Nonetheless, the narrator accords Ferker the 'insight' that Buribunk production can be transferred to the higher realm of the 'spiritual/intellectual', and anoints him as 'ethically elevated'.[136] The text is literally a 'tangle of negated negatives'[137] in its formal use of double negatives and substantive contradictions. Contradictions are evident in the definitions of what is *ethical* (now, solipsism is ethical), and what is *alien* (now, 'nothing human is alien').[138] For if the Buribunks actually believed in their definition of 'alien', their discrimination between true Buribunks and non-Buribunk humans must collapse. Instead, a disordered, topsy-turvy world is produced.

The actual deployment of the phrase '*sine ira et studio*' arrives at the culmination of the litany of Ferker's perversions – perversions apparently alien to buribunkology. Schmitt, like Tacitus, undercuts the phrase immediately after using it. The narrator recites that, due to 'buribunkological discipline', these 'perversions of the human heart' will be interred '*sine ira et studio*' within the 'book of history' – it is claimed that the 'historical reality' is that the second Buribunk leader, Schnekke, has purified Buribunkdom from 'perversions'.[139] While the use of the phrase appears to manifest an even-handedness in developing the Buribunk 'mind', it is subverted immediately and thereafter in the text as the Buribunks readily demonstrate their partiality. Consider the reaction of the narrator and the Buribunks to one of Ferker's perversions – his illicit marriage. The phrase '*sine ira et studio*' is juxtaposed with the narrator's advice that Ferkologists (presumably, Ferker's Buribunk followers) relegate the 'fact' of Ferker's marriage to a '*pudendum*'. While the Latin can be translated figuratively as a derivative of 'shameful' (to describe Ferker's marriage as a 'disgrace'), the Latin plural '*pudenda*' otherwise denotes genitalia. As a result, the narrator's follow-up comment – 'as if there were *pudenda* in Buribunkology!'[140] – is both parodic and confounding. It is parodic given the narrator's evident indignation and seeming prudishness to a fact of Buribunk life; parodic too is the designation of the Ferkologists' so-called 'understandable silence'[141] concerning the fact of the illicit

134 Chapter 2 of this volume, pp 19–20.
135 Chapter 2 of this volume, p 21. See Mehring (2014), p 82.
136 Chapter 2 of this volume, p 21.
137 Chapter 2 of this volume, p 21.
138 Chapter 2 of this volume, p 21.
139 Chapter 2 of this volume, p 21.
140 Chapter 2 of this volume, p 22.
141 Chapter 2 of this volume, p 22. Note the fictive author's assurance that 'Buribunkological discipline' would recognise the fact of this perversion.

marriage. Equally, the comment is confounding because it affirms the 'accusation of scholarly unworldliness' characterising the Buribunks,[142] an accusation that they dispute. Confounding, too, is the narrator's and Buribunks' lack of comment on Schnekke's 'numerous erotic relationships'.[143]

Hence, Tacitus appears to claim an impartiality and necessary insight that would avoid biased imperial histories. But, like *The Buribunks*'s narrator, Tacitus ultimately problematises the practice of history-writing, a target common to the next consideration – *The Buribunks*'s intersection with Juvenal's *Satire* 7.

The Buribunks and Juvenal's *Satire* 7

As a 'satire on scholarship',[144] *The Buribunks* obviously connects with the usual reading of Juvenal's *Satire* 7 – that is, a reading that reflects a broadly negative treatment of the plight of intellectuals. Like Tacitus, Juvenal was a conservative-leaning, nostalgic but acerbic intellectual. *Satire* 7 targets the declining fortune and fame of a list of intellectuals ('*diserti*'),[145] including historians.[146] Described as an 'unsettling read'[147] and an 'enigmatic and controversial work',[148] *Satire* 7 is contentious not least because Juvenal appears to have vanished in favour of a double voice being installed. The question is whether the narrator is satirising intellectuals (due to poetry's vanity, and history's sterility),[149] or is sympathetic to the intellectuals' plight (due to the fickleness of fate, fame, and fortune).

In this sense, *Satire* 7's advocacy of five unfortunate intellectual-types[150] is double-edged, promoting a diverse audience response. Tennant reads Juvenal's central purpose here as sympathetic to intellectuals, but as condemning the Roman elite's failure to nurture poetry and intellectual pursuits.[151] By contrast, Braund discerns an ambivalent treatment of intellectuals, particularly historians, and claims this as perhaps the initial manifestation of Juvenal's new technique of irony with its double point-of-view.[152] By contrast again, Keane reads *Satire* 7

142 Chapter 2 of this volume, p 15.
143 Chapter 2 of this volume, p 23 n 11. Note that, in another subversion, these relationships are a definitive feature of Schnekke's 'inner life'.
144 Mehring (2014), p 16.
145 Juvenal (1918), *Satire* 7, line 31 ('*disertos*', referencing intellectuals).
146 Juvenal (1918), *Satire* 7, lines 98–99 ('*historiarum scriptores*', referencing historians). Note the recognition of the impact of a lack of proper Roman patronage: Keane (2015), pp 23, 86 (heading).
147 Keane (2015), p 98.
148 Bartsch (1994), p 101.
149 Juvenal (1918), *Satire* 7, line 98.
150 Juvenal (1918), *Satire* 7; Tennant (1996), pp 73–4 (the poet, historian, advocate, rhetor and schoolmaster).
151 Tennant (1996).
152 Braund (2007), p 30.

as interested not in intellectuals' success, but in their misery and suffering.[153] This split in scholarly views highlights *Satire* 7's interpretative ambiguity, indirection and even doublespeak.[154] For *Satire* 7's text and style breaks from so-called 'Juvenilian' style,[155] and its sustained *saeva indignatio* or biting invective, and moves instead to a prolonged use of irony and a double point-of-view.[156]

For the purposes of this chapter, *Satire* 7 is of relevance for its introduction containing the Clio quotation, and its subsequent treatment of historians and history-writing. In the introduction,[157] *Satire* 7's narrator begins by applauding Caesar not only as the sole patron of the 'sorrowing' Muses and intellectuals, but as the provider of prospects and hope.[158] But the narrator then reports that Clio, the Roman Muse of history, has been driven by poverty and starvation to commercialism – specifically, to the menial auction-rooms.[159] This twists the topos of a 'goddess leaving her haunt on earth in disgust',[160] and so subverts the historical impulse. The narrator attributes this subversion to the wealthy failing to properly recognise intellectuals' endeavours, and so failing to deliver fair consideration for the labours of the learned and lettered.[161] Yet 'dissonant notes'[162] confound the quality of the intellectuals' standing and outputs. For instance, poets apply to operate bath-houses, bake-houses and auction-rooms, all lowly occupations. Dramatic poems are not described as the traditionally elevated epics, but as 'the climax in a list of second-hand junk' for the auction-rooms, suggesting the 'trashiness of contemporary mythological verse'.[163] Moreover, the five intellectual-types, sequentially considered by the narrator, exhibit descending degrees of *dignitas*.[164]

In *Satire* 7's brief consideration of historians as one of the five intellectual-types,[165] the double-edged approach allows sympathy for the historians' plight to be both established and nullified. The narrator first problematises the

153 Keane (2015), p 92: the 'theme of the neglectful patron' is a 'vehicle of misanthropic meditation'.
154 Bartsch (1994), pp 101, 169.
155 Keane (2015), p 4.
156 Braund (2007), pp 25, 26 and 54ff.
157 Braund (2007), p 34 – usually lines 1–35, or 1–21 less frequently.
158 'On Caesar alone hang all the hopes and prospects of the learned': Juvenal (1918) *Satire* 7, Ramsay translation. Or 'The hopes, the whole business of letters depend on Caesar': Juvenal (2011) *Satire* 7, Kline translation.
159 Juvenal (1918), *Satire* 7, lines 5–6; Wiesen (1973), p 469; Braund (2007), p 30. Note the use of 'sorrowing' Muses and 'auction rooms' per the Ramsay translation, and 'market-place' per the Kline translation.
160 Braund (2007), p 38.
161 Juvenal (1918), *Satire* 7, lines 22–32.
162 Braund (2007), p 30.
163 Wiesen (1973), p 469.
164 Keane (2015), p 93; Keane (2006), pp 132–3. See Braund (2007), p 34: *Satire* 7 is 'potentially disjointed' with 'five clearly differentiated sections'.
165 Juvenal (1918), *Satire* 7, lines 98–105.

profitability of historians' labours, given their limitless consumption of time and 'midnight oil'.[166] For Braund, this establishes sympathy as the narrator deplores the historians' lack of reward; by contrast, for Wiesen, sympathy may be nullified if historians' outputs represent 'very little value'.[167] The narrator then farcically reduces historians' outputs 'to an ever-growing heap of papyrus, to a physical mechanical act'[168] – an evidently 'uncomplimentary image'.[169] That the 'thousandth page' in this 'growing pile' is bankrupting, but that historians continue to harness a 'vast number of facts' and follow the 'laws of the genre',[170] suggests a helplessness that 'detracts from their autonomy and dignity'.[171] For Braund, sympathy is restored with the narrator's report that historians' compensation for the 'harvest' of their labour[172] is less than a newsreader's compensation. However, this traverse of historians' fortunes terminates abruptly with a one-line satiric joke[173] – unexpectedly, a hostile interlocutor brands historians 'a lazy crew that delight in lounging and the shade'![174] Hence, it is ultimately unclear whether the audience should be sympathetic to historians' lack of recognition and compensation, or scornful of their lack of expertise and dedication. But it is clear that the written word is under-appreciated, lesser talent is over-valued, intellectuals are obscured, and 'texts are demeaned and confined'.[175] Keane perceives 'a discernible competition between a vision of progress … and a pessimistic or nostalgic undercutting of that vision'.[176]

Turning to *The Buribunks*, Schmitt does not directly reference Juvenal's *Satire* 7 therein – he extracts its Clio quotation in *Dictatorship*.[177] Schmitt's familiarity, as a classicist, with Juvenal's *Satire* 7 can be presumed as the Clio quotation's proper application relies on understanding its greater context, textually and culturally. Like *Satire 7, The Buribunks* deals with change, perceived progress and ironic decline.[178] In both texts, society fails to nurture learning and letters, and subverts the artistic and historical impulse – intellectuals have exaggerated outputs of diminished quality. Both texts deride the preference for a 'mass of

166 Juvenal (1918), *Satire* 7, line 99.
167 Braund (2007), p 30; Wiesen (1973), p 478.
168 Braund (2007), p 60.
169 Braund (2007), p 61; Wiesen (1973), p 478.
170 Juvenal (1918), *Satire* 7, line 102.
171 Braund (2007), p 61.
172 Juvenal (1918), *Satire* 7, line 103.
173 Braund (2007), p 61.
174 Juvenal (1918), *Satire* 7, line 105. Note '*umbra*' references the topos of 'poetic shade'.
175 Keane (2015), p 97.
176 Keane (2015), p 90.
177 Schmitt was developing *Dictatorship* from 1916 and initially published it in 1921. Note that from 1917, Schmitt was 'feverishly doing research' for *Political Romanticism*: Hoelzl and Ward (2014), p xiii.
178 Keane (2015), pp 23 and 86 (heading).

facts', not a 'wealth of ideas'[179] – intellectuals whose talents are over-valued are parodied. Ultimately, sterility results, as is clear from the Buribunks' promotion of quantity (not quality) and intellectualism (not realism or reality), respectively.

Concerning the quality/quantity tension, the narrator claims that quality (the alleged value of buribunkology) can be derived from quantity (the facts of the '400,000 plus' Buribunk dissertations).[180] Greatly exaggerated numbers are reported in the futile attempt to translate so-called facts to value. Mega-quantities can be instanced in the Buribunk outputs pertaining to the Buribunk institutes ('weekly competitions', 'numerous prizes', 'billions' of research funds[181]), to the 'great Ferker' (a 'library of diaries')[182] and to the Ferker industry ('billions of letters', '200 volumes' of biography).[183] Ironically, the narrator perceives no parody in Ferker being elevated to a Buribunk 'hero', but then being demoted to number '78029 in the collection "Intellectual Heroes"'.[184] Nor can the narrator persuasively distinguish buribunkology from the otherwise derided scholasticism – they both exhibit comparative quantitative 'greatness'.[185]

Concerning the intellectualism/realism tension, the narrator ironically performs this 'satire of detached intellectualism'.[186] As buribunkology's mouthpiece, the narrator is no advertisement for intellectual logic or abstract reasoning, despite approving the 'logic of the facts' and the 'laws of logic' – the narrator's oblivion to the limitations of the arguments is the vehicle for Schmitt's satire. The narrator has defined intellectualism as buribunkology's science and the World Spirit's form. The Buribunk mind is constructed by, and engaged with, intellectualism, and the narrator is interested only with this intellectual 'intensity' of the higher realm of the 'intellectual/spiritual'. But these 'intellectuals' are actually displaced from any separate existence or reality – they merge with the recording machine and recorded word, losing materiality in their quest for absorption within the World Spirit. Like Juvenal's *Satire* 7, this satire parodies intellectuals' over-rated talents that obscure the lack of quality of their over-produced outputs.

The Buribunks, admonitions and dystopia

Finally, adopting Koselleck, *The Buribunks* can be read with an 'admonitory function'.[187] Schmitt was not directly delivering alarms or admonitions – as

179 Wiesen (1973), p 478, concerning *Satire* 7.
180 Chapter 2 of this volume, p 13.
181 Chapter 2 of this volume, p 13.
182 Chapter 2 of this volume, p 20.
183 Chapter 2 of this volume, pp 20, 20 n 8.
184 Chapter 2 of this volume, p 20 n 8.
185 Chapter 2 of this volume, pp 13, 21.
186 Meierhenrich and Simons (2016), p 7.
187 Koselleck (2002), pp 99, 93.

Henderson remarked of Tacitus's *Annales*, the text is 'ironised beyond anything so crude'.[188] But, consonant with satire's purpose of being derisive but serious, *The Buribunks* furnishes cautions – even to the point of reprimands – by drawing on its Roman links.

Cautioning historians and intellectuals, *The Buribunks* indicates that historical 'truth' may be manipulated, as signalled by Tacitus's phrase, '*sine ira et studio*'. Seemingly oblivious to the requisites for impartiality, *The Buribunks*'s narrator presents as an unreliable historian and sub-standard intellectual. The farcical, implausible arguments are a warning against accepting the narrator's assertions at face value. *The Buribunks* indicates too that history's value may be compromised and intellectuals over-rated, recalling Juvenal's *Satire* 7 – the Muse of history flees, and historians over-value their efforts when consuming unlimited time. Juvenal's 'disillusionment in the imperial dream'[189] is expressed in his 'criticism of "contemporary" society in the *Satires*'[190] – ultimately, he stresses that betrayals are a common theme in society's dystopia. Similarly, the Buribunks' military-type productions of 'wads of negated negations' are like Juvenal's historians' mechanically produced 'heaps of papyrus'. Ultimately, the Buribunks fail – 'reading history' means 'meaningful interaction between past and present',[191] but their 'history' transcribes the present to preordain a static, self-referential future.

Cautioning diarists, *The Buribunks*'s message exposes Schmitt's 'complicated relationship' with diarising, a format he perceived to be 'alien' both formally and substantively,[192] but that he ironically embraced like 'one of his "Buribunken"'.[193] *The Buribunks* punctures romantic occasionalism and Buribunk pretensions in their grand theory. Recalling Juvenal's *Satire* 7 again, the image therein of the literary patron betraying his poet so as not to be outshone[194] is integral to Juvenal's dystopia. Similarly, *The Buribunks* warns against buribunkology as totalising, as manipulative of reality and history, and as self-reflexive in relating the ego to the collective – in gazing solipsistically on Buribunkology and themselves, the Buribunks are passive and lack ethics. Moreover, their vanity publishing has sinister implications: Buribunks vanish regardless of whether or not they faithfully discharge their publication role; they are either absorbed within the World Spirit and Buribunk totalitarianism and massification, or excluded and forgotten in history's pages.

Ultimately, then, *The Buribunks* offers a dystopia[195] – Kennedy reads *The Buribunks* as bereft of the 'playfulness' that characterised *Schattenrisse*, Schmitt's

188 Henderson (1998), p 260.
189 Bond (2010), p 33.
190 Bond (2010), p 48.
191 O'Gorman (2000), p 47.
192 Norberg (2011), p 22.
193 Schupmann (2016), p 321, quoting Mehring (2014), p 526.
194 Bond (2010), p 50.
195 Balke (2016), p 633; Koselleck (2002), p 98, describing it as a 'negative utopia'.

pre-war collection of parodies in collaboration with Eisler.[196] In buribunkology's 'rising terror',[197] the 'idealist demand for legibility amounts to a terror campaign'.[198] For Norberg, 'diary writing is arrogant in its elevation of the individual while compliant with an invasive regime of surveillance and classification'.[199] Balke identifies Schmitt's 'actual diagnosis of the crisis of modernity' – here, 'political-public structures and processes'[200] are 'perceived as empty and deceptive disguises, as a veil, a façade, a fake, or a decoration'.[201] But Koselleck's conclusion is the most telling – Schmitt's utopia was ultimately 'fulfilled … even worse than what he parodied'.[202]

Conclusion

Schmitt, the 'consummate "prosecutorial" thinker', developed his 'major works … as attempts to destroy positions he rejected'.[203] He is recognised as an 'eminently citable political philosopher and jurist',[204] but not as a literary force for his satire. Yet the satiric and ironic impulse of *The Buribunks*, his early speculative text, is not too distant from the polemics of his non-speculative intellectual tracts. As an example of the sophisticated genre of satire, *The Buribunks*'s attempted destruction of three main satiric targets – romantic occasionalist diary-writing, progressivist philosophy of history and positivist social science – is 'dressed in parodistic vestments',[205] featuring dense allusions and a wealth of interrelated ideas. But, being satire, it additionally conveys serious messages.

This chapter's exploration has considered *The Buribunks*'s satire, irony and engagement with two classical Roman authors and texts that Schmitt referenced in *Dictatorship* – Tacitus's *Annales* and Juvenal's *Satire* 7. These Roman links are not only models for the use of the double voice, but they diversely engage with history-writing. This chapter, then, contributes to examining how Schmitt's antiquarian sources assisted the development of his intellectual thought, and how intertextual links can enrich and dress up *The Buribunks*'s speculative satire.

Interestingly, Schmitt engaged in lifelong diarising except for the period 1916 to 1921.[206] Musil expressed shock at what he perceived to be *The*

196 Kennedy (2004), p 44. See Mehring (2014), pp 38–40.
197 Koselleck (2002), p 98.
198 Lambrow (2017), p 335, reading Koselleck.
199 Norberg (2011), p 39.
200 Balke (2016), p 631.
201 Schmitt (1986), p 14.
202 Koselleck (2002), p 99.
203 Oakes (1986), p xii.
204 Wolin (1992), p 424.
205 Koselleck (2002), pp 84–5.
206 Bendersky (2016), pp 118, 127.

Buribunks's reflection of his own diary-writing self,[207] whereas Schmitt's diary-writing self was apparently 'trapped in a textual form he detested',[208] struggling between 'an intellectual concern and a private affliction'.[209] Notwithstanding this, Musil appreciated the satire in 1930.[210] For it is derisive but serious – penetrating, creative, admonitory but enigmatic. *The Buribunks*'s satiric force subverts its ostensible rejection of notions of value, quality and freedom. It presents the total lack of political space, voice and visibility in Buribunk philosophy in terms of Schmitt's 'penchant for binaries'.[211] And it exposes the ultimate colourlessness or vanishing of the Buribunks as an existence ironically coloured with shades of mechanisation, delusion and enslavement, then darkened by the eclipse of freedoms and thought. *The Buribunks*'s allusive, imaginative text should attract continued analysis on the question of its intersection with Schmitt's key ideas and positions. For, ultimately, the satiric impulse in this surreal, speculative text echoes the polemical force in Schmitt's non-speculative political, philosophical and conceptual texts. Equally, satire's ambiguity and levels of interpretation reveal *The Buribunks*'s 'admonitory function'[212] – that is, the warning to be gleaned from this future fantasy world's 'rising terror in the medium of writing'.[213]

References

Matthew Arnold (1960–77) *The Complete Prose Works of Matthew Arnold Vol I–XI* (Vol IV), University of Michigan Press.

Gopal Balakrishnan (2000) *The Enemy: An Intellectual Portrait of Carl Schmitt*, Verso.

Friedrich Balke (2016) 'Carl Schmitt and Modernity', in Jens Meierhenrich and Oliver Simons (eds), *The Oxford Handbook of Carl Schmitt*, Oxford University Press, 629.

Shadi Bartsch (1994) *Actors in the Audience: Theatricality and Doublespeak from Nero to Hadrian*, Harvard University Press.

Thomas Oliver Beebee (2011) *Citation and Precedent: Conjunctions and Disjunctions of German Law and Literature*, Bloomsbury.

Joseph J. Bendersky (1983) *Carl Schmitt: Theorist for the Reich*, Princeton University Press.

Joseph Bendersky (2016) 'Schmitt's Diaries', in Jens Meierhenrich and Oliver Simons (eds), *The Oxford Handbook of Carl Schmitt*, Oxford University Press, 117.

Robin Bond (2010) 'The Utopia of Horace and Vergil and the Dystopia of Petronius and Juvenal' 19 *Scholia: Natal Studies in Classical Antiquity* 31.

207 Tihanov (2007), p 124.
208 Norberg (2011), p 27, although Norberg relates this to Schmitt's notebooks from 1947 to 1951; Mehring (2014), p 83, noting that Schmitt ceased diarising for a period after *The Buribunks*.
209 Meierhenrich and Simons (2016), p 12.
210 Lambrow (2017), p 333.
211 Meierhenrich and Simons (2016), p 18.
212 Koselleck (2002), p 99.
213 Koselleck (2002), p 93.

David Boucher (2018) *Appropriating Hobbes: Legacies in Political, Legal, and International Thought*, Oxford University Press.
Susan H. Braund (2007) *Beyond Anger: A Study of Juvenal's Third Book of Satires*, Cambridge University Press.
Jane Fife (2016) 'Peeling the Onion: Satire and the Complexity of Audience Response' 35 *Rhetoric Review* 322.
Carole Fink (1996) 'The Weimar Republic and its "Minderheitenpolitik: Challenge to a Democracy"' 14 *German Politics and Society* 80.
Matthew Fox (2007) *Cicero's Philosophy of History*, Oxford University Press.
Peter Green (1989) 'Juvenal Revisited' 9 *Grand Street* 175.
Dustin Griffin (2015) *Satire: A Critical Reintroduction*, University Press of Kentucky.
Holly Haynes (2012) 'Tacitus' History and Mine', in Victoria Emma Pagán (ed), *A Companion to Tacitus*, John Wiley & Sons, 282.
John Henderson (1998) *Fighting for Rome: Poets and Caesars, History and Civil War*, Cambridge University Press.
Michael Hoelzl and Graham Ward (2014) 'Translators' Introduction', in Carl Schmitt, *Dictatorship: From the Origin of the Modern Concept of Sovereignty to Proletarian Class Struggle* (trans Michael Hoelzl and Graham Ward), Polity Press, x.
Juvenal (1918) 'Satire 7' in *Juvenal and Persius* (trans G.G. Ramsay), William Heinemann (*Satire* 7 in the text).
Juvenal (2011) 'Satire 7 – Patronage' in *The Satires* (trans A.S. Kline), Poetry in Translation (*Satire* 7 in the text).
Catherine Keane (2006) *Figuring Genre in Roman Satire*, Oxford University Press.
Catherine Keane (2015) *Juvenal and the Satiric Emotions*, Oxford University Press.
Ellen Kennedy (2004) *Constitutional Failure: Carl Schmitt in Weimar*, Duke University Press.
Friedrich A. Kittler (1999) *Gramophone, Film, Typewriter* (trans Geoffrey Winthrop-Young and Michael Wutz), Stanford University Press.
Reinhart Koselleck (2002) *The Practice of Conceptual History: Timing History, Spacing Concepts* (trans Todd Samuel Presner), Stanford University Press.
Alexander Lambrow (2017) '14 December 1930: Robert Musil Meets Carl Schmitt' 90 *German Quarterly* 332.
T.J. Luce (1989) 'Ancient Views on the Causes of Bias in Historical Writing' 84 *Classical Philology* 16.
Desmond Manderson and Edwin Bikundo (2019) 'Forms of irony in Carl Schmitt's Political Romanticism, The Buribunks and Ex Captivitate Salus' 28 *Griffith Law Review* 189.
John P. McCormick (1997) *Carl Schmitt's Critique of Liberalism: Against Politics as Technology*, Cambridge University Press.
John P. McCormick (2010) 'From Roman Catholicism to Mechanized Oppression: On Political-Theological Disjunctures in Schmitt's Weimar Thought' 13 *Critical Review of International Social and Political Philosophy* 391.
Anthony McElligott (2013) *Rethinking the Weimar Republic: Authority and Authoritarianism, 1916–1936*, A&C Black.
Reinhard Mehring (2014) *Carl Schmitt: A Biography* (trans Daniel Steuer), Polity Press.
Jens Meierhenrich and Oliver Simons (2016) '"A Fanatic of Order in an Epoch of Confusing Turmoil": The Political, Legal, and Cultural Thought of Carl Schmitt', in

Jens Meierhenrich and Oliver Simons (eds), *The Oxford Handbook of Carl Schmitt*, Oxford University Press, 3.
Ronald Mellor (1999) *The Roman Historians*, Routledge.
Jakob Norberg (2011) 'Day-to-Day Politics: Carl Schmitt on the Diary' 157 *Telos* 21.
Guy Oakes (1986) 'Translator's Introduction', in Carl Schmitt (ed), *Political Romanticism* (trans Guy Oakes), MIT Press, ix.
Ellen O'Gorman (2000) *Irony and Misreading in the Annals of Tacitus*, Cambridge University Press.
Ellen O'Gorman (2018) 'Introduction', in *Tacitus, Histories I: A Selection* (commentary and notes Benedict Gravell), Bloomsbury, 1.
Ruben Quintero (2007) 'Introduction: Understanding Satire' in Ruben Quintero (ed), *A Companion to Satire*, Blackwell, 1.
Brendan Rapple (1997) 'England's Neglect of Higher Education: The Comparative Perspective of Matthew Arnold' 31 *Journal of Educational Thought* 159.
Michael Dylan Rogers (2016) 'The Development of Carl Schmitt's Political Thought During the First World War' 13 *Modern Intellectual History* 123.
William E. Scheuerman (1999) *Carl Schmitt: The End of Law*, Rowman and Littlefield.
Carl Schmitt (1986) *Political Romanticism* (trans Guy Oakes), MIT Press.
Carl Schmitt (2014a) 'Preliminary Remarks to the First Edition (1921)', in Carl Schmitt, *Dictatorship: From the Origin of the Modern Concept of Sovereignty to Proletarian Class Struggle* (trans Michael Hoelzl and Graham Ward), Polity Press, xxxvii.
Carl Schmitt (2014b) *Dictatorship: From the Origin of the Modern Concept of Sovereignty to Proletarian Class Struggle* (trans Michael Hoelzl and Graham Ward), Polity Press.
Karen Schultz (2019) 'Schmitt's Satire in The Buribunks: Intertextual Links in Diary-writing's Dystopia' 28 *Griffith Law Review* 206.
Benjamin A. Schupmann (2016) 'Carl Schmitt: A Biography. By Reinhard Mehring' 23 *Constellations* 320.
Jeffrey Seitzer and Christopher Thornhill (2008) 'An Introduction to Carl Schmitt's Constitutional Theory: Issues and Context', in Carl Schmitt (ed), *Constitutional Theory* (trans Jeffrey Seitzer), Duke University Press, 1.
Donald Sullivan (1976) 'Innuendo and the "Weighted Alternative" in Tacitus' 71 *The Classical Journal* 312.
Tacitus (1876) *The Annals of Tacitus* (trans Alfred John Church and William Jackson Brodribb), Macmillan (*Annales* in the text).
Tacitus (2004) *The Annals of Tacitus: Volume 1, Annals 1.1–54*, commentary R.D. Goodyear, Cambridge University Press (*Annales* in the text).
Peter Tennant (1996) 'The Question of Juvenal's Sincerity in his Seventh Satire' 5 *Scholia: Natal Studies in Classical Antiquity* 72.
Galin Tihanov (2007) 'Robert Musil in the Garden of Conservatism', in Philip Payne, Graham Bartram and Galin Tihanov (eds), *A Companion to the Works of Robert Musil*, Camden House.
Kaius Tapani Tuori (2016) 'Schmitt and the Sovereignty of Roman Dictators: From the Actualization of the Past to the Recycling of Symbols' 42 *History of European Ideas* 95.
Johannes Turk (2016) 'At the Limits of Rhetoric: Authority, Commonplace, and the Role of Literature in Carl Schmitt', in Jens Meierhenrich and Oliver Simons (eds), *The Oxford Handbook of Carl Schmitt*, Oxford University Press, 751.
James Uden (2015) *The Invisible Satirist: Juvenal and Second-Century Rome*, Oxford University Press.

Max Weber (1994) 'The Profession and Vocation of Politics', in Peter Lassman and Ronald Speirs (eds), *Weber: Political Writings*, Cambridge University Press, 309.
David S. Wiesen (1973) 'Juvenal and the Intellectuals' 101 *Hermes* 464.
Wouter G. Werner (2019) 'Buribunks and Foundational Paradoxes of International Law' 28 *Griffith Law Review* 259.
Richard Wolin (1992) 'Carl Schmitt: The Conservative Revolutionary Habitus and the Aesthetics of Horror' 20 *Political Theory* 424.

Part IV

The Buribunks as part of Schmitt's wider oeuvre

Chapter 15

Mephistophelean irony in Carl Schmitt's *Political Romanticism*, *The Buribunks* and *Ex Captivitate Salus*

Desmond Manderson and Edwin Bikundo

The ironic cage of modernity

In the last years of his life, Max Weber warned of an impending spiritual and intellectual crisis. An 'iron cage' of bureaucratic machinery was encasing Europe.[1] Not summer's bloom lies before us, he prophesied in lectures delivered during the last days of the Great War, 'but rather a polar night of icy darkness and harshness'.[2] Goethe was the starting point of Weber's Cassandra-like ruminations. Twice he quotes the same passage from *Faust*: 'Reflect, the Devil is old, so become old if you would understand him.'[3] This reaching out for a religio-literary figure was no mere aberration for, as he wrote elsewhere, 'anyone who wishes to engage in politics at all … is entering into relations with satanic powers that lurk in every act of violence'.[4] Anton Warde, in tracing the genesis of irony in Goethe's *Faust*, contends that Goethe utilised layer upon layer of irony – albeit unconsciously.[5] Johannes Anderegg analyses the play-within-a-play framing role of the *Book of Job* in Faust, whose 'intertextual layers provide a varnish of irony'.[6] Ellis Shookman concurs with Warde that irony enabled Goethe to achieve critical distance from the character of Faust, but also notes that 'Mephistopheles is often called ironic'.[7]

Weber was not alone in his fears and foreboding. The hideous and meaningless violence of the Great War had made the phrase the 'crisis of modernity' commonplace.[8] The complacency of the long nineteenth century had been broken: its promises of technological mastery marching hand-in-hand with peace and social progress had been shown to be naïve – indeed fraudulent. In the arts, too, the self-confidence of European civilisation gave way to a

1 Weber (1958), p 181.
2 Weber et al. (2004), p 93.
3 Weber et al. (2004), pp 27, 91.
4 Weber et al. (2004), p 90.
5 Warde (1975), pp 181 and 184.
6 Anderegg (2006), p 40.
7 Shookman (2009), p 491.
8 Collingwood (2008a), pp 105, 142; Collingwood (2008b), p 233; Simmel (1968), p 23.

DOI: 10.4324/9781003091066-19

profound loss of faith: in God, certainly, but in man too, in progress and science and reason and history. D.H. Lawrence warned in his wartime letters:

> I feel as if the whole thing were coming to an end – the whole of England, of the Christian era … The world is gone, extinguished, like the lights of last night's Café Royal … So it seems our cosmos is burst, burst at last, the stars and moon blown away … So it is the end – our world is gone, and we are like dust in the air.[9]

What, then, could replace these spent faiths? The modernist literature of the post-war years betrays a constant puzzling search for some new Archimedean point. Herman Hesse's *Siddhartha* (also 1922) was only one of many such novels of inwardness. In the work of many other writers, only an abyss seemed to await the unprepared citizens of the twentieth century. Here, for example, is E. M. Forster's *A Passage to India* (1924):

> She had come to that state where the horror of the universe and its smallness are both visible at the same time – the twilight of the double vision in which so many elderly people are involved … Visions are supposed to entail profundity, but – Wait till you get one, dear reader! The abyss also may be petty, the serpent of eternity made of maggots …[10]

These turbulent times radically altered the art, literature and philosophy of the inter-war years. They created no less of a disturbance in the field of jurisprudence. Weimar Germany was the crucible of the 'crisis of modernity' in legal thought. Within the span of a few short years, major works addressed just these questions.[11] For law too had to face not only the death of God and Empire but the death of the empire or god of the System. If the bureaucratic rationality of positivism was not an answer but a cage, then what could be done? Hans Kelsen, whose major work on sovereignty and law appeared in 1920,[12] made conscious reference to the recent work of Freud, with which he was intimately familiar,[13] in defending formal legal structures designed to achieve the '*repression* of sovereignty'.[14] He seems to have had the primal scene in *Totem and Taboo* in mind.[15] In *Modernism and the Grounds of Law*, Peter Fitzpatrick quotes Freud's parting shot at the end of *Totem and Taboo*, itself a repudiation of the famous line from *Faust*, 'in the beginning was the deed'. On the contrary, says Freud, 'In the elusiveness of origins the deed cannot be

9 Delany (1979), p 385; Lawrence (1915), pp 105–106.
10 Forster (2000), p 184.
11 Agamben (2005); Dyzenhaus (1997); Kennedy (2004); Scheuerman (1999).
12 Kelsen (1920).
13 Jabloner (1998); Kelsen (1924); Losano (1977).
14 Schmitt (1985), p 21.
15 Fitzpatrick (2001), pp 11–36; Freud (1999).

known to have happened or known not to have happened.'[16] Fitzpatrick takes as emblematic of modernity the distinction between the neurotic for whom 'the thought is a complete substitute for the deed' and 'primitive men', for whom '[the deed] is a substitute for the thought'.[17]

All these allusions to the ambiguity of modernity, poised Hamlet-like between being and acting, are in Schmitt's sights when he traces a philosophy of the Buribunks. He paraphrases *Faust*: 'In fact I do not capture myself and it through thinking, but writing – for in the beginning there is the deed and not the thought. That means: I am not only the reader of world history but also its writer.'[18] Walter Benjamin wrote 'Critique of Violence' the year after *Totem and Taboo*.[19] The same year, Carl Schmitt wrote *The Dictator*, [20] and in 1922 *Political Theology*.[21] Together, Benjamin and Schmitt were the harbingers of a Weberian doom when it came to liberal conceptions of the relationship between law, sovereignty and violence. *Political Theology* unequivocally rejected Kelsen's repression thesis, and instead sought to let the genie of untrammelled sovereignty out of the bottle once and for all.

The Buribunks

The Buribunks 'is primarily a satire on scholarship'.[22] Schmitt, barely in his thirties, published it as an essay in the Catholic-leaning journal *Summa*.[23] A Buribunk – a word of Schmitt's coinage – is an obsessive self-documenter. In the twenty-first century, they would be blogging and taking selfies and, if academics, engaged in furious auto-citation.[24] In the twentieth century, they kept a diary.[25] In *The Buribunks*, Schmitt 'mocks a self-referential scholarly machinery in which everything and everyone is researched'.[26] As seen in the extract below, Schmitt reveals a deep attraction to the force of irony:

> If the value of every methodological discussion about the status of intellectual activity as a science lies only in reflection on the intellectual means and aims of the work, then this requires a body of work in the first place – in the same way, it is self-evident that there would be no study of America if America had not been discovered, and no buribunkology if there were

16 Fitzpatrick (2001), p 16.
17 Freud (1999), p 187.
18 Chapter 2 of this volume, p 26.
19 Agamben (2005), pp 52–64; Benjamin (1920); Benjamin (1986), pp 277–300.
20 Schmitt (1921, 2012).
21 Schmitt (1985).
22 Mehring (2014), p 82.
23 Schmitt (1918).
24 Tranter (2019), p 131.
25 Payne et al. (2007), p 184.
26 Mehring, (2014), p 82.

> no buribunkologists. [Schmitt inserts a footnote here: 'In this way, the existence of the Buribunks themselves, which is occasionally denied by hypocritical doctrinists in a manner that can hardly be taken seriously, is *a priori* put beyond doubt. As the existence of America follows out of the fact that American Studies exists, the existence of the Buribunks follows from the fact that buribunkology exists.'] Such historicity planted with both feet on solid ground is, at first glance, certainly convincing and does not have to fear any objections.[27]

The philosophical tenets of the Buribunks include 'I write, therefore I am'.[28] A Buribunk is consequently his 'own master'[29] through a continual process of self-archiving. The 'realm of Buribunkerism' is an institution inspired by Schmitt's wartime bureaucratic experience in the Army General Command in Munich.[30] *The Buribunks* crams in references to such disparate themes as Goethe's *Faust*,[31] the scientific method, reflexivity, technology, the world court and many others.

If we focus on the use of a single offensive word (and not just any offensive word, either) in an ironic passage of a satirical work – we can readily acknowledge that on the face of it, Schmitt appears to be sending up racial eugenics:

> If, however, we consider that lesser peoples, Polynesians, Tierra del Fuegians, Baronga Negroes and other tribes incapable of an education, have a relatively small mouth, even though they are cannibals, the close connection between the enlarged mouth and a higher intellect becomes a probability. This probability reaches its ethical certainty through the further assertion that if a small mouth is already sufficient to elevate those primitive races above the level of apes and birds.[32]

We here use the word 'Negroes' to replace the original epithet or 'N- word' which gives the quote much of its highly offensive quality, the original word itself being too offensive nowadays to use: whether ironically, faux-ironically, or otherwise Joseph W. Bendersky states that Schmitt 'never succumbed to a belief in the biological racism of National Socialist ideology. He always considered such ideas absurd.'[33] On closer inspection, however, Schmitt is playing a double

27 Chapter 2 of this volume, p 12.
28 Kittler (1999), p 241.
29 Kittler (1999), p 233.
30 Mehring (2014), p 82.
31 *The Buribunks* contains at least eight references or allusions to Goethe's *Faust*, including: 'In the beginning was the deed' (not the word) approvingly cited. Schmitt at various points quotes from Goethe's *Faust II*, act V, line 11,837, *Faust I*, line 2038 and 2039. Schmitt even creates a pun using the word for fist (Faust) which is also the title of Goethe's Faust to refer to the devil (Mephisto), *Faust I*, line 1939, *Faust II*, act V, lines 12,106 and 12,107 and *Faust II*, act V, lines 11,583 and 11,584. See also Schmitt (2015).
32 Chapter 2 of this volume, p 14.
33 Bendersky (1983), p 208.

game. His ironic use of the word, while seeming to mock a boorish and unsophisticated strand of racism, barely conceals a variant of the same malady disguised only by bourgeois condescension. The irony allows him to support opinions while at the same time scoffing at the ignorance of those who admit to them too openly. The irony gives Schmitt permission to insinuate views while refusing to take any responsibility for them. It is a kind of double-bluff, like the 'purloined letter' in Poe's tale, hidden in plain sight.[34]

Throughout his long career, Schmitt melded together two unrelated forms of creative writing – storytelling by parable on the one hand[35] and fact-creation through legal fiction on the other.[36] He did this by identifying, highlighting and then demonstrating powerfully through example that the standard legal fictions were fundamentally allegorical and spiritual in nature. Revitalising concepts that had become sterile clichés – the state, the sovereign, democracy and so on – he highlighted the close kinship of law to the humanities, mythology, religion, literature and aesthetics. 'In Germany,' he wrote, 'the mind has once again outmaneuvered [*überspielt*] the Leviathan. I conclude from this that the humanities will outmaneuver the natural sciences and will force them to transform themselves into humanities.'[37] No wonder then that Schmitt 'had something about him that led some to compare him to … Mephistopheles': alchemical, unnatural, unstoppable.[38]

Paradoxically, the violent clarity of Schmitt's writing both disguises and reveals his meaning or multiple meanings. This is a kind of deep irony operative on the level of his style. Johan Tralau says simply that 'Carl Schmitt is a master of ambiguity'.[39] Bendersky refers to him as 'this enigmatic thinker'[40] and 'this enigmatic jurist'.[41] The *Oxford Handbook of Carl Schmitt* sees its task as 'locating Schmitt beyond both stigma and enigma'.[42] Schmitt's vertiginous textual power, no less than its political implications, demands a closer reading.

The enigmatic ironies of his texts are not hard to find. Thinkers from both the left and the right show a continuing fascination with his work.[43] The man who openly lamented the demise of the European colonial age[44] is often relied upon by post-colonial theorists.[45] His diaries document lifelong anti-Semitism in spite of intense friendships with, and at times financial dependence upon,

34 Poe (2008), ch 25.
35 Linder (2016), p 157.
36 Teschke (2016), p 389.
37 Schmitt (2017), p 21.
38 Müller (2003), p 91.
39 Tralau (2010), p 435.
40 Bendersky (1988).
41 Bendersky (1987), p 91.
42 Meierhenrich and Simons (2016), p 58.
43 Bargu (2014); Hooker (2009), p 63; Schwab (1992), p 99; Specter (2016), p 58; Wolfe (2004).
44 Schmitt (2003).
45 Koskenniemi (2016), p 607.

Jews.[46] Indeed, his work was held in high esteem by both Walter Benjamin[47] and Jacob Taubes.[48] Furthermore, Schmitt joined the Nazi Party but this did not prevent him from being denounced and almost put in a concentration camp by them, then arrested by the Allies at the end of the war – he only narrowly escaped the Nuremberg trials.[49] He seems strangely malleable – everybody's friend *and* everybody's enemy, to adopt the rough polarity he made famous.[50]

Schmitt's writing is epigrammatic and arresting: 'Sovereign is he who decides the exception', or 'All significant concepts of the modern theory of the state are secularized theological concepts', or 'All political concepts, images, and terms have a polemical meaning' and 'The specific political distinction to which political actions and motives can be reduced is that between friend and enemy'.[51] His use of satire and irony are provocative: 'Humanity is such an abstract idea that even Catholicism appears comprehensible by comparison.'[52] In the course of his implacable critique of liberal internationalism, the same juxtapositions of irony, understatement and oxymoron can be found: 'Humanity as such cannot wage war because it has no enemy, at least not on this planet';[53] 'All modern theories of direct action and the use of force rest more or less consciously on an irrationalist philosophy.'[54] Wit and contempt forever jostled for pre-eminence in his writing. A liberal Pontius Pilate would simply defer the choice between Christ and Barrabas to a committee, he suggested; the liberal dream of a war to end all wars was like 'eating the last cannibal'.[55] These literary manoeuvres are surprising, disorienting and confounding.

Political Romanticism

To better understand Schmitt's complex attitude to the relationship between intention, meaning and responsibility – characterised here in terms of irony – let us turn to *Political Romanticism* (1919), another early work that was published just a year after *The Buribunks*.[56] What makes this book particularly telling is the fact that Schmitt here sets out to diagnose and to skewer not an idea, but a *feeling*. Romanticism is not about particular things, like mountains or monks or

46 Mehring (2014), pp 66, 189; Schmitt (1996).
47 Weber (1992), p 5; Bredekamp (2016).
48 Taubes (2013).
49 Bikundo (2016).
50 Schmitt (2007).
51 Schmitt (2005).
52 Schmitt (2008).
53 Schmitt (2007), p 54.
54 Schmitt (1998).
55 Diken and Laustsen (2004), p 101.
56 Schmitt (1986).

sunsets, he says, because anything can be viewed romantically. Nor can it be associated with a particular politics, since both the revolutionary and the monarchist wrap themselves in its mantle.[57] It is rather a disposition, a way of approaching the world. The romantic is not an object but a subject. What characterises this subject, according to Schmitt, is a 'metaphysical narcissism'.[58] The romantic, he argues, is not interested in rules or judgements or decisions, which attempt to confront the reality of disagreement and conflict, but only in subjective experience, which romanticism elevated to a creative deity. He indulges 'the sphere of irresponsible private feeling'[59] to such an extent that his own response to events serves as his sole criteria for judgement. Action is not done, but felt. The judgement of the romantic is based not on outcomes or morals, but only on the intensity and interest of its emotional states.[60] Conflict or difference are not resolved by decisive action but rather by-passed: the retreat to subjectivity and the retreat to aesthetics are both ways of creating a fantasy of 'aesthetically balanced harmony'.[61] 'Viewed romantically,' as Schmitt puts it – wit and scorn again in equal measure – 'injustice is only a dissonance that is aesthetically resolved in a sacred music, an endless feeling of the higher life'.[62]

Now we turn to the critical relationship between thought and deed. The distancing effect of romantic feeling, according to Schmitt, entirely disables the romantic from taking decisive action in the world. On the one hand, the romantic adopts an *ironic distance* from the world the better to cherish and chart, without ever taking responsibility for, his own feelings in response to it. This irony – key to the Romantic character, he insists – results in a poisonous incapacity to act since it creates an unbridgeable distance between self and world.[63] The courage of commitment, of acknowledging disagreement and accepting the necessity of making decisive and perhaps disagreeable choices through the application of norms or principles, is replaced by a retreat to egotistical feeling. Human activity consists entirely in emotions, not in the application of judgements, evaluations or criticism.[64]

On the other hand, the romantic yearning for some future unity and synthesis replaces all conflict with a vague 'conversation'.[65] 'A class that shifts all political activity onto the plane of conversation in the press and in parliament', wrote Schmitt, 'is no match for social conflict.'[66] He dismissed this

57 Schmitt (1986), pp 2–10.
58 Schmitt (1986), p 139.
59 Schmitt (1986), p 15.
60 See, in particular, Oakes's 'Translator's Introduction' to Schmitt (1986), p xxvi.
61 Schmitt (1986), p 55.
62 Schmitt (1986), p 161.
63 Schmitt (1986), pp 54–6.
64 Schmitt (1986), p 94.
65 Schmitt (1986), p 139.
66 Schmitt (1985), p 59.

'conversation' as simply a way of shirking conflict – 'the enemy of enemies'.[67] 'The essence of liberalism', he wrote, 'is negotiation, a cautious half measure in the hope that the definitive dispute, the decisive bloody battle, can be transformed into a parliamentary debate and permit the decision to be suspended forever in an everlasting discussion.'[68] In the real world, argues Schmitt, enemies must be made and decisions must be taken. But the romantic ultimately retreats to fiction and fantasy, 'without decision, without a final court of appeal, continuing into infinity'.[69] Romanticism, argues Schmitt, is a cult of indeterminacy, since it is only prior to an actual decision that all possibilities remain open. Thus the glorification of primitivism and of childhood[70] – both realms in which human societies on one hand and human beings on the other are marked as 'not yet determined, not yet limited'.[71] For the romantic, that is a kind of untainted perfection. 'Limited reality', by way of contrast, 'is empty, a realized possibility, a decision that has already been made; disenchanted, disillusioned, it has the dull melancholy that a lottery ticket has after the drawing'.[72] If to be human is to choose, the romantic – like *Bartleby the Scrivener* – prefers not to.[73]

Schmitt's diagnosis of irony as the fatal flaw of romanticism is entirely plausible. He was not alone in connecting romanticism to romance and the *roman*, and thus to the role played by fiction and imagination in both rewarding the intensely private feeling of the reader and absorbing without ever confronting all substantive oppositions and differences.[74] M.H. Abrams famously concluded that 'romantic philosophy is thus primarily a metaphysics of integration, of which the key principle is that of the "reconciliation" or synthesis of whatever is divided, opposed and conflicting'.[75] This search for harmony and fusion was both a feature of romantic intellectual life in the work of Coleridge and Wordsworth,[76] and in that of the New Romantics who, in the early years of the twentieth century, turned their backs on the technical and bureaucratic 'separation thesis' or division of powers that characterised modern social life.[77]

Above all, the romantic tradition throughout the nineteenth century sought to resolve conflicts via *transcendence*, the ability of a unique individual to overcome all rules and constraints and thus to carve out a new and higher unity. The genius in Kant or Goethe, Nietzsche's 'Übermensch, or Weber's

67 Dyzenhaus (1997), pp 41–5; Schmitt (1986), p 17.
68 Schmitt (1985), p 63.
69 Schmitt (1986), p 19.
70 Ariès (1979); Plotz (2001).
71 Schmitt (1986), p 69.
72 Schmitt (1986), p 69.
73 Melville (1986), p 1.
74 Miller (1989).
75 Abrams (1971), p 182.
76 Abrams (1971), p 182.
77 Mosse (1964).

charismatic leader are all similar figures. So is Nature and the Artist, one the high priest of the other, in Wordsworth or Shelley or Coleridge or Friedrich.[78] What was sought through these superhuman figures was the attainment of some fantasy world in which human conflict and human choice would be dissolved and unified on a higher plane. The sublime stands against the everyday world and transcends it. New laws, new creations and a new harmony are realised, not by operating within the constraints of work-a-day laws and limits, but rather by an appeal to a wholly unregulated mastery outside them. Schmitt also insists on this point in his characterisation of romanticism. The romantic shies away from the human resolution of definite conflicts, 'constantly escaping from one sphere into another, to the alien "higher" third factor', whose 'higher and true unity' would perfectly satisfy both sides of a problem – a synthesis without remainder, without sacrifice, without violence and without compromise.[79] 'The higher third', he writes, 'is always a way out of the either–or.'[80]

M.H. Abrams terms the Romantics' transcendent impulse the lure of 'natural supernaturalism'. Schmitt dismisses it as nothing but 'subjectified occasionalism'.[81] The term is central to Schmitt's critique of romanticism. By occasionalism he means the theological doctrine that maintains finite beings have no efficient causality of their own; whatever happens in the world comes about only through the continuing intervention of God. On the one hand, this emphasises precisely the transcendent element essential to late romantic thought in particular. They made a choice to purify their thought from the influence of modern civilisation, as Leo Strauss said, and placed their faith in agents of salvation that would transcend the limits of the mundane world.[82]

On the other hand, for the 'occasionalist', an event is not the consequence of an action that leads to a particular result. It is not structured by norms whose applications are predictable causes in the world. An event is rather the vehicle for a feeling to be examined and documented, archived narcissistically and obsessively – exactly the temperament Schmitt set out to satirise fictitiously in *The Buribunks*, and to puncture polemically in *Political Romanticism*.[83] What separates theological occasionalism from its romantic counterpart is that the 'first cause' of this transformative moment ceases to be God or normativity – some firm commitment to right and wrong[84] – and becomes instead nothing but the self-performance of the romantic ego itself. The *occasio* is not realised through responsible action, but through irresponsible creative play.[85]

78 Abrams (1971).
79 Schmitt (1986), pp 87, 145.
80 Schmitt (1986), p 117; Schmitt (1985), pp 54–5.
81 Schmitt (1986), pp 17, 78–108.
82 Strauss (1999), p 371.
83 Schmitt (1986), pp 17–18.
84 Schmitt (1986), p 116.
85 Schmitt (1986), pp 82–5.

Schmitt's *Political Romanticism* is a psycho-portrait, a vitriolic diatribe against the weakness and the perils of a certain character type – an aesthete who does not belong, who has no state, who stands to one side, who cultivates an ironic distance from the conflicts around him, who sees ethical grey areas, who is suspicious of authority, who is devoted to conversation and to the interminable interpretation of texts – futile 'word play'[86] – at the expense of decisive social action. (The name given to this character type among Germany's late romantics was – too often to be a coincidence – The Jew.) Both the romantic's appeal to a transcendental solution *outside* the mundane world, and his ironic refusal of any embodied commitment *within* it, signify two sides of the same coin. Irony, says Schmitt, amounts to a *refusal to take responsibility.*

This makes it all the more shocking that the psycho-portrait that Schmitt paints is his own. Schmitt has been aptly termed a 'reactionary modernist': like Spengler and Junger, or like W.H. Auden, Ezra Pound or D.H. Lawrence, Schmitt responded to the horrors of the war and the instability of the post-war years by turning his back on modernity.[87] But this reactionary modernism was itself simply the last gasp of romanticism. Schmitt's jurisprudence is undoubtedly decisionist: he condemns rules and he glorifies action; he sees in the sovereign the very locus of a decision and a normative force which neither rules nor structures nor discourse can realise. At first blush, this seems exactly the *opposite* of the romantic. But the central feature is that the decision, when and if it comes, is transcendent – it emerges miraculously from *outside* the quotidian world, unpredictable and unconstrained, opposed to all merely human institutions and established social structures. Recall that for Schmitt not only was 'Sovereign is he who decides on the exception',[88] but, 'The exception in jurisprudence is analogous to the miracle in theology.'[89] For Schmitt, the romantic seeks a way out of the iron logic of political reality by appealing to a 'higher third' or transcendent power that would, in the name of History or Absolute Spirit or Nature, accomplish 'the romantic suspension of antitheses by means of another higher factor'.[90] And that is exactly the move – the romantic move – that Schmitt makes in the figure of the sovereign. Schmitt's decisionist philosophy is nothing but the apotheosis of late romanticism. The Sovereign is simply the romantic 'other' – God or Nature or Spirit or Genius – in human guise. If Schmitt dismissed political romanticism as 'the sovereignty of the ego', he substituted for it the *egotism of the sovereign.*

Schmitt's personification of romanticism and his institutionalisation of transcendence sharply differentiate his treatment of sovereignty from that of Walter Benjamin. In 'Critique of Violence', Benjamin acknowledges that Schmitt's

86 Schmitt (1986), p 139.
87 Herf (1984).
88 Schmitt (2005), p 5.
89 Schmitt (2005), p 36.
90 Schmitt (1986), pp 80–8.

ungovernable 'decision' is a necessary implication of 'the curious and at first discouraging experience of the ultimate undecidability of all legal problems'.[91] So Benjamin and Schmitt agree that the exception is endemic to legal decision-making and a logical consequence of the indeterminacy of law. The violence of a free decision, not the passive application of a prior norm, is the necessary predicate of legal judgement. But Benjamin then attempts (perhaps unsuccessfully) to distinguish between different manifestations of violence: first between law-preserving violence and law-making violence – two forms of human power; then between a pure or divine violence outside of the law, which is ecstatic in instead *deposing* the law and thus making real revolution possible. This dream of divine violence finds concrete expression in Benjamin's distinction between the 'proletarian general strike' and the 'political general strike'.[92] While the latter is programmatic and instrumental, the former is not. It annihilates the present in order to open society to an unknowable future. The end of Benjamin's critique reads:

> But all mythic, law-making violence, which we may call 'executive,' is pernicious. Pernicious, too, is the law-preserving, 'administrative' violence that serves it. Divine violence, which is the sign and seal but never the means of sacred dispatch, may be called 'sovereign' violence.[93]

In Benjamin, 'sovereign' is an abstract adjective that describes a certain sort of violence. But Schmitt *literalises* the sovereign; it becomes in his hands a noun – 'he who decides', the sole authorised agent of that violence. By conferring the inevitable violence of decisions beyond the rules on a particular human figure, instrumentalism and political violence become indefeasible. Schmitt's romanticism, his transcendent solution to the problem of indeterminacy, finally reduces everything to human control operating entirely in the interests of the power of the state, whereas Benjamin's transcendence remains irreducible to human control and entirely *outside* the control of the state or the legal order. For Benjamin, Sovereign violence – by being detached from the state – is essentially radical and destabilising. For Schmitt, by being on the contrary yoked to the state, sovereignty essentially becomes reactionary and authoritarian. The sovereign is Schmitt's way of appropriating and taming the Benjaminian divine.

The paradox is that, all protestations to the contrary, Schmitt was at once the most 'political' and the most 'romantic' of legal writers, in his literary style and his appeal to feeling. Indeed, it makes his jurisprudence, more than anything, pre-Raphaelite. The Catholic yearning that underlies his theological works, and that emerges in his metaphor of the 'miracle' in *Political Theology*, betrays a

91 Benjamin (1986), p 293.
92 Benjamin (1986), pp 291–2.
93 Benjamin (1986), p 300.

search for the resuscitation of the mysteries and the emotions that legitimated the pre- and counter-Reformation church.[94] A contempt for liberalism drips from the pages of *The Crisis of Parliamentary Democracy* [95] and comes through in his consistent disdain of 'the chattering classes'.[96] For Schmitt, liberalism and discourse are both cowardly in their avoidance of real, impassioned, winner-takes-all argument. They seek to defuse the intense feeling of political dispute, and remove it instead to the tame and deracinated forum of 'conversation'. At the same time, what is clearest about *The Concept of the Political* is Schmitt's deep anxiety over the instability of government and the indeterminacy of law to which his previous work had drawn our attention. This anxious desire for quietus, for 'total peace … tranquility, security and order'[97] drives Schmitt to extraordinary lengths. And unsurprisingly perhaps, his solution lies precisely in the realm of feeling. In *Political Romanticism,* he castigates Schlegl for arguing that the state ultimately depends on 'feelings of love and fidelity'.[98] Yet in *The Concept of the Political* Schmitt insists on the necessity of one set of feelings – that of hatred for 'the enemy' – in order to instil another set of feelings – that of belonging and fidelity – in members of the nation. On this reading, politics appears as all feeling all the way down: from anxiety and fear, to anger and hatred, and thence to his burning need to revive a collective existence from which all conflict and disagreement have been purged by supreme sovereign will.[99]

The romantics finally did not yearn for the triumph of individual will any more than the triumph of nature. Instead, they yearned for triumph itself – for the visitation of a god-like mastery over the world that would save us from our fallen nature. In that desire and yearning, in that intensely Christian 'pathos of authority', Schmitt undoubtedly partakes. If during the 1930s Schmitt sought 'total peace' through the 'total state',[100] this was his way of governing the riot of emotions within him – the very emotions that in *Political Romanticism* he sought and failed to banish. Schmitt, as is by now notorious, made his peace with the fascist state as early as 1933, with the publication of 'The Fuehrer Leads the Law'. But it was a peace that would come back to haunt him when, arrested and interrogated at the end of the war, he was forced to reflect on and to account for his actions in deeply uncomfortable ways. The results of that process of introspection, such as it was, are to be found in *Ex Captivate Salus.* If Schmitt deploys irony in *Political Romanticism* as a sword, in *Ex Captivate Salus* it becomes his shield.

94 Schmitt (1985), pp 53–66.
95 Schmitt (1998).
96 Schmitt (1985), p 59.
97 Schmitt (2007), p 46.
98 Schmitt (1986), p 113.
99 Balakrishnan (2002); Schmitt (2007); Slomp (2009).
100 Schmitt (1999); Wolin (1990).

Ex Captivitate Salus

Yet irony took two different and opposite forms in modernity. Magnus Zeller's painting *The Orator* (1920),[101] for example, depicts someone very much like Schmitt's 1921 Dictator, his 1922 Sovereign or indeed the 1934 *Führer* who Schmitt argued, 'protects the law'[102] by ignoring it. Zeller's Orator, like them, is a charismatic figure who magnetically draws the rapt and frenzied crowd to him, feeding on their craving for unification and fulfilment. Yet the difference between Zeller's art and Schmitt's jurisprudence is immediately apparent. In *The Orator*, the focus of the picture is the speaker's ecstatic rapture and not, of course, his ideas. In particular, one notes the figure of a boy sitting at the very centre of the painting. He sits at the bottom of the frame gazing up at the orator. His line of sight parallels our own, yet he sits apart from both the crowd and the speaker, an ironic observer of its passions and not a participant. The figure is ironic and distanced from the impassioned action of the crowd, but this irony is by no means an excuse for inaction. On the contrary, irony here serves the purpose of a critique – the real need that the orator satisfies is not that of the crowd but his own craving for adulation.

Mikhail Bakhtin, writing in the 1920s and 1930s, insisted that irony was essential to the modern novel.[103] His understanding of the effects of this distancing is very different from that of Schmitt. By juxtaposing the voices of different characters and discourses in the same frame, including those of the narrator telling the story and the author orchestrating it, there is, argues Bakhtin, a necessary doubleness in the novel. This indirect and doubled speech constantly undercuts any claims to a monologic discourse made by any character within it. Any particular form of speech – particularly that given to characters representing authority, tradition, establishment or power – is consistently being challenged by the voices of others and the multiple discursive frames within which it is set.[104] Irony, argues Bakhtin, *undermines authority*. As Shoshana Felman writes:

> Since irony precisely consists in dragging authority as such into a scene which it cannot master, of which it is not aware and which, for that reason, is the scene of its own self-destruction, literature by virtue of its ironic force, fundamentally deconstructs the fantasy of authority in the same way and for the same reasons that psychoanalysis deconstructs the authority of the fantasy.[105]

101 Zeller, *Der Redner* (*The Orator*), 1920, oil on canvas, 152.4 × 198.12 cm, Los Angeles County Museum of Art, Los Angeles, CA.
102 Schmitt (1934), pp 945–50.
103 Bakhtin (1981).
104 Bakhtin (1981); Holquist (1990).
105 Felman (1977), p 8.

The role of irony, then, is necessarily as a foil to law's demands for finality, certainty and obedience. Irony, on this view, is 'a structure of failed resolution ... an imperfect form of closure, an imperfect form of justification'.[106] This unsettling power reveals the *impossibility* of all projects of transcendence, perfection and closure.

We might call this critical distance *echt* – authentic or modern – irony. But while Schmitt condemns the political perils of irony, he nonetheless uses it himself as a tactic of dissimulation and irresponsibility (let us call this move *ersatz* – false or romantic – irony). In jest at the end of World War I in *The Buribunks*, but in deadly earnest at the end of World War II in *Ex Captivitate Salus*, Schmitt instinctively retreated to this self-defensive position. Schmitt was initially arrested by the Russians in Berlin in April 1945, interrogated and then released.[107] Subsequently, in September 1945, he was arrested by the Americans and interned until March of 1947, during which period they brought him to Nuremberg as a potential defendant in the ongoing international criminal trials.[108] This was with a view to investigating his alleged participation either directly or indirectly in 'the planning of wars of aggression, of war crimes and of crimes against humanity' by providing their 'ideological foundation'.[109]

Ex Captivitate Salus is the title of the prison writings Schmitt wrote during this period, collected and then translated in a small volume, not all of which presently concerns us.[110] *Ex Captivitate Salus,* written in the summer of 1946, is also the title of an essay of the same name published as part of that volume, in which Schmitt said, 'I have spoken of myself here, actually for the first time in my life.'[111] He goes on to say that:

> What I say here is intended neither as a form of journalism nor as an apology ... I speak because I want to send word to a few deceased friends, while I, for one, am still in the clutches of this earthly life; because I want to give a sign to some living friends from whom I am separated and to loyal students in all countries; and, finally, because I think of my daughter Anima and my godchild Carl Alexander. Speaking with them violates no secret [*arcanum*]. We are all bound together by the stillness of silence and the inalienable secret of the godly origins of humanity.[112]

'Conversation with Eduard Spranger', collected in the same volume, was written in 'Summer 1945'. It was therefore written a year earlier than *Ex captivitate salus*. It provides us with a good idea as to why Schmitt at this moment

106 Dimock (1996), p 176.
107 Bendersky (1987), p 91.
108 Bendersky (1987), p 91.
109 Schmitt (1987), p 98.
110 Schmitt (2017), p 21.
111 Schmitt (2017).
112 Schmitt (2017), pp 61–2.

and 'for the first time in his life' should have tried to speak for himself. It also provided the occasion for Schmitt to defensively rely on irony. Eduard Spranger, 'the German philosopher and pedagogue'[113] who Schmitt had even cited in *Concept of the Political*, [114] was no less than the interrogator hired by the Americans to determine whether or not he should stand trial:

> Who are you? *Tu qui es?* This is the unfathomable question. I plunged into it at the end of June 1945 as Eduard Spranger the famous philosopher and teacher, awaited my response to a questionnaire.[115] On this occasion he told me that my lectures were extremely spirited but that I myself – my personality and my essence – remained opaque. That was a serious accusation, which meant that: what you think and say may be interesting and clear; but what you are, yourself, your essence is murky and unclear.
>
> ...
>
> I looked at my interrogator and thought: Who are you, in fact, to question me? Whence your superiority? What is the essence of power that empowers and emboldens you to pose such questions to me – questions that are intended to challenge me and thus are, in their final effect, only snares and traps?
>
> ... Nevertheless I still prefer to be a defendant rather than a prosecutor ...
>
> To me, the prosecutorial is even more sinister than the inquisitorial. Perhaps in my case this can be traced back to theological roots. For Diabolus means 'the prosecutor' [the translator notes that the word for 'devil' in Hebrew shares the same root with the word for 'prosecutor'].[116]

Schmitt's response to this intense questioning concerning his wartime responsibility for German expansionist policy, his precise role in the National Socialist Party establishment and state and 'the Jewish Question'[117] had two elements. First, he argued that he had to accommodate a tyrannical regime because any order is better than disorder; second, that he had to utter many untruths in order to survive an authoritarian regime:[118]

> The mind has its pride, its tactics, its ineluctable freedom, and, if you excuse the expression, even its guardian angel, and it has all this not merely in migration but also inwardly, even in the claws of Leviathan itself. In Europe, the mind has known until now how to find its crypts and

113 Ulmen (1984), p 201.
114 Schmitt (2007), p 59.
115 Schmitt answered more than one questionnaire: see Schmitt (1987).
116 Schmitt (2017), p 14.
117 Bendersky (1983), pp 268–72; Bendersky (1987), pp 91–6.
118 Schmitt (2017), p 6.

> catacombs, its new methods and forms. *Tyrannum licet decipere* ['one is allowed to deceive a tyrant'].[119]

Schmitt goes on to add:

> The silent tried-and-tested tradition of withdrawal to a private interiority subsisted, along with a great readiness for conscientious cooperation with whatever the current legal government mandated.[120]

Both these responses have the air of explaining away or justifying evil. They appear too ingenuous by half.

Schmitt's attempts to excuse his actions during the National Socialist era fundamentally rely on irony, on establishing a distance between the outward actions he took and the words he uttered on the one hand, and the inward or secret reservations by which he refuses to take responsibility for them on the other:

> The mind and intelligence put forward multiple forms of politeness, correctness, and irony, and ultimately their silence, against the clamour of public activity. A judgment regarding achievements in such a situation can thus not simply be passed from the outside. The person judging must remain aware of a few basic sociological truths, above all things regarding the eternal link between protection and obedience.
>
> A researcher and scholar cannot select the political regime according to his wishes either. In general he accepts it initially as a loyal citizen, like every other person.[121]

Schmitt goes on to emphasise the impossibility of external judgment in this regard:

> The duty to unleash a civil war, to conduct sabotage, and to become a martyr has its limits. Here on should grant something to the victims of such situations and should not be allowed to judge only from the outside.[122]

I spoke the words, argued Schmitt, but I didn't mean them; I kept my distance from them; I maintained my irony and thereby my dignity.

Drawing out this theme in his own work, Agamben engages explicitly with Yan Thomas, Carl Schmitt and Hans Kelsen in order to uncover 'the bond that

119 Schmitt (2017), p 18.
120 Schmitt (2017), p 20.
121 Schmitt (2017), p 21.
122 Schmitt (2017), p 22.

ties agents to their action'.[123] Agamben, like Schmitt before him, understands the essence of politics as theodicy – an inevitable descent into violence, inevitably a way of justifying evil.[124] Perhaps the Great War forced this tragic perspective on everyone, for Weber had asked much the same question: 'Can the ethical demands made on politics really be quite indifferent to the fact that politics operates with a highly specific means, namely, power behind which *violence* lies concealed?'[125] Unsurprisingly, excerpts from *Political Theology* were published in 1923 in a volume dedicated to Weber's life and work.[126] Indeed, Schmitt attended both of his famous *Vocation* lectures.[127] For Weber, the Sermon on the Mount – 'resist not him that is evil with violence' – provides no answer to the problem. He concludes with the startling observation that 'the politician must abide by the *opposite* commandment: "You shall use force to resist evil, for otherwise you will be *responsible* for its running amok"'.[128] Weber arrives at this conclusion by distinguishing an ethic of responsibility from an ethic of conviction. Schmitt's irony lies precisely in his purported willingness to protect his real convictions by keeping them secret, and in the process abjuring any public responsibility to act. His convictions he preserved inviolate, but at the price of his inaction – or so he said.

Conclusion

Political Romanticism serves as the sub-text that reveals the very aspect of Schmitt's thought that he most wanted to banish from it, and to nevertheless illuminate the role it played in his writing and his life – a role made painfully clear in the exculpatory rhetoric he developed in *Ex Captivitate Salus*. Reading *Political Romanticism*, against the grain or deconstructively as it were – as a text that defines Schmitt's political position through his heated denial of it – allows us to observe the structural, metaphorical and aesthetic traces it left in his work. In fact, Schmitt marks the critical distinction between *echt* and *ersatz* irony himself, noting that romantic irony is 'essentially the intellectual expedient of the subject that keeps its distance from objectivity', while at the same time observing that any *self*-irony would be thoroughly unromantic, since it would undo the sovereignty and narcissism of the romantic ego.[129] As he showed already in *The Buribunks*, it is possible to relentlessly document and archive oneself without ever developing any insight.

Indeed, *Political Romanticism* tragically foreshadows Schmitt's own trajectory during the 1920s and 1930s. He argues that the desire for a world beyond the

123 Agamben (2018), p 9.
124 Agamben (2018), p 22.
125 Weber et al. (2004), p 81.
126 Balakrishnan (2002), p 101.
127 Balakrishnan (2002), p 101.
128 Weber et al. (2004), p 83.
129 Schmitt (1986), pp xxii, 72–3.

world, for a perfect resolution to human conflict and social pluralism, to a 'higher third' judged by strong feeling, leads the romantic to a place of acute political vulnerability. Romantic irony invites an ideological 'plasticity'.[130] If politics is only the occasion for an aesthetic experience, romanticism can happily accommodate itself to whatever is the active political tendency of the time. The political romantic 'unconsciously submits to the strongest and most proximate power'.[131] At its heart, romanticism nurses a 'lack of inner resistance to the most powerful and immediate impression that happens to prevail at the time'.[132]

The critique is devastating for its apparent lack of self-consciousness. Everyone is familiar with the first sentence of *Political Theology*. But perhaps the last sentence of *Political Romanticism* will equally repay our attention:

> Everything that is romantic is at the disposal of other energies that are unromantic, and the sublime elevation above definition and decision is transformed into a subservient attendance upon alien power and alien decision.[133]

The irony is that, in prophesying the terrible fate of political romanticism in the twentieth century, Schmitt wrote his own epigraph.

References

M.H. Abrams (1971) *Natural Supernaturalism*, W.W. Norton.

Giorgio Agamben (2005) *State of Exception* (trans. K. Attell), University of Chicago Press.

Giorgio Agamben (2018) *Karman: A Brief Treatise on Action, Guilt, and Gesture*, Stanford University Press.

Johannes Anderegg (2006) 'Unrecognized Modernity: Intertextuality and Irony in Goethe's "Faust"' 39(1) *Colloquia Germanica Themenheft: Goethe* 31.

Philippe Ariès (1979) *Centuries of Childhood*, Penguin.

Mikhail Bakhtin (1981) *The Dialogic Imagination: Four Essays* (trans. C. Emerson and M. Holquist), University of Texas Press.

Banu Bargu (2014) 'The Predicaments of Left-Schmittianism' 113(4) *The South Atlantic Quarterly* 713.

Gopal Balakrishnan (2002) *The Enemy: An Intellectual Portrait of Carl Schmitt*, Verso.

Joseph W. Bendersky (1983) *Carl Schmitt: Theorist for the Reich*, Princeton University Press.

Joseph W. Bendersky (1987) 'Carl Schmitt at Nuremberg' 72 *Telos* 91.

Joseph W. Bendersky (1988) 'Carl Schmitt as *Occasio*', in K. Hansen and H. Lietzmann (eds), *Carl Schmitt und die Liberalismuskritik*, Leske & Budrich, 225.

130 Schmitt (1986), pp xxv, 158–62.
131 Schmitt (1986), p 162.
132 Schmitt (1986), p 51.
133 Schmitt (1986), p 162.

Walter Benjamin (1920) 'Zur Kritik der Gewalt' 47 *Archiv für Sozialwissenschaft und Sozialpolitik* 809.
Walter Benjamin (1986) 'Critique of Violence', in *Reflections* (trans. Edmund Jephcott), Schocken Books, 13.
Edwin Bikundo (2016) 'Carl Schmitt as a Subject and Object of International Criminal Law: Ethical Judgment in Extremis' 16(2) *The International Criminal Law Review* 216.
Horst Bredekamp (2016) 'Walter Benjamin's Esteem for Carl Schmitt', in J. Meierhenrich and O. Simons (eds), *The Oxford Handbook of Carl Schmitt*, Oxford University Press, 679.
R.H. Collingwood (2008a) 'Truth and Contradiction', in R. Murphy (ed), *Collingwood and the Crisis of Western Civilisation*, Imprint Academic, n.p.
R.H. Collingwood (2008b) 'What "Civilisation" Means', in R. Murphy (ed), *Collingwood and the Crisis of Western Civilization*, Imprint Academic, n.p.
P. Delany (1979) *D.H. Lawrence's Nightmare*, Harvester Press.
Bülent Diken and Carsten Bagge Laustsen (2004) '7–11, 9/11, and Post-politics' 29(1) *Alternatives: Global, Local, Political* 89.
Wai Chee Dimock (1996) *Residues of Justice: Literature, Law, Philosophy*, University of California Press.
David Dyzenhaus (1997) *Legality and Legitimacy: Carl Schmitt, Hans Kelsen and Hermann Heller in Weimar*, Oxford University Press.
T.S. Eliot (1963 [1922]) 'The Wasteland', in *Collected Poems*, Harcourt Brace.
Shoshana Felman (1977) 'To Open the Question' 55/56 *Yale French Studies* 5.
Peter Fitzpatrick (2001) *Modernism and the Grounds of Law*, Cambridge University Press.
E.M. Forster (2000 [1924]) *A Passage to India*, Folio Society.
Sigmund Freud (1999 [1913]) *Totem and Taboo*, Routledge.
Jeffrey Herf (1984) *Reactionary Modernism: Technology, Culture and Politics in Weimar and the Third Reich*, Cambridge University Press.
Michael Holquist (1990) *Dialogism*, Routledge.
William Hooker (2009) *Carl Schmitt's International Thought: Order and Orientation*, Cambridge University Press.
Clemens Jabloner (1998) 'Kelsen and his Circle: The Viennese Years' 9 *European Journal of International Law* 368.
Hans Kelsen (1920) *Das Problem der Souveranitaat und die Theorie des Volkerrechts*, Mohr-Siebeck.
Hans Kelsen (1924) 'The Conception of the State and Social Psychology – with Special Reference to Freud's Group Theory' 5 *International Journal of Psycho-Analysis* 1.
Ellen Kennedy (2004) *Constitutional Failure: Carl Schmitt in Weimar*, Duke University Press.
Friedrich A. Kittler (1999) *Gramophone, Film, Typewriter*, Stanford University Press.
Martti Koskenniemi (2016) 'Carl Schmitt and International Law', in Jens Meierhenrich and Oliver Simons (eds), *The Oxford Handbook of Carl Schmitt*, Oxford University Press, 592.
D.H. Lawrence (1915) 'D.H. Lawrence to Lady Ottoline Morrell' [9 September], in J. Boulton (ed), *Selected Letters*, One World Classics, 105.
Christian Linder (2016) 'Carl Schmitt in Plettenberg', in Jens Meierhenrich and Oliver Simons (eds), *The Oxford Handbook of Carl Schmitt*, Oxford University Press, 147.
M.G. Losano (1977) 'I rapporti tra Kelsen e Freud' 1 *Sociologia del Diritto* 142.
Reinhard Mehring (2014) *Carl Schmitt: A Biography*, Polity Press.

Jens Meierhenrich and Oliver Simons (2016) '"A Fanatic of Order in an Epoch of Confusing Turmoil": The Political, Legal, and Cultural Thought of Carl Schmitt', in Jens Meierhenrich and Oliver Simons (eds), *The Oxford Handbook of Carl Schmitt*, Oxford University Press, 3.

Herman Melville (1986) *Billy Budd, Sailor and Other Stories*, Penguin.

David Miller (1989) *The Novel and the Police*, University of California Press.

George Mosse (1964) *The Crisis of German Ideology: Intellectual Origins of the Third Reich*, Grosset and Dunlap.

Jan-Werner Müller (2003) *A Dangerous mind: Carl Schmitt in Post-war European Thought*, Yale University Press.

Philip Payne, Graham Bartram and Galin Tikhanov (eds) (2007) *A Companion to the Works of Robert Musil*, Camden House.

Judith Plotz (2001) *Romanticism and the Vocation of Childhood*, Palgrave.

Edgar Allen Poe (2008) *Tales of Mystery and Imagination*, Dover.

W.E. Scheuerman (1999) *Carl Schmitt: The End of Law*, Rowman & Littlefield.

Carl Schmitt (1918) 'Die Buribunken' 1(4) *Summa* 89.

Carl Schmitt (1921) *Die Diktatur: Von den Anf¨angen des modernen Souver¨ anit¨ atsgedankens bis zum proletarischen Klassenkampf*, Munich & Leipzig.

Carl Schmitt (1934) 'Der Führer schützt das Recht [The Leader Protects the Law]' *Zur Reichstagsrede Adolf Hitlers* 945.

Carl Schmitt (1985 [1922]) *Political Theology: Four Chapters on the Concept of Sovereignty* (trans George Schwab), MIT Press.

Carl Schmitt (1986 [1919]) *Political Romanticism* (trans G. Oakes), MIT Press.

Carl Schmitt (1987) 'Interrogation of Carl Schmitt by Robert Kempner (I)' 72 *Telos* 97.

Carl Schmitt (1996) *The Leviathan in the State Theory of Thomas Hobbes: Meaning and Failure of a Political Symbol*, Greenwood Press.

Carl Schmitt (1998 [1926]) *The Crisis of Parliamentary Democracy*, MIT Press.

Carl Schmitt (1999) *Four Articles, 1931–1938* (trans. S. Draghici), Plutarch Press.

Carl Schmitt (2003 [1950]) *The Nomos of the Earth in the International Law of the Jus Publicum Europaeum*, Telos Press.

Carl Schmitt (2005 [1927]) *Political Theology: Four Chapters on the Concept of Sovereignty*, University of Chicago Press.

Carl Schmitt (2007 [1927]) *The Concept of the Political* (trans. George Schwab), University of Chicago Press.

Carl Schmitt (2008) *Roman Catholicism and Political Form*, University of Chicago Press.

Carl Schmitt (2012 [1921]) *Dictatorship*, Polity Press.

Carl Schmitt (2015) *Dialogues on Power and Space*, Polity Press.

Carl Schmitt (2017) *Ex Captivitate Salus: Experiences, 1945–47*, Polity Press.

George Schwab (1992) 'Carl Schmitt Hysteria in the US: The Case of Bill Scheuerman' 91 *Telos* 99.

Ellis Shookman (2009) 'Goethe's Baccalaureus and the Concept of Romantic Irony in Faust' 20(4) *European Romantic Review* 491.

Georg Simmel (1968) *The Conflict of Modern Culture and Other Essays* (trans K.P. Etzkorn), Teachers College.

Gabriella Slomp (2009) *Carl Schmitt and the Politics of Hostility*, Palgrave Macmillan.

Matthew G. Specter (2016) 'What's "Left" in Schmitt? From Aversion to Appropriation in Contemporary Political Theory', in Jens Meierhenrich and Oliver Simons (eds), *The Oxford Handbook of Carl Schmitt*, Oxford University Press, 426.

Leo Strauss (1999 [1941]) 'On German Nihilism' 26 *Interpretation* 353.

Jacob Taubes (2013) *To Carl Schmitt: Letters and Reflections*, Columbia University Press.

Benno Teschke (2016), 'Carl Schmitt's Concepts of War', in Jens Meierhenrich and Oliver Simons (eds), *The Oxford Handbook of Carl Schmitt*, Oxford University Press, 367.

Johan Tralau (2010) 'Order, the Ocean, and Satan: Schmitt's Hobbes, National Socialism, & the Enigmatic Ambiguity of Friend and Foe' 13(2–3) *Critical Review of International Social and Political Philosophy* 435.

Kieran Tranter (2019) 'Die Buribunken as Science Fiction: The Self and Informational Existence' 28 *Griffith Law Review* 118.

Gary Ulmen (1984) 'Book Review: Joseph W Bendersky, Carl Schmitt: Theorist for the Reich' 59 *Telos* 210.

Anton Warde (1975) 'Goethe, Schiller, Faust, and the Ideal: The Genesis of Irony in Faust' 48(2) *The German Quarterly* 175.

Max Weber (1958 [1920]) *The Protestant Ethic and the Spirit of Capitalism* (trans Talcott Parsons), Scribner.

Max Weber, David S. Owen, Tracy B. Strong and Rodney Livingstone (2004) *The Vocation Lectures*, Hackett.

Samuel Weber (1992) 'Taking Exception to Decision: Walter Benjamin and Carl Schmitt' 22(3/4) *Diacritics* 5.

Alan Wolfe (2004) 'A Fascist Philosopher Helps Us Understand Contemporary Politics' *The Chronicle of Higher Education*, 2 April.

Richard Wolin (1990) 'Carl Schmitt, Political Existentialism and the Total State' 19 *Theory and Society* 389.

Chapter 16

Imagined facts, actual enemies

The Buribunks and the political

Attila Gyulai

Introduction

In March 1951, Carl Schmitt, the keen diarist, recorded the following aphoristic fragment in his *Glossarium*: 'So, what remains? Friend and enemy. It is their distinction that remains. Distinguo ergo sum.'[1] Whose self-definition is this? For readers of Schmitt's works, it should be evident that decades after its first appearance, the non-Cartesian figure of the sovereign is declared once again as the ultimate source of authority. According to *The Concept of the Political*, the distinction that explains and – buribunkologically – proves being is formal and existential at the same time; it offers a criterion for the political but – precisely because the distinction is already political – with the same conceptual stroke it points to the enemies of the political who would deny the importance, unavoidability and the rightness of making distinctions.[2] The enemies of the political hide behind many different masks: liberals, pacifists, romantics, positivists and, in Schmitt's 1918 essay, the Buribunks.[3]

Rather than distinctions, the Buribunks define themselves by a series of identifications: 'I think, therefore I am; I speak, therefore I am; I write, therefore I am; I publish, therefore I am.'[4] From thinking to publishing, a typical and ideal Buribunk, the hero of Schmitt's satirical essay keeps a diary to record every moment of their life. A Buribunk does not live to keep a diary but keeps a diary to live. Life becomes experience only through recording. The diaries, then, are collected and catalogued by other Buribunks, who subsequently record this activity in their own diaries, also dissolving themselves in an archive of diary records. Buribunks thus live in a self-written and self-enclosed society, achieving a complete but impersonal unity. How does this make a Buribunk an enemy of the political?

1 Schmitt (1991), p 314.
2 Schmitt (2007), pp 26–7.
3 For a summary of the different attempts to explain the origin and the meaning of the word 'Buribunk', see Heidenreich (2005), p 143; Tommissen (1997), pp 24–8.
4 Chapter 2 of this volume, p 25.

DOI: 10.4324/9781003091066-20

To address this question, this chapter reads Schmitt's *The Buribunks* as a link between the early legal texts and his later works, moving closer to political theory. As will be argued, this fictional text is not a detour isolated among Schmitt's theoretical and scholarly projects; in the case of Schmitt, genre boundaries are permeable. For Schmitt, fiction is a not a problem to be avoided, but one to be taken seriously. Thus, literature, literary criticism or satire should not be disregarded when it comes to Schmitt's theoretical position. To understand Schmitt and, more specifically, the theoretical relevance of the essay, it is important to note that fiction and the fictive are not only accidental in his thought but fulfil a constitutive role.[5] The importance of the essay lies in the interplay between fictional form and political content.

Schmitt's essay presents a rhetorically strong challenge to the neo-Kantian and positivist intellectual and juridical context of the late Wilhelmian and early Weimar period in Germany. The text does not deal with juridical theory or practice directly; furthermore, its sparse legal or political terminology is curiously non-Schmittian. Still, it is not difficult to recognise the debates of the age in the satire. Although there is no consensus in the literature about exactly when and to what extent Schmitt did distance himself from positivist jurisprudence, the essay forcefully demonstrates his objections against positivist self-sufficiency and self-enclosedness. On the most abstract level, by adopting an ironic reversal, the text argues against a self-enclosed configuration of patterns determined solely by the internal relations of its elements without any external intervention.

In this chapter, I will discuss this short text from the viewpoint of political theory and not of jurisprudence – even if, especially in case of Schmitt, they are deeply interlocked. I am interested in how *The Buribunks* addresses problems of the nature of the political and, more precisely, how the text links Schmitt's earliest writings with his more mature understanding of politics. From this perspective, it will be seen that the Buribunks are the enemies of the political who attempt to eliminate authoritative sources of order as well as any kind of political contingency and conflict.

Fictions of factuality

Although Carl Schmitt's approach to the judicial understanding of the state had changed fundamentally by the end of World War I,[6] he recurrently addressed

5 Kennedy (1988), p 234; Kennedy (2004), p 43.

6 Schmitt's position against legal positivism (and neo-Kantianism) is far from unambiguous. It might be argued that, despite the criticism, his works retain strong ties to the positivist tradition as Seitzer and Thornhill (2008), p 14 write; however, Rogers (2016) argues that Schmitt's wartime writings in the early 1910s indicate a substantive transformation in this regard. Reinhard Mehring (2014) shows how Schmitt's tactics against legal positivist in German academia, and in particular Heidelberg, resulted in a distinction between positivism and normativism implying

the limitations of a closed judicial conception of the state from the early 1910s. His early legal scholarship focused on the inner tensions of positivist theory and introduced later key issues such as decision, the non-identity of the legal system and the state, but also the concept of exception, which not only subverts a closed system of norms but also serves as the non-stabilisable foundation of a legal, political or historical order.[7] It is in this context that the Buribunks and their scientific enterprise buribunkology emerge.

Although buribunkology, the fictive science described in the essay is not an explicit legal theory; rather, it constitutes the political system of the Buribunks in the same way as positivism is claimed to validate the conception of a closed and self-sufficient legal system that substantiates the idea of the *Rechtstaat*. Buribunkology, however, is not explicitly based on the relationship between legal measures and jurisprudence, but instead between diary-keeping and its scientific elaboration. Buribunkology is the science of facts, namely the diary records that objectify the living of the Buribunks, but buribunkology is itself a fact to be processed in a buribunkological manner.[8] Buribunkology is not merely the outcome of Buribunks' activity; it is buribunkology that constitutes the Buribunks. To prove the existence of Buribunks, it is enough to refer to the fact of buribunkology; since it exists, develops and flourishes, the question of the existence of the Buribunks is simply presupposed.[9] Self-referentiality thus plays a defining role not only on the level of the individual Buribunk and obligatory self-recording, but also on the conceptual level, which in turn becomes the source of regulation and normativity. The progress of buribunkology becomes completed when, with Schnekke, this self-referentiality becomes gapless and spotless,[10] and the series of identifications that define the activity of Buribunks achieves the level of self-enclosedness. At this point, facts become self-originating and, rather paradoxically, independent from any factual foundations. In other words, facts become fictions.

The problem of fictionality entered Schmitt's thinking well before the *Buribunken* essay. The influence of Hans Vaihinger's philosophy of 'as if' on German legal scholarship and Schmitt in the 1910s is well known. In a short review published in 1913, Schmitt recommended Vaihinger to legal scholars due to his understanding of fiction based on its epistemological usefulness instead of its proximity to reality.[11] Although this conception of fiction kept links to neo-Kantian and even positivist thinking,[12] in Schmitt it offered a way

a possible – temporal – alliance with the former to attack the latter represented foremost by Hans Kelsen.

7 Schmitt (1914, 1917, 1969). For a thorough analysis of these writings, see Hofmann (2010).
8 Chapter 2 of this volume, p 12, 23.
9 Chapter 2 of this volume, p 12.
10 Chapter 2 of this volume, p 22.
11 Schmitt (2017).
12 Thornhill (2007), pp 194, 262; Kennedy (2004), pp 65–8.

out of self-enclosedness and eventually helped to disrupt the seeming internal coherence of jurisdiction and jurisprudence, thereby moving towards the problems of politics, the necessity of external foundations, decision and sovereignty.

According to Vaihinger, fictionality means that knowledge is based on rhetorical tropes, which cannot be grounded or substantiated, yet its 'as if' mode of functioning can still become meaningful. The literary theorist Wolfgang Iser, commenting on Vaihinger's concept of fiction, emphasised that it should be understood as an analogy inasmuch as it acknowledges the impossibility to grasp reality; however, at the same time it also rejects this impossibility of shifting focus from knowledge to production and positing by invoking 'as if'.[13] Thus, fiction should not be understood in Schmitt as a genre or a mode of writing, but as general critique of foundations that are simultaneously impossible and necessary. Fictionality, then, achieved in Schmitt a more profound language-theoretical role, which at the same time points towards an understanding of politics that cannot be contained by a self-enclosed sphere. In his *Der Wert des Staates und die Bedeutung des Einzelnen*, first published in 1914, Schmitt turns once again to the problem of *Rechtsverwirklichung*, the question of how right can be realised under actual circumstances. Just as in *Gesetz und Urteil* two years earlier, in this book the main presuppositions are still neo-Kantian inasmuch as right is claimed to be independent from facts;[14] however, the conclusions foreshadow Schmitt's later anti-Kantian and definitely anti-positivist stance. While *Gesetz und Urteil* introduced the concept of non-deducible decision, in the *Der Wert des Staates* the concept of sovereignty is explained alongside a theological analogy.[15] In the latter work, right retains its ideal origins and the state is linked to the actual; its purpose is to translate the ideal onto the level of the actual, therefore its meaning cannot be understood along universal or generalised concepts. However, this does not just pertain to the concept of the state; it is about the concept of concept in general. Language, writes Schmitt here, is not a mere fact just like any other. Words and concepts do not necessarily overlap because words are surrounded by a 'confusing swirl of associations'.[16] Words, as Thomas Schestag put it when commenting on Schmitt's remarks, are tropes and language is characterised by a tropological factuality.[17] Concepts are not facts, but fictions – which is not an accidental characteristic, but rather their paradigmatic feature.[18] It is a step further from

13 Vaihinger (1922), pp 39–40; Iser (1993), p 147.
14 Kiefer (1990), p 484.
15 Schmitt (1914), p 55.
16 Schmitt (1914), pp 41–2.
17 Schestag (2007), p 545.
18 Several decades later, discussing the rhetorical nature of the language of literature, Paul de Man invoked a remarkably similar metaphor: 'Rhetoric radically suspends logic and opens up vertiginous possibilities of referential aberration. And although it would perhaps be somewhat more remote from common usage, I would not

Vaihinger's useful fictions, and the swirl that has just been opened up is the place where a few years later the concept of the political would take place.

As Vaihinger's concept of fiction contributed to Schmitt's thinking in questioning the correspondence model of language and truth and doing away with factual foundations, the same logic pervaded his early legal theory. Extending its role already in *Gesetz und Urteil*, the concept of judicial decision later became a model for political action where correspondence and positivist self-sufficiency were replaced by a systematic difference, an opening up of any system that claimed to be closed off by factual correspondence. Furthermore, by radicalising the logic of 'as if' into a swirling association of tropes, the logic of fictionality is what leads from Schmitt's early understanding of sovereignty in his *Der Wert des Staates* to *Political Theology* almost a decade later. Already in the 1910s, the concepts of decision and sovereignty imply that order is grounded and disrupted at the same time by the same agent.

In the context of *The Buribunks* and its criticism of positivism, these insights also mean the opening up of any self-enclosed and self-referential system that assumes to be founded on gapless conceptual facts. Factuality is not criticised merely in the name of a non-factual paradigm, but it is shaken from the inside as it turns out that, eventually, the foundation of any fact-based understanding leads us back to non-deducible fictions. It is language as such that does not allow self-enclosedness to stabilise itself. Thus, when Schmitt conceived of buribunkology as the self-referential science of factuality, it should be kept in mind that he wanted to show that any identification between a Buribunk person and a Buribunk diary – or, in general, the Buribunks and buribunkology – is, from the outset, doomed to fail.

Fictional authors and factual utopias

Schmitt's *The Buribunks* is a fictional text about a factual utopia. Its fictional narrative aims at displacing the self-enclosed logic of utopian positivism. It tells us about a completed positivist social arrangement, a fact-worshipping community of diarists. The fact that it is likened to a religion – moreover, that it assumes 'a form of contemporary religiosity'[19] – reveals that the narrative is obviously ironic and that the tropological nature of the text takes precedence over its content.

Fact and fiction are curiously intertwined within and by the text. First, it is a fact that there is an essay titled *The Buribunks*. It is, however, only a fiction that there is a scientific-social enterprise that is called buribunkology. Yet, inasmuch as the essay is a satire and a critique of positivism, Buribunks are rather real; the satire posits that Buribunks exist. The word 'Buribunk' is a polemical and

hesitate to equate the rhetorical, figural potentiality of language with literature itself.' See de Man (1979), p 10.

19 Chapter 2 of this volume, p 21.

therefore a political concept which, as Schmitt put it almost a decade later, is 'incomprehensible if one does not know exactly who is to be affected, combated, refuted, or negated by such a term'.[20] The reader might know for sure who is being targeted here. Buribunkology is strictly based on a positivist understanding of factuality, while fiction, understood as opposed to factuality, is strictly barred from anything that has to do with the Buribunks. Factuality is thus represented by fiction, although the status of this fiction is factual since representation was brought about by the fact of the essay published in the last volume of the short-lived journal titled *Summa*. If buribunkology is real, it is created by a factual act of writing about Buribunks. Facts are ironically created by fiction, which in turn is rooted in a fact. This intertwining of fact and fiction does not mean that Schmitt is just playing with circularity or pointing to regression; rather, it concerns the very problem of positivist jurisprudence, which claims to settle this ambiguity not by looking for a stabilising external source, but by closing off the legal system from every external intervention and, thus, according to Schmitt returning to the criticism of positivism in 1950, rendering it defenceless against the 'existential crises resulting from the split of law into legality and legitimacy'.[21] Therefore, fictionality rooted in facts and facts originating in fiction concern both the need for political foundations and their impossibility. Self-enclosed political or legal systems are delusive since, although they claim the opposite, they require foundations – even if, in the context of modernity and secularisation, these foundations are necessarily fictitious; as might be clear from the section above, this does not imply a rejection of, or a distancing from, reality.

As seen, form and content obviously contradict each other in this pseudo-scientific essay that, adopting a laudatory tone, aims at giving an account of the state and the progress of buribunkology.[22] There does, however, seem to be a barely concealed message in the fact that Schmitt already questions his fictional heroes at the outset. Within the essay, the Buribunks live in a perfectly self-enclosed society, while their historical, theoretical and ethical achievements are contained and closed in a wider frame of a fictitious narrative. Merely the possibility of narrating buribunkology displaces the very principles by which they wish and are expected to live. Writing has two different meanings here. While the Buribunks live to write but, more importantly, write to live in a 'permanent textualisation'[23] to accomplish the perfect unity of self and

20 Schmitt (2007), p 31.
21 Schmitt (1990), p 63.
22 In this regard, *The Buribunks* essay might be read as the direct counterpart of Schmitt's *Die Lage der europäischen Rechtswissenschaft* and the likewise seemingly ascertaining text about parliamentary government and democracy titled *Die geistesgeschichtliche Lage des heutigen Parlamentarismus*. Neither of these writings conceals that when facts are settled and *die Lage* is ascertained, conceptual swirling means political differentiation.
23 Schmitz (2016), p 708.

narration, the objectification of this union necessarily lags behind the desired level of progress. Writing implies acting within the society of the Buribunks. However, telling their history sets the historian out of buribunkology. Precisely by writing the history of the Buribunks, C.S., the historian, distances himself from the praised object. Objectification thus becomes a problem for the strict factuality of buribunkology. Assuming that a Buribunk worthy of this name cannot retain Buribunk-identity and relate this identity at the same time, since this latter move should be also conducted buribunkologically, the form either becomes self-refuting or cannot help but acknowledge the possibility of an extra-buribunkological viewpoint among the Buribunks. However, from this it follows that buribunkological perfection is beyond the reach of those who are not already Buribunks themselves. Of course, this divide between inside and outside is in line with the positivist position Schmitt aims at criticising. It is analogous to the distinction between the positivism of domestic law and international treaties that Schmitt addressed three decades later, surveying the state of European jurisprudence.[24] So fiction, for Schmitt in *The Buribunks*, means the first level of expressing theoretical and political disagreement. Merely by writing his essay, Schmitt had already repoliticised the Buribunks.

In this regard, the use of tropes and figurative language seems to be also meaningful in *The Buribunks*. While the overall wording and composition of the essay fluctuate between a state-of-the-art article and a triumphant report, the proliferation of metaphors sometimes becomes too striking to overlook their obvious intentionality. Figurative language becomes especially spectacular when it comes to those moments in the lives of the most significant arch-Buribunks that reveal their individual errors and non-buribunkological attitudes. Metaphors are used to describe the enormous extent of the loss that follows from the failures of Leporello and Ferker, whose contribution to buribunkology was indispensable yet deficient. Making notes only of his lord's conquests, Leporello failed to become the master of his own history and nor was he seriously interested in facts, so he held the chest (*Schrein*) full of the treasures of buribunkology in vain as he did not hold the key to open it.[25] Ferker, Leporello's successor in the development of buribunkology, surpassed him yet retained too much of his individuality, such as the fear of death and a completely 'unburibunkological' marriage. Therefore he, just like Moses, glimpsed the promised land but was never permitted to enter it.[26] In contrast, Schnekke – the real hero of the Buribunks and the peak of Buribunk history – is praised without the use of such rich figurative language. Although the metaphors – shrine, Moses, promised land – depicting the failure of Leporello and Ferker are vague enough to invoke commonplace knowledge, still their religious connotations have intrinsic value in the essay as they refer to the

24 Schmitt (1990).
25 Chapter 2 of this volume, p 17; Schmitt (1918), p 94.
26 Chapter 2 of this volume, p 21.

residual metaphysical baggage that real Buribunks should be able to shed.[27] The contrast between religious and post-metaphysical factual knowledge is reinforced in the text by a footnote quoting – and denouncing – a certain Carl Schmitt, who dared to challenge buribunkology by claiming the superiority of Christian cultural heritage.[28] It is suggested that metaphysical thinking is represented by a necessarily figurative language, whereas fact-based positivist thinking thrives in a normative but objectified representation.

Given the significance of fiction, it is hardly surprising that the author and the characters of the satire are also subjected to the questioning of self-enclosedness. Schmitt, the supposed but formally absent author of the essay, is distanced from the Buribunk who relates the progress of buribunkology within the text. C.S., who claims authorship in the published version of the text, is the Buribunk who criticises the position from which Carl Schmitt criticises positivism. C.S., whose signature aims at validating buribunkological factuality, is located outside of the main body of the text while he exists within the buribunkological world-view. In contrast, Carl Schmitt, who did not subscribe to buribunkology, becomes a fictional character within the text as someone whose Christian references prove that he is unsuitable to understand buribunkology. As a creator and founder, the author is outside of the text, his authority established by the external position he assumes and from which it becomes possible to generate the fiction of the Buribunks. He invents the fiction that becomes fact viewed from within the textual world of buribunkology. Carl Schmitt as the author of the essay fictionally makes up the factual world of the Buribunks to prove that it is impossible to found and establish a political and legal system without an external intervention. As Reinhart Koselleck explains reading Schmitt's essay as a temporal utopia, the author of the uchronia is different from the author of a classic utopia precisely because the author is not the discoverer of the fictional world anymore, but its sole originator.[29] This intervention, however, cannot be reduced to the role of an external authority that terminates as soon as the order is set in motion. By founding the textual order, the sovereign author becomes inscribed into the system he created. When mentioned by C.S. within the text, the name 'Carl Schmitt' becomes a

27 As an exception, it should be mentioned that at one point the progress of buribunkology is itself described by a Biblical example, namely that of the mustard seed from which the enormous tree (*mächtiger Baum*) of buribunkology could grow. However, it is a crucial difference that while the Biblical tree as a constituted order in the Schmittian context is understood as a result of personal sovereignty, in the essay it is related to the work of the unknowing means in the hands of the world spirit and history. C.S. calls it the 'paradox of origin' that even anti-buribunkological attitudes and acts contribute to the historical progress of buribunkology, which refers also to the several mentions of Hegel throughout the essay. For the mustard seed metaphor, see Chapter 2 of this volume, p 15.

28 Chapter 2 of this volume, p 14 n 2.

29 Koselleck (2002), p 87.

disruptive force, fundamentally questioning the self-referential logic of buribunkology.

Authorship as sovereignty is located both inside and outside of the textual system that conceives itself as self-enclosed.[30] It is far from accidental that without explicitly referring to the problem of sovereignty, *The Buribunks* invokes the position of Schmitt's later *Political Theology*. The answer to the problems of the former text are present fragmentarily in Schmitt's works from the 1910s, albeit without the more straightforward political terminology that appears shortly after *The Buribunks*. However, *The Buribunks* is not less political than *Political Theology* or any other texts published by Schmitt in the 1920s. The political nature of *The Buribunks* reveals itself through its mode of writing – through its fictionality, selective figurative language and sovereign authorship. Politics is not merely expressed by language, but becomes political in Schmitt's sense through language. That is, the mode of writing is not neutral to the 'political content' it conveys, but is political itself.

Buribunkological romanticism

The Buribunks is an essential part of Schmitt's oeuvre, theoretically as important as any other piece from the 1910s and 1920s. More precisely, *The Buribunken* is Schmitt's political theory applied and practised before it was expounded in his later scholarly works, as its most important feature is designating and naming the enemy who claims that there is no need for decisions at all. Positivism is not merely a legal theory anymore, but a world-view[31] that is revealed to be harbouring form-giving political ambitions, which must be met by using political means. Scientific disagreement is therefore transformed in and by the essay into political enmity, and this is what gives the essay its specific place among Schmitt's works. In this regard, the *Buribunken* essay is close to Schmitt's main argument in his *Political Romanticism* and, despite the wavering conceptual framework and shifting emphasis, it might be argued that the fiction of buribunkology is another milestone on the trajectory that leads from the criticism of positivism to the Schmittian understanding of the political.

Beyond the biographical proximity between *The Buribunks* and *Political Romanticism*, the two texts are linked by the Buribunk resembling and melting into the figure of the romantic, as they both believe that by writing world history, the gap between the individual and the universal can be bridged.[32]

30 'Although he [the sovereign] stands outside the normally valid legal system, he nevertheless belongs to it, for it is he who must decide whether the constitution needs to be suspended in its entirety.' Schmitt (2005), p 7.

31 See the first paragraph of *Political Theology II*, Schmitt's last full-length book: 'self-expression, self-affirmation and self-empowerment – one of the many phrases prefixed by "self", a so-called auto-composition are enough to allow a new and unforeseen world to emerge'. Schmitt (2010), p 34.

32 Kennedy (2004), p 47; Lambrow (2017), p 336.

Buribunkology is thus an anti-metaphysical effort that gradually disposed of all the threats that would undermine the self-enclosed totality characterising its fact-based self-understanding.[33] The Buribunks keep their diaries but, as a consequence of buribunkological self-reflection, they are the mere extension of their processed records. Obviously, metaphysics remains inherent in buribunkology precisely due to the belief in historical progress that is thought to be internalised by autobiographical self-reflection. Metaphysics is therefore far from being overcome; it is merely denied the consequences of what will be addressed by Schmitt in the 1920s. However, it is an important step from buribunkology to political theology that in *Political Romanticism* Schmitt writes that 'metaphysics is something that is unavoidable',[34] and it cannot be replaced either by the creative subjectivity of romanticism or the religious factuality of buribunkology.

The idea of authorship plays an obvious role in case of the Buribunks and the romantics alike. Both the Buribunks and the romantics conceive of writing as self-writing, although the implications and consequences are slightly different. Whereas a Buribunk writes to elevate the self onto the level of the universality of buribunkological archives, for a romantic, writing means the creation of the world from the self as its point of origin. Following Schmitt at least, the constitutive nature of authorship is defining in both cases. However, regarding authorship and sovereignty – or, more precisely, rejected and claimed sovereignty – certain differences seem to emerge between the Buribunks and the romantics at this point. Buribunkology dismisses sovereign action as it does not have place in its self-enclosed and self-regulating understanding of collectivity.[35] Even if becoming one's own master seems to be a requirement that Leporello failed to meet,[36] it turns out that personal sovereignty dissolves as soon as – with Schnekke's contributions – buribunkology achieves its highest level, where individual diary records matter only as data for buribunkological analysis. In contrast, romanticism claims sovereignty but, according to Schmitt, it remains feigned. However, as it is well known, Schmitt rejects both that sovereignty could be eliminated and that it could be faked in the subjective occasionalism of the romantic.

Whereas, for the Buribunks, self-enclosedness means a reflexive system of action, observation, analysis and regulatory feedback, the figure of the romantic unites creation of the self and the world in poetic action. The mutual gesture is the belief that a closed system of related elements is attainable without being

33 Chapter 2 of this volume, pp 13–14.

34 Schmitt (1986), p 17.

35 For a different reading, see Heidenreich (2005), p 144, who explains the links between buribunkology and liberalism by emphasising that the Buribunks also claim sovereignty through writing world-history. It should be noted, however, that the Buribunks are not only authors of history but also its derivates, questioning the Schmittian understanding of sovereignty.

36 Chapter 2 of this volume, p 16–7.

open and subjected to an external point that serves as the origin that is uncoverable from within the system of relations. What the Buribunks achieve through institutionalised self-reflection, the romantics establish aesthetically by starting from and returning to the creative subject. Thus, in Schmitt, a thread leads from the positivists through the romantics to the liberals, who essentially all attempt to tame – or at least hide – the nature of the political. The most insightful similarity between the *Buribunken* essay and *Political Romanticism* in this regard is the aestheticised relation of the self to the world, although it is much more explicitly rendered in the latter work while it remains hidden behind the mechanical and technological logic of buribunkology. The common point is the indifference of the content that is created either by the romantic or the Buribunk. Just as, for the romantic, 'everything becomes the "beginning of an endless novel"', to fulfil buribunkological duties, it suffices to keep a diary even if records are about why keeping a diary is pointless.[37] Although in case of the former it serves the self while in the latter it benefits the collective body of the Buribunks, the point is that creation lacks any meaningful choice – or, according to Schmitt, is about avoiding decisions and suspending oppositions.[38] 'Being productive without becoming active' is, according to Schmitt, the core of political romanticism.[39] Similarly, Buribunks also lack real activity because experiences can be called experiences only after they are recorded in a diary and due to their recording in a diary.[40] Keeping a diary is nothing more than the continuous production of data for the buribunkological archive, and even if it relates personal occurrences it merely proves the activity of the irresistible force of history.

Yet, while political romanticism is about producing fiction to establish reality – to maintain possibilities of withdrawal from the world – ironically, buribunkology produces facts to close off the possibility of an external reality that might disrupt the internal order of the diary-keeping Buribunks. Both approaches are deeply antipolitical in Schmitt's understanding. That is, they not only reject politics, but attempt to hide that their politics is fatally dangerous since without meaningful decisions, no question of legitimacy may be answered in times of crisis.

Repoliticising buribunkology

In the late 1910s, by writing *The Buribunks* and *Political Romanticism*, Schmitt repoliticised the jurisprudential discourse in which he was participating as a legal scholar. Confronting the two writings, it becomes clear that in them the earlier points of Schmitt's critique of positivism are transformed into a more

37 Schmitt (1986), p 20; Chapter 2 of this volume, p 24.
38 Schmitt (1986), pp 87–8, 162.
39 Schmitt (1986), p 159.
40 Chapter 2 of this volume, p 16.

general political theoretical position. However, as the theory of the political for Schmitt is always political, always about identifying friend and enemy, the significance of these works consists in taking a side. In this section, Schmitt's repoliticising moves will be scrutinised in the *Buribunken* essay to show how his sovereign authorship disrupted the assumed self-enclosedness of a world founded on buribunkological principles.

The Buribunks does not bring about a break or a turning point in Schmitt's theoretical trajectory. However, it is an especially powerful criticism of positivism precisely because it is not a scholarly contribution. The text of *The Buribunks* is intended to be a devastating critique that does not play by the rules of a scholarly debate. The subversive force of the text is established by the fictitious nature of the science of buribunkology; it is the result of buribunkology conceived and debunked as a fictive science. A satirical fiction about a factual utopia is not meant to be refuted by facts, manoeuvres of logic or literal meaning. The significance of the *Buribunken* essay does not follow from its content, but rather from its implied offensive stance – in other words, from the political surplus it brings about by setting fact against fiction. The text becomes political at the very moment where it hides its position behind its fictional form, but by the same means also highlights it, and it turns into political theory in a truly Schmittian sense where it becomes impossible to distinguish between the descriptive and prescriptive aspects of the text.[41]

In this regard, the markedly non-Schmittian terminology describing the social and political life of the Buribunks is worth considering. Of course, given how Buribunks live and understand their lives, it should not be surprising that although buribunkology does not lack institutionalised order, it barely resembles what concerned Schmitt either before or after *The Buribunks*. Yet little is known about the social order in which the Buribunks live – for example, they do not seem to have a state of their own, or at least not one in Schmitt's sense. The few roughly authoritative positions in the text do not seem to possess any actual authority to make decisions. One of them is the head (*Chef*) of the department responsible for collecting and analysing the data on the development of a given province and a central authority (*Zentralinstanz*), where the local information gathered is summarised. However, before anything could be known about their specific powers to be used in case of a non-buribunkological trend or activity, the text returns to the fundamental principle of buribunkology and repeats that the reason of the process is to grasp Buribunkdom buribunkologically.[42]

41 Of course, the distinction between descriptive and normative approaches of political theory is age-old; however, it has returned in recent debates on political realism. Mark Philp (2012), p 631, for example, emphasises that realism is a 'political theory'. In the literature on Schmitt, Heinrich Meier (1995), p 4 puts it similarly: a theorist of the political must be a political theorist.

42 Chapter 2 of this volume, p 25.

In buribunkological terms, power means the power of writing. It is writing and written power (*schreibenden Macht*),[43] however, it dissolves in the Buribunks' self-referential relation to world history, which is understood as cause and effect at the same time – thus invoking the positivist understanding of the state as being both the origin and the result of the legal system. So, the state gave place to history which does not need any coercive means and measures since conflicts and contradictions are eliminated without any external intervention, while the individual Buribunks remain unknowing subjects and objects of buribunkological progress. In this fundamentally anti-Schmittian understanding, judgement becomes the result of a depersonalised production of history – quite similar to the romantic withdrawal from the world.[44]

Apparently, Buribunks are not particularly interested in politics. The term comes up only twice in the text: the first instance concerns the lack of any awareness about population policy in the registry of Don Juan conquests, while the second is to be found in a list of categories used to process diary-records.[45] Although the categories mentioned specifically – erotic, demonic, satirical, political – are surprising enough in themselves,[46] it is not the content of the categories that calls for an explanation, but the gesture that lists politics as merely one of the many activities or aspects of a Buribunk's life. This suggests that according to buribunkological principles, defining politics merely means contrasting it with the other categories. It is supposed to be possible to decide whether a diary-record is political or not. If not, it is because it belongs to another category listed (or yet to be listed); it is, for example, demonic. That is, categories form a self-enclosed list, suggesting an exhaustive definition of politics; it is exhaustive inasmuch as politics is anything that cannot be categorised as something else. This foreshadows Schmitt's later struggle with describing the political which, according to the first edition of *The Concept of the Political*, was simply a sphere among others (e.g. morality, economics, aesthetics), an autonomous domain that, following the critiques of Hans J. Morgenthau and Leo Strauss, was revised to be understood as the criterion of the degree of intensity of union and separation to mark the political as the authoritative dimension that necessarily becomes primary over all other spheres of human activity.[47] It is not surprising that, according to Schmitt, Buribunks do not conceive politics

43 Chapter 2 of this volume, p 27.
44 For a recent analysis of Schmitt's understanding of history and his rejection of positivist and progressive account of it, see Lievens (2016). In The Buribunks, Schmitt refers to the world court of history, a Hegelian phrase that appeared in 'Resignation', a poem by Friedrich Schiller ('Die Weltgeschichte ist das Weltgericht'). See Chapter 2 of this volume, p 17.
45 Chapter 2 of this volume, pp 17, 23.
46 All of these would deserve a detailed analysis, but 'satirical' seems to be the most insightful as, on the one hand, it directly refers to the status of the text thereby referring to the fact/fiction problem discussed above while, on the other, it explicitly aestheticises politics as just another mode of expression.
47 Schmitt (2007), p 26.

politically; however, it might be telling that in this regard, by attempting to grasp politics exhaustively, Schmitt himself was a Buribunk even in the 1920s – at least partly.

The non-Schmittian 'political' terminology of the *Buribunken* essay reinforces the idea of self-enclosedness and the exclusion of any external and heterogeneous authority that Schmitt claims to be necessary to found, maintain and legitimise political order. Thus, if no such self-enclosed totality is achievable without an 'act of exclusion',[48] it needs to be functioning in the text even if it remains hidden from the eyes of the Buribunks or is deliberately hidden by buribunkology. In the remaining part of this section, the analysis moves to Schmitt's interventions in the text that aim to directly disrupt this self-enclosed totality. The question is thus whether the description of buribunkology is as gapless as it should be according to buribunkological principles.

To answer these questions, the analysis borrows from Schmitt's own approach from his 1938 book on Hobbes's Leviathan, which addressed the problem of how a symbol can establish a political order. According to Schmitt, the Leviathan – which otherwise is considered the first example of a mechanised and positivist understanding of political order and the state as its temporarily successful model[49] – is founded on the differentiation between inner faith and outer confession. While the former is declared free, the latter is decided authoritatively by the state. However, in Schmitt's reading, this moment that allowed sovereignty to become effectual is also the very moment of its undoing. The distinction is more than separation; it is a 'crack' that, at the peak of unity achieved by the Leviathan, brings about its eventual collapse. Schmitt accused Spinoza of exploiting Hobbes's barely visible and supposedly unintended crack, and placing personal freedom in the public sphere ahead of sovereign power within the protection-obligation pattern.[50] Using the relations between unity, exclusion, cracks and sovereignty as an analogy, below we ask whether similar blind spots might render buribunkological self-enclosedness similarly open for repoliticisation. Reading *The Buribunks* as an exposition of the strategies of neutralisation that are hoped to eliminate the fundamental conflicts of an age, the cracks should not only imply the undoing of the depoliticised logic, but also plant the seeds of the emerging new conflict.

Considering the archival system of diaries or the practical and historical role of the typewriter with which the Buribunks become as one, it might be argued that in this case it is technology that eventually separates what was believed to be settled and united.[51] But, apart from this general insight, what is it that might plant disagreement among diary-keeping Buribunks? In other words,

48 Lambrow (2017), p 333.
49 Schmitt (1996), p 45.
50 Schmitt (1996), p 57.
51 Chapter 2 of this volume, p 26. For a detailed analysis of the role of technology and its relation to neutralisation of the political in Schmitt's thought, see McCormick (1997).

how do possible anti-buribunkological moments stir genuine conflict in a seemingly self-enclosed order? The text of *The Buribunks* does not just depict the enemies of the political but, as a political intervention itself, the essay enters the conflict. At least two weak points – or, in the words of Schmitt's *Leviathan*, two 'barely visible cracks' – left the Buribunks vulnerable to the impossibility of their own self-enclosedness. It is not entirely clear that these weak points are the result of C.S.'s work: despite being a Buribunk himself, did C.S. fail to perceive the last open spots of buribunkology – or it was Schmitt who deliberately undermined buribunkology by installing anti-buribunkological mines in the text? Both possibilities could be explained along Schmittian insights.

The first anti-buribunkological moment becomes visible by returning to the character of the fictive author of the text. It might be supposed that C.S. is either one of the Buribunks or someone who, apparently understanding and accepting buribunkological normativity, will become one of them. From this it follows that there has to be a diary containing a record about the writing of the essay and discussing C.S.'s attitude towards his own contribution to buribunkology, just as Buribunks working in the archives are required to keep diaries on their own buribunkological activities. To understand buribunkology, it is important to emphasise that it does not merely involve keeping diaries. At the peak of buribunkological progress, completion occurs when each diary record is processed in the buribunkological archives and this latter act is also recorded in the diaries. This is what C.S. calls '*Doppelregistrierung*'. Don Juan could not even approach real buribunkological attitude since he lacked any consciousness regarding recording data. Leporello, his servant, was not a Buribunk as his records were not really his own, so recording – which is the only meaningful event – had no impact on his own individuality. Although Ferker kept most of his diaries as required, he failed to do it consequently and his records were not processed according to a buribunkological method, since the institutionalisation of buribunkological activities was incomplete in his times. These requirements were met only in Schnekke.[52] To maintain positivistic self-enclosedness, every activity of the Buribunks should be recorded in a diary, which in turn should be processed in the archives. However, this very requirement excludes self-enclosedness, as there cannot be an ultimate level of buribunkological activity. Implicitly referring to the positivist principle of the state preceded by right, but at the same time being the origin of the legal system, the lack of a stabilising external authority such as a diary containing all diaries or an archive processing all buribunkological activities leads to the collapse of the supposed self-enclosedness. Schnekke, who in the history of Buribunks and buribunkology represents the highest point of progress – at least

52 It is also interesting that Schnekke is not described as an unknowing contributor to buribunkological progress as Leporello and Ferker were earlier. His position resembles an impossible lawgiver who laid down the principles of buribunkology – principles that exclude the position of a sole and personal originator.

according to C.S.'s article – did not say anything about this problem. The immanence of buribunkology is conceivable only at the point of ultimate self-reflection, when recording the ultimate note becomes possible. However, it is unconceivable since every note requires a note about the experience of its entry. Buribunkology remains unavoidably open precisely where it is supposed to be gapless and closed. This is the first crack that C.S. did not perceive or did not want to present to readers, but that Schmitt made readable by having C.S. remain silent about it.

The other, much more visible crack or anti-buribunkological moment concerns the possibility of conflict among Buribunks – or, as C.S. puts it, the 'rebellious spirit'.[53] What constitutes the main conflict within buribunkology? Basically, there should not be any or, if a conflict emerges, it is to be settled automatically and harmoniously thanks to historical progress. But then what characterises the 'rebellious spirit'? Is it refusing to keep a diary? According to the essay, it is not. Those who neglect recording the events of their lives gradually disappear from sight; as Buribunks, they become non-existent since they cease to appear in other Buribunks' records and, consequently, they are not processed in the archives anymore. Accordingly, Schnekke's buribunkology does not contain a system of sanctions to be applied; no decision is needed to declare anti-buribunkological behaviour. Since buribunkology is self-sufficient and self-enclosed, declining it automatically leads to the system-immanent consequence of disappearing. What about Buribunks who voice their dissent? Expressing anti-buribunkological views is allowed and even encouraged, as it also contributes to the further development of buribunkology. When a Buribunk records in the diary that keeping a diary is annoying or useless, a valuable record is created from a buribunkological point of view.[54] Although it is claimed to prove the freedom of speech and thought, rebellious Buribunks seem to be neutralised, albeit according to a different logic. They neither disappear nor are eliminated; to the contrary, they remain part of Buribunkdom and retain their Buribunk identity. Eventually, they seem to be harmless. Still, C.S. does not know what Carl Schmitt will know and discuss a few years later: here, enmity has been declared – or, at least, a potential differentiation has been offered between Buribunk and Buribunk. The Buribunks who refuse to keep a diary do not constitute a threat because they are only *inimici*: they are private enemies to the extent that they cannot be seen anymore. However with the type of Buribunk who keeps a diary to express dissent, the figure of *hostis* has appeared on the horizon and, with it, stasis and the threat of civil war.[55] Even if

53 Chapter 2 of this volume, p 24.
54 Chapter 2 of this volume, p 24.
55 Schmitt adopts a similar logic in his post-war *The Tyranny of Values*, where he describes the boundless tolerance and neutrality towards the 'arbitrarily exchangeable' viewpoints on which positivist valuing allegedly rests as 'immediately turn [ing] over into its opposite, into enmity, as soon as it becomes a concretely serious matter of enactment and making valid'. Cf. Schmitt (2018), p 35.

the clash of anti-buribunkological and buribunkological diary records at first seems to be similar to a parliamentary contest, it is a regulated competition of views and positions only up to a certain point. Similar to the crack that opened up the Leviathan, what started as a private record about a private opinion about buribunkology, due to the buribunkological process, becomes public and conflict now reappears on this public stage. And as the political consists not in a mere differentiation between friend and enemy but in the degree of intensity of union and separation,[56] historical progress in itself cannot guarantee that it does not reach the level of enmity in the Schmittian sense, which eventually threatens buribunkological order with disintegration. In his later writings, Schmitt at this point introduces the figure of the sovereign – the external, heterogeneous other whose authority is claimed to be necessary to settle the crisis-like situation. However, in buribunkological self-enclosedness, no such position exists, so being depoliticised in a buribunkological sense means fatal anti-political vulnerability. This second 'barely visible crack' thereby remains open to the political, making the lack of sovereignty apparent and undoing the seeming harmony of buribunkological life.

Conclusion

At first glance, *The Buribunks* seems to be an easily decodable parable. For the contemporary reader, the story, the characters and the moral of the narrative might have been familiar. The loss of individuality and privacy, the beneficial or damaging implications of technological progress, the emergence of the masses both as military and political actors were obviously at hand in the late 1910s. For a scholarly readership, the role of positivism, the philosophy of history or the *sein-sollen* dilemma offered intellectual trenches to be attacked or defended. However, the essay should not be read merely as a parable but much more as an analogy in the Schmittian understanding of the term. That is, these elements of *The Buribunks* are not only hints that simply point to the real-world context; they contribute to a structurally similar establishment of relations. Analogical reasoning in Schmitt is not an epistemic problem, but rather a political one. The elements of the essay and the elements of the real-world context of the essay are structurally similar: they do not just refer to each other metaphorically, but also imply intrinsic relations. The fictitious science of keeping diaries does not merely refer to producing, storing, transmitting and calculating data,[57] but also to the problem of social arrangement – or, more precisely, to the way legal frameworks shape the state and realise normativity in the factual world. Buribunkology is more than a prescriptive reflection on diary keeping; it is a constitutional theory[58] – albeit for Schmitt an impossible and

56 Schmitt (2007), p 26.
57 Kittler (1990), p 369.
58 Omiya (2008), p 136.

delusive one. Schmitt's pseudo-scientific satire on positivism does not adopt its critical potential through ridiculing a contemporary phenomenon; it is not a parody but a political act. It becomes political precisely because it implements the fictitious meanings of the text and attempts to realise them to prove that there is no gapless unity or self-enclosedness achieved without exclusion. In the *Buribunken* essay, Schmitt prepares the ground for his later works to show that bridging the gap and overcoming the cracks caused by the essential separation that prevails in modernity is an impossible but unavoidable political task.[59] For Schmitt, those who denied or tried to hide this were worse than political enemies; they were the enemies of the political.

References

Paul de Man (1979) *Allegories of Reading*, Yale University Press.

Felix Heidenreich (2005) *Mensch und Moderne bei Hans Blumenberg*, Wilhelm Fink Verlag.

Hasso Hofmann (2010) *Legitimität gegen Legalität. Der Weg der politischen Philosophie Carl Schmitts*, Duncker & Humblot.

Wolfgang Iser (1993) *The Fictive and the Imaginary*, Johns Hopkins University Press.

Ellen Kennedy (1988) 'Politischer Expressionismus', in H. Quaritsch (ed), *Complexio Oppositorum*, Duncker & Humblot, 143.

Ellen Kennedy (2004) *Constitutional Failure*, Duke University Press.

Lorenz Kiefer (1990) 'Begründung, Dezision und Politische Theologie: Zu drei frühen Schriften von Carl Schmitt' 76 *Archiv für Rechts- und Sozialphilosophie* 479.

Friedrich Kittler (1990) *Discourse Networks 1800/1900*, Stanford University Press.

Reinhart Koselleck (2002) 'The Temporalization of Utopia', in *The Practice of Conceptual History*, Stanford University Press, 84.

Alexander Lambrow (2017) '14 December 1930: Robert Musil Meets Carl Schmitt' 90 *The German Quarterly* 332.

Matthias Lievens (2016) 'Carl Schmitt's Concept of History' in J. Meierhenrich and O. Simons (eds), *The Oxford Handbook of Carl Schmitt*, Oxford University Press, 401.

John P. McCormick (1997) *Carl Schmitt's Critique of Liberalism: Against Politics as Technology*, Cambridge University Press.

Reinhard Mehring (2014) '"Die Austreibung des Heidelberger Geistes": Carl Schmitt und der Heidelberger Rechtspositivismus', in *Kriegstechniker des Begriffs*, Mohr Siebeck.

Heinrich Meier (1995) *Carl Schmitt and Leo Strauss: The Hidden Dialogue*, University of Chicago Press.

Michele Nicoletti (1988) 'Die Ursprünge von Carl Schmitts "Politischer Theologie"' in H. Quaritsch (ed), *Complexio Oppositorum*, Duncker & Humblot, 109.

Kanichiro Omiya (2008) 'Ein Ende der Mediengeschichte: Carl Schmitts Die Buribunken', in L. Pfeiffer and R. Schnell (eds), *Schwellen der Medialisierung. Medienanthropologische Perspektiven – Deutschland und Japan*, Transcript Verlag.

Mark Philp (2012) 'Realism Without Illusions' 40 *Political Theory* 629.

59 See Kiefer (1990), p 483; Nicoletti (1988), pp 114–17.

Michael Dylan Rogers (2016) 'The Development of Carl Schmitt's Political Thought During the First World War' 13 *Modern Intellectual History* 123.

Thomas Schestag (2007) 'Namen Nehmen. Zur Theorie des Namens bei Carl Schmitt' 122 *MLN* 544.

Carl Schmitt (1914) *Der Wert des Staates und die Bedeutung des Einzelnen*, J.C.B. Mohr (Paul Siebeck).

Carl Schmitt (1917) 'Diktatur und Belagerungszustand' 38 *Zeitschrift für die gesamte Strafrechtswissenschaft* 138.

Carl Schmitt (1918) 'Die Buribunken' 4 *Summa* 89.

Carl Schmitt (1969) *Gesetz und Urteil*, C.H. Beck.

Carl Schmitt (1986) *Political Romanticism*, MIT Press.

Carl Schmitt (1990) 'The Plight of European Jurisprudence' 83 *Telos* 35.

Carl Schmitt (1991) *Glossarium: Aufzeichnungen der Jahre 1947–1951*, Duncker & Humblot.

Carl Schmitt (1996) *The Leviathan in the State Theory of Thomas Hobbes*, Greenwood Press.

Carl Schmitt (2005) *Political Theology*, University of Chicago Press.

Carl Schmitt (2007) *The Concept of the Political*, University of Chicago Press.

Carl Schmitt (2010) *Political Theology II*, Polity Press.

Carl Schmitt (2017) 'Juristische Fiktionen', in *Über Schuld und Schuldarten*, Duncker & Humblot, 172.

Carl Schmitt (2018) 'The Tyranny of Values', in R.A. Berman and S.G. Zeitlin (eds), *The Tyranny of Values & Other Texts*, Telos.

Alexander Schmitz (2016) 'Legitimacy of the Modern Age? Hans Blumenberg and Carl Schmitt', in J. Meierhenrich and O. Simons (eds), *The Oxford Handbook of Carl Schmitt*, Oxford University Press, 705.

Jeffrey Seitzer and Chris Thornhill (2008) 'An Introduction to Carl Schmitt's Constitutional Theory: Issues and Context', in Carl Schmitt, *Constitutional Theory*, Duke University Press, 1.

Chris Thornhill (2007) *German Political Philosophy*, Routledge.

Piet Tommissen (1997) *In Sachen Carl Schmitt*, Karolinger.

Hans Vaihinger (1922) *Die Philosophie des als ob*, Verlag von Felix Meiner.

Chapter 17

Between *The Buribunks* and the Christian Epimetheus

Fabrizio Grasso and Matteo Negro

Translated by Carla Biondi

Science and history

In Carl Schmitt's short and shrewd essay, two terms frequently jump off the page: history and science. This is no coincidence. Today the scientific standardisation of knowledge is the model cultivated by many human science specialists who, fearful of wielding knowledge that is too fatuous and ineffective, seek a solid basis and a reliable methodological lever in the statute of empirical sciences. 'Knowledge is power', philosopher Francis Bacon proclaimed, probably well aware of the impotence and transience that loom over the life of man. Among all forms of knowledge, historical science as well gradually transforms into its opposite when it metamorphoses into objectifying science. History turns to studying processes. This aspect was superbly captured by Hannah Arendt in *Between Past and Future*:

> Technology, the ground on which the two realms of history and nature have met and interpenetrated each other in our time, points back to the connection between the concepts of nature and history as they appeared with the rise of the modern age in the sixteenth and seventeenth centuries. The connection lies in the concept of process: both imply that we think and consider everything in terms of processes and are not concerned with single entities or individual occurrences and their special separate causes. The key words of modern historiography 'development' and 'progress' were, in the nineteenth century, also the key words of the then new branches of natural science, particularly biology and geology, one dealing with animal life and the other even with non-organic matter in terms of historical processes.[1]

From this perspective, the status of science confronts the evolution of technology, by which the classic relationship between nature and subjectivity is somewhat reformulated: thanks to technology, the self returns to the field,

1 Arendt (1961), p 61.

DOI: 10.4324/9781003091066-21

observing nature and its processes with an attentive eye to their reproducibility. Nature is an operational field in which it is possible to intervene, a set of reproducible processes that can carefully and cleverly be manipulated. Similarly, as a history of processes, history is the result of an operation that those in possession of effective knowledge are finally able to show. Likewise:

> The modern age, with its growing world-alienation, has led to a situation where man, wherever he goes, encounters only himself. All the processes of the earth and the universe have revealed themselves either as man-made or as potentially man-made. These processes, after having devoured, as it were, the solid objectivity of the given, ended by rendering meaningless the one over-all process which originally was conceived in order to give meaning to them, and to act, so to speak, as the eternal time-space into which they could all flow and thus be rid of their mutual conflicts and exclusiveness. This is what happened to our concept of history, as it happened to our concept of nature. In the situation of radical world-alienation, neither history nor nature is at all conceivable. This twofold loss of the world – the loss of nature and the loss of human artifice in the widest sense, which would include all history – has left behind it a society of men who, without a common world which would at once relate and separate them, either live in desperate lonely separation or are pressed together into a mass. For a mass-society is nothing more than that kind of organized living which automatically establishes itself among human beings who are still related to one another but have lost the world once common to all of them.[2]

Like science, history is indeed given back to the subject – but to a subject now disembodied, deconstructed, amorphous and devoid of edges. It is a calculable entity, identified with the value assigned by the process itself, and that the flow of information can encode with a number, a function or a proportion. Anyone sufficiently trained in the technique of calculation can ultimately write their own narrative, shaping their own destiny and entrusting exclusively to themself the task of narrating to themselves and narrating the world, thanks to the sounding board offered by the network that no book or newspaper would ever have made available. If such a power is in the mass, nothing outside the mass can dictate or accentuate it. Memory has no future, and we can recreate the past however we wish at any time: one day it attracts us, another it deters us. The difference is that, today, the past reaches us without the mediation of historiography and academic historians are often trapped in restricted and quarrelsome circles.

Schmitt's satire seems to be the product of labour and not of joy: the pages of the Buribunks flooded with contempt for the new world still in gestation.

2 Arendt (1961), pp 89–90.

Despite everything, Schmitt himself will contribute to create such new world by accepting and supporting the mass revolution that has released unprecedented power, the power to free oneself from history and its theology to fall back into the nihilism of projectuality.[3] Carlo Galli grasped this last aspect quite well in his comments on the Buribunks:

> the modern acceleration of time in the prospective form of the project finds its paradoxical truth here, and, in the same way, modern science is accused of being unable to think of a non-tautological relationship between immediacy and the Universal, and therefore of dissolving the concrete in the *logos*.[4]

In line with these findings, two consequences can thus be identified: the self-historicisation of the self and the stripping of history, which here brings us back to technological artificial progress:

> the will to power, implicit in the unceasing insert, through writing, of every moment of life into history, reveals its intrinsic nihilism not only in the subject being just 'a letter from the typewriter of history', but in the destruction, which follows, not only of the life of the subject itself, but also of the objectivity of history.[5]

Regardless of necessary future considerations of the dialectics between event and process, the technological process gives history an unprecedented acceleration.

We could also see here an analogy between the Anthropocene and the accelerations that geological eras have encountered far before historical chronology: causal events have intensified some processes. The geological model applied to human history and its acceleration is perhaps compatible with the Hegelian structure of Schmitt's writings of maturity (particularly in *The Concept of the Political*); nevertheless, in the first phase, a conception of factuality prevails that is completely refractory to the formalism of process intensity. Italian scholar of Schmitt Michele Nicoletti records a reversal of trend, particularly with regard to Hegel, between the young Schmitt of *The Buribunks* and that of his later works. Indeed, if it is true on one hand that in the latter work Schmitt will support the conflictual transformation of the quantity into quality when it assumes such an intensity as to become 'politically relevant', it is equally true

3 Schmitt has in fact emptied the reference to metaphysics and the concreteness of individual being of meaning by progressively projecting itself onto an ontology of super-individual forms. Dallmayr grasped this aspect of Schmitt's philosophy with insight: 'Although he [Schmitt] starts from the acceptance of metaphysical realities, his ideas can lead, and actually did lead, to a strengthening of the "super-ideologies" of modern totalitarian parties.' Dallmayr (1958), p 659.

4 Galli (1996), pp 190–1. Translated by Carla Biondi.

5 Galli (1996), p 190. Translated by Carla Biondi.

that in the former work this transformation is harshly criticised. As Nicoletti aptly argues:

> While, on the one hand, in the early writings the empirical reality appeared to be completely incapable of arriving at a whatever form, idea or quality, here on the other hand [in *The Concept of the Political*] the form of the political appears to be characterized by a certain degree of *intensity* of the existential reality, and therefore from a certain quantity.[6]

If the facts remain irreducibly empirical and ultimately incomparable, extraneous to an overall movement, history remains a type of narrative without other pretensions, in which mystery, uncertainty and conflictual latency cannot be overcome in organic movements. Shortly after the release of *The Buribunks*, Chesterton made an important remark about anti-Catholic historiography: 'Anti-Catholic history fails because history is a story; and here it can never give the beginning of a story.'[7]

From this perspective, the starting point of a story is arbitrary, not necessary; some contradictory facts must deliberately be ignored in order to give rise to the visibility not only of other facts themselves, but moreover of their special function as primary conceptual operators around which all the other facts are coherently organised.[8] If history is not a continuous process, then the single fact can only be the starting point of a delimited and incommensurable narrative. By way of example, the story of Don Juan, skilfully sculpted by Schmitt in *The Buribunks*, is incommensurable and completely irrelevant for the scientist of history:

> Don Juan had no interest whatsoever in the past, indeed just as little as in the future, which for him barely extended beyond his next rendezvous; he lived in the immediate present and his interest in the singular erotic experience did not contain anything in which we could glimpse the beginning of self-historicisation. We do not notice anything of that attitude which distinguishes the Buribunk and which springs from the urge to preserve every single second of one's own being for history: the creating and viewing of oneself as a monument. The diary-keeping Buribunk pounces on every second, as does Don Juan – their psychological impulse

6 Nicoletti (1990), p 264. Translated by Carla Biondi.
7 Chesterton (1920), p 8.
8 Chesterton (1920), p 10: 'Anti-Catholic history, in so far as it is atheist or agnostic, has been a series of sweeping but very depressing scientific theories or generalizations, each applied rigorously to everything and each abandoned abruptly in favor of the next. Among these were the commercial and utilitarian theories of Bentham and Buckle, the theories that referred everything to race, especially to the triumph of a Teutonic race, the economic theory of history of Marx and other materialists. There is probably another coming into fashion by this time.'

> is certainly similar. But instead of consecrating his prey on the altar in the light-filled temple of history, he drags it into the murky depths of brutal hedonism, devouring it like an animal satisfying its base instincts.[9]

The uniqueness and unrepeatability of Don Juan's experiences for the buribunkologist are the emblem of the illusion of singularity and its irrational manifestations, which are otherwise inexplicable.[10]

Schmitt's vision returns the world to factuality and concreteness, and the subject to invincible mortality, which perhaps only Christian eschatology can remedy. Mystery reappears in history, whose theological presuppositions can be reaffirmed: no longer with the semblance of the *logos*, but with that of the *eskaton*. Here the mystery is not the antagonist of factuality; to the contrary, it is the most worthy complement to it, provided it is not conceived as the result of a theological tradition, according to which eschatology is not exclusively related to the expectation of something either not yet existing or happening somewhere in the future. To borrow from the insightful words of Karl Löwith:

> If the last things were only the latest events in a continuous series of secular happenings, the hope in them would be indeed subject to disillusion. Only by their eschatological qualification, as redemptive events, can hope and faith in them be rightly maintained. The Christian hope is not a worldly desire and expectation that something will probably happen but a cast of mind based on an unconditional faith in God's redemptive purpose. Genuine hope is, therefore, as free and absolute as the act of faith itself ... Hence hope can never be refuted by so-called 'facts'; it can neither be assured nor discredited by an established experience.[11]

Experience does not contradict hope. Since hope does not go beyond experience, it does not expect to overcome it, but captures the eschatological implications of the things themselves, their resistance to any approximation. Science, of which buribunkology is an expression, instead rejects any eschatological perspective and is, at the same time, indifferent to the memory of the past. Past and future emerge only in the present moment of their narration:

> In each second of world history, under the rushing fingers of the World-I, the letters rush from the keyboard of the typewriter onto the white paper and continue the historical narrative. Only in the second in which the single letter leaves the senseless and meaningless indifference of the

9 Chapter 2 of this volume, p 15–16.
10 Chapter 2 of this volume, p 27. 'We see through the illusion of singularity. We are the letters that have rushed from the hand of the writing World Spirit and we consciously surrender ourselves to this writing power. In this we see true freedom.'
11 Löwith (1949), pp 205–6.

> keyboard, and hits the lively connections on the white page, a historical reality is created; only this second is the birth hour of life. That is to say, of the past, as the present is only the midwife who delivers the lively historical past from the dark body of the future. Until it has been reached, the future lies there as dull and indifferent as the keyboard of a typewriter, like a dark rat hole from which one second after another (like one rat after another) steps into the light of the past.[12]

The immortality ensured by historical science is limited to history and is not open to an other-worldly dimension, to a future marked by mystery: the process gradually incorporates every element of uncertainty, restoring the linearity of time.[13]

By definition, eschatology delimits the course of history by attributing a superhistorical purpose to it, ultimately to preserve the world and humanity from mortality – exactly what is unacceptable for the Buribunk writer and weaver of history, who wants to defeat mortality by remaining in history without resorting to divine power.[14]

Schmitt's text is engaging and imbued with irony, not that we would expect an unopinionated or impersonal observation of the world's contradiction by such a shrewd author. His refusal to deny negations places him in continuity with the great tradition of classical philosophy, aware of the *logos* but also of its limits. The relationship between *logos* and *physis*, between conceptual forms and substantial forms, has virtually been at the centre of metaphysical discussion

12 Chapter 2 of this volume, p 26.

13 Chapter 2 of this volume, p 26: 'What does, ethically speaking, the Buribunk do who keeps a diary every second of his life? He wrests every second from the future in order to incorporate it into history. Let us remind ourselves of the full magnificence of this procedure: from second to second, the blinking young rat of the present second creeps out of the dark rat hole of the future, out of the nothing of what has not yet been, in order to enter with sparkling eyes in the next second the reality of the historical. In contrast to the mindless human being, for whom millions and billions of rats stream into the immensity of the past without plan or aim and become lost there, the diary-keeping Buribunk is able to capture them one by one and have their well-organised legion perform the big parade of world history. Thus he secures for himself and humankind the biggest possible quantum of historical factuality and awareness. Thus the fearful anticipation of the future loses its horror, for whatever may be, one thing is certain, namely that no second entering the future is lost, no letter of the typewriter will miss the page.'

14 Chapter 2 of this volume, p 27: 'In the realisation that there is true reality only in history, we seek real immortality in history. Not in some after-world. Christianity had "shifted" the heads of people in a literal sense (in full acknowledgement of the relative value of its sublime teachings this needs to be stressed) as it had turned the gaze from the factuality of the past to an after-worldly future, where there is, as we saw, only the dark rat hole of that which not yet exists, but no reality. Therefore we restore the correct direction for the heads towards the real by seeking immortality where it really is: behind us not before us.'

since Plato until today. The temptation to deduce things and facts from epistemic discourse collided in particular with the metaphysics of Thomas Aquinas – to which, as noted by Dallmayr, Schmitt was certainly indebted.[15]

Nevertheless, tensions arose through Thomism itself: the turning point that occurred between the sixteenth and seventeenth centuries certainly accentuated the formal role of reason and the conceptualisation of essences. Well-known Italian scholar of Thomas, Cornelio Fabro, has reconstructed various passages of this evolution that, according to him, culminated in a betrayal of metaphysics and transcendence. It is reasonable to say that the technological expansion of science in mass societies, in addition to its undeniable advantages, has offered totalitarian and un-liberal power the tools to exert an unusual violence on nature with the dual aim of re-finalising it, disrupting the metaphysical link between facts and natural ends, and re-temporalising it, substituting processing and epistemic time for the events-based version, to recall Foucault's seminal distinction. Ultimately, it is in immanence that the Buribunk struggles, the immanence of a consciousness that becomes history and of a science that makes itself a fact. The buribunkological perspective tends to absorb, if not suppress, the limit. Without transcendence, the limit disappears: time, space, nature, the fact, the individual lose the reflection of death, end or finality, surviving in an imaginary totality. Yet even here the 'limit' is around the corner to re-emerge whenever language yields to contradiction and reconstitutes the limits of the world. Therefore, the word inevitably hands us back to transcendence.

Between ontology and the political

This second part of this chapter will follow the metaphysical turns of Schmitt's thought in order to grasp the connection between ontology and politics. It will therefore try to define the extension of immanence with which the Buribunk struggles. In this process, it is useful to discuss a comparison between this figure and that of the Christian Epimetheus.

It seems that the Buribunks imagined by Schmitt have acquired considerable wisdom and achievements in all areas of human knowledge, and what has been shown so far is the intertwining of the history and science of sapid satire, and the consequent issues that it intelligently evokes. Likewise, through the writing of their collective diaries, the Buribunks appear to hold a clear political power over history. It might therefore be helpful to turn our attention to the other side of this intertwining recalled by the author: that of history and power, particularly of history and the political.

The typical and constitutive style of the Buribunks is the procedural capacity to crush, crystallise and simultaneously expand one's consciousness in the dimension of time through the space of the diary. On the one hand, such a space is partly public, becoming collective when the diary is delivered to

15 Dallmayr (1958), p 658.

employees who arrange and catalogue everything. On the other hand, it is private, as it is nevertheless the manifestation of the hypertrophy of the Buribunk's ego – let us not forget that even the detractors are given the freedom to write that they hate writing a diary. In this short circuit of meaning, it is obviously easy to burst into laughter, considering the humorous registry of the work. However, immediately afterwards it is equally easy to glimpse the spectre of totalitarianism that gently and subtly still suppresses freedom.

The power of the Buribunks indeed appears in every way to be absolute, albeit rooted in the sphere of immanence. In one of his passages, Schmitt writes about the fate that awaits those who refuse to write the diary, and consequently make 'inappropriate use of the general freedom of mind',[16] which means the unfortunate 'will be eliminated due to his anti-social disposition'.[17] We can also recognise that the Buribunks are an elite owing to the fact that it is possible to drop, rank by rank, to the lowest class of this society, namely 'the masses who create those external conditions',[18] such as producing the luxurious paper for the valuable diaries to be published, which leads us to notice that even within the elite itself a hierarchy exists.

Therefore, the Buribunks represent an elite, and it is rather simple to see the figure of the intellectual behind them. In this respect, the satiric attack on intellectualism is very clear. In order to look into the intertwining of history and power, we cannot but depart from the abovementioned intuitions of Nicoletti and Dallmayr. On the one hand, the former follows the transformation of the Schmittian ontology; on the other, the latter grasps the sense of immanence of this process. Both scholars have identified and highlighted an issue that cannot be taken as insignificant when trying to comprehend a thought such as Schmitt's, of which the results appear to be marked by an underlying ambiguity. Such ambiguity can arguably be the reason for its charm and fortune.

One can follow the line of this ambiguity deep-rooted in Schmitt's ontological turns also through buribunkology, which is actually founded on one of the most notorious Hegelian formulas, as he argues:

> If it is true that there is a point where – to express it in Hegel's brilliant phrase – quantity turns into quality, then the discussion of the question of buribunkology as a science has to revolve around the cardinal point of whether the factual quantity of buribunkological actualities has reached such an extent that it is only sensible to address it as a quality (which here means as a science).[19]

16 Chapter 2 of this volume, p 25.
17 Chapter 2 of this volume, p 25.
18 Chapter 2 of this volume, p 25.
19 Chapter 2 of this volume, pp 12–3.

The satirical intention is rather evident, and thus it is all the more helpful to read a passage from *The Concept of the Political*, which recalls in an opposite and positive key precisely this concept. In fact, when referring to Hegel, Schmitt writes:

> Of a specifically political nature also is his dialectic of concrete thinking. The often quoted sentence of quantity transforming into quality has a thoroughly political meaning. It is an expression of the recognition that from every domain the point of the political is reached and with it a qualitative new intensity of human groupings. The actual application of this sentence refers to the economic domain and becomes virulent in the nineteenth century.[20]

This observation, although retrospective, can only raise questions about the political nature of a Buribunk society in which the sphere of the political, rather than having vanished, seems to have diluted to such an extent that it totally culminates in reality, and embraces it in the space of the diary, which is above all a head space ruled by buribunkology. The Buribunk appears to have precisely the metamorphic ability needed to transmute quantity into quality in a Hegelian sense. Therefore, he is a real creator of essences. This passage is crucial to understanding two stages of Schmitt's thought: its movement of the ontological process and its mutation. There is undoubtedly a change of perspective between the young and older Schmitt, who theorises the category of the political. Such change is purely ontological.

Restless between the immanence of the political and the transcendent of the theological, in the abovementioned passage Schmitt seems to lean towards a metaphysics and an ontology, such as the Hegelian one, which seals being, essence and existence and leaves little room for transcendence. It is essential to follow the evolution of this ontological turn of the Schmittian thought, as 'The aspect of Schmitt's thought on which it is appropriate to first emphasise on is the metaphysical or (in a traditional way) the ontological one.'[21] In order to do this, it is helpful to relate what is written in this satirical essay to Schmitt's words in another of his works, *Roman Catholicism and Political Form*.[22] An example of the radicalisation and the ontological transformation that affects the language can also be seen in a society such as that of the Buribunks. As Schmitt writes in *The Concept of the Political*, the terminological matters could safely turn into high politics issues among the Buribunks, as 'a word or

20 Schmitt (2007), p 62.
21 Dallmayr (1958), p 659. Translated by Carla Biondi.
22 In fact, Dallmayr writes: 'Unfortunately, it is not possible here to deal with other publications of his that confirm this philosophical orientation, such as "Roman Catholicism and Political form", the title of which is already quite significant …' Dallmayr (1958), pp 659–60. Translated by Carla Biondi.

expression can simultaneously be reflex, signal, password and weapon in a hostile confrontation'.[23]

However, let us come back to the ontological turn. It is once again Dallmayr who highlights that:

> The 'political' thus receives its meaning from different spheres of human life: it does not constitute a separate ontological sphere but rather a degree of intensity. The ambiguity of Schmitt's thought can only be understood if one realizes that – according to him – the degree of intensity reaches the point of transforming the essence; an idea which is similar to Hegel's about the transformation of quantity into quality.[24]

This is a turn that, according to Dallmayr, renders Schmitt irreconcilable with himself as the latter shows a constant shift of ontological paradigm in his works here examined.

In *The Buribunks*, the Hegelian ontology is the object of satire, whereas in *The Concept of the Political*, such ontology is at the root of those ontological matters that become high politics issues. Such shift condemns his thought to the struggle between immanence and transcendence, and thus between the figure of the pagan Prometheus – well represented by the model of the Buribunk – and the Christian Epimetheus, who would be evoked by Schmitt after World War II. At this point, it seems that the political is the result of this transmutation of quantity into quality, which transforms the essence and therefore the reality itself – a position that, rather than adapting the intellect to the thing, is able to transform the thing, and in this case the man himself, into friend or enemy precisely on the basis of the intensity of the dissociation constituent of the concept of the political.

It appears that the ontology itself thus falls into the agonism and antagonism of the political struggle, which is always the struggle for power. This position makes it rather difficult to establish clearly which ontology Schmitt really relies on in his work. Perhaps this occurs because Schmitt is indeed a critic of modernity; however, his critique is limited as his very own thought is an epiphenomenon of modernity. Nevertheless, in order to identify a further aspect of the Schmittian ontology, it is worth recalling what has been said regarding the notion of *complexio oppositorum* developed in *Roman Catholicism and Political Form*. As acknowledged by Galli, this work is 'a privileged access key'[25] to enable observation of Schmitt's intellectual development. On the other hand, according to Albanese – whose opinion is different from Galli's regarding the judgement on the apologetic intent of the work:

23 Schmitt (2007), p 31.
24 Dallmayr (1958), p 674. Translated by Carla Biondi.
25 Galli (2010), p 83.

> The 1923 work is apparently a praise of the Catholic Church, of its remarkable political sense, its flexibility and elasticity ... However, *Roman Catholicism* is not an apologetic work. Quite the contrary. The Roman Church is in fact analysed 'scientifically' as a pure political phenomenon, and more exactly as the only 'political' island in a world in which the political appears hopelessly in decline.[26]

What is this *complexio oppositorum*? Schmitt explains:

> Out of a spiritual promiscuity which seeks a Romantic or Hegelian brotherhood with Catholicism, as with so many other ideas and individuals, a person could make the Catholic *complexio* into one of many syntheses and rashly conclude that he had thereby construed the essence of Catholicism.[27]

Let us start by saying that it is not a synthesis in a Hegelian way, but rather a specific rationality, also from a formal point of view that is able to hold together and encompass in perfect balance reason and life, or in ontological terms essence and existence, without them having to be resolved or one denying itself in the other. According to Schmitt, in the political form of Roman Catholicism, the figure of Christ represents the objective point of transcendence, thus able to hold the opposite tendencies found in reality in a *complexio oppositorum*. This could occur, as the central point is in the historical concreteness of God's son's figure. The latter is seen as a truly objective point in space and time from a historical point of view (of course, this can occur once Catholic religion is accepted in one's world-view) compared with the Romantics' 'indifference point',[28] which for Schmitt is entirely subjective. Given their syntheses, they do nothing but project an illusion of transcendence into the world, accelerating even more the immanent process of secularisation; thus, it is almost as though they were projecting a hologram onto the abyss represented by the true transcendence. When treated in their chronological sequence, the cited works by Schmitt offer a problematic overview of Schmittian ontology, which has a tangled evolution. It has, in fact, been possible to trace three paradigmatic stages of such evolution in *The Buribunks, Roman Catholicism and Political Form* and *The Concept of The Political.* The only lesson to be learned from Schmitt's lack of a clear ontology is that we need to use caution when discussing supreme matters of philosophy, such as those regarding being, essence and existence.

Such caution can be traced to the figure of the Conditioners, outlined by Lewis in his work *The Abolition of Man*, with whom one can partly draw a

26 Albanese (1996), p 23. Translated by Carla Biondi.
27 Schmitt (1996), pp 8–9.
28 Schmitt (1996), p 9. See also Schmitt (2011), p 53.

parallel with the Buribunks. It is therefore useful to mention some of the points of contact which are necessary in order to make even more explicit the risk inherent in the absolute power of a class of men devoted to immanence.

What is the meaning of having absolute power? First, 'we must picture the race extended in time from the date of its emergence to that of its extinction',[29] as this is the only way we can represent the real power that one generation has over the next in our imagination. Both in the case of the Buribunks and in that of the Conditioners, such power is so extensive that it absorbs the dimension of the future.

Indeed, in both cases the man acquires a power that arises from the fact that he is at once subject and object of science, which, to borrow from Lewis, is the knowledge of nature. Both stage the hypothesis of a refined, and therefore extremely seductive, rationalism that the more it progresses, the more it tends to dehumanise the man of flesh and blood in favour of an ideal man who can only be achieved through the total abolition of the real one. Due to this, Lewis's appeal is 'to imagine a new Natural Philosophy, continually conscious that the "natural object" produced by analysis and abstraction is not reality but only a view'.[30]

The Buribunks, like the Conditioners and like any other form of imaginable Prometheism, do nothing but absolutise their point of view. They do this through a compelling logic, using what Schmitt calls 'the laws of logic'.[31] According to Lewis, 'This is one of the many instances where to carry a principle to what seems its logical conclusion produces absurdity.'[32] Moreover, 'Their extreme rationalism, by "seeing through" all "rational" motives, leaves them creatures of wholly irrational behaviour.'[33] The political and social repercussions of the ontological changes that have been examined are all within the sphere of immanence – it will be recalled that Schmitt switches from satire to a retrieval of Hegel – and it is based on the different ontological foundation that the various forms of world government develop.

On the other hand, it is in the figure of the Christian Epimetheus that Schmitt evokes – in the solitude of his cramped cell at the end of World War II, waiting to know whether or not he will be tried in Nuremberg. It is here that a representative of the sphere of transcendence can be found and it is stimulating to point out the features of this figure in order to grasp the difference from the Buribunks. Schmitt borrows the figure born from the imagination of the Swabian-Catholic poet Konrad Weiss, who wrote a poem with the same title in 1933. According to Heinrich Meir, it is 'Schmitt's fixation on the danger of the Antichrist'[34] that 'marks out the horizon in which Schmitt moves

29 Lewis (2009), p 56.
30 Lewis (2009), pp 78–9.
31 Chapter 2 of this volume, p 25.
32 Lewis (2009), pp 71–2.
33 Lewis (2009), p 67.
34 Meier (2011), p 134.

with his political advocacy'.[35] Keeping this fixation in mind, we should perhaps try to give an evaluation of the Schmittian thought. Schmitt cannot escape his destiny as a Catholic, and thus realises that he is already living through the eschatological time that began with the Christian faith. The demonological vision of politics and of its political theology therefore derives from Schmitt's personal faith. According to Agamben, the Christian Epimetheus is an 'assertion',[36] which 'resemble[s] the irresponsible guiltiness (or the guiltless responsibility) which seems to define the ethical situation of our time'.[37]

Perhaps someone might interpret this view of Agamben as a cultured and intellectual way of explaining Schmitt's adhesion to Nazism. However, the matter regarding the meaning of the figure of the Christian Epimetheus is more complex. We have seen that the Buribunks represent an approach to satirical criticism to the figure of the intellectual, so we reserve the right to follow two other hypotheses of interpretation – namely those of Meier, who dedicated to the Christian Epimetheus the entire fourth chapter of his book *The Lesson of Carl Schmitt: Four Chapters on the Distinction Between Political Theology and Political Philosophy*, and Cacciari, who entitled the last chapter of his work *Il potere che frena*, 'The Age of Epimetheus' ('L'età di Epimeteo').

Meier rightly highlights that it is through this figure that the Christian can escape from the 'eschatological paralysis'[38] that is created by the expectation of the end in historical time. Schmitt thus distinguishes the figure of a meek Christian awaiting the end of time from that of a Christian Epimetheus who is an active part of the historical process, although unable to find a meaning to historical development – meaning that it is only present in the gaze of the Christ.[39]

Like Epimetheus, he acts in history, but he only becomes aware of his actions afterwards. For this reason, in the Christian version he can unconsciously become the accelerating factor of Armageddon. In this respect, Epimetheus – who for Cacciari represents another face of Prometheus – contrasts not with only a Promethean society such as that of the Buribunks, but also with the Katechon, which represents a brake on the Apocalypse. To the figure of the Katechon, Schmitt dedicates deep and insightful reflections.

It is interesting that, by following Cacciari's reasoning, another piece is added to the puzzle.[40] According to Cacciari, the Katechon expresses yet another Promethean level, as every Katechon belongs to the Titans' bloodline; thus it is able to foresee and plan a world order, and thereby to suggest a sense to

35 Meier (2011), p 134.
36 Agamben (2005), p 17. Translated by Carla Biondi.
37 Agamben (2005), p 17. Translated by Carla Biondi.
38 Meier (2011), p 162.
39 Cf. Schmitt (2009), pp 167–70.
40 Cf. Cacciari, (2013). In particular, refer to the last chapter, precisely dedicated to a reflection on the contemporaneity of the figure of Epimetheus.

progress. Epimetheus, on the other hand, lacks this capacity. He thus wanders around the world without any reference point that can offer meaning, and therefore an end to his action. It is in this sense that Cacciari says that the age of Epimetheus is that of domination of anomie.

In other words, the political does not disappear from the world but instead becomes more and more immanent, to the point of crushing and shattering into political forms that, only worrying about the formal, legalistic, logical aspects, act with the sole aim of increasing their own power and thus practising a domain of a particular sphere of existence. Epimetheus inaugurated the era of permanent crises in which the very process of politics consists of nothing more than a rapid transition from one crisis to another, in a spiral that shortens the elapsing period between these crises. Cacciari grasps with greater desperation than Schmitt the meaning of an age that raises the model of Epimetheus as its emblem. A reason seems to be given by the fact that Cacciari's speech does not consider the hope in afterlife, but only the fear of an apocalyptic age on a purely human, and therefore immanent, level. If we were to use Schmittian political criteria to measure the intensity of the dissociation, and therefore of enmity, between the Buribunks and Epimetheus, we could easily think that they refer to different kinds of humans. After all, this is the distance that makes Schmitt's thought ambiguous, fascinating and powerful – a thought that, despite turning points (or perhaps it would be better to say contradictions), remains rich in suggestions and images that have marked the century we have left behind. Schmitt's Epimetheus, like Cacciari's, is unaware of the meaning of his actions, and he cannot make science out of history – as in Schmitt's view that 'the insight that all historical truth is true only once, as the *arcanum of ontology*'.[41]

Schmitt committed to conciliating the *arcanum* of this ontology with the power and forms that politics has taken in history. This work has shown the attempts of such commitment, which have been uncertain and oscillating yet fruitful, as they are authentic. Furthermore, it could not have been otherwise given that Schmitt's is 'the poor, unworthy, and yet nevertheless authentic case of a Christian Epimetheus'.[42]

References

Giorgio Agamben (2005) 'Introduction', in Carl Schmitt, *Un giurista davanti a se stesso*, Neri Pozza Editore.

Luciano Albanese (1996) *Il pensiero politico di Schmitt*, Laterza.

Hannah Arendt (1961) *Between Past and Future: Six Exercises in Political Thought*, Viking.

Massimo Cacciari (2013) *Il potere che frena*, Adelphi.

Gilbert K. Chesterton (1920) *Catholic and Anti-Catholic History*, The America Press.

41 Meier (2011), p 123.
42 Schmitt (2017), p 15.

Winfried R. Dallmayr (1958) 'Epimeteo cristiano o Prometeo pagano?' 35 *Rivista internazionale di filosofia del diritto.*
Carlo Galli (1996) *Genealogia della politica: Carl Schmitt e la crisi del pensiero politico moderno,* Il Mulino.
Carlo Galli (2010) 'La gloria e i nemici della Chiesa cattolica', in Carl Schmitt, *Cattolicesimo romano e forma politica,* Il Mulino.
Clive S. Lewis (2009) *The Abolition of the Man,* HarperCollins.
Karl Löwith (1949) *Meaning in History,* University of Chicago Press.
Heinrich Meier (2011) *The Lesson of Carl Schmitt: Four Chapters on the Distinction Between Political Theology and Political Philosophy,* University of Chicago Press.
Michele Nicoletti (1990) *Trascendenza e potere: La teologia politica di Carl Schmitt,* Morcelliana.
Carl Schmitt (1996) *Roman Catholicism and Political Form,* Greenwood Press.
Carl Schmitt (2007) *The Concept of the Political,* University of Chicago Press.
Carl Schmitt (2009) 'Three Possibilities for a Christian Conception of History' 147 *Telos* 167.
Carl Schmitt (2011) *Political Romanticism,* Transaction.
Carl Schmitt (2017) *Ex Captivitate Salus. Experiences, 1945–1947,* Polity Press.

Authors Note: The first part of this chapter was written by Matteo Negro, the second part by Fabrizio Grasso.

Chapter 18

Schmitt's life within the academy since 2001

Lachlan Robb, Charles Lawson, Catherine Pickering and Edwin Bikundo

Introduction

Carl Schmitt (1888–1985) was one of the twentieth century's most controversial political theorists and jurists. While his writings remain entangled with his Nazi associations, recent attention has moved to a broader engagement with his ideas and their explanatory power to account for the modern legal, social and political environment in which we find ourselves. Here we attempt to quantify that engagement in the context of the current discourse about the 'War on Terror'.

The 'War on Terror' can be located to the period following the 11 September 2001 terrorist attacks in the United States and the subsequent global response that continues today. Scholars have addressed this event in some detail, and a number have considered Schmitt in their analyses. In this chapter, we take a new approach to this discourse. We adopt the approach of buribunkology as science and apply the methodology of a Buribunk:

> Every male and female Buribunk is obliged to keep a diary for every second of their existence. Copies of all diary entries are submitted daily and collated by local councils. Their simultaneous inspection results in indexation according to subject matter as well as authorship. Not only are the entries of an erotic, demonic, satirical, political and so on nature grouped together (under the strictest observation of the copyright law pertaining to each entry) but the authors are also catalogued according to their place of residence. Due to an ingenious scheme, later inspection through a card catalogue makes it possible straight away to determine every circumstance of interest pertaining to each person.[1]

This methodology as we have applied it is set out as a diagram in Figure 18.1. In true buribunkian fashion, we take the published articles available in databases

1 Chapter 2 of this volume, p 23.

DOI: 10.4324/9781003091066-22

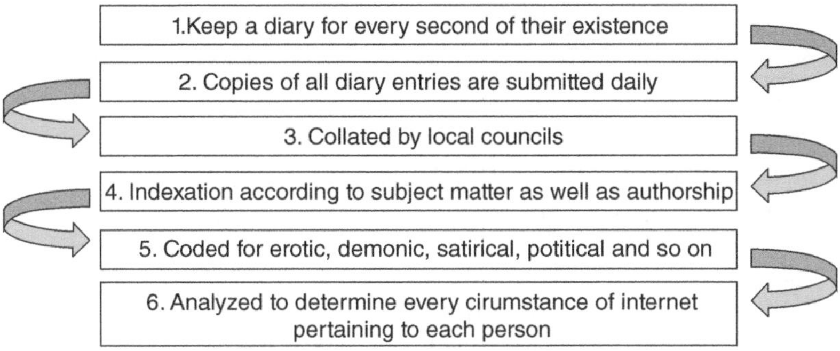

Figure 18.1 The methodology of a Buribunk approaching buribunkology as science.

(diaries) and search systematically for those articles by scholars about Schmitt's work (identifying and collating the diary entries) to see how his work has been used in the literature (indexing and coding). We then apply a mixed-methods approach combining a quantitative analysis with a qualitative account of the details of the discourse (analysis). The outcome of applying these methods is to reveal new insights into the patterns and associations in the uptake of Schmitt's works and to bring new insights and raise new questions requiring further research and analyses. We have asked: What would Schmitt, as he lives in the intellectual archive of the West, look like to a Buribunk? Our analysis reveals that Schmitt's impact is fragmented, spread across disciplines and presented in heterogeneous company. As such, Schmitt is no Ferker, the buribunkian diarist whose methodology of ideas distribution we model with our quantitative analysis using a qualitative account.

Methodology

To undertake a comprehensive analysis of the influence of Schmitt, including the extent of and limits to the current scholarly literature, a systematic quantitative literature review was conducted according to the methodology outlined by Catherine Pickering, Jason Byrne and others.[2] English-language articles were sourced from the electronic databases ProQuest, Scopus and JSTOR. These electronic databases were selected because their coverage of the relevant fields of academic study primarily addressed Schmitt's scholarship, and because preliminary analyses suggested that these databases provided the most comprehensive coverage of Schmitt's scholarship with a range of results specialising in the humanities, arts, law and social sciences. The searches of these databases were carried out in March and April 2017 according to the following sequential steps (see also Table 18.1 and Figure 18.2). Table 18.1 shows the searches of the ProQuest, Scopus and JSTOR databases, the steps taken and the number of hits for the sequential search steps. This outlines the process and actions taken

2 Pickering and Byrne (2014); Pickering et al. (2014).

Table 18.1 Steps 1–12: basic searches.

Step	*Search terms*	*ProQuest*	*Scopus*	*JSTOR*
1	'schmitt'	424,982	3,078	62,753
2	'Carl Schmitt'	9,052	691	8,124
3	'((("Carl Schmitt")) NOT au:"(Carl Schmitt)")'	9,035	691	7,976
4	'((("Carl Schmitt")) NOT au:"(Carl Schmitt)") AND la:(eng OR en)'	7,231	549	3,389
	German – '((("Carl Schmitt")) NOT au:"(Carl Schmitt)") AND la:(de OR ger)'	595	45	3,384
	Spanish – '((("Carl Schmitt")) NOT au:"(Carl Schmitt)") AND la:(spa OR es)'	846	37	220
5	Peer reviewed AND journal articles	3,138	334	3,382
6	'Carl Schmitt' AND subject areas (Table 2 – excluded)	2,357	328	3,264
7	'ti("Carl Schmitt") OR ab("Carl Schmitt") NOT au("Carl Schmitt")'	1,041	–	–
	'TITLE ("Carl Schmitt") AND (LIMIT-TO (DOCTYPE, "ar")) AND (LIMIT-TO (SUBJAREA, "SOCI") OR LIMIT-TO (SUBJAREA, "ARTS")) AND (LIMIT-TO (LANGUAGE, "English"))'	–	137	–
	'(ti:"Schmitt" OR tb:"Schmitt" OR tb:"Schmitt") AND la:(eng OR en) AND "Carl Schmitt"'	–	–	146
8	Subject areas (Table 2 – included)	819	137	145
9	Export as citations	575	137	145
10	Combining citations and removal of duplicates and reviews	578		
11	Individual assessment and removal of non-relevant articles	476		
12	Assessment of articles for engagement with the War on Terror ('War on Terror and 9/11')	67		

to compile the systematic quantitative literature review data. The flowchart in Figure 18.2 outlines the process and actions taken to compile the systematic quantitative literature review: Preferred Reporting Items for Systematic reviews and Meta-Analyses (PRISMA).[3] This establishes compliance with a generally accepted standard for conducting systematic quantitative literature reviews.

The initial search of the databases ProQuest, Scopus and JSTOR was carried out using the search term 'schmitt' (Step 1). These searches returned the following hits: ProQuest – 424,982 hits; Scopus – 3,078 hits; and JSTOR –

3 PRISMA (2014). See also Moher et al. (2009).

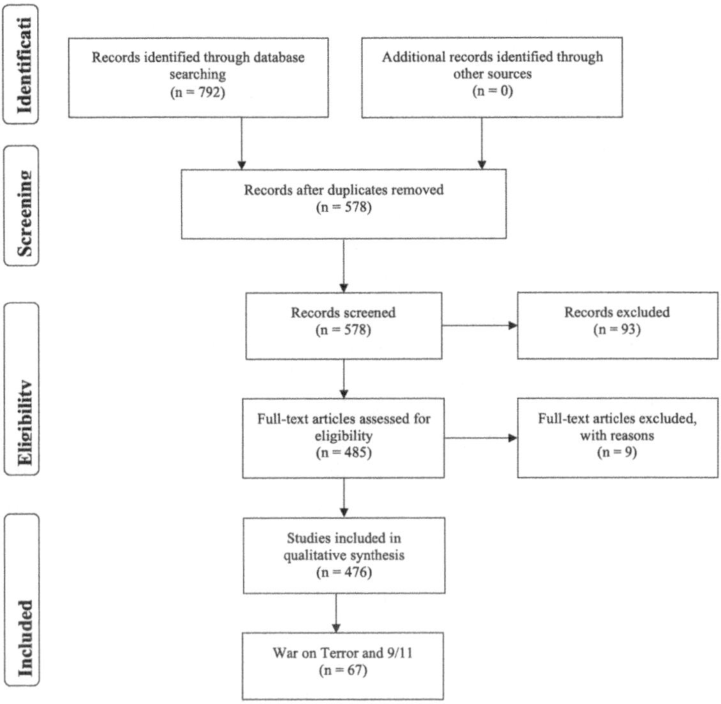

Figure 18.2 Preferred Reporting Items for Systematic reviews and Meta-Analyses (PRISMA) flowchart.

62,753 hits. This was further refined to distinguish between Carl Schmitt and other Carls and Schmitts using the search term 'Carl Schmitt' (Step 2), although not distinguishing between the *actual* Carl Schmitt (1888–1985) and the other Carl Schmitts. These searches returned the following hits respectively: ProQuest – 9,052 hits; Scopus – 691 hits; and JSTOR – 8,124 hits. This was then refined again to remove any results that were for works authored by the actual Carl Schmitt because the analysis is about his influence and not Schmitt's own works. The search terms '((("Carl Schmitt")) NOT au:"(Carl Schmitt)")' were applied (Step 3) returning the following hits: ProQuest – 9,035 hits; Scopus – 691 hits; and JSTOR – 7,976 hits. This was again refined to distinguish between English language and other languages using the search term '((("Carl Schmitt")) NOT au:"(Carl Schmitt)") AND la:(eng OR en)' (Step 4) returning the following hits: ProQuest – 7,231 hits; Scopus – 549 hits; and JSTOR – 3,389 hits. Applying a similar search term for German and Spanish there were the following hits respectively: ProQuest – 595 and 846 hits; Scopus – 45 and 37 hits; and JSTOR – 3,384 and 220 hits.

The selections were further refined to select only peer-reviewed and journal articles (step 5) with the following hits: ProQuest – 3,138 hits; Scopus – 334 hits; and JSTOR – 3,382 hits. To then confine the selected articles to those addressing the *actual Carl* Schmitt, various subject areas were excluded (Step 6) as set out in Table 18.2. After these refinements there were: ProQuest – 2,357 hits; Scopus – 328 hits; and JSTOR – 3,264 hits. To further refine the search to relevant articles, searches were conducted on these results to find those that had 'Schmitt' or 'Carl Schmitt' in the titles or abstracts of the articles (Step 7). The rationale for this was to select only articles with a central focus on the actual Carl Schmitt with the assumption that mention of 'Schmitt' or 'Carl Schmitt' in the title or abstract identifies the focus of the article about the actual Carl Schmitt. Within the databases, some articles did not have abstracts, with the JSTOR database estimating that only about 10 per cent of its database articles included abstracts. This suggests the majority of articles identified in the JSTOR database with the 'Schmitt' or 'Carl Schmitt' terms were according to the titles. The effect of this error was likely to be minimal as the ProQuest, Scopus and JSTOR overlap and most were likely to be duplicates. After these refinements there were: ProQuest – 1,041 hits; Scopus – 137 hits; and JSTOR – 146 hits. The identified articles from these searches were then further refined, again using subject areas (Step 8). These excluded subject areas are also set out in Table 18.2. To confine the selected articles to only those addressing the actual Carl Schmitt, various subject areas were excluded from or included in the table. The subject areas excluded and included are set out for each

Table 18.2 **Excluded and included subject areas.**

Step	*ProQuest*	*Scopus*	*JSTOR*
6	Metaphysics, aesthetics, drama, friendship	Psychology, physics and astronomy, engineering, earth and planetary sciences, computer science, environmental science, medicine, business, management and accounting	Performing arts, music, management and organisational behaviour, linguistics, library science, general science, film studies, art and art history, architecture and architectural history, archaeology
8	Politics, political theory, sovereignty, Carl Schmitt, political philosophy, theology, philosophy, liberalism, law, democracy, Carl Schmitt (1888–1985), philosophers, history, international law	Social sciences, arts and humanities	Bibliography, history, international relations, law, language and literature, philosophy, religion

ProQuest, Scopus and JSTOR databases. After these refinements, there were: ProQuest – 819 hits; Scopus – 137 hits; and JSTOR – 145 hits.

These results were then exported as citations and combined with some loss of data (Step 9). This was because ProQuest limited the available data that could be downloaded to 575 citations out of the 819 identified in the searches and refinements, and some of the JSTOR data downloaded citations in unintelligible code. The citations were then culled of duplicates and reviews (Step 10). The final database of citations was 578 articles. Each of these articles was then downloaded and individually assessed for mention of the actual Carl Schmitt, removing any that appeared in languages other than English and those that had an obvious alternate focus but had eluded the previous screening steps (Step 11). The final number was 476 articles.

The 476 remaining articles were then individually assessed, scored and the count data compiled in a spreadsheet. The dataset and results reported here focus only on those articles that were first scored for 'War on Terror and 9/11', being articles that addressed in substance the War on Terror (Step 12). Of the 476 articles identified in the systematic literature review, 67 were scored for 'War on Terror and 9/11' (see Table 18.1). The count data were then subjected to further analysis using plain counts (Figures 18.3 and 18.4) and ordinations (Figures 18.5–8). Counts were prepared for the geographic distribution of authors' listed affiliations, discipline areas of journals claimed by the journals' editors, concepts articulated by Schmitt (such as political, sovereignty, *Nomos*, and so on), themes iteratively identified from reading the 67 identified 'War on Terror and 9/11' articles (such as terrorism, Guantanamo Bay, human rights and so on), other theorists also addressed in addition to Schmitt (such as Agamben, Hobbes, Kant, and so on) and Schmitt's texts that were cited in the articles (such as *The Concept of the Political* (1927), *Political Theology: Four*

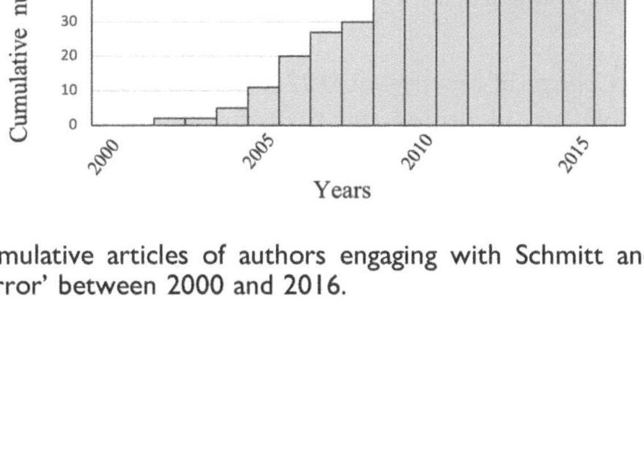

Figure 18.3 Cumulative articles of authors engaging with Schmitt and the 'War on Terror' between 2000 and 2016.

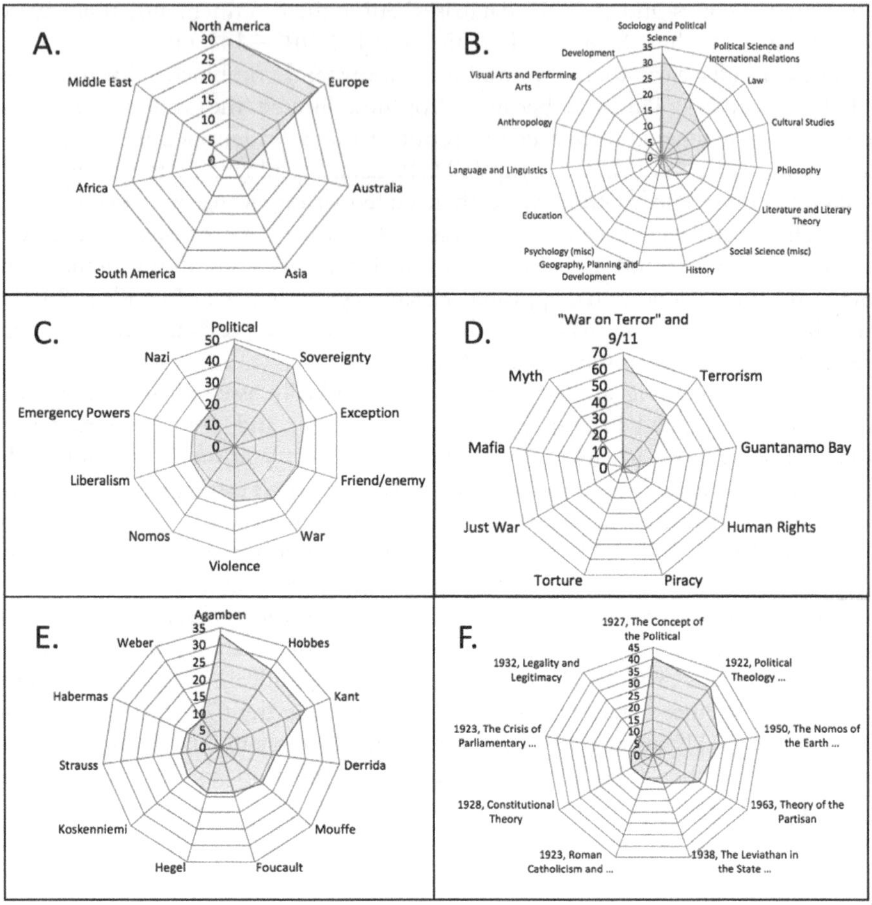

Figure 18.4 Spider web diagrams for the counts of 67 articles engaging with Schmitt and the 'War on Terror' between 2000 and 2016. A. The geographic distribution of articles based on the author(s) listed affiliation. B. The discipline areas of the journals were articles were published. C. The main Schmitt concepts addressed in the articles. D. The main broad themes addressed in the articles. E. The major other theorist also cited with Schmitt in the articles. F. The Schmitt texts cited in the articles.

Chapters on the Concept of Sovereignty (1922) and so on). The count data show whether a variable was identified and then the sum of those counts across the 67 articles for the variable. For example, 33 of the 67 articles include some mention of Agamben, so the sum of counts would be 33 (see Figure 18.4E).

We then applied some standard analysis methods for quantitative data to highlight patterns and relationships among the articles based on their content, and hence to identify emergent properties of the Schmitt literature relating to the 'War on Terror' and 9/11. Specifically, we used non-metric multidimensional scaling (NMDS) ordinations performed in the multivariate statistical package PRIMER (version 6.1.12) to visualise the relationship between the content of the articles. First, the count data for the variables such as the content of the articles were used to calculate (dis)similarity matrices using the Bray-Curtis measures, which gives an estimate of how (un)related each article is compared pairwise with every other article based on (dis)similarity in the content. Then, to visualise these relationships, non-metric multidimensional scaling was used to describe the maximum variation among the articles in two dimensions (NMDS axes 1 and 2) as vectors (Figure 18.5) or tree diagrams (Figures 18.6–8). For a vector example, of the 67 articles, those engaging with the Schmitt concepts of 'Emergency Powers' also engaged with 'Exception' but not with 'Nomos' would be close together on the ordination, but far away from other articles (see Figure 18.5A). For a tree diagram example, the concepts of 'violence' and 'war' were more similarly located in articles (approximately 80 per cent) than 'biopolitics' and 'history' (approximately 30 per cent), and these grouped concepts were only very distantly similar (approximately 10 per cent) (see Figure 18.6).

We also used a text analyser to identify high-level concepts. Specifically, we used the text analyser Leximancer (Version Leximancer V4.5 Desktop Academic) to analyse 64 of the previously identified 67 full text articles (three articles were not available in appropriate formats for analysis) and visualise the relationship between the concepts identified in the articles according to 'themes' (bubbles) and 'concepts' (labels within bubbles). The Leximancer carries out an automatic unsupervised analysis of texts that are imported as individual articles. There are two forms of analysis: a semantic analysis based on the attributes of words and collections of words extracted by its own dictionary of terms; and a relational analysis based on the frequency of occurrence.[4] The Leximancer analysis of the 64 articles amenable to analysis showed five distinct themes (bubbles) consisting of groupings of related concepts (labels within bubbles) (Figure 18.9). The proximity of the theme bubbles and concept labels to one another indicates conceptually similarity, with those clustered together most closely related.

Results

There is a diversity of articles (67) published by a wide range of authors (72) and in a wide range of journals (39) addressing Schmitt's work in relation to the discourse on the war on terror and 9/11 (Table 18.3). Since the first paper on this topic was published in 2002, interest has remained relatively constant, indicating that new engagements continue to emerge with approximately four new articles per year (Figure 18.2). Based on the affiliations of the authors, much of the research is published by academics based in the North America (30), and in particularly the United States (29), followed by Europe (28),

4 Smith and Humphreys (2006).

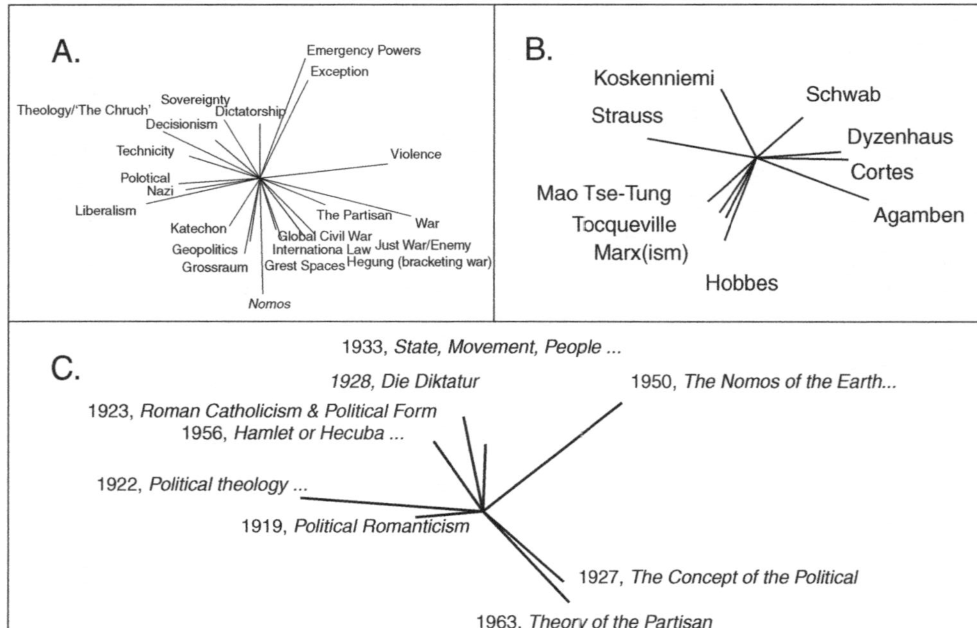

Figure 18.5 The panels display relationships and patterns in the 67 articles based on similarity in their content. Vectors display increasing importance of specific types of content, with clusters of vectors close together reflecting clusters of articles with similar content. A. The main Schmitt concepts addressed in the articles. B. The major other theorist also cited with Schmitt in the articles. C. The Schmitt texts co-cited in the articles.

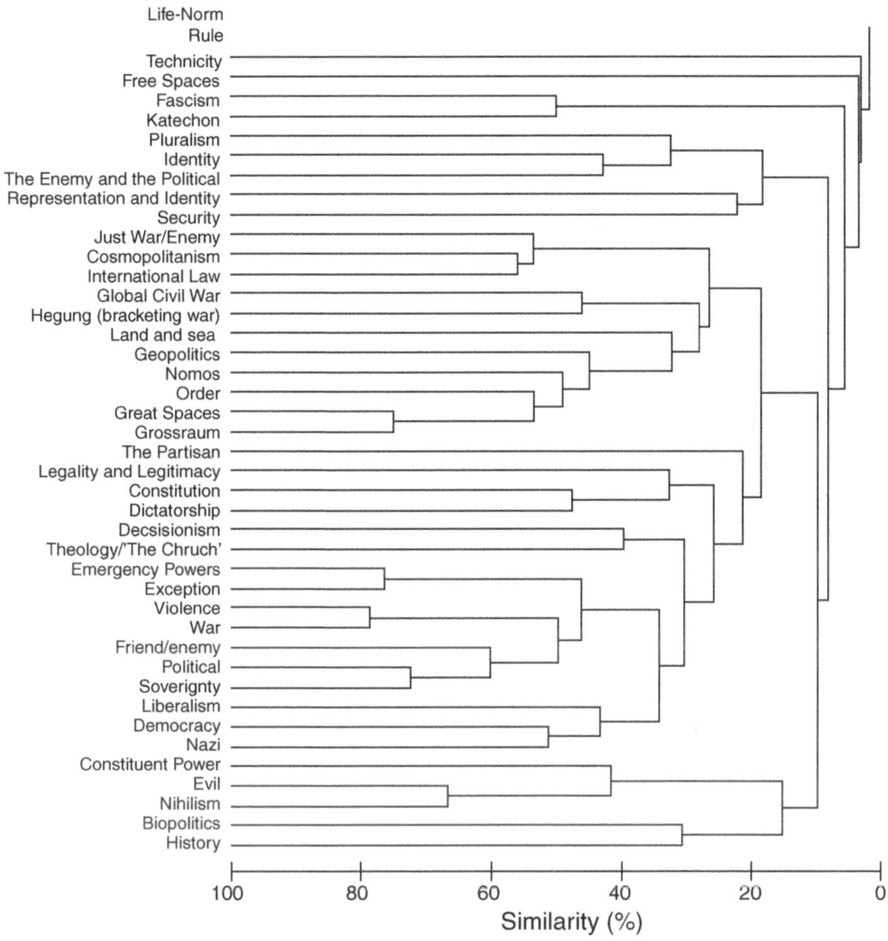

Figure 18.6 Similarity of concepts. A Bray–Curtis visualisation displaying relationships and patterns in the 67 articles based on similarity in their content, with branches joining according to the similarity between the concepts and measured as a percentage of similarity.

including the United Kingdom (13) (Figure 18.4A). Outside this nexus, there were very few papers published with academics who had affiliations to Australia (5), Asia (1) and Chile (1), and none in the rest of South America or Africa (Figure 18.4A). In contrast to the diversity of authors (73), there is a near-absence of a second article on the topic by the same author, with only one, Jason Ralph, authoring a second article (Table 18.3). The most popular journals for work about Schmitt and the 'War or Terror' were: *Telos* (6), *Security and Dialogue* (4), the *South Atlantic Quarterly, International Political Sociology, Leiden Journal of International Law* and *Millennium* (3 each) (Table 18.3). The table lists

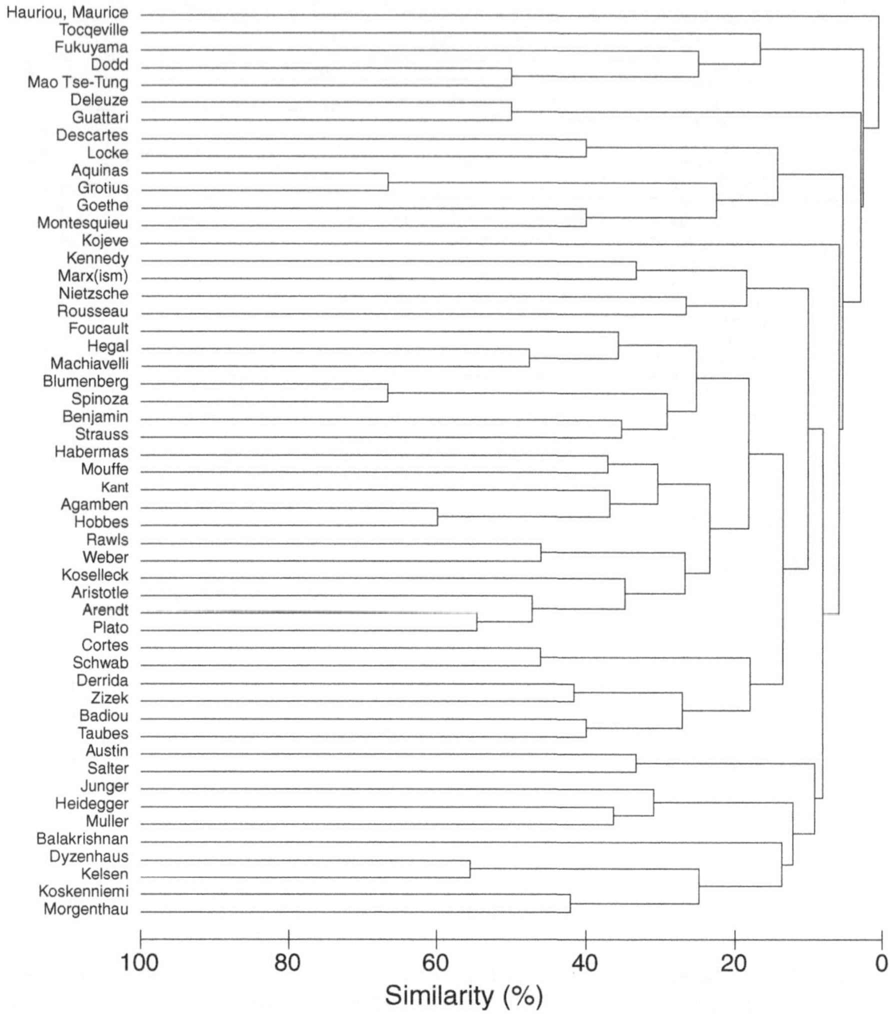

Figure 18.7 Other theorists also cited in the 67 articles addressing Schmitt. A Bray–Curtis visualisation displaying relationships and patterns, with branches joining according to the similarity between the theorists also with Schmitt in the articles and measured as a percentage of similarity.

the articles according to the year, authors, country of author and journal in alphabetical order of the first author's family name. And while the literature is found in 39 different journals (Table 18.3), most of these journals fall within the disciplines of sociology and political sciences (33), political sciences and international relations (21), law (16), cultural studies (16) and philosophy (10) (Figure 18.4B).

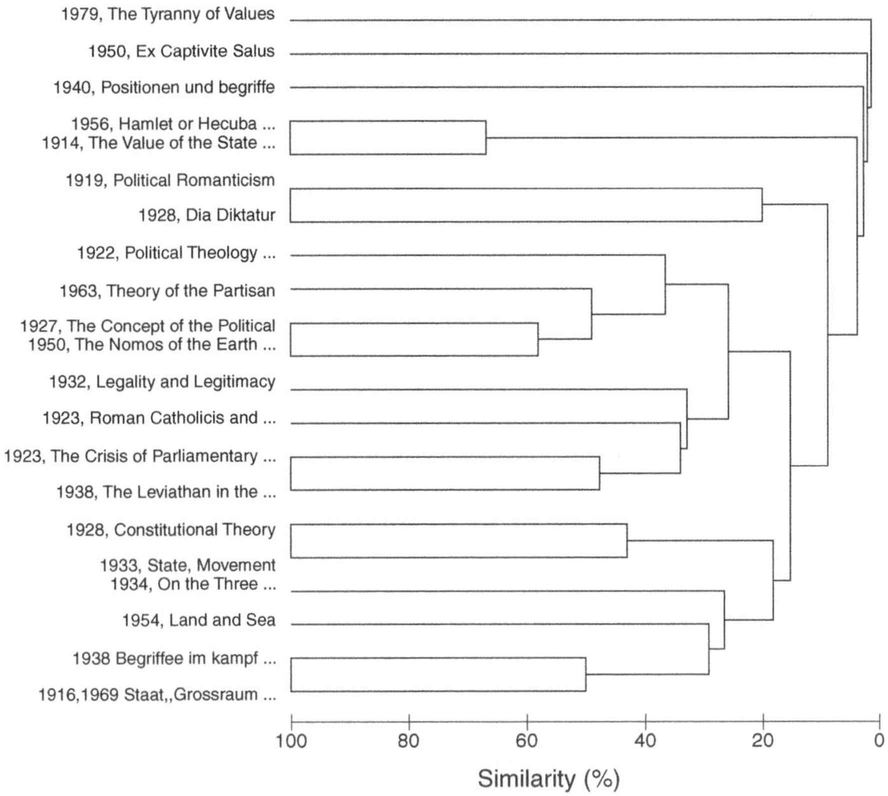

Figure 18.8 Schmitt texts. A Bray–Curtis visualisation displaying relationships with branches joining according to the similarity between the texts and measured as a percentage of similarity.

The kinds of concepts were addressed by reading each article and scoring for concepts. These concepts were iteratively identified from broadly reading the articles and noting the engagement with concepts and then recording the engagement of each article with all the identified concepts. The main concepts addressed by the analysed articles were the political (48), sovereignty (46), exception (34), friend/enemy (31), war (30), violence (26), *Nomos* (23), liberalism (22), emergency powers (21) and Nazis (20) (Figure 18.4C). Within the articles addressing the 'War or Terror', the other themes addressed were terrorism (41), Guantanamo Bay (17), human rights (8), piracy (3) and torture (3) (Figure 18.4D). In the articles addressing Schmitt, there were also references to Agamben (33), Hobbes (27), Kant (27), Derrida (16), Mouffe (16), Foucault (14), Hegel (14), Koskenniemi (13), Strauss (12), Habermas (11) and Weber (10) (Figure 18.4E). The remaining themes addressed were the particular Schmitt texts engaged by the articles: the 1927 publication *The Concept of the*

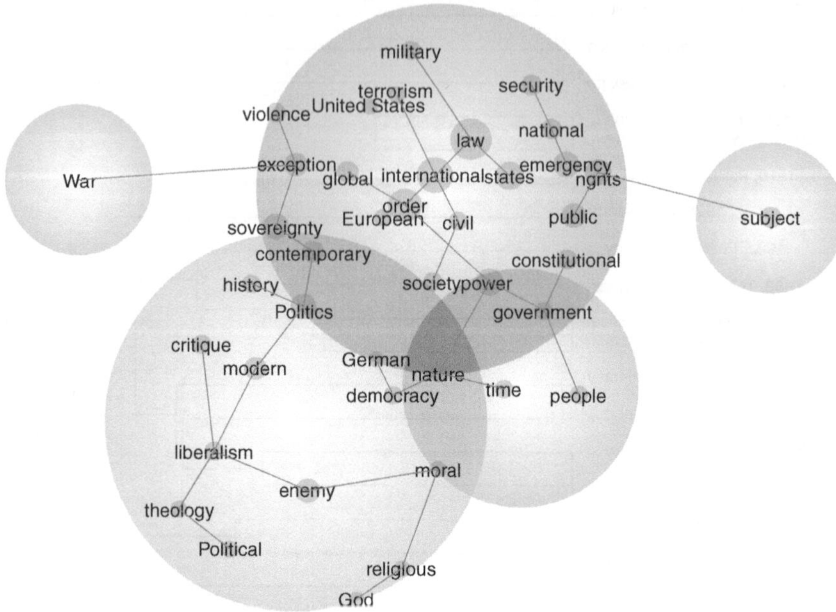

Figure 18.9 Schmitt automated themes and concepts. A visualisation displaying relationships and patterns in the 64 articles based on a Leximancer automatic unsupervised analysis of texts identifying the themes (bubbles) 'law', 'enemy', 'people', 'subject' and 'war', and a range of concepts (labels within bubbles) grouped within each theme. The proximity of the theme bubbles and concept labels to one another indicates conceptually similarity, with those clustered together most closely related.

Political was the most engaged Schmitt text in the articles (41), followed in order by the 1922 publication *Political Theology: Four Chapters on the Concept of Sovereignty* (37), the 1950 publication *The Nomos of the Earth in the International Law of the Jus Publicum Europaeum* (28), the 1963 publication *Theory of the Partisan* (22), the 1938 publication *The Leviathan in the State Theory of Thomas Hobbes* (12), the 1923 publication *Roman Catholicism and Political Form* (10), the 1928 publication *Constitutional Theory* (10), the 1923 publication *The Crisis of Parliamentary Democracy* (9) and the 1932 publication *Legality and Legitimacy* (8) (Figure 18.4F).

To assess more precisely the relationship between the engagements with the concepts, other theorists and texts, various visualisations of the relationships among articles (ordinations) were conducted (Figures 18.5–8). An ordination is a statistical technique for comparing multiple variables (multivariate articles here), where similar articles are near to each other and dissimilar articles are further apart from each other. The relationships between the articles on each of several axes are then characterised graphically. Put slightly differently, the

Table 18.3 Details about the 67 articles engaging Schmitt and the 'War on Terror'.

Year	*Authors*	*Country*	*Journal*
2007	Aradau, Claudia	England	*Third World Quarterly*
2011	Barder, Alexander; Debrix, Francois	USA	*Philosophy and Social Criticism*
2009	Bauman, Zygmunt	England	*Theory, Culture and Society*
2012	Benhabib, Seyla	USA	*Political theory*
2016	Bikundo, Edwin	Australia	*International Criminal Law Review*
2005	Boersma, Jess	USA	*Discourse*
2016	Bradley, Arthur; Cerella, Antonio	England	*Journal for Cultural Research*
2013	Brown, Petra	Australia	*Journal of the Melbourne College of Divinity*
2007	Buck-Morss, Susan	USA	*Rethinking Marxism*
2006	Burchard, Christoph	Germany	*Leiden Journal of International Law*
2008	Casson, Douglas	USA	*Politics and Policy*
2008	Chandler, David	England	*Millennium*
2012	Criddle, Evan; Fox-Decent, Evan	USA	*Human Rights Quarterly*
2016	Croce, Mariano; Salvatore, Andrea	Italy, Belgium	*Ratio Juris*
2012	De Ruiter, Adrienne	Netherlands	*Archiv fur Rechts- und Sozialphilosophie*
2006	Dean, Mitchell	Australia	*Theory Culture and Society*
2007	Dillon, Michael	England	*International Political Sociology*
2013	Ditrych, Ondrej	Czech Republic	*Security Dialogue*
2007	Doty, Roxanne	USA	*International Political Sociology*
2009	Dutton, Michael	England	*Postcolonial Studies*
2008	Emden, Christian J	USA	*Telos*
2014	Falk, Hjalmar	Sweden	*European Review*
2006	Friedrichs, Jörg	Germany	*Leiden Journal of International Law*
2009	Gumz, Jonathan	USA	*Journal of Strategic Studies*
2011	Hansen, Lene	Denmark	*Security Dialogue*
2011	Hartz, Emily; Ugilt, Rasmus	Denmark	*Law and Critique*
2014	Hirsch, Alexander	USA	*Contemporary Political Theory*
2004	Klitsche de la Grange, Teodoro	NA	*Telos*
2006	Kochi, Tarik	Australia	*Law and Critique*
2007	Kutz, Christopher	USA	*California Law Review*
2009	Luoma, Mika	Finland	*International Political Sociology*

Year	*Authors*	*Country*	*Journal*
2005	Marder, Michael	Chile	*Telos*
2010	McCormick, John P	USA	*Critical Review of International Social and Political Philosophy*
2009	McLoughlin, Daniel	Australia	*The Australian Feminist Law Journal*
2012	Minca, Claudio	Nether-lands	*Geopolitics*
2013	Minkkinen, Panu	Finland	*International Journal of Constitutional Law*
2013	Monod, Jean-Claude	France	*The New Centennial Review*
2005	Moreiras, Alberto	USA	*Positions*
2005	Mouffe, Chantal	USA	*South Atlantic Quarterly*
2006	Neal, Andrew	England	*Security Dialogue*
2012	Norman, Emma	Mexico	*Politics and Policy*
2007	Norris, Andrew	USA	*Journal of Law and Society*
2011	Norton, Anne	USA	*Constellations*
2006	Odysseos, Louiza; Petito, Fabio	England, Italy	*Leiden Journal of International Law*
2012	Pan, David	USA	*Telos*
2006	Prozorov, Sergei	Russia	*Millennium*
2010	Ralph, Jason	England	*Millennium*
2009	Ralph, Jason	England	*Review of International Studies*
2004	Rejali, Darius	USA	*Historical Reflections*
2014	Rossi, Norma	England	*Global Crime*
2006	Scheuerman, William	USA	*Constellations*
2010	Schiff, Jacob	USA	*Philosophy and Social Criticism*
2012	Schulman, Alex	USA	*Journal of Political Ideologies*
2016	Schulzke, Marcus	England	*Telos*
2010	Sitze, Adam	USA	*The New Centennial Review*
2013	Stevens, Jason	USA	*Boundary 2*
2007	Suganami, Hidemi	Japan	*Review of International Studies*
2005	Surin, Kenneth	USA	*South Atlantic Quarterly*
2012	Tahmassian, Lena	USA	*Journal of Spanish Cultural Studies*
2011	Teschke, Benno	England	*International Theory*
2002	Turner, Bryan	England	*Theory, Culture & Society*
2002	Ulmen, Gary	USA	*Telos*
2004	Vatter, Miguel	USA	*The New Centennial Review*
2009	Vermeule, Adrian	USA	*Harvard Law Review*
2006	Walker, R.B.J	Canada	*Security Dialogue*
2005	Watson, Janell	USA	*South Atlantic Quarterly*
2010	Werner, Wouter	Nether-lands	*International Theory*

variables' projection represents the relationship among them and groupings close together reveal a closer relationship than those far apart, so that tightly clustered articles are positively related while articles at different ends of the figure have little in common in their content.

For ordinations of concepts, other theorists and Schmitt texts, the vector lines radiating out from the centre are included, with the length of the line indicating increasing strength of correlation while the direction indicates more articles that include that concept (Figure 18.5). Therefore, concepts close together were often used in the same articles. Correspondingly concepts on opposite sides of the figure were less likely to co-occur in articles. The concepts of 'Emergency Powers' and 'Exception', 'Geopolitics' and 'Grossraum', and 'Global Civil War', 'Just War/ Enemy', 'Hegung (bracketing war)', 'International Law' and 'Great Spaces' were grouped (Figure 18.5A). Among the major other theorists in co-occurring articles there were grouping among 'Dyzenhaus', 'Cortes' and 'Agamben' and 'Mao Tse-Tung', 'Tocqueville' and 'Marx(ism)' (Figure 18.5B). Among Schmitt's works cited in articles, the main groupings were '1919, *Political Theology: Four Chapters on the Concept of Sovereignty*', '1919, *Political Romanticism*', '1927, *The Concept of the Political*' and '1963, *Theory of the Partisan*' (Figure 18.5C).

Visualising these ordinations of concepts, other theorists and Schmitt texts using similarity measures in a tree diagram also shows the strength of correlation with higher levels of similarity, meaning concepts close together were often used in the same articles (Figures 18.6–8). These figures show that there was not a high degree of similarity in any of the concepts, other theorists or Schmitt texts, even at the 50 per cent similarity mark (Figures 18.6–8). Comparing the visualisations of groupings according to the vector lines radiating out from the centre (Figure 18.5) with the similarity measures in a tree diagram (Figures 18.6–8) shows that the groupings identified are not very similar, even at the 50 per cent level (Figures 18.5–8). Of the apparent groupings of concepts, 'Life-Norm' and 'Rule', 'Grossraum' and 'Great Spaces', 'Emergency Powers' and 'Exception', 'Violence' and 'War', 'Friend/Enemy' with 'Political' and 'Sovereignty', and 'Evil' and 'Nihilism' show similarity (Figure 18.6). For co-cited similar theorists, the groupings are 'Aquinas' and 'Grotius', 'Blumberg' and 'Spinoza', 'Agamben' and 'Hobbs', 'Arendt' and 'Plato', and 'Dyzenhaus' and 'Kelsen' (Figure 18.7). And for Schmitt's similar texts, '1956, *Hamlet or Hecuba: The Intrusion of the Time into the Play*', '1914, *The Value of the State and the Significance of the Individual*', '1927, *The Concept of the Political*' and '1950, *The Nomos of the Earth in the International Law of the Jus Publicum*' show a similar grouping (Figure 18.8). A better account of these similarity visualisations is that they reveal Schmitt's impact is fragmented, spread across disciplines and presented in heterogeneous company.

To avoid the possible bias in our identifying Schmitt's ideas a scoring them (Figures 18.4–8), an automatic text mining software application, Leximancer, was applied as a machine way to identify high-level concepts (Figure 18.9). The visualisation is of the semantic analysis based on the attributes of words and collections of words extracted from the application's own dictionary of terms, and a relational analysis based on the frequency of occurrence. This appears as five themes (bubbles 'law', 'enemy', 'people', 'subject' and 'war') and a range of concepts (labels within bubbles) grouped within each theme. The discrete themes including a single concept were 'subject' and 'war', while the other themes from the biggest bubble down were 'law', 'enemy', 'people' (Figure 18.9). Within the theme 'law', the concepts included 'international', 'states', 'national', 'security', 'sovereignty' and 'violence', while the theme 'enemy' included the concepts 'democracy', 'theology', 'liberalism', 'religion' and 'modern' (Figure 18.9). These Leximancer machine-derived themes and concepts are broadly consistent with the individually assessed, scored and counted data (Figures 18.4–8), although a direct comparison is not possible because the Leximancer dictionary label may not be the same as the scored label. This is because the Leximancer application builds a list of terms that are ranked according to their frequency of occurrence and interrelationships with each text excerpt based on the machine-generated data to support each concept. Thus, individually assessed, scored and count data relied on human judgement (Figures 18.4–8), while the Leximancer application relies on fixed statistical modelling on semantics and relations (Figure 18.9).

What is a Buribunkian to make of these results?

Leaving Don Juan and Leporello as the 'good buffo',[5] we focus on Ferker. Ferker and Schnekke are for our buribunkian purposes the same, as they both keep diaries, and Ferker's secret love and fear of death[6] are not important for our analyses – although they would be to overcome any 'caprice and to have moulded Buribunkdom in its purest form into a historical reality'.[7] Ferker developed the diary into the quintessential buribunkian endeavour for the distribution of ideas:

> Only Ferker developed the diary into an ethical-historical possibility; he holds the rights of the first-born in the realm of Buribunkdom. Be history yourself! Live so that every single one of your seconds can be recorded in your diary and fall into the hands of your biographer! Coming from a mouth like Ferker's, those were big and strong words which humankind had never heard before. A world confederacy for the distribution of his ideas, which was organised with great skill and which had at its disposal an intelligent press, paved the way for this thought to reach the last corners of the most remote villages. No hamlet is so small for no smith to be there at all, to quote an old folk tune; today we may say with pride that no hamlet is so small for a puff of buribunkian spirit not to blow there.[8]

5 Chapter 2 of this volume, p 16.
6 Chapter 2 of this volume, p 22.
7 Chapter 2 of this volume, p 22.
8 Chapter 2 of this volume, p 19.

Recall that we took this buribunkian endeavour seriously and asked what would Schmitt, as he lives on in the intellectual archive of the West, look like to a Buribunk? In addressing this question, we applied the buribunkian methodology (Figure 18.1) by collecting published articles (diaries), systematically searching those articles (identifying and collating the diary entries), then analysing the text (indexing and coding). This is the quintessential methodology (discipline) of modern science applied to the object of the diary that is the essence of buribunkian endeavour to write a diary, which in turn produces its own object as the written diary (in contrast to the mere record maintained by Leporello of Don Juan's exploits).[9] As such, the Ferker diary is amenable to a science methodology as a 'buribunkian cinematic attitude',[10] while the Leporello record is not beyond the basic counting 'at most the supporting, marginal role of an accompanying incentive'.[11] We therefore applied a mixed-methods approach combining a quantitative analysis with a qualitative account of the details of the discourse (analysis) – this is the 'later inspection through a card catalogue [that] makes it possible straight away to determine every circumstance of interest pertaining to each person'.[12] As the Buribunks might expect, the outcome of applying these methods should be to reveal new insights into the patterns and associations in the uptake of Schmitt's works – like 'a historian of psycho-pathology could reliably determine in a matter of hours which kind of psycho-pathological studies have so far been conducted and … which psycho-pathological motives led to these psycho-pathological studies'.[13] In effect, our hypothesis was that a science methodology would reveal the main ideas of Schmitt by identifying the Schmittian ideas taken up by others in their articles engaging with Schmitt.

We found that Schmitt's work addressing the 'War on Terror and 9/11' was predominantly taken up in North America and Europe (Figure 18.4A), and predominantly engaged with in the sociology and political literature (Figure 18.4B). The main ideas of Schmitt taken up by others were about the 'political', 'sovereignty', 'exception' and 'friend/enemy' (Figure 18.4C) and addressed together with 'Agamben', 'Hobbes', 'Kant' and 'Derrida' (Table 18.4E). The main Schmitt concepts clustered around 'Emergency Powers' and 'Exception', 'Political', 'Nazi' and 'Liberalism', 'Global Civil War', 'International Law' and 'Great Spaces', with 'Nomos', 'Violence' and 'Sovereignty' appearing to be distinctly separated (Figure 18.5A). Visualising these relationships according to similarity, however, revealed that there was very little similarity across the concepts (Figure 18.6), co-cited theorists (Figure 18.7) or texts (Figure 18.8). In contrast, the Leximancer application suggests clear themes and concepts within those themes, showing a relationship between the concepts 'international', 'states', 'national', 'security', 'sovereignty'

9 Chapter 2 of this volume, pp 15–6.
10 Chapter 2 of this volume, p 16.
11 Chapter 2 of this volume, p 16.
12 Chapter 2 of this volume, p 23.
13 Chapter 2 of this volume, pp 23–4.

and 'violence', and the theme 'law'; and the concepts 'democracy', 'theology', 'liberalism', 'religion' and 'modern', and the theme 'enemy' (Figure 18.9).

Most significantly for the purposes of this study, the analyses show that Schmitt's ideas can be traced through the literature using text to identify the locations of where these ideas have been recorded, both the form of location (journal article) and place of location (database) (see Table 18.1, steps 1–11). Text can also be used to distinguish between the different Schmitt ideas (Table 18.1, step 12) according to counting the different ideas (Figure 18.4) and identifying relationships between the different ideas (Figures 18.5–8). This closely tracks the methodology of a Buribunk approaching buribunkology as science (Figure 18.1). The limitation of our analyses, however, is that the specific context or deployment of the Schmitt ideas about the 'War or Terror and 9/11' beyond the tags 'political', 'sovereignty', 'exception', 'friend/enemy' and so on (Figure 18.4C) is not apparent. For example, Agamben is cited in the same article as Schmitt in 34 of the 67 articles identified in the databases (see Figure 18.4E), but this tells us nothing about whether Schmitt's ideas were being compared, contrasted or ignored by Agamben, or the content of the Schmitt ideas being engaged. When we automated the analysis using the Leximancer text analyser, the results appeared more certain because they were not framed with vector or statistical probabilities. However, while the themes and concepts appeared more definite, they too were unable to reveal the specific context or deployment of the Schmitt ideas about the 'War or Terror and 9/11' beyond the tagged themes and concept labels (Figure 18.9). In short, our methodology was unable to determine every circumstance of interest pertaining to Schmitt because the methodology lacked explanatory power to provide an account with explanatory meaning.

As we know, to record buribunkologically for all of Buribunkdom, these outcomes must be reported to the head of a Buribunk department, and then in turn reported to a central agency to create the 'master catalogues published simultaneously in Esperanto'.[14] Applying a mixed-methods approach has revealed some patterns and associations in the uptake of Schmitt's works. But Schmitt is no Ferker dominating the archive; rather, his impact is fragmented, spread across disciplines and presented in heterogeneous company. This is not what a buribunkian expects from recording buribunkologically through a diary to reveal ideas (captured as new insights into the patterns and associations) that can be reported to a Buribunk department and spread to every small hamlet. Instead, our analysis shows that the buribunkian endeavour and methodology for the distribution of ideas are flawed, and that the buribunkian spirit will require more than a mere 'small … puff'.[15] If Buribunkdom requires 'master catalogues',[16] then this mixed-methods approach combining a quantitative analysis with a qualitative account of the details using the diary record will require more nuances and, in particular, an account of what those ideas mean. Our

14 Chapter 2 of this volume, p 24.
15 Chapter 2 of this volume, p 19.
16 Chapter 2 of this volume, p 24.

results do show, in the buribunkian cosmology, 'which kind of psycho-pathological studies have so far been conducted', but not 'which psycho-pathological motives led to these psycho-pathological studies'.[17] In a positive sense, though, our results show that the Buribunk utopia that escapes from the rich experiences of nature into the written diary history that can then be catalogued is not a real (scientific) possibility. As others have detailed living as an informational experience ('as if the Buribunks' immense permeation with data coincided with an automated Buribunkology that could be switched, at the speed of electrical current, from a register of data to a register of persons or even their self-registration'),[18] our contribution is to confirm that the Buribunkian spectre of algorithmic surveillance in the age of information is likely limited. Ferker's failings of secret love and fear of death are likely safe, while Schnekke's 'nothing but a diary-keeper, he lives for the diary, he lives in and through the diary'[19] is an unrealisable surveillance servitude because the buribunkian catalogue can provide the Leporello record but not the rich explanatory meaning that it is assumed Schnekke might reveal in *his* diary. But, 'the language of the upper echelons of leadership … is digitalisation; it transforms sources of accidental noise into absolute all-or-none organs. Otherwise, commands and censures, those two anti-symmetrical instruments of leadership, could not be communicated'[20] – that ironically sovereign act remains the spectre of automated buribunkology and beyond the reach of this chapter.

References

Friedrich Kittler (1999) *Gramophone, Film, Typewriter*, Stanford University Press.

David Moher, Alessandro Liberati, Jennifer Tetzlaff, Douglas Altman and the PRISMA Group (2009) 'Preferred Reporting Items for Systematic Reviews and Meta-Analyses: The PRISMA Statement' 6 *PLoS Medicine* e1000097.

Catherine Pickering and Jason Byrne (2014) 'The Benefits of Publishing Systematic Quantitative Literature Reviews for PhD Candidates and Other Early Career Researchers' 33 *Higher Education Research and Development* 534.

Catherine Pickering, Julien Grignon, Rochelle Steven, Daniela Guitart and Jason Byrne (2014) 'Publishing Not Perishing: How Research Students Transition from Novice to Knowledgeable Using Systematic Quantitative Literature Reviews' 40 *Studies in Higher Education* 1756.

PRISMA (2014) 'PRISMA Statement', www.prisma-statement.org/PRISMAStatement/PRISMAStatement.aspx.

Carl Schmitt (2019) *'The Buribunks: An Essay on the Philosophy of History', trans Laura Petersen and Gert Reifarth 28 Griffith Law Review* 99.

Andrew Smith and Michael Humphreys (2006) 'Evaluation of Unsupervised Semantic Mapping of Natural Language with Leximancer Concept Mapping ' 38 *Behavioural Research Methods* 262.

17 Chapter 2 of this volume, p 23.
18 Kittler (1999), p 244.
19 Chapter 2 of this volume, p 22.
20 Kittler (1999), pp 249–50.

Index

All cited published works are by Carl Schmitt unless indicated otherwise. Page numbers followed by italic *f* refer to figures.

For Product Safety Concerns and Information please contact our EU representative GPSR@taylorandfrancis.com Taylor & Francis Verlag GmbH, Kaufingerstraße 24, 80331 München, Germany